General Ashcroft

General Ashcroft

Attorney at War

Nancy V. Baker

 University Press of Kansas

Published by the University Press of Kansas (Lawrence, Kansas 66045), which was organized
by the Kansas Board of Regents and is operated and funded by Emporia State University,
Fort Hays State University, Kansas State University, Pittsburg State University, the
University of Kansas, and Wichita State University

Library of Congress Cataloging-in-Publication Data

Baker, N. V.

General Ashcroft : attorney at war / Nancy V. Baker.

   p.   cm.

Includes bibliographical references and index.

ISBN 0–7006–1455–9 (cloth : alk. paper)

1. Ashcroft, John D., 1942–   2. Attorneys general—United States—Biography.

3. War on Terrorism, 2001–   4. Civil rights—United States—History.

5. Constitutional history—United States. I. Title.

KF373.A74B35 2006

353.4092—dc22   2006000130

British Library Cataloguing-in-Publication Data is available.

Printed in the United States of America

10 9 8 7 6 5 4 3 2 1

Dedicated to Peter R. Gregware
A true partner

Contents

Acknowledgments

While all of the errors in the book are my responsibility, I recognize that I would not have been able to write it without the support of many people. In writing my acknowledgment of that support, I confess to feeling some trepidation, aware that the vagaries of memory may cause me to omit the name of someone who deserves to be included here. First, I would like to thank those who graciously agreed to be interviewed on the record, taking time from busy schedules to do so: Senators Jeff Bingaman and Orrin Hatch, former attorneys general Griffin Bell and Dick Thornburgh, and former Justice Department official Brick Brewer. Second, I sincerely appreciate the magical arts of Mike Briggs and the staff at the University Press of Kansas, who can transform an unwieldy stack of paper into such a handsome volume. Special thanks go to Lou Fisher for his timely and insightful guidance. I thank my excellent colleagues at New Mexico State University, who make going to work fun, and I particularly wish to thank my dean, Waded Cruzado-Salas, and former department head, Bill Taggart, who carved out a teaching reduction for me to facilitate the writing process. Since no scholar is an island, I appreciate as well the scholarship of my fellow travelers in the Presidency Research Group of the American Political Science Association. Through many years of teaching, I also have come to recognize the role that students play in sharpening our critical thinking skills; among those who have helped on this project, I wish to acknowledge Alison Folsom, April Willeford, and the graduate students in my seminar in civil liberties. For insight into Beltway culture during my research trips to D.C., I wish to thank Dino Montoya and Victor Cornejo. Other dear friends near and far helped me maintain my sense of humor and perspective through more than three years of research and writing. Finally, I deeply appreciate the encouragement and support of my family—Betty, for Saturday morning chats about politics, my siblings, Barbara, Susan, and Michael, my granddaughter, Asia, and her father, Kyle, and Peter, my husband, who helps beyond words. A final tribute is owed to my mother, Dorothy Ellen Baker, who taught me that politics, justice, and freedom of conscience matter. Sadly, she passed away while this work was in progress.

General Ashcroft

Introduction

This study examines the impact of the antiterrorism actions of U.S. Attorney General John David Ashcroft on the constitutional system of divided and checked powers. Underlying this theme is an exploration of the role that an attorney general can play in expanding or shaping presidential power during national crisis.

A study of this nature poses numerous research challenges. The rhetorical excesses that characterize many accounts by and about Ashcroft tended to cloud the factual waters, making a clear and unbiased analysis more difficult. The research task was complicated by the problem of accessing thorough and accurate information about the George W. Bush presidency in the current climate of heightened secrecy. Some potential sources within the Justice Department either refused to be interviewed or asked to remain anonymous out of fear of retribution. Through a spokesperson, John Ashcroft also declined to be interviewed on several occasions in 2004 and early 2005. As a result, I tried to take special care to ensure the evenhandedness of the documentary record, through the use of multiple sources and selected elite interviews.

Some of the research has appeared elsewhere. Some of the material presented in chapters 5, 6, and 7 first appeared in articles published by *Presidential Studies Quarterly* in December 2002 and September 2003, and in a coauthored book chapter in *Courts and Justice: A Reader,* edited by G. Larry Mays and Peter R. Gregware.

There remains much about the Ashcroft tenure that is only tangentially addressed, if at all, in this book, for example, his involvement in the judicial selection process, his opposition to Oregon and California measures legalizing physician-assisted suicide and medical marijuana, respectively, and his insistence on the death penalty against the recommendations of U.S. attorneys in some federal cases. Those issues, while important, did not fit within the confines of the thesis of this book. They do merit future research.

A note on language use is needed. Within and outside government, attorneys general are commonly referred to as "general." White House Press Secretary Ari Fleischer regularly called Ashcroft "general" in the three months following the terrorist attacks,[1] as did his aide Claire Buchan at the White

House press briefing on the evening of September 11, 2001.[2] Many in Congress did so as well; during hearings before the House Judiciary Committee in June 2003, for example, six representatives addressed him as "general" and not "attorney general."[3] Several of the 9/11 commissioners also employed the term during Ashcroft's appearance before the National Commission on Terrorist Attacks upon the United States.[4] The same title was conferred by talk show host Larry King during multiple interviews with the attorney general.[5] According to protocol, however, "Mr. Attorney General" or "Mr. Ashcroft" would have been the correct address. "General" in the title is an adjective referring to the scope of the attorney general's jurisdiction. The fact that it is not used as a noun is clear in the title's plural form: attorneys general. Law professor Michael Herz notes that the usage of "general" continues because "people are reassured, or impressed, by having a general around. The adversary system, litigation 'battles,' . . . all these make the idea of putting a general in charge comfortable." Yet Herz argues persuasively against using "general" instead of "attorney general," on the grounds of good grammar, history, lexicology, protocol, and values such as rule of law.[6]

With apologies to Professor Herz, I use the term in the title of this book to suggest the combative role that this attorney general adopted in the domestic war on terrorism. In an important sense, he served as the "commander of law enforcement's war against terrorism."[7]

1   A Controversial Law Officer

Feared as a fascist and zealot by some, lionized as a godly man of principle by others, U.S. Attorney General John Ashcroft engendered so much impassioned rhetoric among critics and supporters alike that his impact on the office and the larger political system is not easily assessed. His personal attributes and actions in office often led to caricature and exaggeration. He was called "Ayatollah Ashcroft" for his opposition to Oregon's Death with Dignity Act, his registration of thousands of Muslims after 9/11, and his perceived religious intolerance.[1] Even establishment media outlets referred to him in superlative terms, as the "Minister of Fear,"[2] a "steamroller,"[3] and a man with a "messianic sense of his own role in American politics."[4]

Ashcroft's tenure in the administration of George W. Bush has been compared with that of A. Mitchell Palmer,[5] Woodrow Wilson's militantly anticommunist attorney general who rounded up thousands of foreign nationals in 1919–1920 and "violated civil liberties to an extent unprecedented in American history."[6] One commentator argued that Ashcroft is in a dead heat with Palmer as the worst attorney general ever.[7] Another called him "the most dangerous, despised and divisive attorney general since John Mitchell,"[8] Richard Nixon's law officer who spent nineteen months in federal prison for his role in the Watergate cover-up. Liberal columnist Paul Krugman and Democratic hopeful Howard Dean went further, calling Ashcroft the worst in history,[9] even bypassing Mitchell. Several contenders for the 2004 Democratic nomination regularly blasted the attorney general. Richard Gephardt promised to fire Ashcroft "in my first five seconds as president,"[10] and John Edwards received his greatest applause when he asserted, "We cannot let people like John Ashcroft take away our rights, our freedom, our liberty, our privacy."[11] In fact, disparaging references to the attorney general drew the most enthusiastic responses from Democratic crowds during the 2004 presidential primaries.[12]

Liberal Democrats and progressives—while leading the attack—held no monopoly on Ashcroft bashing. Some conservative columnists also criticized the attorney general's actions and demeanor. David Keene, a conservative activist, wrote that conservatives liked him, "but they are wary of what his department has done and wish that in striking a balance between the need for security and the need to preserve our liberties he would be a bit more careful."[13] Fellow conservative Joel Mowbray advised Ashcroft to stop "demonizing those who question certain decisions" and to "tone down some of the tactics" pushed by an overeager FBI.[14] William Safire used stronger language to characterize Ashcroft as "a frustrated and panic-stricken attorney general," whose poor advice led the president to assume "what amounts to dictatorial power to jail or execute aliens."[15] At the announcement of Ashcroft's retirement, Bret Stephens of the *Wall Street Journal* wrote, "He's A. Mitchell Palmer and J. Edgar Hoover rolled into one. He's a national embarrassment. Worse: He's a conservative embarrassment, which is to say, a personal embarrassment to me as a conservative."[16]

But John Ashcroft generated passionate support as well. He was lauded as "a man of tremendous honor and integrity . . . [with an] unyielding code of honor," in the words of a congressman who helped to orchestrate strong lobbying efforts on behalf of his confirmation.[17] During the contentious confirmation hearings, Senator Bob Smith (R-N.H.) called him "the most qualified candidate ever nominated for Attorney General,"[18] and Kay Cole James of the Heritage Foundation testified that "John Ashcroft's long career not only exemplifies the virtue of devoted public service, but it is a testament to his efforts to give validity to his convictions."[19] Once in office, according to a Republican activist, Ashcroft became the "conservative heartthrob" of the administration.[20] His supporters saw him as "a champion of liberty."[21] Orrin Hatch (R-Utah), the chairman of the Senate Judiciary Committee during much of his tenure, called Ashcroft "the right man at the right time. Most people by all measurements would have to say that he was an excellent attorney general of the United States."[22] That assessment was echoed by others.[23] Criticism of the attorney general, according to another supporter, was simply "Ashcroft-phobia raging semi-hysterically on the American left and, also, to some extent, on the right."[24] Ashcroft himself was puzzled by it. Referring to his negative press coverage, he said, "When I read some of those descriptions, I get scared of me."[25]

High-Profile Attorney General

John Ashcroft, unlike most attorneys general, quickly entered popular American culture. He was already widely known at the time of his appointment. Religious conservative voters followed his 1998 candidacy for the Republican presidential nomination; others heard of him when he lost his reelection bid for the Senate in 2000 to a deceased opponent, Mel Carnahan. One poll found that only 17 percent of the public admitted not knowing who he was during his confirmation hearings.[26] The Senate debate over his nomination also generated substantial press coverage, as did his subsequent tenure at the Justice Department. Especially in his first years in office, his outspoken style and controversial antiterrorism policies attracted public attention.

Despite its sometimes unfriendly glare, the media spotlight attracted him as well. For example, after nighttime talk show host David Letterman repeatedly aired a video clip of Ashcroft singing his self-penned anthem, "Let the Eagle Soar," the attorney general made a twenty-minute appearance on the NBC late-night show.[27] He made six appearances on CNN's *Larry King Live* between his confirmation and September 11, 2003; and an additional *Larry King* program looked at the controversy surrounding his acceptance of an honorary degree from Bob Jones University.[28] In comparison, the secretary of defense was a guest only four times and secretary of state three times in the same period.[29]

Ashcroft's tenure was most strongly associated with his counterterrorism measures, and his public visibility increased dramatically in the months following the attacks. In the nine months from his appointment to the terrorist attacks, Ashcroft was mentioned in 124 stories, 52 on his confirmation, on television evening news programs on ABC, CBS, NBC, and CNN. In comparison, 144 stories aired in the few months from 9/11 through the end of the year. As table 1 illustrates, subsequent coverage, while declining, remained relatively high in 2002, with 170 television news stories.[30] Most of this coverage occurred in the context of the war on terrorism. Prior to September 11, 2001, Ashcroft was mentioned in conjunction with terrorism in only 6 stories, compared with 135 news mentions in terrorism stories from 9/11 through the end of that year. In fact, from 9/11 to the end of his tenure, about 75 percent of the network and CNN evening news stories that mentioned him also addressed terrorism.[31] Print media featured the attorney general prominently in its antiterrorism coverage as well. The *Washington Post,* for example, mentioned Ashcroft's antiterrorism role 201 times from 9/11 through the end of the year and 169 times in 2002.[32] Ashcroft became the face of the administration's domestic counterterrorism efforts.

In the process of serving as commander of the law enforcement campaign against terrorism, Ashcroft became one of the most widely covered attorneys general in history. The news coverage he received during his four-year tenure exceeded that of his immediate predecessors. From his nomination on December 22, 2000, through the end of December 2004, he was mentioned 607 times in evening and special newscasts on ABC, CBS, NBC, and CNN.[33] At the halfway point in her eight-year tenure at the Department of Justice, Janet Reno—whose tenure was also eventful—had been mentioned 352 times. William French Smith of the Reagan administration was mentioned 239

Table 1. Television News Coverage of Attorney General Ashcroft

Year	Mentions
2001 Total	268
Pre-9/11	124
Post-9/11	144
2002	170
2003	72
2004	97

Source: Computed from mentions in either the title or the abstract in the Vanderbilt Television News Index and Abstract. Search of archive on April 7, 2005. Available at tvnews.vanderbilt.edu/TV-NewsSearch.

times, and Griffin Bell of the Carter administration, who served slightly less than the full four years, was mentioned 203 times from his appointment until he left office.[34]

Even among other members of the Bush cabinet, Ashcroft garnered substantial public attention. According to a study by Richard Ellis, news coverage typically is higher for inner cabinet officers—state, defense, treasury, and attorney general—than for outer cabinet secretaries, with the secretary of state far exceeding the others. That trend held in the Bush administration as well. But while Ellis found that the attorney general in 1981 received less than 20 percent of the television coverage of the secretary of state, increasing in 1989 to about 30 percent,[35] Ashcroft received almost 50 percent of the television news coverage of Secretary of State Colin Powell (1,227 mentions), as table 2 documents. The only other cabinet officer with higher visibility was Defense Secretary Donald Rumsfeld (1,222). Tom Ridge, as head of the Office and later the Department of Homeland Security, received half of the news references of the attorney general, with 303 mentions. The other major legal adviser in the executive branch, White House Counsel Alberto Gonzales, was significantly less visible, with just 21 stories.[36]

Ashcroft's high public profile drew negative as well as positive attention. His face was painted on an African coffin displayed in one Los Angeles art gallery, to represent the death of affirmative action and abortion rights.[37] He became a staple of humorists, including *Saturday Night Live* and Jon Stewart's *Daily Show* on Comedy Central. His persona was featured in *MAD* magazine as Uncle Sam admonishing readers, "I want YOU to spy on your neighbors,"[38] a parody echoed on multiple Web sites. In one, a menacing helmeted face is emblazoned with "John Ashcroft's watching you."[39] Another featured Ashcroft as the wicked witch threatening Dorothy in Oz, "Watch what you say or I'll get you and your constitutional rights too!"[40] A

Table 2. Television News Coverage of Bush Cabinet Secretaries from Nomination through December 2004

Department	Secretary	Mentions
State	Powell	1,227
Defense	Rumsfeld	1,222
Justice	Ashcroft	607
DHS	Ridge	303
HHS	Thompson	116
Treasury	Abraham	64
Energy	O'Neill*	61
Transportation	Mineta	52
Education	Paige	39
Agriculture	Veneman	27
Interior	Evans	23
Commerce	Norton	22
VA	Principi	9
Labor	Chao	9
HUD	Martinez*	6

*Evening news stories and special news programs on ABC, CBS, NBC, and CNN were counted from the announcement of appointment to March 15, 2004, except for O'Neill and Martinez, who resigned before this date. Their TV coverage is calculated only to the time of their departure.

Source: Computed from mentions in either the title or the abstract in the Vanderbilt Television News Index and Abstract, Vanderbilt University. Search of archive on April 7, 2005. Available at tvnews.vanderbilt.edu/TV-NewsSearch.

blank book, entitled *Everything I Know about the Constitution of the United States of America, by John Ashcroft,* was offered for sale on the Web,[41] as was a pack of playing cards with him appearing as "John 'Leg Chains' Ashcroft" on the ace of diamonds.[42] Web news parodies reported that he ordered the president's dog Spot killed because "the dog knew too much,"[43] that he sent Janet Jackson's right breast to Guantánamo Bay for questioning and a possible military trial,[44] and that he arrested a teacher with a slide rule for being "in the notorious al-gebra movement" and carrying "weapons of math instruction."[45] The Internet also offered lyrics satirizing the attorney general, with titles such as "John Ashcroft Is Hunting You Down" (to the tune of "Santa Claus Is Coming to Town"), "Ashcroft, the New Darth Vader" (to the tune of "Rudolph, the Red-Nosed Reindeer"), and "You Can't Hide from Prying Eyes" (to the tune of "Lying Eyes").[46] His face became so well known that his image was not always identified by name in political cartoons and parodies.[47] On Ashcroft's retirement, the director of the Office of Legal Policy, Daniel Bryant, quipped that the attorney general's caricature "has served as a full-employment program for cartoonists and pundits." Bryant quoted David Letterman: "They say Attorney General John Ashcroft may be stepping down. Apparently he wants to spend more time spying on his family."[48]

Ashcroft's affiliation with the Christian Right added to the sensationalism surrounding some of the news coverage. One of the strangest reports was posted on the Internet by Andrew Tobias, a financial writer and Democratic Party treasurer, alleging that Ashcroft believed calico cats were signs of the devil. Tobias said he based his story on reports from the U.S. embassy in The Hague when Ashcroft's advance team asked about any calico cats on the premises.[49] Another widely reported story was that Ashcroft, offended at the bare breast of the female Spirit of Justice statue in the department's Great Hall, ordered blue curtains to drape the seminude art deco statue and her male partner. A photograph of an early press conference in the Great Hall had revealed the statue's aluminum breast over the attorney general's head. Soon after, the Justice Department spent $8,000 on the drapes. Spokeswoman Barbara Comstock said the curtains were hung to provide a better backdrop for television cameras and that the attorney general was not involved in the decision.[50] Another Justice spokesman, Mark Corallo, said the drapes were requested by the White House advance team, prior to a televised visit by President Bush. Ashcroft denied ordering the drapes or even knowing about them until they were hung.[51] He told some reporters that the curtains were covering a remodeling project.[52] Regardless of the story's veracity, the report of Ashcroft's puritan streak resonated with some frustrated career staff at Justice, where the news about "hiding the statues" circulated through e-mail.[53] Referred to as the blue burka,[54] the curtains also made a tempting item for journalists and satirists. The story even led to a strong condemnation from the singer Cher, who denounced Ashcroft's prudishness in a number of media interviews.[55] Six months after he left office, the blue curtains were unceremoniously taken down.[56]

Because of this extensive coverage, both John Ashcroft's extremism and his role in framing the administration's domestic antiterrorism response are easily overstated. First, while he was the point man on many of the Bush administration's most controversial policies, he did not act independently or contrary to the president's will in framing the domestic response to terrorism. In fact, scholars of the U.S. cabinet note that policymaking increasingly is centralized in the White House itself, with department secretaries, including the attorney general, often relegated to a management and implementation role.[57] The context of the domestic war against terrorism arguably brought greater sharing of the policymaking power between the Justice Department and the White House staff; even so, the attorney general was no maverick. He followed the wishes of George W. Bush, who retained ultimate control. There is little indication that the White House disapproved of his handling of the nation's legal business in the months following the attacks of September 11, 2001. One presidential adviser in 2002 evaluated the attorney general's contribution to the administration: "Ashcroft is more than doing a good job. He is a star."[58] A year later, Bush praised his law officer for doing "a fabulous job."[59]

Second, other government officials share responsibility for domestic anti-terrorism efforts and legal advice. In the first Bush term, these officials included Homeland Security Secretary Ridge, White House Counsel Gonzales, and the vice president's legal adviser David Addington. Ashcroft and his subordinates in Justice did not single-handedly shield the nation from future terrorist attacks, as some—including on occasion the attorney general himself—implied.[60] Nor was he solely responsible for myriad assaults on civil liberties, as others suggested.[61]

Third, some of the policy responses to 9/11 had been framed during the previous administration. Like Bush, President Bill Clinton referred to terrorism as evil.[62] Clinton sought aggressive policies to address terrorism; following the 1995 bombing of the Oklahoma City federal building, his administration successfully pressed for passage of the Antiterrorism and Effective Death Penalty Act of 1996.[63] That law repealed the ban on FBI surveillance of group activities, permitted the use of secret evidence to deport suspected terrorists, and criminalized giving even humanitarian assistance to any group designated by the State Department as terrorist. At the time, some leading civil liberty scholars charged that the 1996 law made "substantial incursions on Constitutional rights."[64] Other tough measures were recommended during the Clinton era, particularly in response to the 1999 millennium bombing plot. Ashcroft noted his reliance on those recommendations when he testified in 2004 about his rigorous enforcement of immigration law.[65] In other words, the Justice Department under Ashcroft did not invent many of the policies for which it was blamed or credited.

Yet the presence of John Ashcroft in the Justice Department on that day in September 2001 has made a difference in the development of U.S. constitutional law. Using Clinton administration policies as a point of departure, he employed the significant discretionary, formal, and informal powers at his disposal to push for fundamental changes in law enforcement and expand executive branch authority to act. A leading "general" in the domestic war against terrorism, Ashcroft was instrumental in framing the nation's response in a way that enhanced presidential power and weakened constitutional checks.

Presidential Power and the Attorney General

From the start, the Bush White House sought to "restore" presidential prerogatives that it argued had been eroded since the Vietnam War and the Watergate scandal, rolling back "30 to 35 years of compromise by presidents of both parties."[66] Vice President Richard Cheney said that he had "repeatedly seen an erosion of the powers and the ability of the president of the United States to do his job."[67] He criticized earlier presidents for acceding to congressional demands and thereby making the presidency "weaker today as an institution."[68] One key power that they planned to reassert was executive privilege, which had been weakened during the Clinton administration.[69] Fulfilling his and the president's plan to reverse that trend, Cheney remarked at the end of Bush's first term that "the proper power of the presidency has finally been restored."[70]

A robust presidency did not seem likely in the administration's first nine months, given the setbacks to presidential privileges and prerogatives during the Clinton years, and Bush's inability to claim a mandate for governance. The likelihood dropped further when the Republicans lost control of the Senate in mid-2001, and Bush's public approval ratings dropped lower than those of any postwar president except Clinton.[71] But the explicit securitization of domestic affairs that came with the terrorist strikes made it politically possible. Now there was a compelling rationale for exercising unilateral executive authority, in both the domestic and the international spheres.

By framing the crisis as a war, the Bush administration could reassert the primacy of the presidency. Deference to the White House is common during wartime, when other political actors customarily unify behind the chief executive. Citizens also rally around the incumbent president, even accepting some limits on their individual rights. Dissenters tend to be silenced—either formally through the law or informally through public disapproval—for giving aid and comfort to the enemy. This deference to presidential authority may be even stronger when the home front is transformed into a battlefront, as in the war on terrorism.

Even absent a crisis, however, a president who seeks to enact policy changes and exercise power can find a useful ally in the U.S. attorney general. Because of the significant discretionary power in the office, the chief law officer of the nation can focus the department's resources on some issues rather than others and interpret federal law in a way that helps legitimize presidential authority and delegitimize claims of competing power centers such as Congress and the courts. Attorneys general also can exercise persuasive power to influence public and congressional perceptions. Within the executive branch, they speak with a special authority on the law and the Constitution, which they can use to reassure a citizenry concerned with rule of law and individual rights as well as with security. And they have formal powers related to law enforcement, investigation, and prosecution.

In many ways, John Ashcroft proved to be an able advocate of the administration's antiterror agenda. He and the president shared a binary conception of the world as good and evil, black and white. They saw the evil of terrorism as best confronted by a strong commander in chief and a muscular federal government. Ashcroft mobilized the Justice Department on a war footing and rallied law enforcement troops. He took the lead in the administration's domestic war against terrorism, from the FBI's reorganization to the criminal trials of suspected terrorists. He was the chief lobbyist for the USA Patriot Act and its chief defender two years later. He pushed for greater surveillance authority, the elimination of Patriot Act sunset provisions, and a broader legal definition of terrorism. He defended presidential authority to designate U.S. citizens as enemy combatants and to create military tribunals, despite reservations he had about how the Pentagon implemented those measures. He oversaw a doubling of the numbers of joint terrorism task forces operating nationwide in coordination with the FBI. On his authority, dozens of organizations were classified as terrorist and more than a thousand people detained in the wake of the 9/11 attacks. He supervised the jailing of scores of potential material witnesses, and the prosecution and deportation of hundreds of people as a result of antiterrorism and immigration investigations. Under his auspices, Freedom of Information Act guidelines shifted the presumption from disclosure to nondisclosure. In addition, blanket closures of certain immigration hearings were ordered, FBI investigatory guidelines were changed, communication barriers between law enforcement and intelligence were lifted, and attorney-client privilege in federal prisons was weakened. On multiple fronts, Ashcroft sought to "enhance local homeland security efforts and make emergency preparedness a part of our daily lives."[72]

Three factors are key to understanding Ashcroft's role and the nation's antiterrorism response at home: the framework of a war against terrorism, the unique legal policy role of the attorney general, and the presence of John Ashcroft in that office. Each of these factors alone is insufficient to explain the impact of Ashcroft's actions on presidential power. However, taken together, they created a context where executive power could be dramatically expanded in domestic affairs. This book is organized to take that context into account. The first part details the relevant institutional and personal factors and then situates them in the larger political environment of the domestic war on terrorism. The second part explores how Ashcroft's counterterrorism actions affected and even eroded the checks on executive power implicit in the separation of powers, criminal procedural rights, privacy rights, and government transparency.

Because of Ashcroft's aggressive efforts to reframe law enforcement after 9/11, he was sometimes called "the hardest of the hardliners"[73] in the administration's antiterrorism efforts. His leadership role led others to consider him "the most powerful attorney general in decades,"[74] and "the most important attorney general since Robert F. Kennedy."[75] His reach may have exceeded even that. In fighting the domestic war on terror, operating within a vastly expanded field of federal authority, John Ashcroft arguably became one of the most powerful attorneys general in the nation's history.

2   The Singular Office of Attorney General

The office of attorney general, while not as visible as those of State and Defense, is a powerful cabinet position, the most powerful of the domestic agencies. Senator Patrick Leahy (D-Vt.) put it well: "There is no appointed position within the Federal Government that can affect more lives in more ways than the Attorney General. . . . What choices the next Attorney General makes about resources and priorities will have a dramatic impact on almost every aspect of the society in which we live."[1] Several attorneys general have been highly trusted presidential advisers on a wide range of issues. Six became justices of the U.S. Supreme Court, two as chief justice, and one attempted to use the position as a springboard to the presidency.[2]

As chief law officer of the nation and head of the Justice Department, the attorney general serves at the nexus of law and politics, well positioned to advance the president's agenda and affect the development of U.S. law. "Being Attorney General is not just about enforcing the law," noted one astute essay published during Ashcroft's confirmation battle. "It is also about changing it, deciding which laws to challenge, how aggressively to prosecute and where to throw your best lawyers."[3] The uniqueness of the office is often noted during Senate confirmation hearings. For example, at John Ashcroft's confirmation hearings, Senator Orrin Hatch (R-Utah) said the attorney general "must demonstrate both a proper understanding of the law and a determination to uphold its letter and its spirit."[4] During Alberto Gonzales's confirmation hearings, even Senate newcomer Barack Obama (D-Ill.) recognized the uniqueness of the post: "The Attorney General is not like the other cabinet posts. Unlike the Secretary of State, who is the public face of the President's foreign policy, or the Secretary of Education, whose job it is to carry out the President's education policy, the Attorney General's job is not just to enforce the President's laws, it is to tell the President what the law is. The job is not simply to facilitate the President's power, it is to speak truth to that power as well."[5] While this is difficult to do, an attorney general who does not fulfill this expectation draws heavy criticism, particularly from across the aisle.

The attorney general's office presents a challenge for presidents and law officers alike because it attracts heightened public expectations and greater congressional scrutiny than most cabinet positions. Edwin Meese III, whose tenure in the Reagan Justice Department was shadowed by special prosecutor probes, captured the difficulty of the job. It was "like being the captain of the Olympic Javelin Team who elected to receive."[6] Another former law officer, Richard Thornburgh of George H. W. Bush's presidency, said the position "is one of the most vulnerable to criticisms." Quoting Eisenhower's attorney general, Herbert Brownell, he said, "Any attorney general who is popular isn't doing his job." Thornburgh then recounted a quip told at the 200th anniversary celebration of the office: "At the end of the day, they tilt Washington up and all of the flotsam and jetsam rolls into the Department of Justice."[7]

Potential for Influence and Power

The attorney general, like the other cabinet secretaries, is appointed by the president and confirmed by the Senate, subject to removal only by the president or by conviction through the impeachment process. The Department of Justice, which he or she heads, handles most of the federal government's legal work, from investigation and prosecution, to imprisonment and parole. Justice officials often take the lead on proposing legislation affecting the courts and law enforcement agencies, as well as civil and criminal law.

The department's policy portfolio is broad; few areas of national interest are beyond its purview. Thornburgh observed, "You really are at the center of most anything that goes on. Not much is peripheral."[8] Senator Edward Kennedy (D-Mass.) echoed that point, "The power and reach of the Department of Justice is vast."[9] The department is the home of more than sixty agencies. Separate divisions handle criminal law, antitrust, civil law, civil rights, tax law, and law related to the environment and natural resources. Located within the department are the Federal Bureau of Investigation, the Drug Enforcement Administration, the Executive Office for Immigration Review, the U.S. Marshals Service, the Federal Bureau of Prisons, and the Bureau of Alcohol, Tobacco, Firearms and Explosives, among others. The Justice Department has links to local law enforcement—through such programs as Community Oriented Policing Services—and international law enforcement, via an office that interfaces with INTERPOL. The Office of Intelligence Policy and Review is responsible for reviewing and filing all surveillance applications with the Foreign Intelligence Surveillance Court. Appendix I outlines the Justice Department's organizational structure. A former public affairs director under Janet Reno described the scope of the department: "Its law enforcement mission is truly global, ranging from al Qaeda to teenagers with nickel bags of cocaine, from wiretaps to whistleblowers, from the Internet to the environment, from Ken Lay and Bill Gates and Martha Stewart to hundreds of thousands of anonymous others whose liberties it alone can take or curtail."[10]

As head of an executive department, the attorney general is required by the Constitution to advise the president "upon any subject relating to the duties"[11] of the office; conventionally, this has included department priorities, budget requests, policy implementation, and proposed legislation. Depending on his or her relationship with the president, an attorney general may give policy advice on issues arising in other departments, such as Education, State, Defense, and Interior. Less frequently than some of the other secretaries, attorneys general have provided direct political assistance to their presidents when they lobby the public on behalf of the administration's agenda.[12]

Unlike other cabinet officers, the attorney general is more than an administrator of a large bureaucracy. He or she also serves as chief law officer of the nation, with distinctly legal responsibilities and a special relationship with the federal courts. The legalistic dimensions of the position are evident in its genealogy. The attorney general's post was created by the Judiciary Act of 1789, the statute that established the federal courts. In the draft of the bill introduced in the Senate, the law officer was to be appointed by the Supreme Court,[13] but the final version omitted the method of appointment, which was understood to mean that the nomination would be made by the president and confirmed by the Senate. The Judiciary Act assigned two responsibilities to the attorney general, both quasi-judicial: "to prosecute and conduct all suits in the Supreme Court for which the United States shall be concerned, and to give his advice and opinion upon questions of law when required by the president of the United States, or when requested by the heads of any of the departments."[14] These duties have largely been delegated to two offices within the Justice Department—the Office of Solicitor General and the Office of Legal Counsel, respectively—yet they remain core responsibilities of the attorney general. Through them, the attorney general articulates and defends the legal position of the U.S. government on many of the great issues of the day. A brief history of the office is provided in appendix II.

Fulfilling the attorney general's responsibilities before the U.S. Supreme Court, the solicitor general's office selects the federal cases to appeal to the high court, argues those cases, and occasionally files friend-of-the court briefs (called "amicus curiae") in cases where the government is not a party but has a policy interest in the outcome. This office has unrivaled success before the Supreme Court, both in winning the Court's acceptance of a case and in winning on the merits, the actual legal question. Amicus support by the solicitor general also translates into a higher rate of success for private litigants. Including its victories in getting the Court to dismiss or deny review of cases brought against the United States, "the government is successful in nearly 96 percent of the cases in which it participates," according to political scientist Rebecca Mae Salokar. In contrast, she notes, "private litigants win a mere 1 percent of their cases against the United States before the Supreme Court."[15] The attorney general also directs the ninety-three U.S. attorneys who serve as the government's principal litigators in districts nationwide; they supervise thousands of assistants who prosecute cases involving the United States in the lower federal courts. In most administrations, the attorney general or a subordinate helps to compile the list of potential nominees for the circuit courts of appeals and Supreme Court, participates in the vetting process, and prepares judicial nominees for Senate hearings.[16] In all these ways, an attorney general can influence the direction of federal law in the courts.

The attorney general also serves as a primary legal adviser to the president and executive branch officials. In the past, the Opinions of the Attorney General have constituted "a considerable portion of the layman's version of the law,"[17] since they generally have been considered binding on the executive branch in areas not yet settled by the courts. The advisory task today is largely handled by the Office of Legal Counsel (OLC). Like the attorney general's official opinions, OLC opinions are accorded deference by the federal judiciary. On occasion, courts have relied on their reasoning or wording. Executive branch legal opinions usually offer "legal analysis of broad aspects of law with consideration of legal interrelationships";[18] in this way, they may extend further than court rulings, which tend to be narrowly tailored.

Constitutional, statutory, and international law all are subject to some degree of interpretation. The language in the U.S. Constitution, for example, is brief and ambiguous in parts, particularly Article II dealing with the chief executive. Compared with the legislative branch, the authority granted to the president seems stingy. Yet certain constitutional phrases—especially the "take care" and "commander in chief" clauses—are notably inexact. Ambiguity also characterizes statutory law. In the classic *Introduction to Legal Reasoning,* Edward Levi wrote that "ambiguity is inevitable in both statute and constitution as well as with case law."[19] The interpretative role provides the attorney general and OLC an opportunity to answer a legal question in the best possible light for an administration. Political scientist Martin Sheffer argued that legal opinions commonly are used to advance presidential claims of power in relation to the other branches.[20] While examples do exist of attorneys general restricting executive action,[21] Sheffer's thesis generally holds.[22] The neutral-sounding legal language used in these opinions can confer credibility on claims of executive power and cloak an administration's ideological or political goals.[23]

In addition to these formal roles, the attorney general often fills an informal role as an authoritative source for the general public on U.S. law and the Constitution. No other executive branch lawyer carries such authority to speak on the law; none other has quite the same "power to persuade." The White House counsel, who usually has a closer working relationship with the president, is more likely to be seen as the president's lawyer and therefore not an unbiased interpreter of constitutional or statutory law. In contrast, the attorney general commonly is perceived to be the people's lawyer, a view expressed during Ashcroft's confirmation hearings. Arlen Specter (R-Pa.) noted that the attorney general is "the lawyer of the American people," as well as the president's lawyer; Joseph Biden (D-N.J.) told the nominee, "You are . . . to become the people's lawyer more than you are to be the President's lawyer."[24] When nominated to replace Ashcroft, Alberto Gonzales noted the distinction between the attorney general's position and that of White House counsel: "I now represent not just one client, but all of you, the people of the United States."[25]

Legal language conveys a special authority in a country like the United States, where a high premium is placed on the rule of law. Some judicial researchers have observed the persuasive power of legal language in court decisions, with "citizens, journalists, interests groups, and public officials" using it to legitimate their preferred policy outcomes.[26] Research into legal consciousness—how ordinary people consciously think about or what they unconsciously assume about the law and legal institutions—suggests that for many Americans, law is a privileged discourse, in some cases even trumping a person's own life experiences as a basis for understanding events.[27] While the literature relating to legal language deals almost exclusively with the courts, legal discourse has an impact throughout the entire political system. That is because there is no bright-line delineation between political and legal issues in the United States, an observation made almost 200 years ago by Alexis de Tocqueville in *Democracy in America.* He noticed the tendency of political issues to be transformed into legal issues in the new republic: "There is almost no political question in the United States that is not resolved sooner or later into a judicial question."[28] Adding to the potency of legal rhetoric is the reverence accorded the nation's founding legal documents. The Constitution and the Bill of Rights, according to sociologist Amitai Etzioni, form part of a civil religion "to which our leaders can appeal and gain some traction."[29] Others also have referred to the Constitution as filling the role of a sacred text in the nation's sense of its history and destiny.[30] By invoking the Constitution, therefore, an attorney general can tap into deep emotional reserves about the nation's identity.

Serving Law and Politics

The attorney general's post encompasses legal as well as political responsibilities. In a sense, the office serves as "a unique bridge between the executive and judicial branches," in the words of law professor and former Justice Department officer Daniel Meador.[31] Senator Mike Dewine (R-Ohio) noted the difficulty of balancing the roles: "His is in many respects the most difficult job because he is the person who must by statute give advice to the President of the United States, but he is also, in essence, the chief law enforcement officer of the country."[32] Due to this unique role, the attorney general potentially encounters conflicting demands between loyalty to the president and fidelity to the law as an officer of the court. No attorney general can entirely ignore either set of obligations, but incumbents have varied in how they have approached their responsibilities. Some have concentrated on the political task of advancing the president's agenda. Others have focused on the legal role, emphasizing rule of law and procedure over substantive policy outcomes. In addition, several norms have emerged that informally define the contours of appropriate behavior. First is the norm of independence from intrusive White House control. As an illustration of this, the White House may guide broad policy at Justice but not interfere in actual cases under consideration. Second, attorneys general are expected to be nonpartisan, giving no special advantage to their own political parties. Loyalty to the president is a third important norm because the attorney general exercises merely delegated authority from the chief executive.[33]

Historically, presidents have preferred attorneys general who could serve as policy advocates. Most modern law officers have had prior political experience and/or political or personal ties to their presidents. In fact, their political expertise and connections may have contributed to their appointments in the first place. Most twentieth-century presidents appointed either a former campaign manager or a leading party official to the top Justice post sometime during their administration.[34] Attorneys general with this experience have often expressed an expansive view of the law as a tool to promote the administration's agenda or presidential power. Examples range from Robert Kennedy in John Kennedy's administration to Edwin Meese in Reagan's. This type of an activist attorney general, if not already close to the president, often became part of the inner circle of White House advisers.[35]

On rare occasions, politically active attorneys general have crossed the line either by violating the law or by violating one of the unwritten norms of independence and nonpartisanship. In a hypersensitive postscandal environment, presidents do not have a completely free hand in selecting their attorneys general. Members of Congress, the press, and the public tend to be critical of a nominee perceived as too close to the White House or "tarnished" by politics. In the past, presidents who ignored this changed political environment in making their appointments encountered stiff Senate resistance to their nominees. This happened to Calvin Coolidge when he ignored the residual political effects of the Teapot Dome scandal and twice appointed a high-profile political figure to the attorney general's office; that nominee was then twice rejected by the Senate.[36] In several postscandal periods, the Senate debated the appropriate balance between law and politics, even considering on a number of occasions the wisdom of removing the Justice Department from White House control entirely.[37]

In contrast to Coolidge, Gerald Ford tailored his nominee to the exceedingly suspicious post-Watergate political climate. He selected Edward Levi, an eminent legal scholar, and Levi was easily confirmed. The former president of the University of Chicago, Levi had not met Ford prior to a brief interview preceding his appointment. Ford said he chose Levi because he wanted an attorney general who "understands the meaning of rule of law and its limits," someone capable of restoring "integrity and trust of our legal system."[38] This type of attorney general often has had little or no prior relationship with the president. Their actions in office tend to be cautious and their advice legalistic. These qualities are well suited to the task of rebuilding national confidence following a scandal, but they also may serve to exclude the law officer from the inner circle of presidential advisers.[39]

Either approach is legitimate. However, in certain political environments, the politically oriented attorney general is dismissed by opponents as a mere hired gun for the White House. The simplistic characterization that the political is bad and the legal is good ignores not only the record of those who have served—such as Robert Kennedy, a political activist who is widely regarded as an excellent attorney general—but the larger constitutional structure. After all, the attorney general is an appointee of an elected president, and it is the president who is constitutionally charged to "take care that the laws are faithfully executed."[40] Former attorney general Elliot Richardson explained, "Advice to a president needs to have the political dimension clearly in view, without a regard for any pejorative attached to the word political. The presidency is by definition a political job."[41] Homer Cummings, Franklin Roosevelt's first attorney general, speculated that "law and government are probably thought of too much as if they were opposites or as if the body social had two organs, one political and one legal," when in fact administration "is both law and government in action."[42] Furthermore, the notion that law is superior to politics is based on a misconception that law is apolitical and static, and that a neutral and trained observer (such as a judge or attorney general) will invariably find the "correct" legal answer by applying law to the relevant facts.

Legal realists writing almost a century ago effectively debunked this mechanistic view of the law.[43] Law actors generally make decisions based not on some idealized nonpolitical calculation but on their own values and political orientations.[44] And those decisions—including ones about the allocation of power—have real policy consequences. In sum, law and politics are distinct but intertwined.

Attorneys general with political pasts, therefore, are not illegitimate interlopers on the legal terrain. In fact, they are the norm, not an aberration. But in polarized political environments, a legalistic law officer benefits from the perception of neutrality, particularly in contentious Senate confirmation hearings.

Breaking Expectations: The Ashcroft Selection

In 2001, the appointment of a legalistic type of attorney general—one not strongly identified with the president or party politics—appeared likely. The political climate was polarized by the contested nature of the 2000 election and the Florida recount, and the electorate and the Senate were evenly split along partisan lines. Furthermore, Bill Clinton's second term had been dominated by an exhaustive special prosecutor investigation and impeachment hearings. The incoming administration appeared in need of a law officer who could shore up its credentials and calm partisan waters. As presidential scholar James Pfiffner noted, "George W. Bush began his presidency with as little political capital as any president since Gerald R. Ford."[45]

But Bush did not follow Ford's example. He did not act like a president who had barely won office and had to contend with a closely divided Congress and public. Instead, to head Justice, he chose John Ashcroft, a man with extensive partisan political experience and a reputation for staking out strong positions on controversial public policies. While neither he nor Ashcroft expected to generate controversy with the appointment, controversy was almost a given in the highly polarized political environment of early 2001.

The nature of Ashcroft's relationship with Bush prior to appointment is not clear. Their gubernatorial terms did not overlap; Ashcroft left the Missouri statehouse two years before Bush was elected governor of Texas. Ashcroft himself said that he knew Bush fairly well prior to his appointment, but the two were not intimate friends.[46] News stories reported that, in December 2000, when Ashcroft was invited to Austin to discuss the position, the president-elect knew him mostly by reputation through his father, George H. W. Bush,[47] who had reportedly considered Ashcroft to head Justice in 1991.[48] The elder Bush might have become aware of Ashcroft during the Reagan administration, when Senator Strom Thurmond (R-S.C.) said he had first recommended Ashcroft to the attorney general's post.[49] It is clear that Ashcroft and George W. Bush knew some of the same key political people. Ashcroft had hired Karl Rove in 1984 to work on direct mail funding solicitations in his first gubernatorial campaign; Rove later worked as a paid political consultant in Ashcroft's successful 1988 race for governor and 1994 Senate race.[50] In addition, George W. Bush and Ashcroft both knew Jack Oliver. Oliver, deputy finance chairman of the Bush-Cheney 2004 campaign, had been an aide to the president's father, then directed Ashcroft's 1994 Senate race and served as his deputy chief of staff.[51] Oliver also had directed Ashcroft's unsuccessful bid to chair the Republican National Committee in 1993.[52]

Ashcroft's initial conception of the attorney general's office is unclear as well: did he see his client as the president, the federal government, or the people of the United States? When he was asked soon after his confirmation if he saw himself as "attorney for the president or the country," Ashcroft answered an ambiguous "Yes."[53] Perhaps he could conceive of no inherent tension between his service to the country and to President Bush. Later, he referred to the American people as his clients, in response to an interviewer's question about his sometimes harsh rhetoric: "I think clarity is one of the most important features in leadership. . . . The American people are the client of this law firm. And we need to let them know exactly how we're handling things. I respect the client at the highest level."[54] Yet the attorney general also knew the importance of being a loyal team player in the Bush administration. Bush told Ashcroft this at their first meeting, saying that he did not want his cabinet members to be "independent operators."[55] Ashcroft seemed comfortable with that approach. Overall, he had worked as a team player during his time in the Senate.

In some ways, the new attorney general appeared to be cast in the mold of his politically active predecessors. His experience in elected office in Missouri and the U.S. Senate was more extensive than that of most other attorneys general. A man who had spent most of his adult life in the public arena, Ashcroft approached issues from the perspective of "broad generalizations—more in the manner of a politician than a lawyer."[56] He considered himself a doer and responded to the law as a tool to advance his conception of good public policy. One opposition press release argued that Ashcroft's strong ideological positions were troubling not in themselves but *because* of his activism—"the way he used the power and resources of his public office to pursue those extreme views."[57] A similar argument was advanced by Edward Kennedy, who argued during Ashcroft's Senate confirmation hearings: "We know that while serving in high office he has time and again aggressively used litigation and legislation in creative and inappropriate ways to advance his political and ideological goals. How can we have any confidence at all that he won't do the same thing with the vast new powers he will have at his disposal as Attorney General of the United States?"[58] But those who shared Ashcroft's policy views were pleased to have an advocate at the highest level of government. Ashcroft's aide David Israelite compared him to former attorney general Robert Kennedy in that "he came here to move the bureaucracy. . . . He came here to change things."[59]

Ashcroft's record prior to joining Justice could be interpreted differently, with less emphasis on the political. Conservative backers emphasized his reputation for integrity, an attribute highly valued in postscandal periods. His Missouri record was cited for its "squeaky clean standards" with no hint of scandal. Supporters felt that this record would appeal to the American public after the lurid news stories and independent counsel investigations of the Clinton administration.[60] In favor of Ashcroft's confirmation, former Missouri governor and senator Christopher Bond testified, "If you were to ask me one word to describe John Ashcroft, it would be integrity, and integrity means a steadfast adherence to a strict moral or ethical code."[61] Similar praises were raised by GOP senators Specter, Thurmond, Jon Kyl (Ariz.), and Sam Brownback (Kans.), who noted Ashcroft's "honesty, his integrity, his devotion to his family and to his Creator, his principled character, and his steadfast belief that each of us is put here on Earth to help our fellow man and to leave this world a better place for all of our children."[62] Even Democratic senators Dianne Feinstein (Calif.) and Joseph Biden, who eventually voted against Ashcroft's confirmation, agreed that he was "a man of honesty and integrity."[63] But Ashcroft's partisan past, coupled with his willingness to engage in hotly contested policy areas, led his opponents to view his selection as "a brazen provocation."[64] Yet even as his critics called him "a relentless crusader for extreme causes,"[65] the same record led supporters to laud him as "a stickler for principle."[66]

John Ashcroft's difficult confirmation hearings, to be covered in greater depth in the next chapter, can be attributed in part to the fact that the nomination of an attorney general with his activist traits was out of sync with the climate in the capital in January 2001. As Leahy noted in opening the hearings, "Fundamentally, the question before us is whether Sen. Ashcroft is the right person at this time for the critical position of Attorney General of the United States."[67]

Another factor could have complicated Ashcroft's confirmation. Cabinet scholar Mary Anne Borrelli argues that ease of Senate confirmation for any secretary-designate varies according to perceptions of his or her "insider" or "outsider" status, or if he or she is a policy specialist, policy generalist, or issue network liaison. Borrelli notes that outsider-generalist cabinet nominees face the most difficult questioning during confirmation hearings, since senators may be concerned about the ability of an outsider to make decisions that "affect the senators' own careers and ambitions."[68] She classified John Ashcroft as an outsider-generalist, because although he had spent six years in the U.S. Senate, four of them on the Judiciary Committee, the bulk of his professional life had been spent in public service at the state level.

Ashcroft's record can be read either way, as an insider or outsider, which senators at his confirmation hearing did, depending on their views about his nomination. Those who opposed his appointment tended to treat him as an "outsider," whereas those who supported it made comments more consistent with an "insider" designation. For example, Leahy's opening remarks outlined the roles and responsibilities of the U.S. attorney general, and Biden presented a lecture on race relations in America.[69] Both Leahy and Biden assumed the role of educator, suggesting that they thought the nominee needed the lessons. Their tone, as Borrelli predicted, was "cautionary, and the committee members refrain[ed] from expressing great confidence" in the nominee.[70] Briefly recognizing Ashcroft's past service on the Judiciary Committee, Leahy downplayed the advantage by adding, "I know that all Senators and the nominee agree that no one nominated to be Attorney General should be given special treatment just because he or she once served in the Senate."[71] Yet special treatment is what former senators customarily receive in the confirmation process.[72]

In contrast, Hatch treated Ashcroft as a Washington, D.C., "insider," presenting a more detailed account of his Senate record and calling him "a leader in many areas, including . . . the assessment of the proper role of the Justice Department." This remark echoed that of Thurmond, who also referred to Ashcroft as "an effective leader in the Senate with a record of legislative accomplishments."[73] Other backers used descriptive terms such as "integrity," "tough positions," and "extremely well qualified." These remarks are consistent with Borrelli's observation that committee members "describe their previous working relationships with the insider men as productive and express their confidence in the nominees' abilities. Accomplishments are attributed to the nominees' independence, strength and courage."[74]

Some of the support for Ashcroft's confirmation also was expressed in terms of customary Senate deference to the president's wishes in selecting cabinet secretaries. Even Democratic senators Maria Cantwell (Wash.), Russell Feingold and Herbert Kohl (Wisc.), and Charles Schumer (N.Y.) noted the expectation of deference. For Feingold, one of just eight Democrats who later voted in favor of confirmation, this deference was the first general principle guiding him: "The Constitution imposes the duty on the President to faithfully execute the laws, and he is expected to propose new laws. To carry out these duties, the President needs advisors and policymakers in the Cabinet to advance the President's program. Over the history of such nominations, the Senate, with rare exceptions, has given the President broad leeway in choosing subordinates."[75]

Yet Ashcroft's confirmation experience was different from that of other Bush nominees because the office to which he was nominated was seen as different. Biden told the nominee that he regretted Ashcroft had not been named to the Departments of Commerce, State, or Defense because the Justice Department was different, since public perceptions of fairness were more critical.[76]

Those opposed to Ashcroft's appointment focused on his reputation as a political activist. Several senators questioned Ashcroft's ability to put aside his own strong views in order to enforce federal laws, including many laws with which he vehemently disagreed. They sought promises from Ashcroft that, if confirmed, he would not be an activist in his use of the law. He tried to reassure them. On the landmark abortion cases, for example, he testified: "I accept *Roe* and *Casey* as the settled law of the land. If confirmed as Attorney General, I will follow the law in this area and in all other areas." Here and throughout the hearings, he sought to portray himself as "law-oriented and not results-oriented."[77] The adoption of a legalistic orientation—effective in defusing criticism from the left—also was reflected in his confirmation remarks: "I am committed to preserving the special history of the Department of Justice by actively confronting injustice. Let me send a clear message today, I will confront injustice by leading a professional Justice Department that is free from politics; that is uncompromisingly fair; a Department defined by integrity and dedicated to upholding the rule of law. The Justice Department will vigorously enforce the law guaranteeing rights for the advancement of all Americans."[78]

Three years later, he continued to reject any characterization of his tenure as political. He told one interviewer, "The president relieved me of the responsibility to think politically when I came here. I don't go to fundraisers. I don't get involved in politics. I don't make political speeches. I don't make political comments. I don't endorse candidates. I just don't, because justice is an arena in which we need to have the capacity to serve . . . without regard to politics. And that's why I'm basically out of politics. And I rejoice in that fact in many respects."[79] In his narrow view of the term, politics for John Ashcroft meant elections and party politics.

Despite these assertions, Ashcroft's actions as attorney general—particularly after 9/11—cannot be described as being "basically out of politics." He was comfortable in the political arena, revealing a more activist orientation to the job. He chose politically experienced people for his top aides, some from his Senate staff. His chief of staff in the Senate, David Ayres, became his chief of staff at Justice. Ayres reportedly was known for "his shrewd political instincts and absolute loyalty to Ashcroft," leading one senior Justice attorney to observe that "he was always looking for a way to put his boss out there in the best light."[80] Other senior staff also had experience in politics. Paul Clement, who served as interim solicitor general in Ashcroft's final year, also had worked for him on the Hill.[81] Among his other key aides, David Israelite had spent three years as the political director of the Republican National Committee (RNC), and Mindy Tucker, Ashcroft's first spokesperson, had been press secretary of the Bush-Cheney campaign and later joined the RNC. [82] Fellow Missourian Larry Thompson, who had advised Clarence Thomas during his Senate confirmation fight in 1991, was named deputy attorney general.[83] This political experience, however, did not mean that some of these aides did not have solid legal credentials. Thompson had served as a U.S. attorney for four years and was a partner with the Atlanta law firm of King and Spalding. Clement also had been a King and Spalding partner and taught law part-time.[84] Viet Dinh was a professor at Georgetown University Law School when he was selected assistant attorney general.[85] Yet the perception of politics held. One observer called it "an intensely political operation, without a career Justice Department employee in the inner circle."[86]

He also was accused of politicizing the selection of new law school graduates through the Attorney General's Honors Program. Before his tenure, the program was operated by career attorneys, but he placed the program under political appointees. Critics said this move effectively filtered out prospective candidates who were liberal or Democrats. Some law school placement officers did confirm that there was "a marked shift to the right in the political makeup of students" who interviewed with the program. Rejecting the contention that politics played any part in the process, Ashcroft's aides defended the move as resulting in a higher-quality applicant.[87] Others in the department said the honors program became "political and partisan" under Ashcroft's stewardship, with candidates who had been associated with the Federalist Society getting "preferential treatment."[88] In addition to the honors program, Ashcroft required political clearance of the release of crime statistics by the Bureau of Justice Statistics and of decisions on research grants. Reporters found that his department tended to "play favorites" with news organizations that were friendlier in their coverage, such as FOX News. These practices also led to charges of politicization.[89]

Ashcroft's high visibility reinforced this sense. He often made the public announcements that other attorneys general, such as Griffin Bell of the Carter administration, left to the Justice Department press office. Bell noted that his earlier experience as a federal judge caused him to eschew the more public role.[90] C. Madison Brewer, a longtime staff attorney, confirmed the impression that the attorney general liked the limelight. "Ashcroft particularly liked to announce indictments," he said.[91] Unlike Bell, Ashcroft regularly announced arrests, indictments, and plea agreements, as well as departmental initiatives and operations.[92] On occasion, Ashcroft's public appearances seemed to eclipse others, such as Homeland Security head Tom Ridge. Sometimes he was accused of self-promotion, of acting "more like a pushy politician with his own agenda than the nation's chief law enforcement officer."[93]

Ashcroft's extensive political credentials—more than his more limited legal experience—may have recommended him to the president-elect. His years as state attorney general, governor, and U.S. senator were cited by Senate Republicans as evidence that he was "the most experienced Attorney General nominee in American history."[94] His public life centered on elective office, and his success in five statewide races in Missouri suggested that voters did not see him as too extreme in his views. At the same time, he brought along a valuable constituency: white Protestant evangelicals who had been essential to the 2000 election outcome and would be critical again for Bush in 2004.[95] Bush may have been motivated by the same electoral factors that had influenced other presidents in selecting their cabinet officers: "past campaign debts and future reelection hopes."[96] One conservative activist described Ashcroft as "good in a chameleon-like way at representing his constituencies within conservatism,"[97] that is, strongly conservative without necessarily appearing to be to those outside the fold. While he lost this chameleon quality once at Justice, Ashcroft would have appeared to be a valuable ally for the incoming president, one with substantial political skills and important connections. And the president may have seen in Ashcroft a law officer willing to be bold in securing executive authority.

Broad Interpretations of Presidential Power

Because of the vagueness in much constitutional language related to the presidency, many contemporary law officers have used legal language to advance an expansive interpretation of executive power, particularly through the Office of Legal Counsel. A memorandum sent to Ashcroft by nineteen former high-ranking attorneys in Clinton's Justice Department opened with the widely held view that the "OLC's legal determinations are considered binding on the executive branch, subject to the supervision of the Attorney General and the ultimate authority of the President."[98]

The two constitutional provisions most often cited as the basis for broad power claims are the designation of the president as the "Commander in

Chief of the Army and Navy," and the charge to the president to "take care that the laws are faithfully executed." As noted, neither of these phrases is clear; in fact, the second phrase may be read as a limit on power rather than a grant. Law professor Louis Henkin observed that, "on the face of it," the president's constitutional powers even in foreign affairs appear to be "strikingly little."[99] As Henkin and most other scholars of the presidency and Constitution have noted, however, twentieth-century presidents have been able to use the terms to expand the powers of the office dramatically. During the Bush administration, Ashcroft interpreted these phrases even more broadly than his predecessors in office, reading the first one to mean "the commander in chief of the nation," and the second to mean a unique grant of executive authority that, under separation of powers, may not be abridged by the other branches. These points will be discussed later in the book.

The importance of the legal advisory role for presidential power is well illustrated by the Justice Department's handling of the question of the status of detainees held by the U.S. military at Guantánamo Bay, Afghanistan, and Iraq. Department lawyers in the OLC argued, in January 2002, that neither the Geneva Conventions, customary international law, nor the 1996 War Crimes Act, a federal law incorporating several Geneva provisions into the criminal code, applied to al Qaeda or Taliban detainees. They determined that al Qaeda, as a violent political movement and not a nation-state, was ineligible to be a Geneva signatory, and that the Taliban militia was "a nongovernmental organization . . . intertwined with al Qaeda," and therefore exempt from the protections of international law. Further, because Afghanistan was a failed state, "the President has the constitutional authority to suspend our treaties with Afghanistan pending the restoration of a legitimate government capable of performing Afghanistan's treaty obligations."[100] Their conclusion expressed a stunningly broad interpretation of executive power: "We conclude that customary international law, whatever its source and content, does not bind the President, or restrict the actions of the United States military, because it does not constitute federal law recognized under the Supremacy Clause of the Constitution."[101] The president might choose, as a policy matter, to extend international law to the situation, but he was not legally required to do so. White House Counsel Gonzales referred to the OLC's novel interpretation in his memo dismissing the counterarguments advanced by attorneys in the State Department and Joint Chiefs of Staff. While conceding that the secretary of state's chief legal adviser disagreed with the OLC, Gonzales wrote, "OLC's interpretation of this legal issue is definitive. The Attorney General is charged by statute with interpreting the law for the Executive Branch. This interpretive authority extends to both domestic and international law. He has, in turn, delegated this role to OLC."[102]

On February 1, 2002, Ashcroft sent a letter directly to the president outlining the advantage of the position that the Geneva Convention did not apply to the conflict in Afghanistan because it was a failed state, over the position that the convention did apply, but not to Taliban combatants because "they acted as unlawful combatants." While he considered both positions legal, he told Bush that the second position would "carry higher risk of liability, criminal prosecution, and judicially-imposed conditions of detainment—including the mandated release of a detainee." The first position was free of such constraints on the executive.[103]

Ashcroft evidently failed to communicate the OLC interpretation to the Office of Solicitor General, thereby creating a very difficult environment for the government's attorney arguing the enemy combatant cases before the Supreme Court. During oral arguments in the cases of *Hamdi v. Rumsfeld* and *Rumsfeld v. Padilla,* both held on April 28, 2004, Deputy Solicitor General Paul Clement was asked directly about coercive interrogations and unchecked executive powers, and he twice reassured the justices that "the United States is going to honor its treaty obligations." That same evening, television news programs began to broadcast photographs of prisoners being abused at Abu Ghraib prison in Iraq.[104] Clement appeared to have been either lying to the justices or out of the loop, a perception that was heightened once the memo was made public a few months later.

This and other OLC memoranda helped to establish legal cover for actions that the administration wanted to take or already was taking in the war against terror. The lead author of the Geneva memo, John Yoo, argued in a memo coauthored with Patrick Philbin that U.S. courts had no habeas jurisdiction over Guantánamo detainees. While they conceded that they "found no decisions that clearly foreclose the existence of habeas jurisdiction there," they argued that "a court should defer to the executive branch's activities and decisions prosecuting the war in Afghanistan."[105] Another draft opinion, authored by former OLC director Jack Goldsmith in March 2004, argued that detainees in Iraq could be transferred to other countries for interrogation, a critical reinterpretation of the Fourth Geneva Convention and one that appeared to sanction the transfer of detainees to countries that permitted torture during interrogations. The memo's legal reasoning was criticized by international law experts. A former senior military attorney, Scott Silliman of Duke University's Center on Law, Ethics and National Security, said, "The memorandum seeks to create a legal regime justifying conduct that the international community clearly considers in violation of international law and the Convention."[106]

Even more controversial was the memo authored by the head of the OLC, Jay Bybee, in August 2002, that argued that domestic and international laws prohibiting torture could unconstitutionally infringe on the president's wartime authority: "Any effort to apply Section 2340A in a manner that interferes with the President's direction of such core war matters as the detention and interrogation of enemy combatants thus would be unconstitutional."[107] The memo also defined torture more narrowly than earlier documents. "Cruel, inhumane or degrading acts" were not necessarily proscribed. To be defined as torture under the OLC's reading of the law, physical pain had to be extreme, "equivalent in intensity to the pain accompanying . . . organ failure, impairment of bodily function or even death," and psychological pain "had to result in significant psychological harm of significant duration, e.g., lasting for months or even years." Interrogation tactics falling short of this, from the government's point of view, were permissible under international law. Furthermore, an agent who causes extreme pain "is guilty of torture only if he acts with the express purpose of inflicting severe pain or suffering," and not—for example—if he acts with the purpose of interrogation.[108] One former administration official defended the position taken by the OLC: "The Department of Justice, the Department of Defense and the CIA were all in alignment that we had to have the flexibility to handle the detainees—and yes, interrogate them—in ways that would be effective" to prevent another 9/11.[109]

The memo's trajectory after leaving the OLC is unclear. A memo of such importance would normally be submitted first to the attorney general; a number of administration officials confirmed that Ashcroft, as well as the head of the criminal division, Michael Chertoff, approved of the memo.[110] It did go to Gonzales at the White House counsel's office, but Gonzales later denied that the president had seen the fifty-page memo. Appearing before the Senate once the document became known, Ashcroft asserted that "this administration opposes torture." He then refused to release that memo and others to the Senate, charging instead that his critics were forgetting that the nation was at war.[111] The memo appeared to have influenced Pentagon policy. A March 2003 report by the Pentagon based in part on the memo said, "In order to respect the President's inherent constitutional authority to manage a military campaign . . . [the prohibitions against torture] must be construed as inapplicable to interrogations undertaken pursuant to his Commander-in-Chief authority."[112] The Defense Department Working Group drew heavily from these memos "for the legal framework for its review of interrogation techniques," according to Senator Carl Levin (D-Mich.).[113] A Defense Department spokesman contradicted that view, asserting that the March report was not a legal analysis and that it had no effect on the interrogation procedures approved by Rumsfeld the following month.[114] Speculation continued, however, that the OLC memoranda relating to international treaties and torture fostered an environment where something like Abu Ghraib could occur. Pressure continued to build. In a highly unusual move, the OLC repudiated much of Bybee's memo in December 2004. One week before the start of the confirmation hearings of Alberto Gonzales to be attorney general, the acting assistant attorney general for the OLC issued a new memorandum that provided a broader definition of actions that constitute torture. The claim of extensive presidential power in interrogations was not repudiated, however.[115]

Through the power to issue legal interpretations, the Justice Department sought to recast international and statutory law to give executive branch officials greater flexibility in detaining and interrogating prisoners at Guantánamo and elsewhere. The memos also were intended to establish potential legal defenses should criminal charges against government agents ever arise. This feature of the memos also appears unusual. As constitutional scholar Louis Fisher has written, "How often does the Justice Department and the OLC offer helpful hints and litigation strategies to those who violate the law?"[116]

Ashcroft and the Bully Pulpit of Law

In addition to the formal powers to affect the development of the law—through OLC memoranda, the solicitor general's litigation priorities, and the selection of judges to federal courts—the attorney general exercises an informal power to recast how the public, the press, and others in government think about particular laws. The attorney general's perspective on a legal issue is highly persuasive, even when it counters established Supreme Court precedent.

Ashcroft's efforts to reframe the Second Amendment illustrate how an attorney general can utilize the bully pulpit of the office in a way that affects public perceptions and potentially alters the development of the law. For half a century at least, the Justice Department interpreted the Second Amendment's provisions as establishing a collective right—through a government-sponsored militia—to bear arms. According to a number of academic studies, this interpretation accorded with the few Supreme Court precedents on the subject.[117] But soon after entering office, Ashcroft asserted a different view in a letter to the executive director of the National Rifle Association, arguing instead that the Second Amendment recognized an individual right to gun ownership. Political scientist Robert Spitzer argued that the widely disseminated letter so mischaracterized precedent and the framers' views that "Attorney General Ashcroft was attempting in this letter to invent a legal past for the Second Amendment that simply does not exist."[118] Even a supporter of Ashcroft's view of an individual right, law professor Eugene Volokh, noted that the view had fallen from favor by the 1930s.[119] In November 2001, Ashcroft sent a directive to all of the U.S. attorneys, telling them to adopt his interpretation of the Second Amendment.[120] Later, Solicitor General Theodore Olson, who had not been consulted in this legal shift, slipped footnotes embracing the individualistic view into briefs filed with the Supreme Court in two gun-related prosecutions.[121] In upholding the prosecutions in both cases, the justices did not remark on the footnotes. The Justice Department's actions, coupled with the Court's silence, resulted in an immediate flurry of litigation challenging gun control laws under this new interpretation of the Second Amendment.[122] More than 130 challenges were filed against federal gun laws just in Virginia and Washington, D.C.[123] In just one year, from May 2001 to June 2002, Ashcroft was able to transform a legal view that was inconsistent with long-established case law into a credible and viable alternative interpretation of the Constitution. In 2004, in a memorandum for the attorney general, the Office of Legal Counsel solidified the interpretation that "the Second Amendment secures an individual right to keep and bear arms."[124]

On the expanded new powers authorized by the Patriot Act, Ashcroft's reassurances were unequivocal and may have helped to ensure its passage with virtually no dissent. Speaking in favor of the bill, he declared, "We will preserve the rule of law, because it is that which makes us civilized. . . . We will, as in the past, never waver in our faith and loyalty to the Constitution. And we will never tire in our defense of the rights that are enshrined in the Constitution."[125] Perhaps placated by this remark and other reassurances, most members of Congress and the news media avoided asking difficult questions about the impact of the law on civil liberties, either during the congressional debate or immediately following the vote. Even Leahy, the usually critical Democratic chairman of the Senate Judiciary Committee, described the measure as "a good bill . . . that allows us to preserve our security . . . but also protect our liberties."[126]

The attorney general frequently repeated these reassurances to answer growing concerns about the Patriot Act and other antiterrorism actions. The words "law," "legal," and "Constitution" appeared regularly in his speeches, interviews, and press releases, often juxtaposed against dark warnings of the terrorist threat. He told the House of Representatives in 2003: "We must never forget that we are in a war to preserve life and liberty. We must not forget that our enemies are ruthless fanatics who seek to murder innocent women and children and men to achieve their twisted goals. We must not forget that in the struggle between the forces of freedom and the ideology of hate, our challenge in this war against terrorism is to adapt, to anticipate, outthink, outmaneuver our enemies while honoring our Constitution."[127]

Ashcroft made similar statements before the Senate. When discussing the department's handling of the war against terrorism, he told senators that the changes he advocated—for example, ending informational barriers between federal prosecutors and intelligence officers—were "rooted in our Constitutional liberties."[128] Similarly, he told a conference of U.S. attorneys in October 2002, "Our actions are firmly rooted in the Constitution . . . and consistent with the laws passed by Congress,"[129] the same phrase he employed a week later when addressing the International Association of Chiefs of Police.[130] At one press conference, Ashcroft answered a reporter's query about allegations that the department's tactics violated individual rights with this assertion: "We believe that we have conducted this investigation in complete accord with the constitutional guidelines—the rules of the Constitution, the principles of it, and within the limits and proposed guidelines of specific legislation."[131] He reassured federal appellate judges that "our post–September 11 policies have been carefully crafted to prevent terrorist attacks while protecting the privacy and civil liberties of Americans."[132] He told members of the Federalist Society that the Patriot Act uses "court-tested safeguards and time-honored ideas to aid the war against terrorism, while protecting the rights and lives of citizens."[133] The language of legal precedent and authority predominated in his announcement of the transfer of American citizen José Padilla to Defense Department custody. "We have acted with legal authority both under the laws of war and clear Supreme Court precedent," Ashcroft asserted.[134] His spokesman responded to the release of the OLC memo on torture, already mentioned, by invoking the law as well: "The department does not comment on specific legal advice it has provided confidentially within the executive branch. It is the policy of the United States to comply with all U.S. laws in the treatment of detainees—including the Constitution, federal statutes and treaties."[135]

The attorney general regularly referred to the language of civil rights as well. The headline of a three-page *Parade Magazine* piece proclaimed his message, "We're Not Destroying Rights, We're Protecting Rights."[136] He described the interrogation process whereby federal agents questioned thousands of foreign nationals as one that exhibited "full respect for the rights and dignity of the individuals being interviewed."[137] He called the revised guidelines permitting FBI agents to monitor public gatherings and infiltrate groups a demonstration to the American public that the agency would protect them from terrorism "with a scrupulous respect for civil rights and personal freedoms."[138] Along a similar line, Ashcroft used a 2002 television appearance on Martin Luther King Jr. Day to emphasize the department's respect for "rights of the individual."[139] In his last days in office, Ashcroft repeated his reassurances, "Rights have not been infringed. Human dignity has not suffered. It's been enhanced and it has not carried a cost or toll on the civil liberties of America."[140]

While insisting that constitutional rights and rule of law were not sacrificed in the quest to secure the country, Ashcroft sent conflicting signals as well. He expounded a view numerous times that civil liberties, judicial process, and open government were vulnerabilities that could be exploited by terrorists. In addition, he seemed to harbor a deep ambivalence about the utility of the law in tackling terrorism effectively. The dichotomy between those viewpoints will be discussed later in the book.

Conclusion

Ashcroft's advisory role in the administration, unlike the activist role of some of his predecessors, such as Robert Kennedy and Edwin Meese, may have been limited despite his own extensive political experience. His daily meetings with the president, to be discussed later, were brief and appear to have been designed to provide the president with information more than consultation. On matters related to presidential power, he was often overshadowed by others. Alberto Gonzales, who was closer to the president both figuratively and literally, played a key advisory role, although both Ashcroft and Gonzales may have been eclipsed by Cheney's legal counsel, David Addington.[141] The dominance of the White House in legal policymaking could be part of a larger trend identified by cabinet scholars, the shifting of policymaking to White House staff, leaving policy implementation to the secretaries. Ashcroft's OLC did issue several significant memos, as discussed, but the advice proffered appears to have accorded with views already held by the White House. The intent of the memos appears to have been to advise others outside the Oval Office, including military officers and courts that might adjudicate future cases.

Even so, as attorney general, Ashcroft had substantial authority. He was situated near the top of the U.S. legal system, heading a massive agency charged with legal as well as administrative responsibilities. There, he could advance the president's goal of reasserting executive power, an administration objective from the start. He also had the opportunity to inaugurate a proactive mission for the Justice Department, one with important consequences for executive authority and civil liberties. Ashcroft used the tools within his reach—litigation and lobbying, reassuring rhetoric and expansive legal interpretations—to try to achieve the twin goals of promoting presidential authority and countering the terrorist threat. As the next chapter will explore, Ashcroft's personal worldview and political experience were critical factors in determining how he approached that task.

3   Understanding Ashcroft

John Ashcroft's presence as U.S. attorney general at the time of the September 11 attacks was central to how the national government responded. His choices particularly affected counterterrorism policy and personnel, but his actions also influenced myriad other areas where law and policy intersect, including the death penalty, gun control, drug enforcement, and the right to die. Despite his policy impact, Ashcroft became known more for what he symbolized than for the specific policies he pursued. Because of this, his portrait is little more than a caricature drawn with broad strokes and little shading. He was fodder for comedians, a foil for administration critics, a lightning rod for the president, and a guiding light for the faithful. This chapter examines his personal and political history, policy orientations, and relationships to help explain the effect he had on legal developments in the Bush administration.

John Ashcroft of Missouri

Born in Chicago in 1942, John David Ashcroft was raised in Springfield, Missouri, where he continues to maintain a 155-acre farm. He preceded George W. Bush at Yale University by a few years and earned a bachelor's degree with honors in history in 1964. Three years later, he received a juris doctorate from the University of Chicago School of Law, where he met his wife, Janet. The young couple moved back to Springfield that year. Ashcroft taught business law at Southwest Missouri State University until 1972 and coauthored two college business law textbooks with his wife, *It's the Law* and *Law for Business.*[1] A key feature of his upbringing, according to his 1998 memoir, *Lessons from a Father to His Son,* was his father's religious instruction.[2] His father and grandfather were ministers in the Assemblies of God, "the largest and most influential white Pentecostal denomination in the United States."[3] His father also served as president of a religious college in Missouri.[4]

Ashcroft's political life began in 1972 with a run for the Republican nomination to Congress. He lost to the GOP incumbent in a tight race. He describes this in his autobiography as the first political crucifixion of his life. But the political death was soon followed by a political resurrection, when the closeness of the race drew the attention of Missouri Republican leaders, and Governor Christopher Bond appointed him to a midterm vacancy as state auditor. When Ashcroft campaigned for the auditor's post in 1974, he lost again. The first election following the Watergate scandal and Richard Nixon's resignation, 1974 was a bad year for Republicans, including a fresh newcomer. But another opportunity arose when Missouri attorney general John Danforth hired him to be an assistant attorney general, where he served with another young attorney named Clarence Thomas. When Danforth went to the Senate, Ashcroft twice won election as state attorney general, serving from 1977 until 1985.[5]

Starting with his tenure as state attorney general, Ashcroft established a solid conservative record, one that drew support from religious and social conservatives and increasing hostility from women's and civil rights organizations. In 1979, he used the Sherman Antitrust Act against the National Organization for Women (NOW), seeking injunctive relief because of its convention boycott of states like Missouri that had not ratified the equal rights amendment. Ashcroft's application of federal antitrust law to go after a political organization was innovative and—to some—unsettling. It was also unsuccessful; the U.S. district court denied relief, a ruling that was reaffirmed by the Eighth Circuit Court of Appeals. The court found that NOW's actions fell within the scope of the First Amendment because the group's goal was not economic but political—to pressure those states into ratifying the ERA.[6] Ashcroft drew conservative acclaim when he argued the abortion case *Planned Parenthood of Kansas City v. Ashcroft* before the U.S. Supreme Court. Planned Parenthood was challenging Missouri's requirement that second-trimester abortions necessitated hospitalization, pathology reports, second physicians, and parental or judicial consent for minors. Ashcroft partly lost the appeal; by a 4 to 3 vote, the justices determined that Missouri's requirement for second-trimester hospitalization was unconstitutional.[7]

Ashcroft's high-profile record fighting court-ordered school desegregation in St. Louis and Kansas City, Missouri, helped to cement his reputation among conservatives. He blamed the desegregation plans for imposing high costs on Missouri taxpayers, which he estimated to be $100 million.[8] One old acquaintance said, "There was this image of Ashcroft not quite standing in the schoolhouse door but giving voice to Missourians' complaints."[9] The St. Louis case had originated with a 1972 class action lawsuit that alleged racial segregation in the schools. The Eighth Circuit agreed with plaintiffs and ordered that a desegregation plan be submitted. By 1983, a five-year voluntary desegregation plan was accepted by the city and county school boards and approved by the federal district court. As state attorney general, though, Ashcroft repeatedly challenged the plan, even though the twenty-two surrounding white school districts approved of the desegregation order.[10] With the assistance of Edwin Meese, at the time a key counselor in Ronald Reagan's White House, he persuaded the Justice Department to oppose the St. Louis plan.[11] When it was largely upheld by the Eighth Circuit, Ashcroft appealed to the Supreme Court, but review was denied. Regardless of the judicial setbacks, he continued to resist implementation of the plan even after he became governor. His efforts reportedly almost earned him a contempt of court citation.[12] Ashcroft's record on race became an issue again when, as governor, he twice vetoed laws designed to increase voter registration in St. Louis, a city with the state's lowest voter registration and among the highest concentration of black voters.[13]

His socially conservative voting record on abortion and affirmative action continued throughout his two terms as Missouri governor, an office he held from 1985 until 1993. His policy choices often reflected his conservative moral values. He helped to block a father's efforts to move his brain-damaged daughter, Christine Busalacchi, to another state for a second medical evaluation. Ashcroft praised the state authorities who intervened when the father sought another doctor's evaluation so that he could have the daughter's feeding tube removed if her condition was hopeless.[14] Ashcroft also supported measures to restrict minors' access to cigarettes and violent movie rentals, and he vetoed a bill permitting liquor sales on Sunday.[15]

Yet his Missouri record was not uniformly conservative. According to former governor Bond, Ashcroft as state attorney general issued opinions that sometimes conflicted with his religious views. Three examples are notable: he determined that state law did not require a death certificate for a fetus less than twenty weeks old, the state education board could not authorize the distribution of religious material on public school property, and a state commission could grant a set-aside program for minority businesses.[16] Later, as governor, Ashcroft focused on balanced budgets, low taxes, and school funding. He signed a hate-crimes bill into law and supported the "battered women's syndrome" defense in homicide cases involving abused women.[17] No scandal tainted his administration, other than a minor flurry over his young son's after-hours access to the state library for a homework assignment.[18]

With this record, Ashcroft was able to attract moderately conservative voters in Missouri, reaching beyond his religious base. A broad appeal was critical in a swing state like Missouri, which, unlike his hometown of Springfield, is not a bastion of deep Republicanism.[19] He benefited from the early sponsorship of Danforth and Bond, considered to be pillars of the Missouri Republican establishment.[20] In the 1980s and 1990s, he won five statewide races, some with broad support.[21] In his second gubernatorial race, for example, he received 64 percent of the vote. His win was unusual; no Missouri governor had been elected to a second consecutive term in twenty years.[22] A similar pattern emerged in his first run for the U.S. Senate, where he won every county in the state.[23] In addition, Ashcroft garnered support from his peers nationwide as both state attorney general and governor, elected as president of the National Association of Attorneys General (NAAG) and later as chairman of the National Governors Association.[24] In 1993, he won the NAAG's Wyman Award for his efforts to achieve the association's objectives.[25] The Republican Policy Committee in the Senate pointed to these accomplishments during Ashcroft's heated confirmation hearings to be attorney general: "If John Ashcroft's execution of these earlier public trusts was as far 'out of the mainstream' as his critics now claim, *wouldn't his fellow state attorneys general or governors have noticed?*"[26] His success with his peers may have been attributable to a personal style in informal settings described by some as "very charming" and "likeable, engaging and funny."[27]

When he left the governor's mansion, Ashcroft sought the post of chairman of the Republican National Committee. He had more political experience than either of his rivals, Haley Barbour and Spencer Abraham; even so, he lost to Barbour.[28] Meanwhile, he reestablished his association with the St. Louis law firm Suelthaus and Kaplan, maintaining the affiliation until 2000. But he soon found another opportunity in public life when Danforth retired from the U.S. Senate. Following again in Danforth's footprints, he won that Senate seat in 1994.[29]

Serving in the U.S. Senate

In the Senate, Ashcroft was appointed to the Judiciary Committee, where he was chairman of the Subcommittee on the Constitution, Federalism and Property Rights. He also served on the Committee on Foreign Relations and the Committee on Commerce, Science and Transportation, where he was ranking member of the Subcommittee on Consumer Affairs, Foreign Commerce and Tourism.[30]

Generally speaking, his one term, from 1995 to 2001, was not noteworthy. His highest-profile legislative action was promoting the charitable choice provision in the welfare reform law, which enabled religious groups to more easily solicit federal funds to provide social services. Like George W. Bush, he believed that the notion of "separation of church and state" had been used to justify discrimination against religious organizations. He explained in 1997 that religious entities had avoided seeking federal funds in the past out of "fear of having to compromise their religious integrity or being hobbled by excessive government regulation and intrusion."[31] He wanted to rectify that situation.

Ashcroft also drew public attention by being the first senator to call on President Bill Clinton to resign following allegations that he had lied in his deposition in the Paula Jones case. When Clinton demurred, Ashcroft voted in favor of both articles of impeachment, arguing that the president had engaged in perjury and obstruction of justice. To Ashcroft, these were "high crimes and misdemeanors," because they "undermine public confidence in government and strike at the integrity of our systems of government and justice." [32] However, should the Senate fail to convict Clinton in the impeachment trial, Ashcroft pragmatically advised his colleagues to return to legislative business and not pursue some other punishment. "To accomplish legislative goals for the nation, it will be necessary for Congress and the President to work together," he said.[33]

On the issue of abortion, he cosponsored the Human Life Act of 1998, which declared that life begins at fertilization,[34] a constitutional amendment to recognize a "right to life" at every stage of fetal development, including fertilization,[35] and a resolution calling for a constitutional amendment to ban abortion even in the case of incest or rape.[36] His religious views also underlay his support of bans on human embryo cloning and physician-assisted suicide.[37] In fact, as a senator, he pushed the Reno Justice Department to go after Oregon's physician-assisted suicide law, and he advocated congressional action to change state rules relating to who could write medical prescriptions.[38] He was a vocal critic of the National Endowment for the Arts, which he believed squandered taxpayer money on obscene artistic expressions.[39] Ashcroft also supported school vouchers and state-sanctioned school prayer and voted in favor of a ban on flag desecration. He fought gun regulations and opposed the inclusion of sexual orientation in civil rights and hate-crime laws. He often spoke against an activist liberal judiciary. As a longtime supporter of states' rights, he rejected federal sanctions on states to enforce lower speed limits.[40]

His record of success in the Senate was mixed. He unsuccessfully fought confirmation of Clinton's choice of David Satcher to be surgeon general; Satcher opposed a ban on so-called late term abortions.[41] However, he was successful in derailing Clinton's appointment of Ronnie White to the federal bench. White was the first African American to serve on the Missouri high court and had received a unanimous qualified rating from the American Bar Association. White's federal judicial appointment was killed on the Senate floor after Senator Ashcroft characterized him as "pro criminal." Both during White's confirmation hearings and later in Ashcroft's own hearings, Ashcroft said he opposed the nomination because White was soft on crime, pointing to White's dissent in a state death penalty case. Yet their history extended further back and over other issues; years before, White had served in the state legislature while Ashcroft was governor, and the two men had particularly clashed over abortion legislation.[42]

In terms of executive power, Ashcroft's Senate votes did not uncritically support either military funding or broad presidential power in military affairs. In 1999 and 2000, Ashcroft favored terminating funds to the executive branch for the continued deployment of U.S. ground troops in Yugoslavia and Kosovo, respectively, unless the deployment was authorized by Congress. He also voted against presidential authority to impose sanctions on medicine and farm products against certain countries without the approval of Congress. In other ways, however, his votes reflect a willingness to accede to executive authority. In 1995, he had supported the item veto bill permitting an executive veto of individual spending items, subject to a veto override by two-thirds of each house.[43] Two years later, he favored granting the president the authority to make selective cuts of "individual spending items, limited tax breaks or new entitlement programs from larger bills already signed into law," and he backed a cloture vote to end a filibuster on fast-track trade pacts.[44]

As in Missouri, Ashcroft's Senate record garnered high ratings from conservative organizations. The National Right to Life Committee announced that he had a 100 percent voting record on its issues. On the Christian Coalition's scorecard—which tracked votes on such issues as education, arts financing, abortion, and the budget—he also garnered a rating of 100 percent.[45] In addition, he received a 100 percent rating from the Eagle Forum in his last year in the Senate. Conversely, he received ratings of 14 percent from the American Civil Liberties Union and zero percent from the National Organization for Women and the League of Conservation Voters.[46]

Yet, like his record in Missouri, his Senate career cannot be characterized as uniformly conservative. He cosponsored reauthorization of the Violence against Women Act, and he and Democratic senator Russell Feingold held hearings on racial profiling before the Constitutional Subcommittee of the Senate Judiciary Committee.[47]

Ashcroft weighed a run for the White House in 1998. A Senate colleague, Jeff Bingaman (D-N.M.), said it was "when he began to be mentioned as presidential timber [that] he became more and more outspoken on the very conservative end" of a lot of issues.[48] In seeking the party's nomination, Ashcroft began to emphasize his pro-life credentials in public appearances, carrying a Missouri Right to Life banner to one antiabortion meeting and comparing the pro-life movement with the civil rights movement of the 1960s: "We have the most noble and worthy objective that we could have."[49] Money from conservative religious organizations and individuals poured into American Values, a friendly political action committee based in Virginia.[50] Pat and Adelia Robertson gave him $10,000 for the race.[51] The Christian Coalition of Florida, the Liberty Foundation, and Focus on the Family were among the groups that paid his travel expenses for twenty-eight trips in 1998.[52] In February that year, a sizable plurality of Christian Coalition leaders endorsed his possible candidacy; with their support, Ashcroft beat George W. Bush in a May 1998 straw poll in South Carolina.[53] He also received indications of support from Phyllis Schlafly of the Eagle Forum, James C. Dobson of Focus on the Family,[54] and Paul Weyrich of the Free Congress Foundation. Other social conservative backers included Tim LaHaye of the Council for National Policy, Donald Wildmon of the American Family Association, and Michael Farris of the home-schooling movement.[55] The *National Review* predicted that he had "a legitimate chance to emerge as the most electable conservative in the presidential race" because of his political experience and "sterling ethical record."[56] Columnist George Will called him the "pinup candidate for social conservatives in 2000."[57]

However, Ashcroft's candidacy faced numerous obstacles: low national name recognition and a speaking style described as wooden. He faced competition for the social conservative vote from Steve Forbes and others. He had particular difficulty attracting economic conservatives to his campaign.[58] In January 1999, determining that he did not have the support necessary to win the GOP nomination, he decided to seek reelection to the Senate.

That race was tight. Then, shortly before the election, his opponent, Mel Carnahan, was killed in an airplane accident. It was too late to reprint the ballots, so Carnahan's name was left in place. Missouri's Democratic governor pledged to appoint Carnahan's widow, Jean, to the seat should voters select Carnahan. Voters did by a narrow margin. It must have been a bitter loss to Ashcroft; he and Carnahan were political foes from the days when Carnahan was lieutenant governor while Ashcroft was governor. Under Missouri law, Ashcroft could have had grounds to contest the election, since a deceased person is arguably not a resident of the state as required by the Missouri constitution.[59] Some supporters encouraged him to challenge the outcome, but Ashcroft conceded defeat, saying: "Some things are more important than politics, and I believe doing what's right is the most important thing we can do. I think as public officials we have the opportunity to model values for our culture—responsibility, dignity, decency, integrity, and respect. And if we can only model those when it's politically expedient to do so, we've never modeled the values, we've only modeled political expediency."[60] His gracious concession impressed George Bush and established goodwill among Senate Democrats, at least for a while.[61]

The Nomination

To head the Justice Department, the president-elect initially considered Marc Racicot, the former governor of Montana. Racicot had helped Bush during the 2000 Florida recount battle and—though a pro-life Republican—was not considered too controversial. In fact, at one point in his governorship, he garnered an impressive 87 percent public approval rating, the highest of any governor at the time. [62] But he had attracted adverse publicity as well, when, in the severe winter of 1997, he ordered state-paid marksmen to kill starving wild buffalo that wandered away from Yellowstone National Park. It was an effort to protect domestic cattle herds from buffalo-carried disease, but the images of so many wild buffalo being slaughtered raised an outcry. [63] Even so, that event may not have been as decisive in derailing his selection as his reputation as a moderate on the charged issues of homosexuality, school choice, and even abortion. Those positions reportedly troubled Catholic as well as Protestant conservatives, who worked together behind the scenes to discredit Racicot among other conservatives. Later, when Racicot declined the nomination, some activists on the religious right claimed that they had forced his withdrawal.[64]

Reportedly, the next person considered was Oklahoma governor Frank Keating, who had served as associate attorney general in Ronald Reagan's administration. Keating contacted Vice President Dick Cheney to express his interest in the post. Despite a positive public image due to his and his wife's handling of the emotional trauma arising from the Oklahoma City bombing, Keating had also attracted negative coverage when he advocated an antiabortion litmus test for national Republican candidates and made insensitive public remarks about minorities.[65] Complicating his selection, he had accepted a number of large cash gifts from a Wall Street financier during his time in government, which though legal raised a perception of impropriety.[66]

In the end, Ashcroft—another former governor—was selected. He had written to the president weeks earlier expressing his interest in the attorney general position.[67] He reportedly had been considered by the Bush campaign team a likely attorney general appointment as early as the summer of 2000.[68] At the time, the appointment of Ashcroft appeared less controversial than that of either Racicot or Keating. Key moderate GOP senators had informed Cheney that Ashcroft would be "a fine attorney general," and some Democratic senators had also promised Ashcroft their support.[69] Having just left the Senate, he was expected to sail through his confirmation hearings,[70] a perception shared by the president-elect, who believed that senators would support one of their own.[71] That was not an unreasonable expectation. The Senate's 1989 rejection of former colleague John Tower to be defense secretary marked only the second time in history that a former senator had been denied confirmation to a cabinet post.[72]

With Racicot no longer in the running, white Protestant evangelicals rallied to Ashcroft. Bush owed the Christian Right for its early support of his nomination, especially in states like South Carolina where it is active and influential. Further, Ashcroft had given him a crucial endorsement during the South Carolina GOP primary.[73] During his race for the nomination, Bush had promised a group of social conservative leaders that he would not forget their support when someday picking his cabinet. As one of those leaders later reported, "He is keeping that promise. John Ashcroft is an example of that."[74]

To ensure that the new president did not forget his pledge, religious leaders made regular phone calls during the transition period, according to Bush aides. The calls stressed the importance of a socially conservative attorney general. Among those calling were Carl Herbster, the president of the American Association of Christian Schools,[75] and David Barton, a heavyweight in Christian Right circles and later vice chairman of the Texas Republican Party.[76] Also influential in lobbying for Ashcroft's nomination was the chairman of the Religious Liberties Practice Group of the Federalist Society, Robert P. George.[77] Ashcroft's electoral importance in 2000 and potential importance in 2004 could have been a key factor in his appointment.

For social conservatives, Janet Reno's tenure at Justice had been a major failure on important issues such as abortion, affirmative action, gun control, drug policy, and school prayer. Her handling of the Branch Davidian standoff at Waco, the Elian Gonzales custody case, and Clinton administration scandals also infuriated conservatives.[78] Ashcroft embraced the opposite policy positions. The post at Justice represented a major prize for the president's religious constituency. Thomas Jipping of the Free Congress Foundation noted, "I don't think there will be any department where there will be a bigger change represented by a single appointment than at Justice."[79] As one *Wall Street Journal* commentary noted of Ashcroft's appointment, "This was an attorney general selected as a cultural warrior."[80] In a sense, the outspoken conservative posture that he had endorsed in his presidential bid "may have helped him get nominated by President Bush," said Senator Bingaman, adding that it also "made it more difficult for him to get confirmed without a lot of controversy."[81] Considered by some "the most socially conservative figure to become Attorney General in many years,"[82] Ashcroft was appointed not to placate or negotiate but to advance a conservative values agenda through legislative proposals, judicial selections, legal interpretations, and prosecution.

In announcing the appointment, Bush called John Ashcroft "a man of deep convictions and strong principles" who "will perform his duties guided by principle, not by politics."[83] There was speculation at his appointment that the administration someday planned to elevate him to the Supreme Court,[84] possibly to replace Chief Justice William Rehnquist, should he retire. Ashcroft was considered by some to be a less contentious choice to head the Court than Associate Justice Antonin Scalia.[85]

Yet others warned that Ashcroft might not be the predictable and inconspicuous cabinet secretary that the Bush administration seemed to prefer. One news account quoted a Republican strategist as warning, "The risk will be that about every six months, [Ashcroft] will do something that he thinks is clever or politically interesting, and they will open their papers at the White House and say, 'What the hell is he doing?'"[86] His tough Senate confirmation would only be the start.

The Fight for Confirmation

Initially, the Ashcroft nomination triggered little controversy. In the first week of January 2001, *U.S. News & World Report* noted that "no senators have announced opposition to him."[87] A number of senators, including Democrats, made positive comments, including that they liked him on a personal level.

Early estimates were that he would receive seventy votes for confirmation.[88] But within weeks, the nomination became polarizing, with active interest group lobbying on both sides. By mid-January, public opinion polls revealed majority support for all of Bush's cabinet nominees except Ashcroft. According to a CBS News poll, 25 percent supported confirmation, 17 percent opposed, and 59 percent reported not being sure.[89] A CNN/*USA Today*/Gallup poll reported a similar trend, with 34 percent of Americans having a favorable opinion toward Ashcroft, 28 percent negative, and 38 percent no opinion.[90] Although no organized opposition had emerged by January 18, when both poll results were announced, negative sentiments were coalescing quickly. The strongest opposition came from African Americans and supporters of abortion rights,[91] two groups deeply concerned about his record in Missouri and the Senate. Ashcroft's reputation, as some noted at the time, "stands in sharp contrast to the generally inclusive and unifying themes" on which Bush ran for president.[92] The nomination seemed to undermine the president's pledge to create an inclusive administration.[93]

Soon an opposition coalition of more than 200 groups emerged,[94] including the NAACP, Planned Parenthood, the Sierra Club, People for the American Way, the Human Rights Campaign, the Leadership Conference on Civil Rights, the National Abortion Rights Action League (NARAL), and the National Gay and Lesbian Task Force, among others. People for the American Way launched a Web site entitled "Oppose Ashcroft," which chronicled his record in Missouri and the Senate and argued that he was "unfit to lead the Justice Department."[95]

On the other side of the confirmation battle, a supportive North Carolina congressman sent 20,000 e-mails to voters in his state to rally support for the nomination. He noted that the American Conservative Union, Americans for the Bush Cabinet, and more than 140 other groups had compiled an exhaustive database on the Internet on behalf of the lobbying effort.[96] Conservative organizations such as the Wednesday Group and Issues Management Center also organized support for the nomination, including radio ads.[97]

The Bush transition team appeared to be caught off guard by the mounting opposition; some GOP senators reportedly complained of "sloppy Bush teamwork," which failed to take advantage of the initial support of some Democratic senators.[98] Ashcroft's confirmation was important for the Bush White House to win. The administration had just suffered a highly visible loss in the appointment of Linda Chavez to head the Department of Labor.[99] Assessing the strategic importance of the fight, one conservative columnist wrote, "If Ashcroft is denied confirmation, Bush's presidency will go a long way down the toilet, too."[100]

Some observers maintained that, minus the unexpectedly strong interest group opposition to Ashcroft's appointment, the confirmation would have sailed through. Democratic senators would have acceded out of deference to a former colleague and to a president's cabinet choice. But with organized opposition, they argued, "the controversy had all the appearances of another outbreak of our ongoing culture wars."[101] Many culture battles are fought on Justice Department turf. The attorney general can push "some of the hottest buttons in American life,"[102] such as affirmative action, drug policy, religious practice, and abortion. It is not remarkable, then, that a nominee's policy positions are scrutinized.

The three-day confirmation hearings covered many policy areas within the purview of the Justice Department, with questions about gun control, abortion, and antitrust dominating the discussion. Drugs, the death penalty, victim's rights, the independent counsel law, affirmative action, and the environment drew some questions from the senators as well. A few senators also focused on the judicial nomination process. Only one question was raised dealing with international terrorism.[103]

Ashcroft was asked pointed questions about his key role in killing the confirmation of Judge Ronnie White. White came to the hearings to testify against Ashcroft's confirmation, telling the Senate Judiciary Committee, "My record as a judge shows that the personal attacks [Ashcroft] made on me were not true."[104] Ashcroft's handling of White's nomination, in tandem with his fight against St. Louis school desegregation efforts, led some to question his commitment to civil rights. The perception of racism was fueled when it became known that he had accepted an honorary degree from Bob Jones University, which barred interracial dating at the time, and that he had given an interview to *Southern Partisan,* a pro-Confederacy magazine. As Joseph Biden (D-Del.) told Ashcroft during the hearings, many in the black community "are suspect because they believe that your ideology blinds you to an equal application of not just the law but the facts."[105]

The Senate Judiciary Committee also examined his position on homosexual rights, particularly a report that he had queried a prospective employee about his sexual orientation in 1985 and had opposed James Hormel's nomination as ambassador to Luxembourg in 1998 because of Hormel's homosexuality. At the time of Hormel's nomination, news accounts quoted Ashcroft as opposing the nomination on the basis of Hormel's "gay lifestyle," but in the 2001 hearings, Ashcroft insisted that Hormel's homosexuality was not a factor in his opposition to the nomination.[106]

In addition to these lines of inquiry, many of the questions raised during the confirmation hearings suggest that a larger issue loomed than simply Ashcroft's conservative policy positions on specific issues, that is, his independence and his commitment to enforce existing federal laws. The unique role of the attorney general was mentioned many times. Ashcroft's reputation for employing the law and legal process as policy tools led some Democrats to question his ability to apply the law evenly, despite his assertions otherwise.[107]

Ashcroft's well-known religious views led some senators to note that he might be guided more by his religious principles than by congressional enactments when enforcing the law of the land.[108] The nominee told his former colleagues that he was "a man resolutely committed to the American ideal," as well as "a man of faith [and] a man of common-sense conservative beliefs."[109] His supporters, including John Kyl (R-Ariz.) and former senator John Danforth, used this expression of religious faith as grounds for accepting Ashcroft's assurances that he would follow the law. Danforth said, "When he tells this Committee and tells our country that he is going to enforce the law so help him God, John Ashcroft means that. That is exactly what he is going to be doing."[110] Critics outside of Congress did not believe Danforth's reassurances and called Ashcroft's remarks an insincere "confirmation conversion."[111]

Some senators expressed concern regarding Ashcroft's willingness to answer their questions. Senators expect that nominees will be available for "extensive briefings, courtesy calls, and other consultation," as cabinet scholar Mary Anne Borrelli notes.[112] In Ashcroft's case, senators submitted hundreds of questions to the nominee, seeking clarification of some of his comments and actions as a senator. Edward Kennedy (D-Mass.), an opponent of the nomination, accused Ashcroft of being "deleterious in answering the questions, filling out time, not being responsive." Orrin Hatch (R-Utah), a supporter, criticized the critics, calling such questioning "a dangerous and unprecedented intrusion into Senatorial deliberation."[113] For Hatch, the process exemplified Democratic partisanship. As he commented, "We are seeing a much greater propensity to rough up Republicans than Democrats" in confirmation hearings. He added that Ashcroft "was very badly mistreated by the Democrats."[114]

Senators barely supported Ashcroft's confirmation by a vote of 58 to 42, dividing largely along party lines.[115] This was the closest vote of any Bush cabinet member. More significantly, for those confirmations with recorded Senate votes, it was the closest vote of any successful attorney general nominee in history, as is documented in appendix III.[116] On February 1, 2001, John Ashcroft was sworn in as the seventy-ninth attorney general of the United States.

Ashcroft at Justice

For the Christian Right, the post of attorney general was the highest political position it had ever achieved. Ashcroft had won "the highest-ranking post a conservative, card-carrying Evangelical has ever had," according to John Green, politics-and-religion scholar.[117] The movement embraced "the triumph of one of its own."[118]

In his first months as attorney general, Ashcroft did not live up to conservative hopes. Jipping of the Free Congress Foundation remarked, "There was increasing concern that he wasn't playing as high profile a role as conservatives thought he would."[119] Ashcroft initially evinced a diffidence and hesitation, not the confidence of a conservative firebrand. Perhaps for this reason, he reportedly had "tenuous relations with President Bush" during his first eight months in office.[120] "There was no sense of his mission or theme," said one Justice official.[121]

The agenda Ashcroft laid out after his first week in office did not capture the conservative imagination. He said he wanted to "stop gun violence. I want to reinvigorate the war against drugs. I want to end discrimination wherever I find it. If it's in voting rights, in housing—violence against women is something that we can focus on that's similar to what Janet Reno focused on. These fundamental things are the kinds of protections of persons, their rights and their property that individual citizens have a right to expect of government, and I want to make the Justice Department a place where they get it."[122] Even opponents of his nomination noted that, as of July 2001, he had not "invoked the hard-right ideology for which he was known as a U.S. senator and governor of Missouri." Only cautiously, critics said, was he "moving the agenda on civil rights, police misconduct, abortion, sentencing, drug and gun enforcement, and corporate (non)regulation" to the right.[123]

He also did not have a major role in identifying potential judicial nominees and shepherding them through the confirmation process. Despite the hope of some religious conservatives that Ashcroft would help to move the federal courts to the right, the judicial nomination process has changed in a way that minimizes an attorney general's impact. Beginning in the 1980s, presidents began to recognize the potential of court appointments to advance their agendas long after they left the Oval Office, and they began to shift the judicial selection process from the Justice Department to the White House.[124] Justice attorneys did continue to assist in vetting and preparing nominees for confirmation hearings. This trend continued under George W. Bush. As presidents realized the potential policy impact of the judiciary, senators did as well, with the result that senators more aggressively question and oppose nominees now "on policy and judicial philosophical grounds."[125] More contentious confirmation battles have resulted, particularly since the 104th Congress (1995–1996). Bush and Republican senators were particularly irked at successful Democratic efforts to filibuster ten nominations during the 108th Congress (2003–2004). The president subsequently gave two of the nominees recess appointments, which in turn upset Senate Democrats.[126] In this highly polarized environment, an attorney general with good relations on Capitol Hill—particularly one who had served on the Judiciary Committee itself—might have been able to facilitate the confirmation of the president's choices. Ashcroft was not able to play this role, however.

Initially, Ashcroft maintained an unusually sane working schedule of 8:30 A.M. to 6:00 P.M. and chafed at the security detail assigned for his protection.[127] His management style was described as "big-picture, results-oriented leadership."[128] But to some career staff, he appeared isolated and disengaged; a joke circulated that he needed the drug Ritalin to address attention-deficit disorder.[129] He rarely met with rank-and-file attorneys in the Justice Department. Even the deputy attorney general reportedly was not a regular participant in his morning staff meetings. Instead, Ashcroft relied heavily on his chief of staff, David Ayres, who had served with him in the Senate,[130] and on David Israelite, the deputy chief of staff. Reportedly, the two men were known around the department as "The Davids."[131] One report described the role that Ayres played as gatekeeper in the Justice Department: "Though not a lawyer, Ayres was heavily involved in department operations, acting more as a second deputy AG than a traditional chief of staff. Any matter requiring Ashcroft's attention first had to go through Ayres. Even presidentially appointed division heads and U.S. Attorneys rarely dealt with the AG."[132] Ayres's association with John Ashcroft continued after both men left the Justice Department. In May 2005, they opened a lobbying firm called the Ashcroft Group, LLC.[133] Among their first clients were two corporations whose services had been used by the department in the war on terror: Oracle Corporation and ChoicePoint.[134]

Ashcroft's reliance on Ayres—which continued throughout his tenure—may have intensified because the new attorney general was operating under several handicaps. The confirmation process had left him with little political capital on the Hill. And, despite his self-deprecating jokes about the confirmation battle, he may have felt some bitterness toward former Senate colleagues. Within the administration, his role as the president's legal adviser was eclipsed by White House Counsel Alberto Gonzales, a longtime Bush friend and eventually Ashcroft's successor.

Overall, Ashcroft seemed restless and bored by the demands of running a mammoth bureaucracy like Justice. He toyed with the idea of another run for elective office, according to Terry Eastland, publisher of the conservative *Weekly Standard* who had served in the Reagan Justice Department.[135] Others speculated that he wanted to campaign against Jean Carnahan for his old seat.[136] Even the possibility of terrorism did not ignite him, according to testimony by the acting FBI head at the time, Thomas Pickard. Pickard told the bipartisan commission examining the 9/11 attacks that he had briefed the attorney general about the terrorist threat during the summer of 2001, but that Ashcroft seemed uninterested; he did not request additional funding for counterterrorism in the department's 2003 budget proposal, as the FBI had asked, and turned down its appeal of that decision.[137]

Any political listlessness that Ashcroft might have felt in the office ended on September 11, 2001. In fact, 9/11 altered the role and agenda of most of the Bush cabinet. Cabinet secretaries assumed greater responsibility and visibility, particularly Donald Rumsfeld of Defense, Colin Powell of State, and John Ashcroft of Justice. In the administration's first months, White House aides and not cabinet secretaries dominated the policy process.[138] Department heads were expected to be team players, "very regimented, very tight message discipline."[139] But with the terrorist attacks, as presidential scholar John Burke predicted, "Any department with important homeland security concerns instantly moved up a notch on the power ladder in Washington."[140] This was notably so in Ashcroft's case. He emerged from the crisis as "one of the most formidable members of the Bush administration,"[141] due to the enactment of broad new law enforcement powers centered in the Justice Department.

Ashcroft was energized by the task of fighting terrorism. He described spending the first "hours, days and most of the first weeks . . . in the FBI's Strategic Information and Operations Center."[142] His workdays became long, often twelve to fourteen hours, beginning at 6:30 A.M. FBI director Robert Mueller gave him an intelligence briefing at 7:00, and together they went to the White House to meet the president for twenty minutes.[143] Eight months after entering office, Ashcroft became part of a new national narrative: now he was the chief warrior in the domestic war on terror. Describing the attorney general as "serious" and "thoughtful," Rumsfeld reassured the public that "he is working very closely with the president."[144] Ashcroft's unsmiling demeanor and staunch religious faith—which had once been parodied—now seemed to embody resolve and strength of character. He was someone who could be counted on.

The Administration Lightning Rod

As a high-profile attorney general with a confrontational style, John Ashcroft was able to absorb political heat for aggressive domestic antiterrorism measures, deflecting blame and political risk from the president. This may have been the president's intention from the start. In a televised interview soon after Ashcroft's difficult confirmation hearings, Barbara Walters asked President Bush directly, "Did you really expect [Ashcroft] to be as much of a lightning rod?" Bush answered yes.[145]

Allies and opponents recognized early that Ashcroft was playing the role of administration lightning rod, defined by political scientist Richard Ellis as "a relationship in which an unpopular adviser deflects criticism away from the president."[146] A pro-Ashcroft commentator noted in 2002 that "he does Bush the favor of being the administration's lightning rod, its big fat target."[147] Another news analysis called the attorney general a "useful political foil for President Bush."[148] His role as administration "spear catcher," in the words of one official, "allowed the president to have the running room he needs to get a lot of policies through."[149] Ashcroft enabled the administration to expand executive power without triggering a political or institutional backlash, aiding the president in his dealings with Congress, the press, and the public by drawing political lightning away from the Oval Office.

In the early months, cabinet secretaries in the Bush administration were expected to provide the president with political coverage. Their role was secondary to White House staff, according to a senior aide, who added, "I think the cabinet officers realize that a large part of their job is to be shields."[150] But Ashcroft and Donald Rumsfeld, secretary of defense, were different; they continued to fill this role in the administration after 9/11. Both men were "most often on the hot seat over the policies," with Ashcroft a "lightning rod for the administration's get-tough police tactics."[151]

Ashcroft is not the first attorney general to provide cover for an administration. Early in the Clinton administration, Janet Reno drew fire for the botched government raid at the Branch Davidian compound in Waco, Texas.[152] She explicitly accepted the responsibility for that disaster. Reagan also benefited from the presence of a high-profile law officer, Edwin Meese III, because Meese was able to absorb "political shots intended for the President."[153] John Kennedy relied on his brother and attorney general Robert Kennedy to absorb the political heat on the administration's civil rights policies. But Ashcroft was unique in that he served as a lightning rod in multiple policy areas, playing the role much more extensively than his predecessors. In part, this is a predictable outcome of the expansion of federal authority in the past twenty years, a trend that accelerated in the post-9/11 atmosphere. In part, it was a product of the controversial new policies adopted by the Justice Department, and in part it was due to his combative style.

Ashcroft's handling of the premature release of the so-called Patriot Act II, the proposal to further expand federal law enforcement powers, provides a case in point of his ability to absorb political heat for the president. An unnamed Justice Department employee released an eighty-six-page draft bill in February 2003. The measure called for vast new law enforcement authority, including an administrative subpoena power that Congress had deleted from the original Patriot Act and a proposal to strip citizenship from Americans who provide material support to groups designated by the attorney general as terrorist. Both of these were contentious proposals. Although Justice Department spokesmen called it "an early discussion draft" and not a bill, the leaked document had a cover memo to the Speaker of the House and the vice president and appeared ready for release at a propitious political moment. Meanwhile, Ashcroft and others had repeatedly reassured Congress that no new legislation was in the works.[154] Soon after the document was posted on the Web site of the Center for Public Integrity, members of Congress responded angrily to what they saw as Justice Department misrepresentation, and both the American Civil Liberties Union[155] and the American Conservative Union[156] condemned the measure. In a previously scheduled appearance before the Senate a few weeks later, Ashcroft successfully deflected questions by announcing the capture of a high-ranking al Qaeda member, which he characterized as proof that the government was winning the war on terrorism.[157] In the end, one media critic wrote, "Patriot Act II was at best a one- or two-day story, and it washed out in TV's 24-hour news cycle."[158] President Bush himself was never associated with the proposal, even in the press releases and commentaries of opposition groups.[159] Instead, the focus remained on Ashcroft and the Justice Department. It was Ashcroft who "readies new assault on civil rights," according to a guest column's headline in the *Los Angeles Times.*[160] It was the Justice Department that "drafts sweeping expansion of anti-terrorism act," according to the press release of the Center for Public Integrity.[161] Ashcroft made it possible for the president to stay above the fray.

A similar strategy minimized the adverse impact of a report that criticized the government's handling of more than 700 people detained after the terrorist attacks. The report was issued by the Office of Inspector General, an independent agency within the Justice Department charged with investigating "allegations of waste, fraud and abuse in DOJ programs and personnel."[162] Documenting abusive detention conditions and other problems, the report was released in June 2003, on the same day that Ashcroft was appearing in a public roundtable discussion. Asked questions by the press about the report, he stoically ignored them and later refused to concede any wrongdoing on the department's part.[163] Again, the press criticism focused on Ashcroft and Justice, and not the responsibility of the White House for the policy and its implementation. It was the Justice Department that "mishandled the post–September 11 detention process,"[164] and the attorney general who "employed some old, discredited means."[165] The story soon faded from news columns.

But this strategy is not without costs. Perhaps for this reason, Senator Herbert Kohl of Wisconsin admonished Ashcroft during his confirmation hearings that an attorney general had "to be a role model and not a lightning rod for certain causes."[166] The opposition party in the Senate embraced the "lightning rod" analogy, seeing Ashcroft's potential for becoming "a vivid rallying point in the years and battles to come."[167] As pointed out in chapter 1, Ashcroft's name did become synonymous with civil liberty abuses. With so much focus on the attorney general, the president was able to escape excoriating criticism from the right as well as the left.

In time, however, Ashcroft began to attract heat to the administration, not deflect it. At this point, his utility for the White House ended. First, Ashcroft's management of the Justice Department did not always merit the president's approval. When Bush received news, for example, that the Immigration and Naturalization Service had approved the visa requests of two of the 9/11 hijackers six months after the attacks, he described his reaction to reporters: "I was stunned, and not happy. Let me put it another way—I was plenty hot. And I made that clear to people in my administration. I don't know if the Attorney General has acted yet today or not, I haven't seen the wire story. He got the message. And so should the INS. . . . But, yes, it got my attention in a negative way."[168] Later, Ashcroft's public remarks drew criticism from the president. In May 2004, Ashcroft reportedly irritated the White House when he issued a terror warning that al Qaeda was "almost ready to attack the United States," a warning that appeared to conflict with the tone of remarks earlier the same day by Homeland Security head Tom Ridge. Only Homeland Security was authorized to issue public warnings, and then only after interagency approval that included the White House. The attorney general's comments brought a rebuke from White House aides and some congressional Republicans.[169] Ashcroft also was criticized for his intemperate testimony before the 9/11 commission, particularly his smear of Jamie Gorelick, a commission member and Clinton's deputy attorney general; he laid responsibility for 9/11 on Gorelick's 1995 memo outlining department policy on the sharing of information between intelligence and law enforcement agencies.[170] He ignored the fact that his deputy, Larry Thompson, also had endorsed the Gorelick policy prior to September 11. The backlash from Ashcroft's remarks forced the White House to distance itself. Spokesman Scott McClellan told reporters, "The president does not believe we ought to be pointing fingers in this time period." McClellan also sought to distance the president from Ashcroft's hasty decision to declassify and electronically post more than two dozen pages of internal documents that related to the Gorelick memo.[171] Ashcroft's use of selective declassification for political reasons will be examined further in chapter 8.

The impact of Ashcroft's post-9/11 policies on civil liberties reportedly was one of "various incidents that have distracted the Bush team."[172] The mixed public response to Ashcroft's pro–Patriot Act tour in the autumn of 2003 also may have triggered the administration's efforts to sideline the attorney general. There is some evidence that his tour accelerated public concerns. The Gallup Organization found that, in September, early in his speaking tour, "most Americans are not worried that their civil liberties are in danger."[173] By the following November, however, Gallup reported that "Americans are growing more likely to say that the Bush administration has gone too far in restricting civil liberties,"[174] a shift in attitude that might be attributed to the dialogue about the Patriot Act and civil liberties inspired by the attorney general's national tour. In addition, Americans began to express a measure of anxiety about greater government surveillance, which they associated with Ashcroft and the Justice Department. One study dealing with Americans' privacy concerns found that the Office of Attorney General ranked the lowest on the Privacy Trust Score among forty-four agencies, followed by the Department of Justice. The study was designed to assess how much confidence U.S. citizens have that their personal information would be safeguarded by the federal government.[175]

As a result of the poll numbers and specific incidents, "well-placed Republican sources say the President has gone out of his way to take the spotlight off the Attorney General at high-profile law-enforcement-related events." In fact, some Bush insiders started to predict that "Ashcroft will not be the A.G. by Christmas if Bush wins," replaced by a less confrontational personality such as Larry Thompson, Ashcroft's former deputy attorney general. Although no longer at Justice, Thompson reportedly was asked by the White House to sit next to Ashcroft during the attorney general's 9/11 commission testimony.[176] The signal intensified in May when it was Thompson who joined President Bush for a speech on the Patriot Act in Buffalo, New York.[177] By late June 2004, "well-connected Republicans in Washington" had started to complain about Ashcroft that he "too often pursues his own agenda rather than that of President Bush." This was not the view of Christian conservatives, who continued to hold him in high esteem. But some in the GOP felt that his presence was too polarizing and undercut his ability to be an effective advocate of the president's agenda, including the Patriot Act. His supporters explained his response to these internecine attacks; said Justice spokesman Mark Corallo, "The last couple of weeks have been a little rough, but he keeps saying, you've got to keep focused, you've got to persevere and keep going."[178] Despite health problems in early 2004,[179] Ashcroft made it known publicly that he would be willing to continue as attorney general should Bush win a second term and ask him to stay. He was not asked. Instead, a week after the election, Ashcroft announced his intention to leave office as soon as his successor was confirmed.[180]

Ashcroft recognized the danger to his own political popularity as the face of the administration's aggressive antiterrorism efforts at home. One associate said, "Ashcroft has been amazingly effective, but at great cost to his public persona. It's a role he accepts."[181] He felt a duty to the office, according to Michael Chertoff, who served as the head of the Criminal Division under Ashcroft. "I've always felt that he sincerely believed in the trusteeship element of public service and was very concerned about living up to his obligation."[182] His religious beliefs may have driven that sense of commitment, his determination to face down the critics and continue to serve. His religious beliefs also may have driven his sense of what he was up against: that the war against terrorism was a struggle against a great evil.

Favorite Son of the Christian Right

John Ashcroft is known for his devout religious faith as much as his conservative political ideology; indeed, the two appear to be intertwined. Ashcroft's view that religion plays a large role in politics is clear from several comments he made throughout his public life. As a U.S. senator, he expressed hope that his religious belief "affects the way I do politics and government."[183] He wrote in his autobiography about the "need to invite God's presence into whatever I'm doing, including the world of politics."[184] "If only our government had a heart closer to God's," he said on another occasion.[185] It was not empty rhetoric. As governor and senator and during his first months as attorney general, he regularly started his workday with office devotionals and Bible study. He wrote that his father anointed him with oil prior to his becoming governor and senator, following the biblical practice of anointing kings in the book of First Samuel.[186] His father had died by the time he was named attorney general, so he was anointed by his longtime friend Associate Supreme Court Justice Clarence Thomas, who also swore him into office.[187] He described his political career as a series of crucifixions followed by resurrections because after every loss, he achieved a higher office. At the Justice Department, he sponsored internship and employment opportunities for students at Regent University, founded by television evangelist Pat Robertson.[188] His connections with Robertson continued after he left Justice. In March 2005, Ashcroft gave the keynote address on the opening night of Robertson's seventy-fifth birthday weekend in San Antonio,[189] and soon began offering short courses on "leadership in times of crisis" at Regent University, where Robertson remained chancellor.[190] In July 2005, he became a Distinguished Professor of Law and Government at the university's Law and Justice Institute, formed to provide research assistance for lawsuits involving Christian values. Accepting the appointment, Ashcroft complimented the school for providing "an academically rigorous graduate education based on a biblical foundation."[191]

His unabashed religiosity brought Ashcroft the strong endorsement of other religious political conservatives. Considered "a favorite son of the modern Christian political movement," he received heavy campaign contributions from the Christian Right. In fact, as a senator, he was "the leading recipient of campaign contributions from clergy and religious organizations."[192] The role of the Christian Right in securing his nomination as attorney general has already been explored.

The Christian Right is "a social movement dedicated to restoring 'traditional values' in public policy by mobilizing evangelical Protestants and other conservative religious people to political action," according to political scholar John Green.[193] Yet the Christian Right movement, while cohesive, is not monolithic. Important doctrinal differences exist between the Assemblies of God and Christian fundamentalism and evangelicalism.[194] Politically as well, the Christian Right is not monolithic. It began to experience a widening gap in the late 1990s between political pragmatists who accept the occasional need to compromise, like Ralph Reed, former executive director of the Christian Coalition, and purists who "support absolute policy pronouncements and strong moral and religious condemnations of behavior they believe to be sinful."[195]

Ashcroft on occasion could sound like a purist. Numerous times, he expressed a disdain for political compromise, writing in his autobiography: "There are some things we must be strongly, even passionately, committed to."[196] Regarding the issue of abortion, Ashcroft told a Christian Coalition convention that "confronting our cultural crises is the true test of our courage and true measure of our leadership. It is time for us to reacquaint our party with the politics of principle. We must not seek the deal, we seek the ideal."[197] He reportedly asserted during his 1998 White House run, "There are voices in the Republican Party today who preach pragmatism, who champion conciliation, who counsel compromise. I stand here today to reject those deceptions."[198] He repeated the sentiment as he was leaving office, emphasizing the need "to focus on the principled and noble, rather than the pragmatic and doable."[199] Commentator Brian Doherty of *Reason* magazine said that this did not make Ashcroft a Cotton Mather, the fiery eighteenth-century clergyman. Instead, Ashcroft has "always been more Ned Flanders [a character on the *Simpsons* television program]. . . . A gentler kind of modern religious man." Doherty added, "He's never fought back at his critics with fire and brimstone."[200] Others had a different experience, arguing that Ashcroft's devout religiosity and expressions of rock-solid principles could make him rigid, even self-righteous. For example, Harriet Woods, the former lieutenant governor who served under him in Missouri, said his "amiable, open countenance with the public and his peers" changed when he felt crossed. She explained, "A sense of righteousness and ordained destiny can make it hard to brook criticism."[201] Another observer, a former Bush administration official, also hinted at two sides to the attorney general. He said Ashcroft had an almost "Jekyll and Hyde quality" when it came to "the more political aspects of the job."[202]

Ashcroft's political behavior suggests that his purist impulses were balanced against a pragmatic understanding of politics. Ralph Reed insisted, "He is not an insurgent," evidenced by his success as a mainstream political figure for so many years in Missouri. Even so, he maintained "a strong political base within the conservative wing of the Party."[203] Ashcroft on occasion expressed a political pragmatism at odds with his other remarks. He wrote, "While I believe in absolutes, there are many times where honest, well-meaning people can disagree."[204] A pragmatic strain also surfaced in his campaigning. In running for governor, for example, he accepted campaign contributions from Anheuser-Busch, even though he disapproved of beer and banned alcohol in the governor's mansion.[205] In addition, he softened his pro-life language during his 1998 run for the GOP nomination for president. He generally made clear the importance that he attached to the pro-life position; in a *Meet the Press* television interview, for example, he asserted that he would "outlaw abortion" if he had to choose between that and cutting taxes.[206] Yet following the Republican Party's poor showing in the November 1998 midterm elections, he shifted his campaign speeches to focus on "the kinds of issues that proved to be Republican winners," such as tax cuts. He told elite business leaders in December that the Republican Party was in danger of being defined by its internal divisions. He added, "We must never confuse politics and piety."[207] That comment—as well as his pointed silence on the issue of abortion and the Clinton-Lewinsky scandal—did not sit well at the time with purists, who thought Ashcroft was beginning to sound like "an echo of Gov. George W. Bush of Texas," another pragmatic religious conservative.[208]

Ashcroft also evinced a libertarian and individualistic strain in his political practice. Christian evangelicalism as a whole includes a strain of intense individualism, but the Assemblies of God faith of John Ashcroft in particular is individualistic.[209] The importance he attached to individual choice explains his statement in his autobiography, "It is against my religion to impose religion on people,"[210] an assertion he repeated at his Senate confirmation hearings. Some Justice colleagues confirmed that he "never invoked religion in policy or procedural discussions," an indication of his respect for individualism.[211] On certain policy issues, his individualism was expressed as conservative libertarian thinking. For example, in 1997, Senator Ashcroft opposed government regulation of the Internet. In a press release entitled, "Keep Big Brother's Hands Off the Internet," he argued that "the state's interest in crime-fighting should never vitiate the citizens' Bill of Rights."[212]

The impact of his religious principles on his political choices was more complicated than many of his critics or supporters expected. An example is Ashcroft's position on the right to die, which many would expect him to oppose on religious grounds, illustrated by his actions as governor to block the father of Christine Busalacchi from seeking a second medical opinion about her chances of recovery. Conflicting with this expectation, however, was his action as Missouri's governor at the time when the case of Nancy Cruzan erupted. Cruzan was a young woman who had been in a persistent vegetative state for eight years; for the last three years, her parents fought for the authority to remove her feeding tube so that she could die "with dignity." The state of Missouri blocked the removal of her life support, and the case traveled through the court system to the U.S. Supreme Court, which, in 1990, determined that Nancy could not be removed from life support absent "clear and convincing evidence" that this would have been her wish.[213] By late 1990, the family had provided that evidence to a Missouri judge, and the feeding tube was removed. At that time, an antiabortion organization called Missouri Citizens for Life sought to have the tube reinserted; its appeal to Governor Ashcroft was unsuccessful.[214] Because of the governor's refusal to intervene, the head of the Center for Christian Activism named Ashcroft in its civil rights suit seeking a temporary order to restore the feeding tube. Randall Terry of the antiabortion group Operation Rescue called on Ashcroft and the state attorney general to intervene in Cruzan's case, saying "Don't betray the pro-life movement." Terry led protests outside the hospital.[215] After Cruzan's death, state legislators considered a bill to permit health care surrogates to make medical decisions for incapacitated relatives. The bill's supporters feared that Ashcroft would veto the measure, due to remarks in his 1991 State of the State address.[216] However, Ashcroft said he supported the idea of permitting people to designate health care surrogates, as long as "the legislation is sufficiently tight to prevent any abuse."[217] The final bill did not give surrogates full health care decision-making power; food and hydration tubes could be removed only with a patient's prior written authorization. Despite the concerns of opponents that the bill would permit the extermination of "unwanted and disabled people,"[218] Ashcroft said there were sufficient safeguards, and he signed the bill.[219]

His position in *Cruzan* also seems inconsistent with his strong opposition to Oregon's Death with Dignity Act, a state law permitting physicians to prescribe federally controlled drugs in lethal amounts to assist the terminally ill to commit suicide.[220] Because the drugs involved are federally regulated under the Controlled Substances Act (CSA) of 1970, the Ashcroft Justice Department threatened to suspend the licenses of any physicians prescribing them for this purpose.[221] In contrast to Ashcroft's interpretation of the CSA, the Reno Justice Department ruled that the law dealt with medical practice, which was left to the states to regulate. Ashcroft's position was that use of these drugs to assist terminally ill patients to commit suicide does not qualify as a medical practice and therefore cannot be legitimated by state law.[222]

His libertarianism seemed to evaporate on September 11, but it surfaced in relation to a few issues during his attorney generalship. Operation TIPS was proposed by the Justice Department to encourage citizen watchfulness of suspicious behavior of neighbors and business customers. Although he never publicly criticized it because he was "a team player," Ashcroft himself was "uncomfortable with the project."[223] His discomfort was shared by some other high-ranking Republicans, and the program was scaled back. Ashcroft's position on gun control also may reflect the individualistic ethic of his religious faith. As noted in the previous chapter, he believed the Second Amendment to the Constitution conferred an individual right to gun ownership, not "only a 'collective' right of the States to maintain militias."[224] The position sparked controversy because it altered a long-standing executive and judicial interpretation of the Second Amendment and appeared to run counter to the fight against terrorism. However, Ashcroft did emphasize vigorous prosecution of those who commit crimes with guns, reflecting his core belief in individual choice.[225] For Ashcroft, individual choice was not merely about rights but also about consequences. His stands on the death penalty and criminal law are the products of this deep personal belief.

Ashcroft on occasion disappointed some on the religious right. In the antiabortion movement, for example, he fulfilled his confirmation promise regarding federal enforcement of the 1994 Freedom of Access to Clinic Entrances Act (FACE Act). The conservative group Concerned Women for America said he "went beyond the law" in February 2002 when he obtained a federal injunction against a pro-life group gathering outside Washington, D.C., abortion clinics. Said the group's leader, "For Attorney General Ashcroft to use the weight of the Justice Department to keep peaceful pro-lifers from praying on a public sidewalk is an abuse of power."[226] Under Ashcroft, the solicitor general also filed friend-of-the-court (amicus curiae) briefs that effectively argued against certain strategies of the antiabortion movement. In 2002, for example, Solicitor General Theodore Olson filed an amicus *against* granting Supreme Court review of an appeal brought by the American Coalition of Life Activists. The antiabortion group sought to overturn a lower court ruling that the group's "Wanted" posters of abortion doctors were not protected speech but amounted to "true threats" under the FACE Act.[227] The Supreme Court did not grant review. Olson also filed an amicus brief on the merits in two cases involving disruptive antiabortion protests outside of abortion clinics. The National Organization for Women had sued the protest groups under the Racketeer Influenced and Corrupt Organizations Act (RICO) for engaging in extortion, as defined by the Hobbs Anti-Racketeering Act. The solicitor general rejected the ability of a private party like NOW to seek injunctions under RICO, but he found that the Hobbs Act could apply to such protests, supporting the argument advanced by NOW.[228] In fact, the Justice Department's position went further than the Supreme Court did; eight justices ruled that neither federal law could be applied to abortion clinic protesters.[229] As of August 2003, Ashcroft's Justice Department had brought seven of the forty-three criminal prosecutions brought under the FACE Act. The same month, Justice filed an appeal of a federal district court ruling that struck down the act as unconstitutional. Abortion rights proponents noted that he appeared to be living up to the pledge he had made about enforcing the law.[230]

Liberal and feminist opponents of Ashcroft also could not fault other actions that his Justice Department took that appear driven in part by his religious values. Early in his tenure, for example, Ashcroft established an initiative to combat human trafficking, slavery, and sexual servitude. Three years later, he announced the results of the effort, including the convictions of those who had held Vietnamese and Chinese garment workers in virtual slavery and others who had kept young Mexican women as sex slaves. "These crimes," he said, "extend beyond the bounds of law. They are an affront to human dignity, an assault on the nation's core belief . . . that every human life is precious."[231] The issue of sex trafficking clearly resonates with the religious right. By the late 1990s, evangelicals became involved in anti–sex trafficking efforts;[232] Bush featured the initiative in his remarks to the National Association of Evangelicals Convention in 2004, along with the ban on late-term abortion and the Unborn Victims of Violence Act.[233] The Ashcroft Justice Department also sided with plaintiffs in cases involving sexual harassment and religious freedom. In March 2004, Justice moved to intervene on behalf of four female students in a Title IX sexual harassment lawsuit brought against a New York school district.[234] Later that month, the department filed a complaint and sought to intervene in a private lawsuit brought against an Oklahoma public school district for suspending a sixth-grade Muslim girl because she refused to remove her hijab (or religious head scarf).[235] Ashcroft also expanded the Office on Violence against Women, making it a stand-alone agency under the direction of a presidentially appointed and Senate-confirmed head.[236]

Yet Ashcroft's religious views did trigger concerns about other individual rights. As attorney general, he employed activist legal measures in enforcing the law banning late-term abortions, signed by the president in November 2003. The Partial Birth Abortion Ban Act provides an exception when a woman's life is in danger, but not when a woman's health is in danger because, in the language of the act, "a partial-birth abortion is never necessary to preserve the health of a woman."[237] Planned Parenthood brought a legal challenge, claiming that late-term abortions can be medically necessary. In framing its defense of the new law, the Justice Department subpoenaed medical records of hundreds and possibly thousands of women at Planned Parenthood clinics around the country. Justice attorneys argued that federal law "does not recognize a physician-patient privilege," a position apparently at odds with the Bush administration's earlier support of medical privacy. Then the Justice Department agreed to accept redacted records with no identifying patient information. After a few weeks of intense media attention and a mixed judicial response to the subpoenas, the Justice Department announced that it would not pursue the records for the time being.[238] A few days after this announcement, the Seventh Circuit Court of Appeals quashed the subpoena given an Illinois hospital, on the grounds that the government had not adequately explained the relevance of the records for its defense of the law.[239]

Beyond the social conservative agenda, Ashcroft's religious views also seemed to motivate his response to the terrorist attacks of September 11. A deeper rationale than national security may have driven his aggressive actions. His comments suggest that he was impelled by the imperative of fighting evil. He called terrorism "a conspiracy of evil"[240] and "a calculated, malignant and devastating evil."[241] In the war against terrorism, he asserted, "We fight to secure victory over the evil in our midst."[242] The idea of evil has explanatory power for Ashcroft. One friend noted that he "believes in the existence of evil, of Satan. He will work to the point of exhaustion to defeat evil."[243] To the attorney general, a religious response to 9/11 was as necessary as a military one; in one law school commencement address, he remarked that American values "must be defended, not just with military might, but with deeper devotion."[244] He repeatedly referred to freedom as a gift of God, and not the U.S. Constitution.

Ashcroft and Bush shared this point of faith. Both understood the attacks in terms of a national struggle of good against evil, with evil exploiting the nation's core values—such as the freedom of movement and speech—to a destructive end. The common vision between the president and the attorney general reportedly enhanced their post-9/11 working relationship for a while.[245] The metanarrative of good and evil appeared repeatedly in the president's remarks following the tragedy, most memorably in his reference to the "axis of evil" in his 2002 State of the Union address.[246] He told the National Association of Evangelicals that "America is a nation with a mission . . . we are called to expand the realm of human liberty. . . . Yet I know that liberty is not America's gift to the world—liberty and freedom are God's gift to every man and woman who lives in this world."[247] The sense that he acted on behalf of a divine mission also appeared in an interview with journalist Bob Woodward in late 2003. Bush talked about praying to God, after giving the combat order for Iraq, "that I be as good a messenger of His will as possible."[248]

For George Bush, the narrative of good and evil at home necessitated a strong attorney general, unwavering in his aggressive application of the law as a weapon in the war against terror. For John Ashcroft, the narrative drove the need for a hegemonic presidency, a hero to lead the nation in dark times. The struggle against the evil of terrorism was too critical to permit debate or power sharing with other political actors. A conflict framed in this way—as a war with the nation's very survival at stake—had serious consequences for the system of divided and checked powers.

4   Framing 9/11 as a War on Terrorism

When commercial planes slammed into the Pentagon, the World Trade Center, and a Pennsylvania field, conventional conceptions of security disappeared. The enemy was here at home, the weapon of choice as common as it was so terribly effective. The Bush administration, in framing the nation's response, could have considered many alternatives, but it immediately chose the framework of a war on terrorism, announced publicly by the president the day after the attacks.[1] That choice has had profound repercussions for the U.S. legal system.

Commanding most of the investigative and prosecutorial forces of the federal government, John Ashcroft became a key general on the domestic front. He saw 9/11 as transforming towns, roads, and shopping malls into battlefields, telling Congress, "We must not forget that this great fight for freedom did not end in Kabul. It will not end along the banks of the Tigris and Euphrates. The fight continues here, on America's streets, off our shores and in the skies above."[2] To meet that enemy, he transformed the nation's law enforcement as well, charging the Justice Department with a new proactive mission and furnishing it with broad legislative and administrative powers. Now the department would wage a preemptive military-style campaign, as well as traditional reactive investigations and prosecutions.

To understand how this transformation occurred and its larger implications for the legal system, this chapter will address the impact of the war on terrorism on the securitization of the domestic sphere and expansion of presidential power. It also examines the administration's selective borrowing from both the law enforcement and war models in confronting potential threats within the United States. Situating Ashcroft's efforts within the context of the war on terrorism, the chapter explores the possible implications of the Justice Department's new wartime mission on the nation's constitutional architecture.

Presidential Power during Wartime

The ambiguity of the language in Article II, Section 2, of the U.S. Constitution, particularly the meaning of the commander-in-chief provision, has permitted presidents to claim broad powers during wartime. Security is paramount; resources must be mobilized; government administration must be centralized. Congress, the courts, and the press—which ordinarily exercise checks on executive authority—look to the president to act. Military action may boost public approval ratings as well, which can translate into success for the president's broad policy agenda. Administration critics appear partisan, self-serving, or even treasonous, sowing discord and disunity and weakening the nation's ability to respond. There may even be electoral benefits for a president if voters are wary of changing leadership in the midst of crisis.

A war against terrorism may enhance executive authority even more because it blurs the distinction between domestic matters and international fronts. Historically, a wartime expansion of presidential power has applied almost exclusively to the international sphere. Domestically, even during wartime, legal and political restraints tied the president's hands. Constitutional scholar Laurence Tribe writes that "domestic executive power remains limited, requiring congressional justification—even during times of national crisis."[3] The classic expression of this occurred in the case of *Youngstown Sheet and Tube Co. v. Sawyer.*[4] During the Korean War, Harry Truman ordered his secretary of commerce to take over the operation of many of the nation's steel mills to avert a threatened strike. Congress had not sanctioned the action. The solicitor general, defending the seizure of the steel mills, claimed the source of the president's authority to act unilaterally lay with his constitutional commander-in-chief role during a war, as well as with his duty to "take care that the Laws be faithfully executed." But the Supreme Court, in a 6 to 3 vote, rejected Truman's argument. Presidential power to act in domestic affairs, even during wartime, needed congressional authorization. Associate Justice Robert Jackson, in a well-known concurring opinion, wrote, "That military powers of the Commander in Chief were not to supersede representative government of internal affairs seems obvious from the Constitution and from elementary American history."[5]

Presidents have had greater success making power claims in the international sphere.[6] They have had the benefit of Justice George Sutherland's language in the 1936 case of *Curtiss Wright Corp. v. U.S.* The question before the Supreme Court was the constitutionality of a congressional joint resolution that delegated authority to the president to institute an arms embargo in the Chaco conflict in South America, should the president determine that an arms embargo would help to reestablish peace in the region. The justices upheld the delegation, but Sutherland went much further than that in his opinion, using the case as an opportunity to promote his own view that—in foreign affairs—the president has independent and inherent authority to act.[7] Sutherland called it "the very delicate, plenary and exclusive power of the President as the sole organ of the federal government in the field of international relations—a power which does not require as a basis for its exercise an act of Congress."[8] Despite the historic and legal flaws in Sutherland's reasoning and despite its status as a dictum or judicial "aside," this part of the opinion regularly appears as the foundation for claiming broad executive power in foreign affairs. Shoring up that foundation is the Supreme Court's decision forty years later, which upheld the unilateral actions of the Carter administration to freeze Iran's U.S. assets and suspend related court claims in an effort to pressure Tehran to release American hostages captured in 1979.[9]

Political scientist Aaron Wildavsky argued in 1966 that presidential success in domestic versus international arenas differed so much that there were essentially "two presidencies": one domestic, where power is shared with Congress, and one international. "Since World War II," Wildavsky wrote, "Presidents have had much greater success in controlling the nation's defense and foreign policies than in dominating its domestic policies."[10] In recent decades, however, scholars have started to note that international and domestic affairs are no longer so distinct.[11] Many so-called domestic policy issues—such as labor, environmental protection, and the budget deficit—have international dimensions, while international issues relating to immigration, tariffs, trade, foreign aid, and even diplomatic recognition have domestic implications and have triggered domestic interest group activity and increased congressional scrutiny of executive action. In a sense, foreign affairs have become "domesticated."

A countertrend toward "internationalizing" domestic affairs also emerged as a result of the declaration of a war on drugs and efforts to combat drug trafficking. The events of September 11—particularly the ramming of commercial planes into a civilian building in the country's largest city—fully shifted domestic matters into the national security arena. That day, many people within and outside government began to conceive of the home front as a battlefront. Threats that had been external, and therefore handled with fewer legal scruples by the government, were now internal. The old internal rules—related to sharing power between the branches, providing public access to nonclassified government information, following due process in detaining suspects, among others—were now seen as obstacles to confronting the new threat. This blurring of lines between international and national increases the authority of the White House to act. There is just one presidency now, with the attributes of Wildavsky's international presidency.

George W. Bush moved quickly to demand the enhanced presidential power that customarily comes during wartime. According to some close observers of his administration, he made a successful, if not fully anticipated, transition into a strong leader in the months following 9/11.[12] Benefiting from—and perhaps helping to create—a strong and lasting rally effect, he was able to reinvent "his image as the nation's heroic leader" in those first difficult eighteen months, said presidential scholar Jon Roper.[13] Political scientist Nancy Kassop charted the "network of laws and policies" that Bush put into place, resulting in a centralization of "decision making in the executive branch to an unprecedented degree."[14]

The securitization of domestic affairs began in earnest immediately after the attacks. Concerned about biological weapons, Bush granted the secretary of health and human services the original authority to classify documents, a step he repeated with the Department of Agriculture in September 2002 and the Office of Science and Technology Policy in September 2003.[15] These actions moved traditional domestic agencies into the national security bureaucracy. Other clientele-oriented departments also were recast as national security actors. For example, in November 2001, Bush named the heads of the Departments of Labor, Health and Human Services, Housing and Urban Development, Transportation, Energy, and Veterans' Affairs to the Task Force on Citizen Preparedness in the War on Terrorism. They were joined by Justice and Treasury and six executive branch offices, all under the direction of Homeland Security and the Domestic Policy Council.[16] By bringing these departments into the security ambit, the president institutionalized greater executive control over their functions.

Relying on war terminology, Bush in his first term encountered little resistance to an exercise of power that arguably matched or exceeded that of any president. On the international stage, his unilateralist approach and doctrine of preemptive war drew much scholarly attention.[17] In *America Unbound,* for example, Daalder and Lindsay described the president's ambitious course in foreign policy as "revolutionary":

> In his first thirty months in office, he discarded or redefined many of the key principles governing the way the United States should act overseas. He relied on the unilateral exercise of American power rather than on international law and institutions to get his way. He championed a proactive doctrine of preemption and de-emphasized the reactive strategies of deterrence and containment. He promoted forceful interdiction, preemptive strikes, and missile defenses as means to counter the proliferation of weapons of mass destruction, and he downplayed America's traditional support for treaty-based nonproliferation regimes.[18]

In many ways, this passage also describes what the president accomplished at home. Wartime concerns about security, secrecy, and capturing enemies justified similar unilateralist and preemptive strategies for federal law enforcement within the United States.

The president regularly referred to his role as leading a domestic as well as an international war on terrorism. Bush told journalist Tim Russert in early 2004, "I'm a war president,"[19] and he clearly envisioned waging that war at home. In his radio address about two weeks after the strikes, he made clear that this war was different, "much broader than the battlefields and beachheads of the past. This war will be fought wherever terrorists hide, or run, or plan,"[20] including a domestic front. Bush repeated this message throughout his first term. In a 2003 speech at Quantico, Virginia, he said: "As we wage this war abroad, we must remember where it began, here on our homeland, this new kind of war. . . . Our methods for fighting this war at home are very different from those we use abroad, yet our strategy is the same. We're on the offensive against terror. We're determined to stop the enemy before it can strike our people."[21] Law enforcement officials would be "on the front line" in the country's defense against "a ruthless enemy."[22] His 2004 State of the Union Address, which included the word "war" a dozen times and "terrorist" fourteen times, reiterated that the war began "inside the United States."[23] Vice President Cheney explained the president's new role since 9/11: Bush "must look at security in a new way, because our country is a battlefield in the first war of the 21st century."[24]

Bush often "cast himself as the steady commander in chief of what he portrayed as the nation at war."[25] This reference was not limited to the president; others also regularly referred to him as "the commander in chief of a nation at war"[26] and "our commander in chief."[27] The attorney general expressed a similar understanding of the president's wartime authority during Senate testimony in 2001: "The Constitution specifically delegates to the President the authority to 'take care that the laws are faithfully executed.' And perhaps most importantly, the Constitution vests the President with the extraordinary and sole authority as Commander-in-Chief to lead our nation in times of war."[28] The president's authority to establish and oversee military tribunals specifically came "out of his responsibility as Commander-in-Chief of a nation in conflict," Ashcroft added.[29]

This conception of the president as the commander in chief of the citizenry or nation is worth noting because it differs significantly from the language of the U.S. Constitution and the intent of the Constitution's framers, which confer a much more limited wartime authority on the chief executive. Article II, Section 2, of the Constitution makes the president "the Commander in Chief of the Army and Navy of the United States, and of the Militia of the several

States, when called into the actual Service of the United States."[30] Alexander Hamilton, although a proponent of a strong executive, explained that this authority "would amount to nothing more than the supreme command and direction of the military and naval forces, as first General and admiral of the Confederacy."[31] A commander in chief of the nation, by contrast, could claim broad authority over domestic affairs. A president also benefits psychologically from the title. As historian Arthur Schlesinger Jr. recognized thirty years ago, "The title Commander in Chief . . . acquired almost a sacramental aura, translating its holder from worldly matters into an ineffable realm of higher duty."[32] When that higher duty includes the defense of innocent lives on American soil, the title casts a special aura of nobility and heroism. All these factors contribute to a climate favorable to expansive claims of executive power.

Thinking about 9/11: War or Crime?

Despite the widespread use of the term "war" to apply to the nation's response to domestic terrorism, this was not the only approach open to the administration. Bush could have framed 9/11 as a heinous crime, as did previous U.S. administrations and most countries in Europe in response to earlier terrorist acts. Traditional law enforcement had produced successful prosecutions of those who bombed the World Trade Center in 1993 and the Murrah Federal Building in 1995. In addition, traditional investigation techniques uncovered and foiled the millennium bombing plot in 1999, eventually resulting in another successful prosecution. The U.S. embassy bombings in Kenya and Tanzania, while triggering military strikes against targets in Afghanistan and the Sudan, were treated as "big crimes with a small war component" by the Clinton administration.[33] Clinton stayed within the law enforcement framework in his directive that the government vigorously seek the return of indicted terrorists to the United States for prosecution, by force if necessary.[34] The same framework should apply post 9/11, according to international law scholar Harold Hongju Koh, who argued that police and courts could handle the terrorist threat.[35]

Attorney General Ashcroft's initial response to the attacks reflected the law enforcement approach. In a press briefing that evening, he outlined the known facts and then said, "Crime scenes have been established by the federal authorities. . . . The full resources of the Department of Justice . . . are being deployed to investigate these crimes and to assist survivors and victims' families."[36] The law enforcement model could have been extended globally, with the terrorist attacks declared a gross violation of international law, even a crime against humanity or a war crime. This seemed to be the approach of Secretary of State Colin Powell. The attacks of September 11, he said, constituted "a crime against the United States . . . a crime against humanity."[37]

Soon after 9/11, however, the president expressed distrust of the efficacy of law and regular judicial processes to address the terrorist threat. Bush told journalist Bob Woodward that he had to show "the resolve of a commander in chief that was going to do whatever it took to win. No yielding. No equivocation. No lawyering this thing to death."[38] In January 2004, he asserted, "After the chaos and carnage of September the 11th, it is not enough to serve our enemies with legal papers. The terrorists and their supporters declared war on the United States, and war is what they got."[39] Repeating this line, he told an audience of supporters at a campaign reception in Los Angeles in March 2004: "Some are skeptical that the war on terror is really a war at all. My opponent said the war on terror is 'far less of a military operation and far more of an intelligence-gathering, law enforcement operation.' I disagree. Our nation followed this approach after the World Trade Center was bombed in 1993. The matter was handled in the courts and thought by some to be settled—but the terrorists were still training in Afghanistan, plotting in other nations, and drawing up more ambitious plans."[40]

Ashcroft also disparaged the utility of legal process for bringing terrorists to account. For example, after Senate Democrats suggested that some legal protections be instituted in the military tribunals, the attorney general implied that the alternative to the president's military order for those captured in Afghanistan was "to read them the Miranda rights, hire a flamboyant defense lawyer, bring them back to the United States to create a new cable network of Osama TV."[41] In his testimony before the commission investigating the 9/11 attacks, he faulted lawyers and the "snarl of laws" with contributing to the devastating strikes against American targets. He told commissioners: "There was a covert action program to capture bin Laden for criminal prosecution, but even this program was crippled by a snarled web of requirements, restrictions and regulations that prevented decisive action by our men and women in the field. When they most needed clear, understandable guidance, our agents and operatives were given instead the language of lawyers. Even if they could have penetrated bin Laden's training camps they would have needed a battery of attorneys to approve the capture."[42]

If anything, the Bush administration countered, the legalistic approach made the United States appear weak, increasing the likelihood of a terrorist strike.[43] This belief was underscored in Bush's press conference in April 2004, when he implied that the previous administration's policy was one of appeasement: "Over the last several decades, we've seen that any concession or retreat on our part will only embolden this enemy and invite more blood-shed. And the enemy has seen, over the last 31 months, that we will no longer live in denial or seek to appease them."[44]

Many international law scholars agree that the 2001 attacks justify the administration's use of the war terminology. The resulting casualties were comparable to conventional warfare,[45] and Article 51 of the UN Charter recognizes an "inherent right of self-defense in responding to such violent attacks."[46] The president's declaration of war, however, went beyond targeting the attackers to targeting terrorism, an age-old strategy of violence. This meant it would not be a small war carefully targeted but, in legal scholar Kim Lane Scheppele's terms, "a world war."[47] National Security Adviser Condoleezza Rice noted the president's decision in her testimony before the commission investigating the 9/11 strikes: "We could fight a narrow war against al Qaeda and the Taliban, or we could fight a broad war against a global menace. We could seek a narrow victory, or we could work for a lasting peace and a better world. President Bush has chosen the bolder course."[48]

The "bolder course" has implications that a more narrow declaration does not. A concern raised by many European states is that a war approach complicates the fight against terrorism. It antagonizes entire Muslim and immigrant communities from which a handful of terrorists have emerged, and obscures the root causes of terrorism, making them more difficult to address. European governments instead have relied on a law enforcement approach over the past several decades: intelligence gathering and cooperation, police work and the courts. "Europe is not at war," said the European Union's foreign policy chief.[49] Another European official remarked, "We call it the fight or battle against terrorism, and we do think the distinction makes a difference."[50] The director of the Foundation for Strategic Research in Paris noted, "What Bush calls the war against terrorism is the war which Bush chose to wage in Iraq."[51] The rejection of the war framework, particularly the administration's conflation of the Iraq war with a war on terror, strained relations between many European governments and the Bush White House.

The European response differs from the American in part because of different lessons taken from World War II, according to Scheppele. While the United States took the message that appeasement with a dictator leads to war, European states saw the war as stemming from Hitler's rise to power in the first place, which was accomplished largely through an extraconstitutional seizure of power in response to national emergency. As a result, Europe is less sanguine about a strong executive pushing beyond established constitutional principles in the service of national security. In contrast to the U.S. administration's suspicion of legal mechanisms, Scheppele writes, "Many of America's allies have seen 9/11 not as a moment when the rule of law should be suspended, but precisely a moment when the rule of law needs to be strengthened."[52]

The notion of a war on terrorism posed numerous conceptual problems. As one scholar observed, "Wars have typically been fought against proper nouns (Germany, say), for the good reason that proper nouns can surrender,"[53] and hostilities will end. This war, in contrast, is not bound by time, as Cheney made clear soon after the attack: "There's not going to be an end date that we say, 'There, it's all over with.'"[54] Rice repeated that observation, "We will remain at war until the terrorist threat to our nation has ended."[55] No terrorist attack is acceptable, so the war must be total and comprehensive. In contrast, European policy has sought to minimize and manage the threat of terrorism, while acknowledging the impossibility of eradicating the threat entirely. Because the strategy of terrorism has been used for a thousand years, a war against it could be temporally open-ended. And because it is a war against a strategy, and not a nation-state or even a communist or jihadist ideology espoused by a nation-state, it is geographically open-ended. It extends strategically and tactically into the United States itself, adding to the transformation of the home front into a battlefront.

The administration itself seemed to realize the conceptual problems inherent in the phrase "war on terrorism" in mid-2005, switching to the phrase "global struggle against extremism." General Richard Myers of the Joint Chiefs of Staff said "war on terrorism" defined both the threat and the response only in military terms, ignoring diplomatic and political aspects. But others in the administration emphasized that the new language did not represent a change in thinking or approach since 9/11.[56] In other words, the military paradigm that grounds the preemptive law enforcement remained intact. By late August 2005, the administration had returned to using the phrase "war on terror."[57]

Maximizing Freedom of Action

The actual approach employed since 9/11 is not solely military or civilian but an unprecedented hybrid. Despite the administration's repeated use of the phrase "war on terrorism," it has shifted between military and legal frameworks depending on the desired outcome. Legal scholar Noah Feldman predicted this development: "To maximize flexibility, the U.S. government would probably try to give itself the option of invoking either the crime paradigm or the war paradigm at any moment. If the terrorist can be killed, and is killed, then the U.S. will call that war. If the terrorist surrenders or is captured, the paradigm will be crime. Whatever happens operationally can then be justified according to one of the two paradigms in question."[58]

Each framework creates different opportunities and imposes different limits on government action. While the president may disparage the limits imposed by "legal papers," even the war approach mandates certain rules of conduct. Under international law, enemy combatants may be killed without warning before they have attacked, and collateral damage—that is, the killing of noncombatants—may be permissible in the pursuit of combatants.[59] Yet, once captured, enemy soldiers are considered prisoners of war, who cannot be punished for being combatants or subjected to threats, insults, or poor treatment if they refuse to cooperate during interrogations. In addition, they must be released when hostilities are over.[60] The law enforcement model applies a different set of restrictions. Criminals "may not be killed by their pursuers if they pose no immediate threat, but may be punished after capture," including capital punishment. However, under U.S. law, they are presumed innocent until proven guilty and "must be tried and afforded due process." Furthermore, law enforcement agents must be careful not to harm innocent bystanders in the process of conducting an arrest.[61]

During the first term, the Bush administration sought to exploit the advantages and minimize the constraints inherent in each model. It shifted between the war and law frameworks, gaining more power with fewer limitations by picking and choosing between them. This hybrid approach became most visible in the international arena, where the administration used whatever approach provided the greatest flexibility and authority. In the midst of war on Iraq, for example, the president referred to bringing Iraqi "thugs and assassins" to justice, implying legal recourse. This led one commentator to ask, "Is it accurate for us to think of Baghdad as a genuine war zone, or just a city wracked by explosive lawlessness?"[62]

Admittedly, neither the legal nor the military model may be adequate to address the type of threat posed by terrorism, because terrorism blurs the distinctions between international and domestic, war and crime, state and non-state actors. The 9/11 commission seemed to recognize this when noting that al Qaeda's terrorist actions did not neatly fit either war or crime: "Its crimes were on a scale approaching acts of war, but they were committed by a loose, far-flung, nebulous conspiracy with no territories or citizens or assets that could be readily threatened, overwhelmed or destroyed."[63] An entirely new approach may be warranted.

However, this blending of military and legal approaches in order to bypass constraints on government power raises serious concerns, particularly regarding consistency and arbitrary treatment. These concerns become particularly acute when the government shifts between models in the same case. The situation of the detainees at Guantánamo Bay, Cuba, illustrates this point. One senior Defense Department official explained, "What we're doing at Guantánamo is more understandable in the war context."[64] Guantánamo Bay detainees are captured enemy soldiers with no right of access to American courts or due process of law; these were the chief questions before the U.S. Supreme Court in *Rasul v. Bush,* which will be examined more fully in chapter 5. At the same time, the administration declared the detainees to be "unlawful combatants," in other words, not prisoners of war under the Geneva Convention. President Bush informed his top policymakers, "The war against terrorism ushers in a new paradigm [which] requires new thinking in the law of war." While the principles of the Geneva Convention related to humane treatment of detainees would be followed, he said, it would be as a matter of policy and not of law.[65] The men held at Guantánamo Bay fell outside the protections of either domestic or international law and therefore could be subjected to coercive interrogations, continued detention after cessation of hostilities, military trial, and even execution. Their situation illustrates the difficulty of applying a mixed war-crime model in a way that is consistent with the rule of law.

The president considered "the best way to protect American people is to stay on the offensive . . . at home" as well as overseas.[66] This has led to military engagement in domestic law enforcement. Under the Posse Comitatus Act, U.S. troops have been formally barred from enforcing domestic law since 1878. Even before September 11, however, the barrier on military involvement within the United States was eroding, according to a former military attorney who wrote in 2000, "Through a gradual erosion of the act's prohibitions over the past 20 years, posse comitatus today is more of a procedural formality than an actual impediment to the use of U.S. military forces in homeland defense."[67] Interpretations of the law following 9/11 have furthered speculation that posse comitatus legal restraints are now gone. The Office of Legal Counsel, for example, issued an opinion in October 2001 that found that the 1878 law "does not forbid the use of military force for the military purpose of preventing and deterring terrorism within the United States."[68] Consistent with that interpretation, the military has since intervened in domestic antiterrorism efforts. For example, in February 2004 an army intelligence agent visited the University of Texas law school, demanding information on "three Middle Eastern men who had made 'suspicious' remarks to Army lawyers" at an academic conference there.[69] The military was also deeply involved in designing new technology to set up a massive data warehouse, including data on U.S. citizens. The program, called Total Information Awareness, was intended to track suspicious patterns in such everyday transactions as credit card purchases, medical histories, and employment records.[70] Privacy concerns triggered Congress to cut off funding for the project.[71] A less ambitious version of the program may still exist, and government agencies continue to contract with private data-mining intelligence services like ChoicePoint.[72]

The military orientation to fighting terrorism at home raises potentially troubling questions, particularly as related to the presumption of innocence, privacy, and open government. As Nancy Kassop notes, "More than just the correct metaphor is at stake here, for there are very real distinctions in how a government conducts itself, depending on whether it engages in a war under the jurisdiction of the military, or in criminal prosecutions within the judicial system."[73] Incorporating the war model into the law model creates "a system that imprisons people for their intentions rather than their actions, and that offers the innocent few protections against mistaken detention or inadvertent death through collateral damage," according to David Luban.[74] The impact of this war imperative has led to an unprecedented expansion of federal law enforcement authority, under the aegis of the attorney general.

Attorney at War

At the center of many of the administration's antiterrorist efforts since the 9/11 attacks, John Ashcroft was present at the early National Security Council meeting where the entire philosophy of domestic law enforcement changed in regard to terrorism. On September 17, 2001, the president charged the attorney general and the directors of the CIA and the FBI with the task of "protecting America from future attacks."[75] Until then, the Justice Department, including the FBI, had primarily been a reactive agency, focused on investigating and prosecuting crime. But Ashcroft told senators that this changed on 9/11: "From that moment, at the command of the President of the United States, I began to mobilize the resources of the Department of Justice toward one single, over-arching and over-riding objective: to save innocent lives from further acts of terrorism."[76] In testimony supporting passage of the USA Patriot Act,[77] he said the new mission was defensive, to stop future terrorist attacks. The atmosphere at the Justice Department after the strikes was ad hoc and intense, according to one government prosecutor: "Everyone was shifting on the fly. We didn't know if we'd get hit again the next day."[78]

Responding to this new reality, Ashcroft instituted a "wartime reorganization and mobilization" of the Justice Department. He told employees that "the men and women of Justice and law enforcement" were on the front lines, to "lead America in the battle against the enemy at home."[79] He described federal agents and prosecutors as "warriors" in his testimony to the commission investigating the terrorist attacks.[80] During his national tour to promote the Patriot Act, the attorney general told local law enforcement officers that "you are the soldiers . . . on the ground and in the trenches."[81] To House members in June 2003 he said, "The United States Department of Justice has been called to defend America," adding, "We accept that charge." The old way of doing business, "being reactive, waiting for a crime to be committed . . . , didn't seem to us to be an appropriate way to protect the American people."[82]

The attorney general made the different approach clear to FBI director Robert Mueller III at a meeting of the National Security Council the day after the attacks. In outlining the FBI investigation under way, Mueller reportedly noted the importance of not tainting evidence to ensure that a conviction of accomplices would stand. According to Woodward's account in *Bush at War,* Ashcroft interrupted, "Let's stop the discussion right here. . . . The chief mission of U.S. law enforcement . . . is to stop another attack and apprehend any accomplices or terrorists before they hit us again. If we can't bring them to trial, so be it."[83] In time, Ashcroft joined others in the administration who opposed holding Osama bin Laden and other al Qaeda leaders for a criminal trial. According to one source, he and CIA director George Tenet agreed that bin Laden's trial and execution "would discomfit Arab and Islamic allies and transform some al Qaeda sympathizers into active recruits." A better solution, from their point of view, was to kill him quietly, to let him "fade away." Others disagreed with the notion that a military trial would increase the risk, arguing that al Qaeda could not mount more terror against the United States than it already had.[84]

The proactive wartime mission represented an important conceptual shift in federal law enforcement, and it had repercussions. It drove Ashcroft's "deliberate campaign of arrest and detention" of anyone suspected of planning a future attack, even without hard evidence, to be covered in chapter 6. It also drove an aggressive policy of prosecuting minor charges that arguably would have been ignored in the past. For example, government attorneys did not file charges in May 2000 against two Arab grocers caught stealing cases of Kellogg's cereal; prosecutors were not convinced that the theft "rose to the level of a federal crime." However, following 9/11, the federal government found the men to be suspicious and charged them and a third Arab grocer with the cereal heist. Along the way, the government investigated them for a possible terrorist connection; no such link was found.[85]

A Justice Department spokesperson justified the vigorous proactive approach: "We are at war, facing a terrorist threat from unidentified foes who operate in covert ways and unknown places."[86] At war, we needed domestic weapons. Telling Congress to "make terrorism the priority in our laws,"[87] Ashcroft pressured legislators to act quickly in passing the USA Patriot Act, soon followed by the Homeland Security Act. The Patriot Act, in Ashcroft's words, was "our laser-guided weapon to prevent terrorist attacks." He explained the role it played in the nation's wartime arsenal: "Al Qaeda wants to hit us and hit us hard. We have to use every legal weapon available to protect the American people from terrorist attacks. Like the smart bombs, laser-guided missiles and predator drones employed by our armed forces to hunt and kill al Qaeda in Afghanistan, the Patriot Act is just as vital to targeting the terrorists who would kill our people and destroy our freedom here at home."[88]

War references appeared often in his public remarks about the new law. He referred to the provisions of the Patriot Act as "constitutional weapons that you have provided to make the war against those who fight freedom a war whose conflict will be resolved in victory."[89] The removal of statutory barriers between the FBI and CIA is "critical to our strategic mission and to our victory," Ashcroft said.[90] He used similar language to put critics of the government's expanded powers on the defensive, even those in Congress. He called opponents obstructionists and people who preach "defeatism and surrender."[91] His strong language was effective. When he went on a verbal attack during Senate Judiciary Committee hearings in December 2001, for example, senators who had intended to challenge the president's unilateral creation of military tribunals were conciliatory instead.[92] As the next chapter will explore, such an aggressive posture tended to undermine the ability of the other branches to exercise meaningful oversight.

Law enforcement's wartime mobilization had repercussions within the Justice Department as well. More of the department's budget and personnel were shifted to fight terrorism, necessarily leaving fewer resources for a host of other legal areas, from civil rights to the environment.[93] Critics charged that civil rights enforcement had particularly suffered as the department's priorities shifted. In 2002, for example, the Disability Rights Section of the Justice Department initiated 181 fewer investigations than it did in 2001. The Employment Section, which annually had filed two to four cases claiming a "pattern or practice" of discrimination, filed only one. The Housing Section filed only two cases in 2002 and 2003. The head of a Justice Department watchdog group remarked, "The focus on September 11 has left the daily operations of the Department of Justice largely overlooked."[94] Ashcroft explained, "We cannot do everything we once did because lives now depend on us doing a few things very well."[95]

The new war framework also brought increased control over many career Justice employees. "Main" Justice in Washington, D.C., is exercising greater control now over the U.S. attorneys, according to C. Madison Brewer, who started out as an assistant U.S. attorney in 1969 before moving to other positions in the department and who recently retired. Brewer noted that a terrorism expert now operates out of each of the ninety-three U.S. attorneys' offices. That and other actions taken by "Main" Justice under Ashcroft felt like "micromanaging" to some frontline government lawyers, he said.[96] Additionally, more control was exercised over the U.S. attorneys when they were classified as national security offices because of their involvement with antiterrorism task forces. Although Ashcroft also classified the Criminal Division, National Drug Intelligence Center, Office of Intelligence Policy and Review, and National Central Bureau–INTERPOL in this way, the national security classification was more controversial with the U.S. attorneys. U.S. attorneys traditionally have acted with a degree of autonomy from "Main" Justice, and the classification meant that they and others so classified lost the right to bargain collectively under the Federal Labor-Management Relations Program. They would no longer be permitted to organize collectively, much less strike.[97]

The department's new war-oriented mission had the most impact on the FBI, converting it from "a primarily case-oriented criminal justice agency into a domestic investigatory body."[98] Counterterrorism was not new to the bureau. A joint terrorism task force was first set up in New York City in 1980, and a small counterterrorism unit was formed in the 1990s. The FBI honed antiterrorism investigative skills following the first World Trade Center bombing, the Oklahoma City federal building bombing, and the attacks on the Khobar Towers in Saudi Arabia and on U.S. embassies in Kenya and Tanzania. But the resources to focus on counterterrorism were not there until after the strikes on September 11. To respond to 9/11, the FBI sent 60 percent of its field agents to investigate.[99] Ashcroft announced a reorganization of the FBI in 2002,[100] and issued new investigative guidelines for the bureau in 2002 and 2003, which included protocols for collecting intelligence and sharing it with other federal agencies. But the transition to a proactive force in the war against terrorism was not easy. Even though the number of FBI terrorist investigations tripled and the number of terrorist-related surveillance requests quadrupled in the fourteen months following the attacks, some government officials continued to complain that agents "still aren't looking at this as an intelligence agency but as cops."[101] To some at the FBI, the preventive approach had serious downsides that were not adequately addressed. For example, the new policy to arrest suspects quickly to prevent a possible attack had an adverse effect on the bureau's ability to develop informants, exhaust leads, and build a full case for a successful prosecution.[102] In addition, the focus on gathering intelligence rather than criminal evidence could waste finite law enforcement resources, according to one former FBI agent, because agents now felt obligated to follow every lead to exhaustion.[103]

Despite his general embrace of the war framework, Ashcroft occasionally felt frustrated by it. He reportedly objected to the Pentagon's handling of the detainees at Guantánamo Bay, seeing the open-ended detentions there as damaging the country's relations with allies, undercutting international counterterrorism efforts, and ultimately undermining presidential power.[104] He grew increasingly impatient with the slow pace of the military trials and the improvised nature of the review process. Officials in Justice and the FBI pushed for stronger cases to prosecute and more rapid Pentagon action. Two participants in one meeting reported Ashcroft's frustrated observation that "Timothy McVeigh was one of the worst killers in U.S. history. But at least we had fair procedures for him."[105] The assistant attorney general for legal policy during this time, Viet Dinh, later noted that "there was not a real process for determining who was an enemy combatant. And the ad hoc nature of that process gave a lot of power to the Pentagon."[106]

Ashcroft also apparently disagreed with the administration's aggressive legal position—promoted by Cheney's counsel, David Addington—that no attorney was required for Yaser Hamdi or José Padilla, designated as enemy combatants by the president. Addington reportedly advocated an aggressive position regarding Hamdi and Padilla unless and until the courts told the administration to stop. This more extreme position, Ashcroft believed, opened the executive branch to judicial reversal, and that would have a long-term negative effect on presidential power. The attorney general advised a more moderate position, with the idea that the Supreme Court might not feel the need to accept a court challenge for review. On this issue as well as others involving presidential power, however, Addington prevailed.[107]

Conclusion

The framework of a domestic war against terrorism shifted the paradigm at the Justice Department. Accepting that the nation was engaged in a military-like struggle against terrorism at home, Ashcroft established a preemptive and aggressive approach to law enforcement. The war framework brought greater deference to the president and a steady erosion of legal constraints on executive action. The remainder of the book will seek to delineate these changes and evaluate what they mean in post-9/11 America.

5   Presidential Action and Separation of Powers

Those who designed the framework for the new government in 1787 believed that a declaration of democratic principles alone would not provide sufficient protection from the threat of tyranny. Pragmatically, the Constitution's framers adopted a system of institutional checks to keep power from centralizing in either the legislative or the executive branch. Such centralization would be "the very definition of tyranny," in James Madison's words.[1] "It will not be denied, that power is of an encroaching nature, and that it ought to be effectually restrained from passing the limits assigned to it," he wrote in *The Federalist* Number 48. The most effective restraint would be institutional, with power "so divided and balanced among several bodies of magistracy, as that no one could transcend their legal limits, without being effectually checked and restrained by the others."[2]

Madison argued that the separation of powers works because various institutional actors have "personal motives" to "resist encroachments of the others." In this way, he asserted in *The Federalist* Number 51, "private interest . . . may be a sentinel over the public rights."[3] But this formulation poses a problem during a national crisis. Congress and the courts face powerful incentives to forgo their own constitutional prerogatives and defer to the executive branch. At such times, "personal motives" and "private interest" are almost impossible for either branch to assert without appearing guilty of self-promotion, parochialism, and obstructionism. The chief executive, in contrast, can claim to represent a national constituency. A president can act with greater secrecy, speed, and flexibility than the large and fragmented legislative branch, and with greater democratic accountability than unelected judges. Small wonder, then, that national security concerns are easily transformed into trump cards to support expansive presidential authority. Because it is so difficult to challenge, the national security–driven centralization of power poses special risks.

Referring to the post–World War II period, historian Arthur Schlesinger described the effect in mystical terms: "The high priests had only to utter their incantation—'national security'—and international actions and policies of the United States were supposed to vanish into some *sanctum sanctorum*" of the Oval Office. The result, he wrote, was "the doctrine so commonly voiced . . . and so profoundly anti-democratic, 'We must trust the President because only he knows the facts.'"[4] This sentiment solidified in the 1950s and 1960s as the nation faced two hot wars and a cold war nuclear threat. Schlesinger observed that the separation of powers "began to disappear in the middle distance" as presidents increasingly pursued independent courses of action.[5]

After Vietnam and Watergate, however, Congress sought to impose statutory restraints on executive action in foreign affairs, such as the War Powers Resolution of 1973, intended to guard against creeping, undeclared wars, and the Case-Zablocki Act of 1972, to require the president to inform Congress of international agreements made without congressional input. Neither measure lived up to its potential. The War Powers Resolution, for example, evolved not as a check on executive power to commit troops but as "de facto congressional permission to commit troops abroad for a time period of up to sixty days."[6] The Case Act was hampered by executive maneuvers to avoid reporting to Congress.[7] In fact, instead of being restrained in the late twentieth century, "the American presidency is as strong, if not stronger than ever,"[8] with both branches acceding to a more aggressive interpretation of executive power in the U.S. Constitution. Yet George W. Bush believed that executive powers had been seriously eroded since the 1970s, powers that he and his administration were determined to restore. On numerous occasions, the president made clear that "I'm not going to let Congress erode the power of the Executive Branch. I have a duty to protect the Executive Branch from legislative encroachment."[9]

An important presidential ally in this task, Attorney General Ashcroft facilitated the centralization of decision making in the White House. He used his office to draft and lobby for legislative changes, enact administrative rule changes, issue new interpretations of existing law, and frame the government's position in litigation. In this way, he assisted in the task of expanding presidential authority to an unprecedented degree and, in the process, discounting the constitutional balancing role to be played by either Congress or the courts.

Congress

The national emergency triggered by the attacks of 9/11 built on the existing cold war predilection for executive hegemony in national security affairs. This time, with the securitization of the home front, there was an even more compelling rationale for unilateral presidential action. In the initial aftermath, Democrats in Congress joined Republican colleagues to vote overwhelmingly in favor of enhancing presidential power. They were conscious, said one, of not "showing disunity at a time when we wanted to have unity" and not "tying the hands of the Commander in Chief."[10] At the same time, legislators did not intend to vacate their own constitutional powers. Some members soon tried to reassert their institutional prerogatives, but they encountered difficulty partly of their own making. They had given the executive branch two statutory tools—the Authorization for the Use of Military Force (AUMF) and the USA Patriot Act—which the president and his attorney general were able to exploit to dominate antiterrorism policy. The administration also relied on rule changes and reinterpretations of existing law to further that goal. In response, some legislators called for more oversight, which sparked a battle over access to information. One particularly vocal member on the necessity of checking executive power was Senator Robert C. Byrd (D-W.V.), who complained that "this administration shows little appreciation for the constitutional doctrines and processes that have preserved those freedoms for more than two centuries."[11]

Legislative Action

The country was still in shock, and members of Congress themselves were locked out of their offices due to the anthrax threat when legislators considered the administration's call for greater authority to address the nation's security needs. They quickly complied. The first bill was the Authorization for the Use of Military Force, which passed by a stunning vote of 98 to 0 in the Senate and 420–1 in the House. The measure granted the president the power "to use all necessary and appropriate force against those nations, organizations, or persons he determines planned, authorized, committed, or aided the terrorist attacks that occurred on September 11, 2001, or harbored such organizations or persons, in order to prevent any future acts of international terrorism against the United States by such nations, organizations or person."[12] Legislators characterized the AUMF as "specific statutory authorization within the meaning of . . . the War Powers Resolution."[13]

According to some members of Congress, their goal in drafting the AUMF was to provide sufficient but defined authority for the White House to respond to the September 11 attackers. Their intent was to avoid the type of open-ended authority that characterized the 1964 Tonkin Gulf Resolution authorizing use of force in Southeast Asia. President Bush had submitted to Congress a more expansive draft, "far too broad for most of us," according to Senator Carl Levin (D-Mich.). In the House, Representative Peter DeFazio (D-Ore.) called the early draft "unprecedented, open-ended . . . far beyond that necessary to respond to the terrorist acts on our people, even far beyond that ceded to FDR in World War II." The issue, DeFazio asserted, was not partisan but institutional. "The earlier drafts ceded too much authority to the executive branch," he said.[14] In contrast, the final version explicitly tied the president's authority to the September 11 attacks and situated it within the War Powers Resolution. It was in this light that a bipartisan group of legislators endorsed the strikes against Afghanistan in October 2001.[15]

Regardless of the legislative intent, the president interpreted the measure as a broad grant of executive authority. In his signing remarks, Bush said the resolution authorized a "direct, forceful and comprehensive response" to any terrorism that is "directed against the United States and its interests."[16] In other words, it was not limited to eradicating the al Qaeda threat. Further, the president noted obliquely, "I maintain the longstanding position of the executive branch regarding the President's constitutional authority to use force, including the Armed Forces of the United States and regarding the constitutionality of the War Powers Resolution," by which he meant that, like his predecessors in office, he did not consider the War Powers Resolution to be a constitutional check on his authority. Most significant, despite the language in the law, the president did not consider the AUMF to provide "specific statutory authorization." Instead, Bush claimed that his authority to act emanated from the Constitution itself, which Congress simply recognized in the AUMF. He said that the legislation "recognizes the seriousness of the terrorist threat to our Nation and the authority of the President under the Constitution to take action to deter and prevent acts of terrorism against the United States."[17]

The AUMF, as Public Law 107-40, was cited by the president when he issued the military order of November 13, 2001, authorizing detention and military trials for "certain non-citizens";[18] it was cited again by the president and Congress in the use of force authorization against Iraq in 2002.[19] Bush reiterated his view that the AUMF merely recognized—and did not grant— the president's authority to act, and that the authority applied generally to international terrorism: "The President has authority under the Constitution to take action in order to deter and prevent acts of international terrorism against the United States, as Congress recognized in the joint resolution on Authorization for Use of Military Force."[20] Later, in key legal briefs related to the war against terrorism, the Justice Department also cited the AUMF with this understanding. Government attorneys argued in *Hamdi v. Rumsfeld* that AUMF was evidence that Congress recognized that "the President has authority under the Constitution to take action to deter and prevent acts of international terrorism against the United States."[21] Constitutional law scholar Jamin Raskin warned that "the grant of power to the president in the resolution was so expansive and boundless that Congress may have dealt itself out of the hand."[22] Others also noted that the White House employed the measure to claim an almost open-ended delegation of power.[23]

The Patriot Act strengthened executive claims as well, again despite the intent of some legislators to fashion a less ambitious law. The act, which will be examined in more detail in chapter 7, passed overwhelmingly, reflecting the widespread desire in Congress to do something dramatic and meaningful to minimize the terrorist threat at home. Members were cognizant of the necessity of protecting both national security and their own reputations, since inaction could be seen as failure to stop a future attack. Ashcroft insisted that the bill pass immediately if Congress wanted "to prevent acts of terror."[24] The legislative process broke from customary norms, with just one hearing in a House committee and none in the Senate. House rules and Senate leadership ensured that amendments would not be added. Shortly before the vote, the House version, which had received bipartisan committee support, was replaced with a different bill. Most members had not had a chance to read it by the time the vote was called. Ashcroft was pivotal in pushing for the mammoth measure and reassuring wavering legislators about the bill's constitutionality.

An unusual coalition of representatives warned against moving too precipitously. Bob Barr, a conservative Georgia Republican, and Maxine Waters, a liberal California Democrat, were among those in the House who unsuccessfully opposed the bill. Barr lamented, "It's very difficult to get members of Congress to do anything that might appear to the untrained eye [as] not to be going after the terrorists."[25] Morton Halperin of the Council on Foreign Relations explained the atmosphere in Congress: "At the time the Patriot Act was passed, the message from the administration was, 'If you don't give us what we want, the next terrorist act will be on your head.' Congress doesn't stand up very well to that kind of demagoguery."[26] Ashcroft on a number of occasions made this type of threat. On the second anniversary of the attacks, he warned an audience in New York City that "more Americans will die" if Patriot Act powers are rolled back.[27] He urged the Senate not to let the "sunsetted provisions" of the Patriot Act expire, "unless we want simply to let down the guard of the United States against terror."[28] Such hyperbolic language put Congress on the defensive.

As with the AUMF, legislators had resisted the administration's calls for even greater powers. Members did not provide the government with broad administrative subpoena power, for example, something the White House sought again in the unsuccessful Domestic Security Enhancement Act (called Patriot II) and in the Patriot Act reauthorization in 2005. Nor did Congress completely acquiesce to Ashcroft's demands that Foreign

Intelligence Surveillance Act (FISA) warrants be available more generally, an issue to be examined later in this book. Yet, as chapter 7 will document, the attorney general succeeded in shepherding through Congress broad new executive powers and then using his interpretative role to extend them even further.

Resisting Oversight

With the statutory authorities in place, the administration sought to act with minimal interference from the legislative branch. The struggle between the executive and Congress over access to information long predates 9/11, but it intensified in subsequent years as the Bush administration—particularly the attorney general—resisted releasing information sought by legislators about the antiterrorism efforts of the executive branch, including the administration's handling of the al Qaeda threat before the attacks and its implementation of the Patriot Act.

Some members, joined by proponents of open government, criticized the administration's tight hold on unclassified as well as classified information, "without scrutiny and input from Congress or the public."[29] Justifying the greater secrecy, the White House asserted a compelling need to protect national security. Government transparency is dangerous in a time when terrorists "exploit our openness," in the words of the attorney general.[30] Not simply the press and public but also Congress and the courts were advised against pushing for disclosure. Bush explained his reasoning when he refused to release to Congress a key memo he received a month before the attacks:

> One of the things that is very important . . . is that the information given to the President be protected, because we don't want to give away sources and uses and methodology of intelligence-gathering. And one of the things that we're learning is in order to win this war on terror, we've got to have the best intelligence-gathering possible. And not only have we got to share intelligence between friends—which we do—but we're still at war, we've still got threats to the homeland that we've got to deal with. And it's very important for us to not hamper our ability to wage that war.[31]

The core of his argument appears to be this: sharing information with friends would aid the war on terror, whereas sharing information with Congress would undermine it. Congressional oversight would interfere with the president's exercise of his constitutional wartime authority and thus could threaten national security.

Separation of powers figured prominently in many arguments for confidentiality. For example, when Representative Henry Waxman (D-Calif.) sought information relating to meetings between Vice President Cheney's energy task force and executives of the failed energy giant Enron, the administration based its refusal to comply on the grounds that disclosure would undermine the president's ability to receive advice and input from the electorate. Spokesman Ari Fleischer explained, "[A] very important principle is involved here. And that is the right of the government and all future presidencies . . . to conduct reviews, to receive information from constituents regardless of their party or their background."[32] The administration's refusal to share information brought a Government Accountability Office (GAO) investigation at the request of Waxman and Representative John Dingall (D-Mich.).[33] When the GAO, the nonpartisan investigative agency of Congress, sought the documents, the vice president's office again refused to comply. The GAO then sued for release of the documents, and the Justice Department filed a motion to dismiss on separation of powers grounds. A Justice spokesperson said: "The GAO's assertion of virtually unlimited authority to investigate the Executive Branch would revolutionize and violate the separation of powers doctrine that has made our nation's government so strong."[34] The federal district judge, John Bates, weighed the separation of powers arguments advanced by both sides and the appropriateness of judicial mediation of such a dispute. He noted, "Historically, the Article III courts have not stepped in to resolve disputes between the political branches over their respective Article I and Article II powers."[35] This case, Bates concluded, was not the appropriate one to break that precedent because it did not involve a subpoena by Congress itself. He granted the government's motion to dismiss, and the GAO decided not to appeal.[36]

One of the government's reasons for maintaining a high degree of secrecy vis-à-vis Congress was a concern with news leaks. The administration's efforts to investigate one leak appeared to undermine separation of powers. It started when someone leaked to CNN the substance of two Arabic conversations intercepted on September 10, 2001, by the National Security Agency.[37] The leaks may have originated with the House or Senate intelligence committees that were jointly examining intelligence failures prior to 9/11. Under House and Senate rules, news leaks are investigated internally, by each chamber's ethics committee.[38] However, with the invitation of the committees' chairmen, the FBI began to investigate committee members and their staff. The Justice Department requested at least seventeen senators to voluntarily provide their daily schedules, calendars, appointment books, e-mail messages, and other documents relevant to the inquiry. In an unprecedented move, some were also asked to voluntarily submit to lie detector tests.[39] Several refused the polygraphs, pointing to a conflict with the constitutional separation of powers.[40] Senate majority leader Tom Daschle (D-S.D.) and minority leader Trent Lott (R-Miss.) were among those citing separation of powers concerns when they advised members not submit to the FBI's polygraph request.[41] In fact, the appropriate body for investigating the allegation of news leaks was Congress itself, not an executive agency.

John Ashcroft interpreted the doctrine of the separation of powers differently from members of Congress, to mean a strong commitment to defending executive prerogatives. For example, when asked by Senate Judiciary Committee members to provide the Office of Legal Counsel memo issued in 2002 that reportedly sanctioned torture, he demurred on the grounds that the memo constituted private legal advice to the president. He said he based his refusal not on executive privilege but on the grounds that "any confidential memorandum provided to members of the executive branch is considered by the department to be important that we maintain it, that we not provide it outside the executive branch. . . . We believe that to provide this kind of information would impair the ability of advice-giving in the executive branch to be candid, forthright, thorough and accurate at all times, and so that the disclosure of such advice and the threatened disclosure that all memos would be in some way provided would impair our ability to conduct ourselves in the executive branch."[42] He saw congressional oversight as a potential infringement on core executive authority. On another occasion, he told senators that the administration wanted to work with Congress to fight terrorism, but added, "Congress' power of oversight is not without limits."[43]

One limit related to Congress's access to executive branch personnel. Ashcroft informed senators that he was not constitutionally obligated to testify before them unless instructed to do so by the president.[44] This was a change from the historic norm that government officials testify unless they are under a presidential grant of privilege. Throughout his tenure at Justice, Ashcroft seldom appeared before the judiciary committees of Congress, even after Republicans won control of both houses in 2002. When criticized for this, he cited his busy schedule at the Justice Department. But congressional critics pointed out that he did find time to give numerous public speeches. A review of his activities on the Justice Department Web site confirms this. He testified before congressional committees seven times in 2001 and four times in 2002. His public addresses and announcements for those years numbered seventy-two and seventy-six, respectively.[45] In 2003, he again met four times with Congress while giving forty-seven public addresses, not including the Patriot Act lectures he presented nationwide in the fall. His absence at a Senate Judiciary Committee hearing in October 2003 was particularly noteworthy because the hearing was reviewing "criminal terrorism investigations and prosecutions," an area squarely within the attorney general's purview.[46] The pattern held in 2004, when Ashcroft gave twenty-three addresses, half of them outside of the District of Columbia, but testified only once before Congress.[47] In contrast, according to a report in *Roll Call,* both Donald Rumsfeld and Colin Powell made regular appearances and provided classified briefings before the House and Senate Armed Services Committees and the House International Relations and Senate Foreign Relations Committees, respectively.[48]

The attorney general apparently supported the FBI's resistance to providing Congress with access to an FBI informant who had rented a room to two of the September 11 hijackers. The joint congressional committee investigating the attacks, the predecessor of the 9/11 commission, had sought to question the informant. When the FBI refused to produce him for questioning, the committee issued a congressional subpoena, but then the FBI refused to serve it on the informant.[49]

Ashcroft also sought to shield executive branch documents and information from Congress. He was slow in responding to congressional requests for information and sometimes ignored letters from members of Congress. For example, he did not respond to a letter sent by Democratic senators Russell Feingold (Wisc.), Jeff Bingaman (N.M.), Edward Kennedy (Mass.), Richard Durbin (Ill.), and Jon Corzine (N.J.), formally requesting that he voluntarily release the names of the hundreds of individuals detained following 9/11.[50] He resisted sharing information with Congress regarding the implementation of the Patriot Act, even though the act itself mandates that "on a semiannual basis, the Attorney General shall fully inform" the House and Senate intelligence committees on Foreign Intelligence Surveillance Act warrant requests, and the House and Senate judiciary committees on the numbers of applications made and orders granted for FISA searches.[51] Ashcroft used different ploys to delay disclosure. When the House Judiciary Committee sought information about how many times resident legal aliens and U.S. citizens were being monitored electronically as part of the terrorism investigation, the Justice Department did not directly refuse to release the documents but simply announced that the information would be released to the House Intelligence Committee instead. The intelligence committee, however, did not have oversight responsibilities for that portion of the Patriot Act.[52] Interestingly, the previous November, Ashcroft had identified the congressional judiciary committees as the appropriate ones to oversee his department's handling of the antiterrorism investigation.[53] Furthermore, judiciary committee members and staff had the requisite security clearances to review the classified material. In the late summer of 2002, the chairman of the judiciary committee, James Sensenbrenner Jr. (R-Wisc.), threatened to issue a subpoena to Ashcroft if his committee did not receive the answers it sought.[54] Sensenbrenner told reporters, "I've never signed a subpoena in my five and a half years as a chairman. I guess there's a first time for everything."[55] The *Congressional Quarterly* noted that "monitoring the effects of the anti-terrorism law would be hard under any circumstances because of the secretive nature of the counterterrorism investigations. But the Justice Department has aggravated the problem by refusing to share with Congress even general information about how the law is being used."[56] By April 2003, however, Ashcroft had reassessed his reluctance to disclose information to Congress. This time, when Sensenbrenner and ranking member John Conyers Jr. wrote to the attorney general for information on implementation of the Patriot Act, they had to wait only eight weeks for a response from Justice.[57]

Similar battles over access occurred between Justice and the Senate. One struggle involved the Senate Judiciary Committee's access to the department's proposed new rules regarding electronic eavesdropping warrants issued by the Foreign Surveillance Intelligence Court. In a private meeting with the committee chairman Patrick Leahy (D-Vt.) and Senators Arlen Specter (R-Pa.) and Charles Grassley (R-Iowa), a Justice official had said in passing that new rules had been drafted for conducting electronic surveillance of suspected terrorists and their supporters.[58] At the time, Judiciary Committee members were debating a relaxation in FISA warrant requirements and believed the information was relevant to their lawmaking function.[59] However, when the senators asked to see the administration's new rules, the Justice Department declined, essentially saying that "the rules for doing secret surveillance are secret."[60] The Justice Department explained that the proposed rules could not be released because of pending litigation. One Senate staff member complained, "We actually want to help [the Justice Department] by crafting the best legislation possible, but they're too secretive to let us do it."[61] Because the FISA judges had reviewed the department's proposed regulations, the senators asked the Justice Department for a copy of the unclassified FISA opinion. Again, the department refused. The three senators then took the unprecedented step of asking the FISA court itself to release its opinion, and the court did so. That was the first time the Senate oversight committee knew "what Ashcroft was proposing" in his new FISA guidelines. The level of secrecy rankled even his supporters. A Republican Senate aide explained, "There is nothing in there that gives away the keys to the kingdom for a terrorist or spy."[62]

Patrick Leahy continued to clash with the attorney general over access to documents even after he lost the chairmanship to Senator Orrin Hatch (R-Utah). In June 2004, he chastised Ashcroft for his failure to produce a copy of the OLC memorandum that seemed to condone the torture of enemy detainees. Leahy had only seen the memo after it was leaked to the press. He complained,

"I've been asking for copies of post–September 11th policy memos for over a year, but your department has repeatedly said such documents are classified, or they simply won't release them. I asked you for the specific memo that was reported in the press 10 days ago and received no response." He added, "You denied information to members of this committee on both sides of the aisle, and so we conduct our oversight view of what we learn in the press."[63]

The following exchange between the two men illustrates both the attorney general's ability to obfuscate his answers and the senator's growing frustration:[64]

SENATOR LEAHY: Does your answer mean that there has or has not been any order directed from the president with respect to interrogation of detainees, prisoners or combatants?

ATTORNEY GENERAL ASHCROFT: The president of the United States has not ordered any activity which would contradict the laws enacted by this Congress or previous Congresses . . .

SENATOR LEAHY: Not quite my . . .

ATTORNEY GENERAL ASHCROFT: . . . or the Constitution of the United States . . .

SENATOR LEAHY: Mr. Attorney General, that was not my question.

ATTORNEY GENERAL ASHCROFT: . . . or any of the treaties.

SENATOR LEAHY: That was not my question. Has there been any order directed from the president with respect to interrogation of detainees, prisoners or combatants, yes or no?

ATTORNEY GENERAL ASHCROFT : I'm not in a position to answer that question.

SENATOR LEAHY: Does that mean because you don't know or you don't want to answer? I don't understand.

ATTORNEY GENERAL ASHCROFT: The answer to that question is yes.

SENATOR LEAHY: You don't know whether he's issued such an order?

ATTORNEY GENERAL ASHCROFT: For me to comment on what I advise the president . . .

SENATOR LEAHY: I'm not asking . . .

ATTORNEY GENERAL ASHCROFT: . . . what the president's activity is, is inappropriate if—I will just say this: that he has made no order that would require or direct the violation of any law of the United States enacted by the Congress, or any treaty to which the United States is a party as ratified by the Congress, or the Constitution of the United States.

SENATOR LEAHY: Well, it doesn't answer my question. But I think my time is up.

Ashcroft's assertions were more opaque than they may appear because—as noted in chapter 2—the memo in question had defined torture so narrowly that many highly coercive interrogation techniques would not qualify as torture under it, and therefore would not be illegal from the OLC's perspective.

Continuing its efforts to shield its actions from congressional oversight, the administration revived the doctrine of executive privilege over certain Justice documents. This occurred even at a cost to the administration's partisan interests. For example, the House Committee on Government Reform in 2001 subpoenaed confidential Justice Department documents relating to Janet Reno's decision in 1996 not to appoint a special counsel to investigate allegations of campaign finance wrongdoing. The House hearings on Reno's decision potentially could embarrass the preceding Democratic administration. However, Ashcroft and the president viewed the subpoena as "inconsistent with the constitutional doctrine of separation of powers," as well as a burden on internal deliberations regarding criminal charges and a potential politicization of the criminal justice process. Bush invoked executive privilege and instructed his attorney general not to release the documents.[65]

Ashcroft's reluctance to share documents with Congress extended even to those involving cases long closed. In 2002, for example, the same House committee sought thirty-four-year-old Justice Department documents pertaining to a 1968 federal murder prosecution in Boston. The two men convicted of the crime had their convictions overturned in 2001, and the House committee began an investigation into the FBI's knowledge that perjured testimony had been used to convict them. When the committee sought the relevant documents, however, Justice refused to release them, citing executive privilege. The assistant attorney general for legislative affairs explained the underlying principle: that their release would have a chilling effect on current and future prosecutors. The committee chairman, Representative Daniel Burton (R-Ind.) continued to press for their release; he rejected the Justice Department's offer to describe the contents of the documents. At one point, fellow Republican Bob Barr of Georgia said they were willing to sue to get the documents.[66]

Defending the Justice Department's record on cooperating with Congress, Justice press secretary Mark Corallo said that the volume of requests from Congress was higher than the department could handle, since its personnel were preoccupied with a "massive terrorism investigation."[67] On another occasion, Corallo said the department had responded to more than 7,000 letters from members of the 107th Congress, with Justice staff members testifying at 247 hearings.[68] Some legislators also defended the department and attorney general. Senator Jon Kyl (R-Ariz.), for example, said he was not convinced "that we are somehow missing the boat by not having a lot more oversight hearings." Regarding the release of documents, Kyl said that the attorney general sometimes was slow to comply "but it's never been a reluctance to cooperate."[69] Senator Hatch resisted calls for greater oversight issued by Leahy, Grassley, and Specter. Hatch chided his colleagues: "Some of these guys would have [Ashcroft] up here every day. The attorney general is always on the griddle, and some people want to embarrass him every chance they can. I don't think we should use the attorney general so we can get the media to come."[70]

But many on Capitol Hill shared the perception that Justice was not responsive to them. The attorney general's lack of openness arguably complicated the ability of Congress to conduct its business. Sensenbrenner's spokesman explained what was at stake: "A lot of times people think congressional oversight is just looking for scandals, but this is an area where they just want to know how the law is being implemented, what's working and what's not and those sort of good-government type questions."[71] The executive branch's zeal in securing its own constitutional prerogatives effectively undercut the ability of legislators to fulfill theirs.

Defending Unilateral Action: Military Commissions

In addition to shielding documents, the Justice Department asserted a constitutional basis for unilateral executive action to address terrorism. One of the most contested actions concerned the president's order to create military tribunals. On November 13, 2001, Bush issued a military order to authorize the detention and military trial of "certain non-citizens." The president claimed a wartime authority to establish tribunals absent specific congressional authorization. He based the order on "the authority vested in me as President and as Commander in Chief of the Armed Forces and the laws of the United States of America, including the Authorization for the Use of Military Force Joint Resolution."[72] As noted earlier, Bush did not consider the AUMF to be the source of his authority to act. Many legislators and scholars rejected the administration's claim of unilateral authority. They believed that military commissions were Article III courts, that is, federal courts inferior to the Supreme Court, which, under the Constitution, "the Congress may, from time to time, ordain and establish."[73]

Under the military order, the president would determine who would be subject to military trial, and the Defense Department then would detain and prosecute those individuals under procedures promulgated by the secretary of defense. Except for the judge advocate general, the military judges need not be trained in the law. The secretary of defense or his designee could review either a conviction or a sentence, with the president having the final say on a case outcome. Civilian courts were barred from exercising judicial review. In fact, defendants were not "privileged to seek any remedy" in regular court—either federal, state, foreign, or international. Because the executive branch would create the tribunals, establish the rules, appoint the judges and military attorneys, identify individual defendants, adjudicate the cases, and hear appeals, the system would rest entirely on a single branch of government. Further, the civilian Justice Department—despite its legal expertise—was not mentioned in the order, except implicitly as one of the "departments, agencies, entities and officers of the United States" charged to assist the secretary of defense.[74] This omission seemed to surprise Specter and Leahy in Senate Judiciary Committee oversight hearings held two weeks after the order was issued.[75]

Ashcroft may have been involved in helping to draft the order.[76] At the least, he was informed that the military order was under consideration. In late November 2001, Senator Hatch recalled that Ashcroft had "indicated that such tribunals were under consideration" in his Senate testimony the previous October 18, even though the attorney general did not explicitly "commit at that time to creation of such tribunals."[77] The fact that the senators themselves had not been specifically informed irritated some members. Leahy, for example, asked Assistant Attorney General Michael Chertoff why the government had not asked for authorization during the six weeks that the Patriot Act was under construction; after all, he and Ashcroft were in contact a couple of times each day during this period, discussing the need to expand the legal tools to fight terrorism. Congress could have included an authorization for military commissions at that time. Chertoff replied that the president was acting in his capacity as head of law enforcement in discussions related to the Patriot Act, and therefore shared powers with Congress. But the military order did not require consultation with Congress because, "from the administration's perspective, the issue of military tribunals is a matter that comes under the jurisdiction of the Department of Defense as an extension of the President's power as Commander-in-Chief."[78] In other words, law enforcement and military decision making are distinct constitutional roles, necessitating different levels of presidential consultation with Congress.

Ashcroft and attorneys under him defended the constitutionality of the order. The attorney general told the Senate in December 2001, "It is my position that the president has an inherent authority and power to conduct war and to prosecute war crimes," including the creation of military tribunals. "For centuries, Congress has recognized this authority and the Supreme Court has never held that any Congress may limit it," he said.[79] Ashcroft also did not concede a role for Congress in creating the procedures to be followed by the tribunals. If legislators wanted to give their input, he said he would pass along their suggestions to the Pentagon.[80] Reassuring senators that the military order was "carefully drawn to target a narrow class of individuals—terrorists," he added that the president's action was consistent with precedent and custom.[81]

In fact, the language of the act would apply it to "any individual who is not a United States citizen,"[82] conceivably including the between 15 and 20 million foreign nationals legally in the United States. People would be designated foreign terrorists by the president without any independent court review, a problem that did not concern the attorney general, who said, "Foreign terrorists who commit war crimes against the United States, in my judgment, are not entitled to and do not deserve the protection of the American Constitution."[83]

Louis Fisher, author of two scholarly books on military tribunals, disputed Ashcroft's reading of history that a long line of precedent supported military tribunals as established through the president's military order in 2001. The authority to establish earlier tribunals had been provided by Congress, and the procedures to be followed mirrored those of regular courts-martial. The tribunals were emergency measures instituted in combat zones or occupied territories.[84] Further, Fisher argued, the application of the military order to a "broad class of non-citizens"—not just the eight tried in *Ex Parte Quirin,* the case of the Nazi saboteurs—constituted another significant break from precedent.[85]

Ashcroft's argument that prosecutorial and investigatory powers are solely executive also is subject to challenge because it ignores the Supreme Court's opinion upholding the constitutionality of the Independent Counsel Act in 1988. In that case, Justice Antonin Scalia had argued unsuccessfully that—because an independent counsel was appointed by a judicial panel rather than the executive—the law violated the separation of powers. But the court majority rejected Scalia's view that the conduct of criminal prosecution rested solely with the executive branch.[86]

Neither the "take care clause" nor the "commander in chief clause" of the Constitution provides the unequivocal authority for expanded presidential power that Ashcroft asserted. In fact, numerous judicial precedents[87] and constitutional scholars[88] provide contradictory interpretations of the relevant constitutional language and history. Even Alexander Hamilton, that champion of presidential power, distinguished the U.S. president from the British monarch on these grounds because in the new republic the powers to declare war and raise and regulate the armed forces "would appertain to the legislature," and not the executive, under the Constitution.[89]

Repercussions with Congress

Ashcroft's tendency to ignore Congress's institutional concerns may have contributed to increased congressional scrutiny of the administration's antiterrorism legislation. It need not have been that way. Fellow Republicans controlled the House of Representatives during his entire term in office and controlled the Senate for more than two years. This arguably provided him with a partisan advantage that was not enjoyed by the previous Republican administrations of Nixon, Ford, Reagan, and Bush. Yet partisanship alone was not sufficient to guarantee a close working relationship; a law officer perceived as aloof and incommunicative could alienate even party allies on Capitol Hill. Responding to Ashcroft's call for greater law enforcement powers, for example, Representative Sensenbrenner reminded the attorney general, "My support for this legislation is neither perpetual nor unconditional."[90] His colleague Darrell Issa (R-Calif.) explained his reaction to Ashcroft's lack of cooperation: "It's been disappointing. He came out of the Senate and has been a leader in the Republican Party at every conceivable level. I would have expected more."[91] Arlen Specter in the Senate expressed a similar disappointment. He told Ashcroft, "When you sat next to me on this dais a couple of years ago, I think it is accurate to say that you shared my frustration about getting responses from the attorney general. How do we communicate with you? Are you really too busy to respond?"[92]

Despite this evident level of frustration with the attorney general, during the first term of the Bush administration, Congress as a whole avoided confrontation with the White House in its handling of the domestic war against terrorism. Members of the legislative branch generally deferred, despite their own "substantial constitutional powers" to shape national security policy.[93] Nor did legislators press their need to have access to the information necessary in order to oversee executive branch actions in the national security arena. The administration's actions in relation to Congress "seem to advocate a farreaching transformation of the separation of powers," in the words of Steven Aftergood, a critic of government secrecy and head of the Project on Government Secrecy of the Federation of American Scientists.[94] Congressional expert Thomas Mann of the Brookings Institution observed, "This is the most executive-centered team in the White House in memory."[95] Congress itself was criticized for acceding too much constitutional turf to the White House; one editorial admonished that the legislative branch was "unwilling to get involved in defining reasoned boundaries" on presidential authority, leaving the judiciary "the only realistic check on the Bush administration's unilateral assertions of power."[96] The next section will examine the degree to which courts enforced any "reasoned boundaries" on the chief executive.

Judiciary

Reliance on the judiciary to define and enforce "reasoned boundaries" posed its own perils. The judicial branch, famously called by Alexander Hamilton "the least dangerous" in *The Federalist,*[97] ran into challenges when framing its institutional response to presidential action after 9/11. More so than legislators, judges prefer to defer when faced with issues that could involve them in a "political thicket" and thus undermine their credibility and prestige. Called the doctrine of political questions, it involves a determination of an issue's justiciability; that is, does the issue lend itself to judicial resolution, or does it concern "matters as to which departments of government other than the courts . . . must have final say"?[98] If the latter, courts customarily have avoided the issue, deferring to the so-called political branches.

The judiciary need not defer to the political branches and, historically, often did not. Since World War I, and particularly since the Vietnam War, however, the courts have tended to cite the political questions doctrine to avoid taking cases that involve foreign affairs and presidential war power.[99] This caution has strengthened executive power, as noted in chapter 4. By the time of 9/11, many members of the judicial branch reacted timidly to executive claims, accepting the administration's assertion that the issues raised were outside of a court's competence. There were notable exceptions, however, with some judges revealing a willingness to be more critical in evaluating the administration's antiterrorism actions.

Limiting Court Oversight

The administration was clear: the domestic war against terrorism would be fought by the president, with Congress providing the arsenal. Law and legal systems had little to do with winning the war, from Ashcroft's perspective. This view underlay his court briefs, statutory interpretations, and administrative rule changes. His efforts to minimize the judiciary's role ranged from limiting judicial review of immigration appeals and expanding the reach of administrative subpoenas, to holding material witnesses for months without access to a courtroom and denying judicial authority over cases of designated enemy combatants. Some of these measures will be addressed in later chapters.

Even in traditional law enforcement matters, where the executive branch conceded the need to share power with the other branches, the Justice Department sought to carve out areas where the executive could act without court interference. For example, the Bureau of Prisons in the Justice Department created a special administrative measure permitting prison authorities to monitor communications between certain federal inmates and their attorneys without a court order.[100] The earlier policy had required judicial approval before attorney-client privilege could be breached.[101] Special administrative measures (SAMs) also could be used to restrict some detainees' access to counsel. This occurred in the case of Richard Reid, the man who tried to detonate explosives packed in his shoes on a transatlantic flight. Ashcroft issued twelve pages of special rules that included barring Reid from meeting psychiatrists retained by the defense, other defense experts, and the nonattorney staff of the federal public defender's office. The rules were "pettifogging, illogical, . . . absurd," according to defense counsel Owen Walker.[102] When the U.S. attorney pressured Walker to sign the SAM as a condition for seeing his client, he refused and lost contact with Reid. The defense attorney argued, "That Congress has given the Attorney General, a federal defendant's adversary, unilateral power to set rules for the conduct of the defense is a startling suggestion."[103] The government responded that the SAMs were legal and necessary for national security. The district court judge intervened, issuing a protective order that permitted the attorneys to meet with Reid but barring them from repeating to third parties the substance of his comments.[104]

In military matters, the Justice Department went further, asserting an executive sphere of action virtually immune from judicial review. The government's legal briefs in the enemy combatant cases argued that the courts could not "second-guess" the executive's military judgment and "were not competent" to assess matters related to intelligence. The Office of Legal Counsel told the Defense Department's general counsel, "Federal courts lack jurisdiction over habeas petitions filed by alien detainees held outside the sovereign territory of the United States," including the U.S. naval base at Guantánamo Bay, Cuba.[105] Those cases are examined in the following chapter.

The president's military order formally marginalized the role that civilian judges and law enforcement could play in cases involving defendants subject to military trial. It seemed premised on the view that regular court processes could not be relied on to address the threat posed by terrorists.[106] The OLC memo relating to the legal status of al Qaeda and Taliban fighters held by the U.S. military also reflected this view. It concluded that neither international treaties on the laws of war nor the War Crimes Act, which incorporated many treaty provisions into the federal criminal code, created legal constraints on how the executive could treat these fighters.[107] For Ashcroft, judicial deference was mandated not only by separation of powers but also by national security demands. Following court losses in the enemy combatant cases, for example, he said the lack of deference to the president was dangerous and could "put at risk the very security of our nation in a time of war." He added, "Dangerous and constitutionally questionable judicial action raises the stakes for our nation."[108] As with his rhetoric scolding and browbeating Congress, Ashcroft's remarks appeared designed to create pressure on judges to yield to executive determinations. Overall, said one former federal prosecutor, the

Justice Department's aggressive handling of terrorism cases seemed to reveal "a distrust of lawyers or an attempt to cut lawyers out of the process."[109]

Debating Judicial Deference

Many of the federal judges hearing challenges to the government's antiterrorism actions echoed Ashcroft's call for greater deference to the executive branch. For example, district court judge Richard Leon, in dismissing petitions for writs of habeas corpus filed by seven foreign nationals held at Guantánamo Bay, expressed this opinion when he wrote, "Simply stated, it is the province of the Executive branch and Congress, should it choose to enact legislation relating thereto, to define the conditions of detention and ensure that United States laws and treaties are being complied therewith."[110] He added, "The Founders allocated the war powers among Congress and the Executive, not the judiciary. As a general rule, therefore, the judiciary should not insinuate itself into foreign affairs and national security issues."[111] Some federal judges echoed this view, but others did not. For example, Judge Joyce Hens Green of the D.C. District Court found that precedent, particularly *Rasul v. Bush,* required "the recognition that the detainees at Guantánamo Bay possess enforceable constitutional rights," which necessarily brought their cases within the judicial ambit. Far from Leon's deferential attitude, Green then struck down the Combatant Status Review Tribunals instituted at Guantánamo for failing to satisfy due process guarantees.[112]

In several cases, the district and appellate courts disagreed on the level of deference due the executive's determination. Opposite rulings were reached in *Hamdan v. Rumsfeld, Hamdi v. Rumsfeld,* and *Padilla v. Bush.* These cases illustrate the separation of powers issues embedded in antiterrorism litigation.

Bin Laden's Chauffeur

Salim Hamdan was Osama bin Laden's driver in Afghanistan when he was captured by Afghani militia in November 2001 and then turned over to U.S. forces. Among the first detainees at Guantánamo scheduled for a military tribunal, he was given a formal hearing before the Combatant Status Review Tribunal, which affirmed his enemy combatant status. In July 2004, he was charged with conspiracy to attack civilians and to commit terrorism, among other charges. Meanwhile, Hamdan filed a habeas corpus petition in federal court. The government moved to have it dismissed, arguing that the district court lacked jurisdiction to accept the petition, since the president had already determined that Hamdan was a member of al Qaeda, and "presidential determinations in this area are due 'extraordinary deference.'"[113] But in *Hamdan v.*

Rumsfeld, district judge James Robertson denied the government's motion. He ruled that a competent neutral tribunal had not yet determined that Hamdan was an enemy combatant. Hamdan's status had to be determined by a tribunal, and "the president is not a 'tribunal.'"[114] Furthermore, under the Constitution, Congress and not the president has the authority to establish military commissions, and the procedures to be followed must be consistent with the Uniform Code of Military Justice in order to comply with U.S. law and the 1949 Geneva Convention.[115]

Reversing the lower court, however, the U.S. Court of Appeals for the District of Columbia Circuit upheld the constitutionality of military tribunals as established by the president. The appellate judges pointed to the AUMF and two federal statutes as sufficient congressional authorization for the creation of military commissions, although none of the three measures provided explicit authorization. Deferring to the executive's view that the Geneva Convention did not apply to Guantánamo detainees, Circuit Judge Raymond Randolph wrote for the majority, "Under the Constitution, the President 'has a degree of independent authority to act' in foreign affairs and, for this reason and others, his construction and application of treaty provisions is entitled to 'great weight.'"[116] The Supreme Court granted Hamdan's petition for review during the October Term 2005.

Hamdi and Habeas Corpus

In the case of Yaser Hamdi, the government also asserted the need for judicial deference, arguing in its legal brief that civilian courts lack standing to intervene once the military has designated a person to be an enemy combatant. The district court rejected that position, finding instead that the factual record presented by the government to support Hamdi's classification as an enemy combatant was not sufficient. The district judge ordered the government attorneys to provide more evidence. On appeal to the Fourth Circuit Court of Appeals, the government again argued for the courts to defer: "The Court may not second-guess the military's enemy combatant determination. At the very most, given the separation of constitutional powers in this unique area, a court could only require the military to point to some evidence supporting its determination. Either way, no evidentiary hearing is required to dispose of a habeas petition in this military context."[117] Government attorneys asserted that the decision to classify someone an enemy combatant "is a quintessentially military judgment, representing a core exercise of the Commander-in-Chief authority."[118]

The Fourth Circuit Court found the government's argument persuasive and overturned the district court. Hamdi's habeas petition was dismissed. Asserting that "jurisdictional limitations have their roots in the respect courts owe the other branches of our government,"[119] the appellate judges determined that the district court had overstepped separation of powers when it ruled that Hamdi had a right to raise a habeas corpus appeal. The only issue that federal courts could consider was the legality of his detention under the president's war powers and the AUMF. The specific facts supporting Hamdi's detention were off limits.[120]

The Supreme Court, however, did not confirm the Fourth Circuit's reasoning. Instead, the justices vacated and remanded the case by a 6 to 3 vote. The plurality found that "due process demands that a citizen held in the United States as an enemy combatant be given a meaningful opportunity to contest the factual basis for that detention before a neutral decision maker."[121] Justice Sandra Day O'Connor reasserted that the Constitution envisions a role for "all three branches when individual liberties are at stake." She explained:

> We necessarily reject the Government's assertion that separation of powers principles mandate a heavily circumscribed role for the courts in such circumstances. Indeed, the position that the courts must forgo any examination of the individual case and focus exclusively on the legality of the broader detention scheme cannot be mandated by any reasonable view of separation of powers, as this approach serves only to *condense* power into a single branch of government. We have long since made clear that a state of war is not a blank check for the President when it comes to the rights of the Nation's citizens.[122]

Despite the stirring language, O'Connor did not find that Hamdi had a right of access to civilian courts, only to a "neutral decision maker," which could include well-designed military tribunals. Furthermore, Hamdi carried the burden of proof in establishing his innocence, and he was guaranteed access to counsel only for the limited purpose of challenging the government's factual record.[123] The justices did not overturn military tribunals, although they disagreed on the basis of the president's authority to create them. Four of the justices in the majority found that the AUMF provided the necessary authorization, but two did not. Two of the dissenters—Justices John Paul Stevens and Scalia—argued against the majority's deference to any legislative authorization short of a congressional suspension of the writ of habeas corpus; in their view, Hamdi had to be released or charged. Justice Thomas alone believed that the president's inherent constitutional authority was sufficient to establish military tribunals.[124]

Of note in terms of separation of powers, the Justice Department used language similar to the *Hamdi* brief in challenging one defense offered in June 2002 by the attorneys for John Walker Lindh, the U.S. citizen captured in Afghanistan but transferred to civilian court. When Lindh's attorneys tried to invoke a defense of combat immunity, prosecutors argued that the president had already determined the Taliban to be unlawful combatants, and the court should not "second-guess" him. To permit the combat immunity defense "would contradict a publicly stated determination by the president in his capacity as Commander in Chief in the midst of an ongoing war," they argued. The court rejected the defense.[125] The government later agreed to a plea bargain with Lindh.

Padilla v. Bush

The case of another U.S. citizen, José Padilla, followed a slightly different track from Hamdi's in terms of judicial deference. In *Padilla v. Bush,* the district court evidenced a greater willingness to affirm the president's lead than did the circuit court.

Padilla had traveled to Afghanistan and Pakistan in 2001, allegedly to contact al Qaeda and prepare to conduct terrorist operations in the United States. When he returned to the country on May 8, 2002, he was seized by federal marshals at Chicago's O'Hare Airport and held for a month in New York as a material witness in a grand jury investigation. Padilla refused to testify, however, and federal officials decided not to build a criminal case against him.[126] Then, on June 9, the president classified him as an enemy combatant and transferred him to military custody.[127] His transfer to a high-security naval brig in South Carolina enabled the government to hold him incommunicado, without charges or access to his New York attorney, where military interrogators could freely question him.[128] His attorney, Donna Newman, filed a habeas corpus petition on his behalf in the Southern District of New York, where he had been held as a material witness.

Contesting the authority of civilian courts to oversee an enemy combatant case, Justice attorneys asserted that judicial review could not go beyond a mere confirmation of the existence of *some* factual basis for Bush's decision. The factual basis relied on by the president was an affidavit filed by a political appointee in the Pentagon named Michael Mobbs. The Mobbs Declaration summarized the material gathered by the Defense Department about Yaser Hamdi and José Padilla, including interrogations of captured Taliban and al Qaeda fighters.[129] The declaration provided the basis for the president's designation of the two men as enemy combatants; there was no other review of the evidence. The government argued that, if the courts examined the substance of the Mobbs Declaration, they would become entangled "in highly sensitive judgments about the reliability of foreign intelligence sources and the assessment of military justifications." For that reason, the declaration should be accepted at face value. The government filed a motion to dismiss: "The judiciary is ill-equipped to conduct that manner of second-guessing of sensitive executive judgments, which lie at the heart of the President's exercise of his authority as Commander in Chief in wartime."[130] The district judge, Michael Mukasey, deferred to the executive on most of these points, including an affirmation of the president's power to detain citizens as enemy combatants. Even so, he did not accept that the courts had no role to play. Padilla had a right to challenge the factual basis for his classification as an enemy combatant, and, for this limited purpose, he also had a right to counsel.[131] Even though the government won the significant issue in the case, the Justice Department appealed.

The Second Circuit Court of Appeals issued a clear repudiation of the president's unilateral power to designate citizens enemy combatants. "Where, as here, the President's power as Commander in Chief of the armed forces and the domestic rule of law intersect, we conclude that clear congressional authorization is required for detentions of American citizens on American soil." The judges cited the Non-Detention Act, which requires specific congressional authorization before a citizen can be detained; the act was passed in 1971 partly in response to the internment of Japanese Americans during World War II. The AUMF was not sufficient to clear that legal hurdle. The Second Circuit remanded Padilla's case to the district court and ordered that he be released from military custody within thirty days.[132]

The Justice Department appealed to the Supreme Court. In the government's petition for a writ of certiorari, the solicitor general argued, "A detention 'ordered by the President in the declared exercise of his powers as Commander in Chief' is 'not to be set aside by the courts without the clear conviction that [it is] in conflict with the . . . laws of Congress.'"[133] Padilla's case reached the Supreme Court in the same month as Hamdi's. By a vote of 5 to 4, the justices delayed ruling on the merits of the case and instead focused on the narrow question of jurisdiction, ruling that Padilla's attorney, as next friend, had brought the habeas petition to the wrong district court.[134] Padilla's attorney refiled in the appropriate district court and won, but the Fourth Circuit Court of Appeals reversed, finding that the president could detain Americans who were linked to al Qaeda. Padilla petitioned the Supreme Court for review in October 2005, and observers expected the high court to accept the case. A decision on the merits of Padilla's case had not been made at the time of this writing.

Padilla's experience dramatizes the attorney general's role as defender of broad unilateral executive power during wartime. According to Ashcroft, even the transfer and virtually open-ended military detention of a U.S. citizen arrested on U.S. soil—one whose case was already in the civilian court system—were beyond the scope of judicial review. Not only did the attorney general not object to the transfer of Padilla from Justice Department jurisdiction, Ashcroft reported that he had recommended that course of action.[135] It was Ashcroft who made the dramatic announcement about Padilla's capture, interrupting a trip to Moscow "to announce today" that a "known terrorist" had been captured and an "unfolding terrorist plot" had thereby been disrupted. He characterized Padilla as "an al Qaeda operative" whose U.S. citizenship would enable him to "travel freely in the U.S. without drawing attention to himself." The attorney general also asserted that Padilla had been planning to detonate a "highly toxic" radioactive dirty bomb in the United States that could cause "mass death and injury." His tie with al Qaeda was confirmed from "multiple independent and corroborating sources."[136] The announcement sparked immediate protest because it misrepresented the facts in Padilla's case, apparently an effort to appeal to people's fears. Padilla had not just been caught; he had been in custody more than a month. Nor was there solid evidence of an unfolding plot; some federal law enforcement officials later said there was no evidence that a plot was even under way.[137] Finally, experts disputed Ashcroft's contention that a dirty bomb would kill large numbers of people. A dirty bomb was less likely to be fatal than to trigger panic and illness. Critics also pointed out that Ashcroft made the announcement just as the FBI and CIA faced heavy criticism for failing to cooperate in the fight against terrorism. In fact, the attorney general used his statement to highlight their close cooperation in Padilla's capture.[138]

The Justice Department's handling of Padilla's case continued to raise questions. For example, James Comey, the deputy attorney general who had led the government's case against Padilla as U.S. attorney, told the news media in June 2004 that Padilla had planned to use "uranium wrapped with explosives" and natural gas to target apartment buildings. Again, scientists questioned how lethal "uranium wrapped explosives" would be, many concluding that such a bomb would be a dud.[139] The timing of Comey's remarks also triggered concerns, since the Supreme Court was poised that week to issue its decision on Padilla's habeas corpus petition. Comey's announcement could have hurt Padilla's appeal. That issue will be addressed in chapter 8.

Second Thoughts

By 2002, some observers were expressing concern that the courts were being excluded unnecessarily. An editorial in the *Christian Science Monitor,* for example, argued, "Federal judges can be trusted just as much as Pentagon or Justice Department officials to sift through the same intelligence information and find reasonable suspicion of a security threat. And the methods of how the intelligence data were collected can also be protected by a federal judge."[140] Some members of the judiciary began to articulate similar reservations.

In *Rasul v. Bush,* for example, the Supreme Court found that the federal courts did have the authority to review "the legality of the Executive's potentially indefinite detention of individuals who claim to be wholly innocent of wrongdoing."[141] The case involved a challenge brought by fourteen men detained at Guantánamo seeking a meaningful procedure to establish their innocence. They had been captured in Afghanistan and Pakistan and were accused of being al Qaeda or Taliban supporters. Justice Department attorneys had argued that the judiciary did not have authority to review their claims, and the lower court agreed.[142] The Supreme Court, however, did not. In his concurrence, Justice Anthony Kennedy directly addressed the issue of judicial deference to executive authority over military affairs under the separation of powers. "There is a realm of political authority over military affairs where the judicial power may not enter," he wrote. Yet, he added, "There are circumstances in which the courts maintain the power and the responsibility to protect persons from unlawful detention even where military affairs are implicated."[143] Military necessity on a battlefield might justify such a detention for weeks, but not for years.[144]

Scalia's dissent in *Rasul* illustrates how compelling the deference position can appear when it is phrased in terms of supporting troops in the field during wartime. He quoted a 1950 Supreme Court case: "It would be difficult to devise more effective fettering of a field commander than to allow the very enemies he is ordered to reduce to submission to call him to account in his own civil courts and divert his efforts and attention from the military offensive abroad."[145] Scalia then added, "The Commander in Chief and his subordinates had every reason to expect that the internment of combatants at Guantánamo Bay would not have the consequence of bringing the cumbersome machinery of our domestic courts into military affairs."[146]

Some international law scholars challenged the government's legal reasoning. They assert that the facts behind the three precedents often cited by Justice—*Ex Parte Quirin,* involving an American-born member of a group of German saboteurs, *Johnson v. Eisentrager,* a post–World War II case involving German soldiers captured in China and imprisoned in Germany, and a case involving a U.S. citizen who had joined the Italian army during World War II—did not have facts similar to the enemy combatant cases.[147] Members of Congress also began to question "the rationale of taking such individuals out of the criminal justice system,"[148]and some legislators considered the possibility that the detentions of Hamdi and Padilla violated the Non-Detention Act.[149]

Among those with second thoughts was Viet Dinh, who had served in the Ashcroft Justice Department as head of the Office of Legal Policy. After leaving office, Dinh said that he had reconsidered José Padilla's case and came to view the government's position as "unsustainable." Dinh had helped to draft the Patriot Act and other antiterrorism measures, which he continued to defend, but he considered Padilla's continued detention problematic because the government had not created a mechanism for Padilla to respond. While the president "had the unquestioned authority to detain persons during wartime, even those captured on 'untraditional battlefields,' including American soil," there still had to be "an actual process or discernible set of procedures to determine how they will be treated," he said.[150] The president, in other words, could not operate beyond some constraints, even if those constraints were in the executive branch and not a true separation of powers.

Ashcroft's Response

Prior to becoming attorney general, John Ashcroft already had established a reputation as a critic of an activist federal judiciary. He regularly chastised liberal judges who "insist on creating laws and constitutional rights where there are none." He added, "What these activist judges fail to see is that where the Constitution is silent, that silence expresses the will of the people."[151] As a senator, he and House majority whip Tom Delay of Texas had reputations as the courts' harshest critics. He reportedly saw "some sitting judges as arrogant, unresponsive to the public and prone to 'activist' rulings that overstepped their constitutional role of applying, rather than creating, the law."[152] His Senate opposition to three of Clinton's judicial nominees—Ronnie White, Margaret Morrow, and Frederica Massiah-Jackson—was based not on their policy positions per se, he said, but on their failure of the litmus test of judicial restraint.[153]

Ashcroft's distrust of the judiciary surfaced as well in his support for a more circumscribed court role in adjudicating antiterrorism cases. In 2003, he told a House committee, "When a person is part of a war against the United States as a combatant against the United States, that person is subject to detention under the power of the president to protect the United States. And the courts have not interfered with that in any significant way. And I don't think courts will. I think there is—in that kind of time of peril, there is that responsibility and duty of the president."[154] A year later, after some federal courts began to question unilateral executive action, Ashcroft became highly critical. He told members of the Federalist Society in late 2004 that judges "are not equipped to execute the law. They are not accountable to the people. And they lack the knowledge and expertise essential for the effective administration of government." He warned his listeners about the dangers posed by judicial activists: "We are now confronted by a profoundly disturbing trend in our national political life: the growing tendency of the judicial branch to inject itself into areas of executive action originally assigned to the discretion of the president. These encroachments include some of the most fundamental aspects of the president's conduct of the war on terrorism."[155]

Despite Ashcroft's alarm about overreaching and activist judges tying up presidential power, the courts since September 11 generally have been deferential. Although the expansive litigation positions argued by the Ashcroft Justice Department have not prevailed completely, most judicial rulings in the domestic war against terrorism to date have not fashioned substantial checks on the presidency. In fact, many cases that appear on the surface to impose restraints—such as the Supreme Court's *Hamdi* decision—actually concede the broader executive claims. Legal commentator Michael Dorf observed that the *Hamdi* and *Rasul* Supreme Court rulings "give the government wide latitude to afford enemy prisoners fewer procedural protections than civil libertarians would deem necessary."[156] And as of this writing, José Padilla remained in detention with the Supreme Court yet to rule on the constitutionality of a U.S. citizen arrested in the United States being classified an enemy combatant solely on the president's determination.

In addition to litigation, the attorney general utilized administrative and statutory measures to remove certain executive actions from judicial review. Overall, the events examined here suggest that "the judicial branch has experienced a significant lessening of its authority under the antiterrorism measures of 2001 and 2002, resulting in an expansion of executive power."[157]

Conclusion

John Ashcroft's understanding of the doctrine of separation of powers was captured in that Federalist Society speech. Although he extolled "the fragmentation of power and the separation of authority," his remarks make clear that he saw the executive as the dominant branch. He reinterpreted the historical record to claim that the framers' concern with a weak presidency under the Articles of Confederation drove the effort to craft a new constitution in the first place. The Constitution's Article II, he claimed, solved the deficiencies of the Articles of Confederation.[158] This is a novel theory, ignoring the key gaps in the Articles of Confederation that historically have been blamed for the early republic's problem of governance, such as its failure to provide the necessary authority to the national government to enforce its legislation. James Madison, for one, did not share Ashcroft's concern about a weak executive. He did not mention it in any of the eleven weaknesses he identified in the Articles of Confederation.[159] Edmund Randolph, later to become the first attorney general, also did not consider the lack of a strong executive to be one of the defects of the articles; instead, Randolph cited the "defect of congressional power."[160]

In addition to this misreading of history, Ashcroft's comparison of Article I, dealing with Congress, and Article II, dealing with the presidency, also is flawed. He characterized Article II as a "comprehensive grant of all executive authority to the president, subject only to specified exceptions and qualifications." In contrast, he said, Article I "grants to Congress only limited and specifically enumerated legislative powers, such as the Senate's participation in the appointment of principal officers and in the making of treaties."[161] Not only does this ignore the "necessary and proper" clause in Article I, under which Congress has acted beyond its enumerated legislative powers, but the attorney general's reading blithely ignores the problem of concentrated power that so preoccupied the framers.

Since 2001, the doctrine of the separation of powers has become increasingly relevant. As this chapter has illustrated, both the White House and the Congress regularly accused the other branch of violating the doctrine. As cases traveled through the judicial system, the courts weighed in as well. The administration argued that its core powers must be safe from the encroachment of the other branches of government. Many legislators countered that powers must be divided so that no single branch can become too powerful.

These seemingly contradictory positions are reflections of the two ways of thinking about the separation of powers. As constitutional scholar Laurence Tribe has written, the concern of the first perspective is that another branch will "reduce the necessary range of authority and flexibility within a branch or level of government." The concern of the second perspective is that "the power of one branch or one level of government" will swell to dangerous levels.[162] The Bush administration—which has aggressively asserted the first perspective—appears to have the more difficult case to make when it claims that unilateral power is consistent with the doctrine of separation of powers, particularly when it argues that the judiciary lacks competence even to review its assertions.

The more established conception of the doctrine as it developed in the United States is that branches share powers. William Gwyn, a scholar of the history and theory of the separation of powers, concluded that the system adopted by the framers was not one of fragmented power jealously guarded. The framers were as concerned with efficiency as with checking abusive and arbitrary power, he noted, and that called for a system of interdependence between the branches.[163] James Madison, in *The Federalist* Number 48, understood separation of powers in this way. Even the title of this document captures that sense: "These Departments Should Not Be So Far Separated as to Have No Constitutional Control over Each Other." He warned, "Unless these departments be so far connected and blended as to give to each a constitutional control over the others, the degree of separation which the maxim requires, as essential to a free government, can never in practice be duly maintained."[164] This historical understanding of the doctrine was largely lost in the positions advanced by John Ashcroft and the Bush White House, particularly in the drive to centralize power to fight the war on terror at home.

6   Security and Liberty

The appropriate constitutional balance between national security and civil liberties received much attention in the months and years following the 2001 attacks within the United States. News reports and editorials regularly commented on the tension,[1] as did more scholarly work.[2] Noting the importance of the liberty-security debate, Paul Rosenzweig, a senior legal research fellow at the Heritage Foundation, told one congressional committee, "I have said often since September 11 that the civil liberty/national security question is the single most significant domestic legal issue facing America today, bar none."[3] Assessing the material witness warrant and other post-9/11 expansions of government authority, he offered a defense of the expanded national security powers exercised by the Justice Department. Critics, he asserted, confused the potential for abuse with actual abuse.[4] This chapter will evaluate that claim to determine what adverse impact, if any, the actions of the Ashcroft Justice Department had on criminal procedural rights.

Rights as Weapons

John Ashcroft's public remarks reveal that he believed an effective response to terrorism required new thinking, breaking with the past. In one press interview, he said, "I may be the person more responsible for trying to shape the national consciousness in saying that prosecution is not enough for the Justice Department anymore. It has to be actively involved in prevention."[5] The lesson of September 11 was that both terrorist targets and weapons were abundant in a free society; in fact, it was the very freedom of the society that provided opportunities for terrorists to instill terror. As Ashcroft famously told senators in December 2001, "We are at war with an enemy who abuses individual rights as it abuses jet airliners: as weapons with which to kill Americans."[6] Our freedoms, he said on another occasion, are turned against us, as "a means of freedom's destruction."[7] Ashcroft meant that terrorists could use the free press to rally support for their cause, hide behind privacy laws, and use their freedom of movement to melt into American society; further, terrorists held as prisoners could use their access to counsel to communicate with colleagues outside. Ashcroft's conception of the threat logically led to a new way of thinking about civil liberties in wartime. During previous national emergencies, government restrictions on liberty occurred but were considered regrettable by-products of security measures. Now, government restrictions on liberty were the security measures.

Ashcroft did not admit to this underlying logic, however. Instead, he repeatedly denied that the administration's antiterrorism response had any adverse impact on individual rights. His rhetoric, as noted previously, reiterated that the government's security measures were fully consistent with civil rights and liberties. Because of this denial, no full public debate could be held on the trade-offs citizens might be willing to make between liberty and security. Over time, he began to conflate liberty with security. He told the American Enterprise Institute in August 2003, "For two years, Americans have been safe. Because we are safer, our liberties are more secure."[8] In other words, efforts to secure the nation from terrorism served civil liberties by providing a safer environment for the citizenry. Security ensures liberty, he said at other times.[9] The equation of freedom and security is evident as well in the name of the Web site he instituted to promote the USA Patriot Act—"Preserving Life and Liberty."[10] "The law," Ashcroft said, "is what enshrines freedom. It doesn't undercut freedom when it is properly done."[11] In a speech before the Heritage Foundation soon after leaving office, he made the same argument: "The debate about liberty is really a debate about the rule of law and the role of law. The notion that the law can enhance, not diminish, freedom is an old one. John Locke said the end of law is "not to abolish or restrain but to preserve and enlarge freedom." George Washington called this "ordered liberty." Ordered liberty is the reason we are the most open and the most secure society in the world. Ordered liberty is a guiding principle, not a stumbling block to our security."[12]

Many times as attorney general, he defined the Justice Department's efforts to counter hate crimes and religious intolerance against Muslims as protecting freedom. For example, he cited the department's success in winning a consent degree to protect the right of a twelve-year-old Muslim girl to wear her hijab to school as evidence that the war against terrorism was fought for the girl and "for freedom-loving people everywhere."[13] He also pointed to Justice prosecutions of hate crime as an effort to deflect negative fallout from an internal Justice report documenting dozens of credible complaints of civil rights violations by department employees.[14]

Others in government shared Ashcroft's sense that civil liberties could be exploited to make the nation vulnerable to attack. Approving of the attorney general's actions, Senator Orrin Hatch (R-Utah) remarked that "these new terrorists, who do not wear conventional, military uniforms and are unaffiliated with specific nation states and whose ultimate goal is nothing less than to destroy our way of life, would like nothing more than the opportunity to use all of our traditional due process protections to drag out the proceedings, tie the government for prosecutors in knots, and make publicized political speeches."[15] Secretary of State Colin Powell also argued that 9/11 was not an average or routine crime, and it required exceptional measures. In response to a question about the detentions of foreign nationals following the attacks, Powell said: "What Attorney General Ashcroft is trying to do is go against these immediate vulnerabilities we have and do it as quickly as possible." He added, "As we find ourselves more secure again, . . . some of the things that are inconveniences now will go away and go back to our normal way of doing business."[16]

Yet there were critics inside and outside of government. In the Senate, Jeff Bingaman (D-N.M.) argued, "The Attorney General would have us accept with no dissent that extraordinary times require extraordinary measures, even if it is at the expense of individual civil liberties."[17] Fellow senator Arlen Specter (R-Pa.) admonished the attorney general, "There has to be some concern about how [the Justice Department] addresses civil rights."[18] House Republicans also expressed concern. It was majority leader Dick Armey of Texas who killed the Operation TIPS program, which would have established a nationwide network of postal workers, utility repairmen, and others in the community to report suspicious activity to the government.[19] Armey reportedly insisted on it as a condition for supporting the president's bill to create the Department of Homeland Security.[20] One of Armey's colleague in the House, Butch Otter, successfully attached an amendment barring the expenditure of federal funds on so-called sneak and peek or delayed notification searches that had been authorized in the Patriot Act.[21]

While criticism was aimed at particular policies and proposals, however, few in government objected to the overarching war framework adopted to fight terrorism at home. Fighting a war meant preventing attacks, and this was captured in the Justice Department's new proactive mission. Aggressive, preemptive law enforcement measures would be necessary. "Your agenda can be reshaped very quickly by events, most dramatically something like 9/11," explained former attorney general Richard Thornburgh. Events like that "shift the role of the department and its components from law enforcement after the fact to prevention before the fact." That, he added, requires "enormous changes in the culture and rules of engagement and procedures that you follow."[22]

The Preventive Approach

The Justice Department's preventive approach marked an important shift from its historic priorities of investigation and prosecution. The department would not wait for a threat to emerge. Ashcroft asserted that "America is not sitting back while terrorists wage war against us. We are waging war on them."[23] The motivation for taking strong and early action was not simply to stop an attack; it was also to avoid the appearance of failing to stop an attack. No one wanted to be the person who missed a critical clue or released a covert terrorist from detention. The preventive approach in federal law enforcement drove Ashcroft's "deliberate campaign of arrest and detention" of anyone suspected of planning a future attack, even in the absence of evidence.[24] It justified relying on secret evidence and closing more than 700 "special interest" immigration hearings,[25] barring the release of names and locations of detainees, holding scores of people as material witnesses, and restricting attorney-client privilege for certain federal prisoners. Ashcroft said he would confront the threat of terrorism as aggressively as his predecessor Robert Kennedy had confronted organized crime. For anyone suspected of wrongdoing, even minor infractions of the law would be prosecuted to the fullest. In October 2001, he explained this approach:

> Attorney General Kennedy made no apology for using all the available resources in the law to disrupt and dismantle organized crime networks. Very often, prosecutors were aggressive, using obscure statutes to arrest and detain suspected mobsters. . . . Robert Kennedy's Justice Department, it is said, would arrest mobsters for spitting on the sidewalk if it would help in the battle against organized crime. . . . It will be the policy of this Department to use the same aggressive arrest and detention tactics in the war against terror. . . . We will use every available statute. We will seek every prosecutorial advantage. We will use all our weapons within the law and under the Constitution to protect life and enhance security for America.[26]

The result was a new policy, what one official called "a separate track for people we catch in the war."[27] Federal law enforcement vigorously pursued those guilty of relatively minor immigration or other offenses as if they were major terror suspects. Even those not tied to terrorism got swept up in national security investigations. Crimes for which detainees who were cleared of terrorism were later deported included lying on a loan application and marriage fraud.[28] One such case involved a naturalized U.S. citizen from Pakistan with a Ph.D. in toxicology and a job with the Environmental Protection Agency (EPA). She had misrepresented herself as a citizen to get the EPA job in 1998 because she was only a legal resident at that time, and then lied on her naturalization application in 2001 when she said she had never falsely claimed to be a U.S. citizen. She was arrested and deported in 2004. Her arrest on immigration charges and that of hundreds of others resulted from an aggressive antiterrorism strategy that relied on immigration law.[29] Immigration law was often employed to hold those suspected of ties to terrorism when there was insufficient evidence to make the terrorism charge directly. The judge at the bail hearing of Sami al-Hussayen, for example, found little to suggest that he was dangerous even though the government alleged that he had provided material support to terrorists by helping with their Web pages. When the judge agreed to release him pending trial, the government immediately switched his case to immigration court, where it could have him detained.[30] His case will be discussed in the next chapter.

A preventive approach does have repercussions for civil liberties. First, it conflicts with the presumption of innocence. People suspected of being potential terrorists are held even in the absence of evidence because a preventive approach necessarily means that a crime has not yet occurred at the time of arrest. One defense lawyer—whose client was later acquitted—called his client's prosecution a reversal of the "normal order of business. . . . The typical situation would be a crime gets committed and you go and find the people you think committed it. In this situation, [the government] instead focused on people they were suspicious of and set about trying to prove they had indeed committed a crime."[31] In many detention cases after 9/11, there was no evidence even of a conspiracy to commit a crime. This did not stop the attorney general from assigning guilt. For example, Ashcroft stated that the hundreds of foreign nationals immediately detained after September 2001 had prior knowledge of the terrorist attacks.[32] This was well before any investigation was completed, any charges brought, or any trial held. In the end, none was convicted of a terrorism offense. Yet he continued to conflate possible criminality with actual criminality. In some cases this led him to overstate the government's evidence. For example, in announcing the indictment of Zacarias Moussaoui, Ashcroft charged that he had "engaged in the same preparation for murder as the 19 co-conspirators who carried out the September 11th hijacking,"[33] when, in fact, Moussaoui had not. Unlike the nineteen hijackers, he had made no effort to blend into U.S. society.[34]

A similar pattern of pretrial prejudicial remarks emerged in other cases, making the selection of an unbiased jury more difficult. In the so-called Detroit terror-cell case, Ashcroft made prejudicial remarks on three different occasions. Just after the arrest of the three men, he announced that they had prior knowledge of the 9/11 attacks, a claim that federal prosecutors had not made and that never was raised in their subsequent trial.[35] Later, violating a gag order, Ashcroft told reporters that the testimony of the prosecution's chief witness was of "substantial value" in the fight against terrorism. The district judge, Gerald E. Rosen, criticized him for the remark: "I was distressed to see the attorney general commenting in the middle of a trial about the credibility of a witness who had just gotten off the stand." The judge added later, "The attorney general is subject to the orders of this court. . . . The attorney general has specifically been put on notice about the scope of its gag order."[36] Eight months later, Judge Rosen rebuked the attorney general again for making statements that "could have compromised the defendants' rights to a fair trial." He reportedly considered charging Ashcroft with contempt of court.[37] Ashcroft issued a written apology.[38]

The conflation of possible and actual wrongdoing is particularly apparent in the operation of the material witness law, despite the fact that those persons were not arrested for any crime. For example, when a U.S. citizen named Abdullah al Kidd was arrested in order to ensure his testimony in the terrorism trial of another man, FBI director Robert Mueller III told Congress his arrest was a success in counterterrorism efforts, never mentioning that al Kidd was not charged with a crime. Al Kidd's name was further tainted because his arrest was mentioned along with the capture of the man wanted as "the mastermind of the September 11th attack." Al Kidd was never called to testify and eventually was released, but his reputation, he said, was ruined.[39] One senior Justice Department official explained the government's attitude about those detained on material witness warrants: "If someone has material information who will not come testify, it tends not to be a nun who walks out of a monastery who happens to see a crime from afar."[40] A number of these cases, however, involved people who were willing to testify, including some who already were cooperating with the FBI at the time of their arrests.

A policy of prevention also led the Justice Department to modify and adopt an approach used in foreign intelligence, called the mosaic theory, to the disadvantage of many of those detained after 9/11. Historically, the analogy of a mosaic was employed by the CIA to justify keeping secret seemingly innocuous information because enemy states might fit the pieces together to reveal U.S. government secrets. After the terrorist strikes, however, federal law enforcement increasingly used the mosaic analogy to support detentions without arrest or charges. Detainees might know bits of information, perhaps without realizing it, and they had to be held until they shared that information with authorities. The FBI explained the approach in a seven-page affidavit used by federal prosecutors: "Thousands of bits and pieces of information that may seem innocuous at first glance" need to be collected in order to "reveal how the unseen whole operates." The affidavit added, "What may seem trivial to some may appear of great moment to those within the FBI or the intelligence community who have a broader context."[41] As some critics pointed out, the mosaic analogy justified holding even an innocent person on the grounds that he—or something he knows—might fit into the larger security picture. Two critics wrote to the attorney general, "That legal argument makes it nearly impossible for a defense attorney to prevent her client from being detained."[42] The mosaic theory also served as a key justification for the blanket closures of immigration hearings. This time, the government argued that terrorists could construct a mosaic out of details disclosed in the hearings. In one case to be covered in chapter 8, *North Jersey Media Group v. Ashcroft,* the appeals court accepted the mosaic metaphor that appeared in an affidavit filed by the FBI's counterterrorism chief. The judges agreed that "even details that seem innocuous in isolation, such as the names of those detained, might be pieced together by knowledgeable persons within the terrorist network, who could in turn shift activities to a yet-undiscovered terrorist cell."[43] A slightly different version of the mosaic theory was advanced in two government affidavits filed to defend the closures in *Center for National Security Studies v. Department of Justice.* In rejecting a request for information filed under the Freedom of Information Act, the circuit judge relied on the government's position that "the aggregate release of the names . . . rather than the release of each in isolation . . . could assist terrorists in piecing together the course, direction and focus of the investigation."[44]

The preventive law enforcement approach did have critics within law enforcement, who believed it hampered the counterterrorism effort. Many were particularly concerned with the aggressive application of minor criminal and immigration violations as justification for detention, especially because it alienated the very community—Muslims—from whom investigators were trying to solicit information. Some immigration officials also objected to the FBI's "hold until cleared" policy applying to every immigrant detained as a result of the terrorist investigation, without any particularized suspicion of a link to terrorism. Initially, the Immigration and Naturalization Service (INS) had deferred to the FBI, believing that the clearance process would take only days or weeks. But when detentions continued for months, immigration officials decided to move ahead with deportations unless the FBI could make a case for holding the immigrant further. One immigration official said that those detained "will no longer automatically be considered a special interest case just because they happen to go to the same flight school or register at the same Department of Motor Vehicles office as one of the hijackers."[45] Frustration with the preventive approach also appeared among some in the FBI. Former director William Webster, for example, argued that the policy of preemptive arrest—while possibly disrupting a terrorist plan—did not eradicate the threat. More effective, he argued, would be long-term criminal investigations in tandem with intelligence gathering. He said that, using this approach, the FBI prevented 131 terrorist attacks from 1981 to 2000. The added benefit, Webster said, was that the approach did not "jump all over people's private lives."[46]

The preventive approach adopted by the Ashcroft Justice Department drove the policies and practices that most affected criminal procedural rights. The remainder of this chapter will focus on detentions, material witness arrests, material support and other prosecutions, and the enemy combatant detentions undertaken in the war against terrorism.

The Detentions

Responding to a threat of unknown dimensions, Attorney General Ashcroft initiated a broad sweep of terrorist suspects in the days following 9/11. He called it a "preventative campaign of arrest and detention" of people who might pose a threat.[47] The department's goal was to remove them from the streets until their innocence could be ascertained. As noted earlier, there was no presumption of innocence. Some of those swept up in the initial September 11 investigation were U.S. citizens, but most were foreign nationals. A few were released after a couple of weeks; hundreds were held for months for immigration violations and then deported. Some were charged with federal crimes, particularly perjury for lying to FBI interrogators or grand juries. A handful were prosecuted for more serious offenses related to terrorism. A few convictions were won; many more defendants took plea bargains; some were acquitted or had the charges dismissed. In one case, the Justice Department itself asked for the convictions to be dismissed.

At the time Ashcroft stopped publicly releasing the head count, 1,087 people were being held in the terrorism investigation. At the Senate Judiciary Committee hearings a month later, an estimated 1,182 individuals were reported as detained.[48] The tally included those held on criminal charges, as material witnesses, and for immigration violations. Additional foreign nationals were picked up as a result of other Justice Department initiatives; more than 1,100 were apprehended by early 2003 under a program to locate and expel 5,000 immigrants from certain countries who had fled previous deportation orders.[49] More than 2,700 were arrested after they came to register with the National Security Entry-Exit Registration System established under the Patriot Act.[50] One estimate is that "somewhere between 4,000 and 5,000" people were detained as part of the preventive campaign.[51] Because so many were foreign nationals, one critic called Ashcroft "the unaccountable czar of immigrants."[52]

The perpetrators of the 9/11 attacks had entered the country legally. Even so, the Justice Department focused its antiterrorism efforts on foreign nationals who had overstayed their visas, lied on their applications, or otherwise violated immigration law. These minor crimes ordinarily do not merit detention, but according to Ashcroft's chief policy adviser, Viet Dinh, such detentions are "within our prosecutorial discretion. If we suspect you of terrorist activity, we will use our prosecutorial discretion to keep you off the streets."[53] Using minor violations of immigration law to hold foreign nationals of certain nationalities marked a change in policy.

Through the Patriot Act and administrative rule changes, the government undertook numerous programs to monitor foreign nationals, particularly those from selected countries in the Middle East and South Asia.[54] The most controversial policy changes affecting immigrants, however, were those pertaining to the length of detentions permissible under immigration law. One week after the 9/11 attacks, the INS promulgated a rule that permitted the agency to hold detainees suspected of immigration violations for "an unspecified 'reasonable time' in a national emergency."[55] Then the Patriot Act passed with the following provision: "The Attorney General shall place an alien detained [on the grounds of endangering national security] in removal proceedings, or shall charge the alien with a criminal offense, not later than 7 days after the commencement of such detention."[56] Once the removal proceedings are over and a final removal order issued, the government has ninety days to make arrangements with another country to deport the alien, according to the Immigration and Nationality Act of 2000[57] and the Supreme Court ruling in *Zadvydas v. Davis*.[58]

The Justice Department, however, wanted greater flexibility to detain some aliens after 9/11 in order to ensure a complete investigation. One government prosecutor noted, "It would have been suicidal to release people before we could check them out."[59] In a 2002 opinion, the Office of Legal Counsel issued an interpretation of immigration law to permit detentions of up to six months. The OLC argued that the law allowed extensions beyond 90 days if they were necessary to fulfill federal immigration law or policy. An investigation related to terrorism met that standard, the OLC argued, since a hasty deportation of someone who turned out to be a terrorist would endanger U.S. national security and undermine foreign relations with countries that had accepted the deportee.[60] With this reasoning, immigrants were held for an average of 80 days and up to 244 days, according to the Office of the Inspector General (OIG). In 2003, the OIG examined the processing, bond decisions, timelines, access to attorneys, and prison conditions of 762 foreign nationals picked up as part of the FBI's initial 9/11 investigation.[61] In its 198-page report issued in June 2003, the internal Justice Department agency found that many immigrants were held for months without notice of charges, instead of the seventy-two hours established in INS policy.[62] The lengthy detentions, according to Inspector General Glenn Fine, were due to slow implementation of the FBI's hold until cleared policy; long delays were reported in clearing immigrants of any ties to terrorism so that they could be released or deported. The FBI was understaffed, but it also did not give priority to clearing people already in prison. Clearances were put on hold while the FBI focused on those not yet detained. Some immigrants were held even after they had received final orders for removal and were willing and able to leave the United States.[63] A blanket "no bond" policy also applied to all the detainees picked up during the September 11 investigation. In fact, the OIG determined, the FBI "made little attempt to distinguish between aliens who were subjects of the FBI terrorism investigation . . . and those encountered coincidentally."[64] This meant that a detainee guilty only of overstaying his visa could be wrongly classified as "high interest" and imprisoned for months.

The OIG report documented other problems related to the detentions, particularly for the eighty-four prisoners held at the Metropolitan Detention Center (MDC) in Brooklyn, run by the Bureau of Prisons and under the attorney general's authority. First, detainees experienced an ongoing difficulty in getting access to counsel. Initially it was due to a communications blackout imposed after 9/11. Even after that, attorneys, family members and even law enforcement were unable to contact those detainees who were classified as "witness security" inmates. When the MDC staff did provide lists of pro bono attorneys, the information sometimes was outdated and incorrect. Many detainees were not informed that they could make one telephone call per week to try to contact an attorney. The OIG also substantiated allegations of unduly harsh conditions and a pattern of physical and verbal abuse at the MDC. Detainees were under lockdown for twenty-three hours a day, with twenty-four-hour lighting in their cells for months on end. When outside their cells, they were restrained with handcuffs, leg irons, and a waist chain to restrain their arms. Some correctional officers slammed detainees against the wall and verbally taunted them. The report concluded with twenty-one recommendations for changes.[65]

The attorney general's reaction was intractable, reflecting a deep suspicion of any criticism. Although he refused to answer press questions about the report, he told the generally friendly House Judiciary Committee that "all of the individuals, the subject of that report, were in the United States illegally" and therefore had no right to bail or bond. He added, "We do not apologize."[66] Many top aides also were unrepentant. His spokeswoman, Barbara Comstock, issued a statement that asserted that the report "is fully consistent with what courts have ruled over and over—that our actions are fully within the law and necessary to protect the American people," even though the inspector general's report had documented the opposite. Reiterating that the department's practices were legal, despite the OIG's findings otherwise, Comstock continued, "Our policy is to use all legal tools available to protect innocent Americans from terrorist attacks. We make no apologies for finding every legal way possible to protect the American public from further terrorist attacks."[67] Others in the department also defended the practices. Michael Rolince of the FBI justified the agency's slow pace in investigating and clearing detainees of terrorism links. "Given the choice between finishing checks on those already in custody or locating and neutralizing the seemingly endless threats that were still being reported and investigated, we made a conscious decision to prioritize the 'neutralize potential threats' first."[68] The innocence of an individual detainee of any terrorism link was subsumed in the larger investigative effort. Furthermore, Justice officials repeatedly noted, these detainees had violated immigration law; they were not innocent. As he was leaving office, Ashcroft reiterated that point, "No one was arrested without being in violation of the law. The law regarding immigration is the law."[69] A driving motivation to hold on to detainees was the possibility of another terrorist strike. An attorney in the criminal division argued, "If we had released or granted bond to an illegal alien who went on to commit another terrorist attack, we would have failed in our responsibilities to keep America safe."[70] Even the harsh conditions at MDC were justified as necessary by the director of the Federal Bureau of Prisons because the detainees were suspected of terrorist ties and therefore capable of violence.[71]

Neither Ashcroft nor his top aides conceded that the OIG report directly contradicted the attorney general's assertion that his department respected the law and civil rights. However, unlike Ashcroft, most of the Justice officials immediately noted the need for some reform. The department quickly announced that it would institute at least twelve structural changes and consider another nine of the OIG's recommendations. One key change, according to officials, would be clearer guidelines for the FBI to use in separating terrorist suspects from ordinary illegal immigrants. Deadlines would be established for releasing those cleared. In addition, the department would create a crisis management plan for handling a similar emergency in the future. While not admitting that civil liberties had been violated, Assistant Attorney General Michael Chertoff did note, "These enhancements would further reduce the potential for impinging on civil liberties."[72]

The OIG conducted follow-up reviews of the status of detainees. In July 2003, it reported on thirty-four credible complaints of civil liberty violations by Justice Department employees, many of them in the Bureau of Prisons. One substantiated complaint involved verbal threats by a prison doctor; another alleged that an immigration officer held a loaded gun to a detainee's head.[73] In December 2003, the OIG announced that MDC videotapes finally had been located that documented the abuse reported earlier. The tapes provided additional evidence that detainees were subjected to unnecessary strip searches and had their arms twisted. Many had their attorney-client privilege violated; more than forty conversations between detainees and their attorneys had been taped, in violation of prison rules.[74]

More rules and training were instituted. The Bureau of Prisons notified all prison personnel that they could not monitor or record attorney-client conversations. Staff at the Brooklyn prison received additional training on use of force and restraint.[75] By 2004, the responsibilities of the INS had been divided, with Immigration and Customs Enforcement (ICE) housed in the new Homeland Security Department. Homeland Security established new rules to ensure that each request for a detention was authorized by a high-level FBI official and then reviewed by the ICE.[76]

While the OIG in 2004 continued to substantiate incidents of verbal and physical abuse of Muslim inmates by prison personnel, these incidents were less common and did not establish the pattern of abuse ascertained two years earlier. Only one new incident in the latter half of 2004 was under investigation in the March 2005 report to Congress, involving a Muslim detainee who alleged that federal prison officials had "humiliated and abused Muslim inmates." A few ongoing investigations of similar allegations continued. The OIG also continued its investigation into how the FBI and federal prosecutors had handled the case of Brandon Mayfield, the Portland, Oregon, attorney falsely linked to the Madrid train bombing.[77]

In addition to the inspector general's reports, the abuse of detainees has been alleged in a number of lawsuits brought against Ashcroft, Mueller, and officials at the Metropolitan Detention Center. The plaintiffs charge that the conditions under which they were held were so abusive that their constitutional rights were violated. One class action lawsuit was brought by men from Pakistan and Turkey, who asserted that they had been classified as persons of "special interest" and targeted for abuse solely on the basis of their nationality and religion; the government had never criminally charged them or established any evidence of a terrorist connection. The district court permitted discovery to continue over the government's objections.[78] Ashcroft sought to have another lawsuit dismissed on the grounds that "regulations written in peacetime cannot circumscribe the government's discretion at a time of national emergency from foreign threats." Rejecting that argument, the district judge responded, "This proposition, which suggests that, as a matter of law, constitutional and statutory rights must be suspended during times of crisis, is supported neither by statute nor the Constitution."[79] At the time of this writing, neither lawsuit had been resolved.

The experience of Nabil al-Marabh, chronicled by the Office of Inspector General, is worth recounting here, because it illustrates how immigration law was aggressively used to hold people even after they had been cleared of suspicion. Al-Marabh, one of the inmates at the MDC, was tangentially associated with the Detroit terror cell case to be discussed later; FBI agents had been looking for him when they searched his former Detroit apartment and then arrested the new tenants. Initially, al-Marabh was on the FBI's terrorist watch list after being erroneously identified as an associate of Osama bin Laden's.[80] In addition, as he later admitted, he had taken advanced weapons training in Afghanistan in the early 1990s.[81] He was apprehended at work on September 18, 2001. Authorities soon determined that he was simply an undocumented immigrant from Syria without ties to terrorism. Even so, he was detained for more than eight months in solitary confinement, without seeing an attorney or a judge in that time. Following his interview with the OIG, he finally was given a list of lawyers, officially placed under arrest for violating immigration law, and brought before a federal judge. By then it was late May 2002.[82] From Ashcroft's point of view, al-Marabh had no legal right to see a judge, since he had already been deported once and had illegally returned to the country. Under immigration law, the attorney general could reinstate the earlier deportation order without the review of an immigration judge.[83] Under those circumstances, however, the detainee ordinarily would be removed from the country within ninety days. Al-Marabh's case was complicated by his tenuous link to the government's prosecution of the so-called Detroit terror cell. In that trial, the prosecutors even referred to him as an unindicted co-conspirator, but the district judge intervened, pointing out that the government had had eighteen months to charge al-Marabh and had not done so; the government now could not try him without charges.[84] Civil rights groups have called his experience "one of the more extreme cases of how the government has violated the due process rights of hundreds of people swept up in the nation-wide terrorism investigation."[85]

Overall, the effectiveness of using immigration law in the fight against terrorism is difficult to ascertain because the Justice Department continues to count many of those cleared of terrorism links and charged with minor offenses as part of its antiterrorism tally. Prosecutors liked using immigration law because of its value as an intelligence tool; attorneys did not need to be present, hearings could be closed, and detainees could be pressured into becoming informants.[86] A counsel to Ashcroft during this time, Kris Kobach, explained that immigration charges did not negate the possibility that those detained were terrorists. "Just because the FBI hasn't gotten to the point of applying the terrorism label, it doesn't mean the individual is not a terrorist," he said.[87] Spokeswoman Comstock echoed his view: "[If] an alien was deported rather than prosecuted does not mean that the alien had no knowledge of or connection to terrorism. . . . An individual may have been deported on grounds seemingly unrelated to terrorism, if the assertion of specific terrorism cases could have compromised ongoing investigations or sensitive intelligence matters."[88] Unsaid is the converse, that their detentions, interrogations, and deportations were also not evidence that they were terrorists. A preliminary report issued by the 9/11 commission concluded that the department's policy of detaining immigrants had been largely ineffective in terms of identifying potential terrorist threats.[89]

Material Witness Arrests

Though less widely employed than immigration charges, another statutory tool for federal law enforcement was the Material Witness Statute of 1984. In the wake of the attacks, it was used to hold people for questioning and testifying before a grand jury.[90] A number of material witness arrests later led to criminal charges, particularly related to lying to investigators or a grand jury. When criticized for using the law so aggressively, the Justice Department denied that it was widely applied, telling Congress that fewer than fifty people had been detained as material witnesses as of January 2003 in connection with the 9/11 investigation. In August 2004, Human Rights Watch and the American Civil Liberties Union (ACLU) said the number was closer to sixty when terrorism investigations in general were included.[91] Almost a year later, the two organizations reported that they had identified seventy men who had been arrested as material witnesses, seventeen of them U.S. citizens. Because the Justice Department has kept material witness cases secret, the actual number of material witness arrests is unknown.[92]

The relevant section of the statute reads as follows:

> If it appears from an affidavit filed by a party that the testimony of a person is material in a criminal proceeding, and if it is shown that it may become impracticable to secure the presence of the person by subpoena, a judicial officer may order the arrest of the person and treat the person in accordance with the provisions of Section 3142 of this title. No material witness may be detained because of inability to comply with any condition of release if the testimony of such witness can adequately be secured by deposition, and if further detention is not necessary to prevent a failure of justice. Release of a material witness may be delayed for a reasonable period of time until the deposition of the witness can be taken pursuant to the Federal Rules of Criminal Procedure.[93]

Since the eighteenth century, federal law has authorized the brief detention of people who have relevant knowledge of a criminal act yet are reluctant to testify. Other, less onerous mechanisms to secure a person's testimony are more common: a subpoena, a contempt of court citation (fines or jail), or the threat of jail for failure to appear in court.[94] In the exceptional case when those less drastic measures would not "deter the witness from absenting himself," the Supreme Court ruled in 1927 that the witness could be arrested.[95] The vast majority who are detained today are people who have sought illegal entry to the country and are held in order to testify against their smugglers. The Justice Department reported that 90 percent of the 3,679 people arrested as material witnesses in 2001 met this description. The law's application to terrorism investigations is a new legal development, according to Mary Jo White, former U.S. attorney in Manhattan. Noting that its use in investigating the 9/11 attacks was her idea, White and others at the Justice Department defended the measure as an important tool. Among the safeguards provided material witness detainees, she noted, was access to counsel. Further, every detention was supported by a judicial finding that the person had information material to a grand jury investigation. However, White did concede that "some of the criticism that has been leveled at it is not wholly unjustified."[96]

Allegations of civil liberty violations plagued many of the material witness arrests associated with the terrorism investigation. The subjective nature of the material witness process resulted in religious profiling, according to Anjana Malhotra, a fellow with Human Rights Watch/ACLU.[97] His 2005 report for Human Rights Watch found that all but one of the seventy men it identified were Muslim, and all but two were Middle Eastern, South Asian, African, or African American. They had come to the FBI's attention either because they lived in communities where the nineteen hijackers had lived or visited, or because of some other suspicious connection: flying lessons, a tip from a neighbor, a name similar to that of a terrorist suspect. Seven were eventually charged with providing material support to a terrorist organization. Most were found to have no knowledge of terrorism; forty-two were released without any charges. In thirteen cases, the government issued apologies for wrongful detentions.[98]

Material witness detainees were not always read their Miranda rights at the time of their arrests, or permitted to consult immediately with their lawyers.[99] Some were arrested at gunpoint, even when they had been voluntarily cooperating with the FBI.[100] Most of them were classified as high-security inmates and subjected to more severe treatment than convicted inmates. The district judge in the case of Osama Awadallah, for example, chronicled his treatment by authorities: solitary confinement; no contact with his family; no phone calls; repeated strip searches; leg shackles and a waist shackle on his arms when taken from his cell; food that did not comport with his religious diet; and restricted showers. When he testified before the grand jury, he was hand-cuffed to a chair. He also alleged that guards had physically abused him.[101] Another material witness, Abdullah al Kidd, reported a "terrifying and humil-iating ordeal," which included being "made to sit in a small cell for hours and hours and hours buck naked. I was treated worse than murderers." Kidd, an American citizen who had converted to Islam as a college student and changed his name, charged that the experience had cost him his marriage, good job prospects, and a scholarship for graduate studies in Saudi Arabia.[102]

While most detentions were relatively brief—the Justice Department re-ported that half of detainees were held 30 days or less, and 90 percent were detained less than three months[103]—there were instances of much longer de-tentions. One man was in custody at least 432 days.[104] Under stressful prison conditions and prolonged interrogations, people held as material witnesses were sometimes liable to make verbal misstatements, which exposed them to prosecution on perjury charges. Human Rights Watch called such interroga-tions "perjury traps."[105] A material witness might even make a false confes-sion, as happened to an Egyptian national named Abdallah Higazy.

When Higazy arrived in the United States to attend graduate school under a grant from the U.S. Agency for International Development, he checked into a hotel across the street from the World Trade Center. That was his location at the time the airplanes struck on September 11.[106] For reasons of safety, he and the other guests were evacuated and barred from returning until mid-December 2001, when he was permitted to retrieve his belongings. At that time, FBI agents confronted him, accusing him of owning a ground-to-air radio transceiver, which the hotel security guard said he had found in the safe in Higazy's hotel room, along with his passport and the Koran. The govern-ment believed that he might have used the transceiver to communicate with the hijackers. Higazy repeatedly denied owning the radio. Instead of a crimi-nal charge, however, he was arrested on a material witness warrant. While held in solitary confinement for three weeks, he underwent several FBI interroga-tions. Although ostensibly a material witness, he was never brought to testify before a grand jury. Anxious to prove his innocence, Higazy asked for and was granted a polygraph test. He accepted the FBI stipulation that his attorney could not be present at the polygraph exam. He said later that during the ques-tioning he had felt faint and anxious, convinced that he would be found guilty despite his protestations. In a break between questions, an FBI agent began a conversation with him without the presence of his attorney, and Higazy con-fessed. The government charged him with lying about the radio and interfer-ing with its investigation. Four days later, however, an American pilot arrived at the hotel to claim his belongings, which included the transceiver. The charges against Higazy were dropped, and he was released. He had been held 34 days.[107] Higazy sought redress. He brought a lawsuit against the hotel for his unlawful arrest and imprisonment due to the actions of their security guard. The lawsuit was dismissed.[108] Another judge determined that the government agents could not be sanctioned by the court because they had relied on the security guard, who was then being prosecuted for making false statements. Regarding Higazy's confession without counsel, Justice attorneys asserted that the issue was irrelevant, since the only remedy—excluding the confession from trial—was not available. However, the government did assure the court that it was conducting an internal investigation.[109]

Despite the potential for abuse, the judicial branch largely deferred to extensive use of the material witness statute. In only one case did a court find that the FBI had inappropriately applied the law. That decision, involving a Jordanian student named Osama Awadallah, was later overturned by a federal appellate court. The facts of that case illustrate how the FBI utilized material witness warrants in the months following September 11 and how the courts responded.

Awadallah's first name and an old phone number had been found in the car of one of the hijackers, Nawaf Al-Hazmi. Living in San Diego at the time, Awadallah was approached by FBI agents ten days after the strikes. The agents were suspicious because he had not come forward with information immediately after the attacks. In questioning the first day, he admitted to knowing Al-Hazmi the year before. Meanwhile, an FBI search of his apartment and two cars produced two videotapes of Bosnia, a computer print of Osama bin Laden's photograph, and a pair of box cutters. The latter, found in his second unused car, evidently had been used by Awadallah to install a carpet. The search was conducted after he was in detention and without a warrant based on probable cause that he was involved in a crime. After Awadallah was arrested as a material witness, he was subsequently moved to four different prisons, finally arriving in New York to testify before the grand jury investigating the terrorist attacks.[110] In his initial grand jury testimony, he admitted an acquaintance with Al-Hazmi and described another man with him, but denied knowing a man named Khalid. The prosecutors produced an exam booklet in which he had written the name Khalid, but he denied writing it. Five days later, however, he amended his testimony, saying that his memory had been refreshed, and he did know Khalid. Then he was charged with the crime of making misleading statements. Awadallah's counsel challenged the admissibility of his grand jury testimony, as well as the physical evidence from the search, because the basis for both was his arrest as a material witness, and that arrest was illegal. The attorney argued—and District Court Judge Shira Scheindlin agreed—that the material witness statute did not apply at the grand jury stage but only in a criminal proceeding, after an indictment has been issued. The judge characterized the application of the law to grand juries as "an attempt to fit a square peg into a round hole."[111] Because Awadallah's arrest was unlawful, his grand jury testimony had to be suppressed, and the judge dismissed the indictment.[112] On appeal, however, a three-judge panel of the Second Circuit Court of Appeals disagreed and reinstated the indictment.[113] In no other instance did the judiciary question this use of the material witness statute in the months following September 11.

The application of the material witness law to terrorism investigations constitutes an important change, according to Ronald Carlson, an expert on that law. As he explained, "The law was designed to hold Mr. A, the material witness, to testify about a crime committed by Mr. B, the suspect. Now they are locking up Mr. A as a material witness to the crime of Mr. A. The notion is, 'We'll hold him until we develop probable cause to arrest him for a crime.'"[114] A senior Justice Department official rejected that characterization,[115] but the records of a number of material witness cases suggest that law enforcement did see these individuals as terrorism suspects and not witnesses. As already mentioned, law enforcement agents had found Awadallah's first name and old phone number in a car of one of the 9/11 hijackers, and Higazy was thought to have owned a suspicious ground-to-air transceiver in close proximity to the World Trade Center towers. Authorities in al Kidd's case were interested in "three red flags": he "sold tapes and books containing the teachings of radical sheiks," he owned a video on the September 11 attacks, and he had listed on a Web site his interest in "jihad."[116] Al-Marabh also was initially picked up on a material witness warrant; when no criminal charges were possible, he eventually was charged with immigration violations.[117] In addition, Brandon Mayfield was held on a material witness warrant while the government was building its case against him. Some of the material witness cases did develop into terrorism charges. Among the high-profile defendants who started as material witnesses were Zacarias Moussaoui, charged with conspiracy in connection with 9/11, and James Ujaama, indicted for providing material support to al Qaeda.[118] Maher "Mike" Hawash, a naturalized U.S. citizen and software engineer, was seized on a material witness warrant as well and held for five weeks before being charged with providing material support for terrorism. Hawash had been part of a Portland group that had tried to enter Afghanistan through China in late 2001.[119] Two of the men later classified by the president as unlawful enemy combatants, José Padilla and Ali Saleh al-Marri, also initially were held as material witnesses.

An additional indication that the government used the material witness statute to hold actual suspects is the fact that many were never called to testify before a grand jury or court. The *Washington Post* reported in December 2002 that in twenty of the forty-four cases it had reviewed, witnesses had never been called to testify before a court or grand jury.[120] Human Rights Watch said in June 2005 that at least thirty of the seventy witnesses it identified had never testified.[121] Michael Chertoff, Ashcroft's assistant attorney general for the criminal division, defended this use of the law: "It's an important investigative tool in the war on terrorism. Bear in mind that you get not only testimony—you get fingerprints, you get hair samples—so there's all kinds of evidence you can get from a witness."[122] That evidence, of course, would tend to implicate the witness more than anyone else. In fact, federal agents regularly relied on interviews with the witnesses and searches conducted after their arrests to gather the evidence to bring criminal and immigration charges against them, even though the arrests and searches were not based on probable cause. In the end, according to the Human Rights Watch report, nonterrorism criminal charges—involving either making false statements to the FBI or bank and credit card fraud—were brought against twenty material witnesses. The report explained the constitutional problem: "In evading the requirement of probable cause of criminal conduct, the government bypassed checks on the reasonableness of its suspicion. . . . The rule of law itself suffers when a law is used as a pretext to sidestep longstanding checks on the arbitrary exercise of executive power."[123]

Those who accused the government of using the material witness statute as a device for rounding up and holding people—part of the attorney general's policy of preventive detention—might not have been far wrong. As one defense attorney and former federal prosecutor said, the government's actions "would tend to indicate that the use of the material witness statute was more of a ruse than an honest desire to record the testimony of that person."[124] If federal law enforcement needs the tools of preventive detention, law professor Carlson argued, then it should seek that authority from Congress. "The Justice Department should ask Congress to confront whether it wants to enact some sort of terrorism detention statute. They should not be using this law for a purpose it was never intended."[125]

Terror Prosecutions

The terrorism investigations that followed 9/11 resulted in several high-profile prosecutions: Zacarias Moussaoui, John Walker Lindh, Richard Reid, Iyman Faris, and suspected terror cells in Oregon, Michigan, and New York. They constituted a small percentage of the thousands of cases pursued by the Justice Department as part of its proactive terrorism investigation.

The preemptive approach, however, did not necessarily result in solid successes in the campaign against terrorism. The *New York Times* reported in 2003 that "75 percent of the convictions that the [Justice] department classified as 'international terrorism' were wrongly labeled. Many dealt with ordinary crimes like document forgery."[126] In addition, the General Accounting Office found that about 46 percent of the convictions identified as terrorism-related were misidentified by the Justice Department.[127] It is important to note that document forgery and fraud could be related to the support of terrorism; in the words of the GAO report, such cases could be "acts in preparation of terrorist activities."[128] Conversely, the crimes might have been motivated by simple greed but unintentionally benefited terrorists, as in the case of the men who provided two of the hijackers with false Virginia identification papers, or may have had no link to terrorism. An exhaustive study at Syracuse University suggests that the vast majority of cases did not involve serious terrorism-related charges. In the first two years after the attacks, approximately 6,400 people were referred for charges, but only about one-third of them—or 2,000—eventually faced criminal charges. Of those who did, 879 people were convicted, and 373 went to prison. The sentences in most cases were light, suggesting that serious crimes were not involved. In fact, the median sentence was fourteen days, and some of those convicted received no jail time. Almost 70 percent of those convicted and imprisoned—or 250—resulted in sentences of less than one year, and another 100 received sentences of less than five years. In the two years after 9/11, just 23 men were sentenced to five years or more; those numbers are comparable to the two years prior to 9/11, when 24 people were.[129]

Justice officials disputed the view that the figures showed a low success rate in the fight against terrorism. The figures do not capture other legal channels pursued by the government against suspects, including immigration violations, document and credit card fraud, and perjury charges. According to a listing of cases identified with the war on terrorism compiled by the Web site Findlaw.com, ten cases involved charges of providing material support to terrorists or designated foreign terrorist organizations, but the most common charge was not terrorism-related per se—twenty-seven cases were brought alleging identification document fraud. Charges related to false statements or false declarations before a court or grand jury accounted for at least nine. Other criminal charges against those arrested during the terrorism investigation included immigration fraud, mail fraud, bank fraud, credit card fraud, racketeering, possession of firearms, forgery, embezzlement, money laundering, and graft.[130] Although the Findlaw.com list is not exhaustive, it is suggestive of the forceful strategy employed by the Ashcroft Justice Department as part of its preventive campaign, fully exploiting whatever laws were available. It also illustrates how minor violations could be summarily classified as terrorism cases. Due to the secrecy surrounding the government's evidence in these cases, the actual level of terrorist activity found and prosecuted is unknown.

A tougher law enforcement approach also was apparent in the expanded use of special administrative measures (SAMs) that apply to certain federal prisoners suspected of seeking to disclose classified information that could pose a threat to national security and endanger lives. First instituted in 1997, the SAMs authorize prison oversight of an inmate's communication with the outside world; however, conversations with counsel had been exempt. That changed with 9/11; in October 2001, the Bureau of Prisons issued new rules that expanded its authority. SAMs now could be imposed on an inmate for a year, up from 120 days. In addition, the standard for triggering SAMs dropped from "threat to the national security" to "reasonable suspicion,"[131] a standard more easily met by the government. Finally, the new rules permit the bureau "to monitor mail or communications with attorneys" in cases "where the Attorney General has certified that reasonable suspicion exists to believe that an inmate may use communications with attorneys or their agents to further or facilitate acts of violence or terrorism."[132] The infringement on attorney-client privilege is new. According to the Justice Department, the infringement is limited because procedural safeguards are in place, including the fact that prisoners receive prior notice of any monitoring.[133] Ashcroft considered this advance notification to be an important distinction between Bureau of Prisons monitoring and unlawful eavesdropping.[134] Other safeguards, according to Ashcroft, included the requirement for a court order before any information gathered from the monitoring could be used at trial, and the fact that the federal agents who monitored conversations would differ from those involved in building criminal cases.[135] Other rule changes were made, and stringent SAMs were applied to some suspects in custody, including Richard Reid, whose case was discussed in the previous chapter. Answering the concern of senators that SAMs violated important principles, Ashcroft testified in late 2001 that only 16 prisoners and their attorneys were affected by them, out of 158,000 federal inmates.[136]

The Justice Department's aggressive prosecutorial approach against any suspect, coupled with the application of special administrative measures, deeply affected the prosecution and confinement of those arrested in connection with terrorism. This section will review four terrorism cases to examine the civil liberty effects, as well as explore the complexity of fitting law enforcement into the framework of a war against terrorism.

The 9/11 Prosecution: Zacarias Moussaoui

Zacarias Moussaoui, an admitted member of al Qaeda, was picked up in Minnesota for immigration violations a month before the attacks on the World Trade Center and the Pentagon. A French citizen of Moroccan origin, he was arrested after arousing suspicion at a flight school. Despite the fact that he was in federal custody on September 11, Moussaoui was indicted in December on six counts of conspiracy related to 9/11, four of them capital offenses.[137] He was the only person charged in the United States in connection with the terrorist strikes. Unindicted coconspirators in his case included Osama bin Laden and Ayman al-Zawahiri.[138] Ashcroft's announcement of the indictment was made on the three-month anniversary of the attacks, and he promised the families of the victims an opportunity to follow the case through a soon-to-be established Web site and toll-free telephone number.[139] In time, Moussaoui became known as the twentieth hijacker, who would have been the fifth terrorist on the airplane that crashed in a Pennsylvania field had he not already been in custody.[140] He was never charged with that crime, however.

Moussaoui's self-incriminating rants made during his first months in custody contributed to the government's portrayal of him in the news media as a serious terrorist threat associated with the September 11 attacks.[141] However, he repeatedly denied that he was part of the 9/11 conspiracy, asserting that his brothers in al Qaeda would confirm his innocence of that charge.[142] When he demanded the right to represent himself in April 2002, district judge Leonie Brinkema was concerned enough about his mental state to order a psychiatric evaluation first; she also assigned his defense attorneys as standby counsel. His request was granted, which pleased prosecutors and disadvantaged the defense. As the U.S. attorney noted, "The standard for competency to stand trial is the same as the standard for competency to waive counsel."[143] Therefore, if Moussaoui was found competent by the court-appointed psychiatrist to represent himself, he was competent enough to stand trial, and competent enough to plead guilty, as he did three years later.[144] Moussaoui, as an indicted terrorist, was at a particular disadvantage representing himself because he was barred access to the classified information used as evidence against him. He could not attend certain closed hearings or read certain documents. He had to rely on his standby counsel, whom he did not trust.[145] His attorneys continued to question his competency and brought in two additional mental health experts. His confusion was particularly evident in 2003, when he announced he would plead guilty to the conspiracy charges in order to get rid of his attorneys; he recanted when he learned he could not switch his plea during the sentencing phase of the trial in order to avoid the death penalty.[146] The paranoia evident in his handwritten filings may have been exacerbated by the conditions of his imprisonment, which included solitary confinement, twenty-four-hour lighting, and sleep disruption.[147]

His unpredictable and insulting behavior continued, leading the judge to admonish him. Eventually, she removed him from the case.[148] Despite his agitated mental state, Moussaoui did make a credible claim that he had a Sixth Amendment right to compel the testimony of favorable witnesses, specifically three high-ranking al Qaeda members held as enemy combatants by the U.S. military overseas. In addition to the constitutional right of compulsory process for witnesses for the defense, federal law requires that any evidence "favorable to the accused" that is held by prosecutors, law enforcement agencies, and other agencies "actively involved" with the prosecution must be disclosed to the defense.[149] Under the Classified Information Procedures Act (CIPA) of 1980, exculpatory material that is classified must be available to defendants or the charges dropped, according to judicial precedents.[150] Moussaoui and his counsel argued that the testimony of the three men would exonerate him of the charge that he conspired in the 9/11 attacks; at minimum, their testimony would be important during the sentencing phase of the trial.

The judge took Moussaoui's claim seriously. In early 2003, she ordered the government to give the defense access to the first witness it sought,[151] a man described by prosecutors as "the central intermediary between Mr. Moussaoui and the plotters of the Sept. 11 attacks."[152] Brinkema found that "the defense has made a significant showing" that this man's testimony could rebut the most serious charge of conspiracy in the 9/11 attacks.[153] After the capture of two more al Qaeda operatives, the defense sought their testimony as well, to which the judge agreed. However, she rejected defense requests for access to other detainees because there was not "a sufficient showing that their testimony would be material or exculpatory."[154] Justice attorneys argued that Moussaoui was seeking to expand overseas the reach of Sixth Amendment compulsory process, which would interfere with military operations.[155] Federal prosecutors then refused to grant access to the three men, citing a national security exemption to the Sixth Amendment's right of compulsory process,[156] an exemption that is unprecedented, according to many legal scholars.[157] But the prosecutors may have had little choice. The men were not in civilian custody, and both the Pentagon and the CIA refused to grant any outside lawyer access to them.[158] The prosecution filed an appeal of Brinkema's order with the Fourth Circuit Court of Appeals; the appellate court instructed the parties to come to a compromise. Brinkema proposed a closed-circuit televised deposition of the witnesses, but the prosecution rejected it as setting a bad precedent for future military detainees.[159] The government countered with its own proposal to provide the court with classified summaries of certain parts of the intelligence interrogations, but both the judge and the defense rejected the summaries as "unreliable, incomplete and inaccurate,"[160] with the likely effect of misleading a jury.[161]

Prosecutors continued to defy Judge Brinkema's order. In response, she barred any evidence or argument pertaining to 9/11, since Moussaoui would be unable to produce witnesses who arguably could rebut his involvement.[162] She also struck the government's notice of intent to seek the death penalty because Moussaoui would not be permitted to present mitigating testimony as he had a right to do in a capital case. She noted that Moussaoui could still be tried on the broader conspiracy charge of participating in al Qaeda efforts to attack the United States.[163] The government again refused to produce the witnesses and appealed to the Fourth Circuit, arguing that Brinkema's actions "will deny the jury key evidence and deny the public and the victims of September 11 full justice."[164]

For many, the appeal raised a broad constitutional question about the government's power to fight terrorism versus fundamental criminal procedural rights. Law professor Stephen Saltzburg framed it this way: "If a court were to say there is a national security exemption to the right to confront witnesses, even when you are subject to the death penalty, that would be staggering. There would basically be no limits to what the government could do."[165]

A three-judge panel of the Fourth Circuit gave its ruling in April 2004. The judges reinstated the death penalty and the 9/11 evidence, but they agreed with the district judge that the testimony of the three al Qaeda witnesses would likely help the defense and that government summaries were not a sufficient substitution.[166] After additional filings by the government, the Fourth Circuit issued its final decision that September. Again, the government's proposed substitutions were rejected, but the judges also said they were cognizant of the national security needs related to the ongoing interrogations of the al Qaeda detainees, and they instructed the district judge—and not the government—to compile a written record of the al Qaeda testimony for the jury trial, based on the classified summaries of sections designated by the defendant.[167] This ruling primarily benefited the prosecution.

Moussaoui appealed to the U.S. Supreme Court, which did not grant certiorari, leaving the Fourth Circuit's opinion intact.[168] A month later, in April 2005, Moussaoui again decided to plead guilty, this time accepting the possibility of a death sentence imposed by a jury.[169] In May, he tried to fire his attorneys again, but the judge refused. Moussaoui's sentencing trial was slated to begin in February 2006 in the Eastern District of Virginia.

The case of *U.S. v. Moussaoui* was symbolically important to the Justice Department. Moussaoui's indictment, in the words of the attorney general, meant that "Al Qaeda will now meet the justice it abhors and the judgment it fears."[170] An official at Justice later explained that the government and the public "were looking for the criminal justice system to do what it was designed to do—offer some justice for a great crime."[171] In addition, the case presented an opportunity for the department to demonstrate its capacity for handling terrorist prosecutions in the regular criminal justice system, in contrast to the Pentagon's preferred reliance on military tribunals. The attorney general insisted that the regular criminal justice system could successfully prosecute suspected terrorists.[172] Ashcroft called military tribunals a good tool for the president to try war criminals, but said that the attorney general had the responsibility "to bring charges against those who commit crimes and are to be tried in the criminal justice system."[173]

These factors resulted in two critical decisions by Justice. First, Ashcroft insisted on the death penalty. The government's notice of intent to seek a death sentence said Moussaoui shared responsibility for "the largest loss of life resulting from a criminal act in the history of the United States of America."[174] But the attorney general's refusal to offer a plea bargain and take the death penalty off the table meant that there was no inducement for Moussaoui to "tell what he did know about how Al Qaeda operated."[175] From an intelligence point of view, this was a mistake, particularly given the questions about Moussaoui's actual complicity in the 9/11 conspiracy.[176] The prosecutorial mission trumped the needs of intelligence gathering.

Second, the Justice Department's overriding desire to retain the case and win a conviction meant that prosecutors employed strategies that were unconventional and, in some cases, constitutionally questionable. The fact that it was a capital case meant that the government had a heavier burden to meet and may have felt greater pressure to cut corners in pursuit of a conviction. Among the strategies employed was moving Moussaoui's case to the appellate circuit most favorably disposed toward the government, the Fourth Circuit Court of Appeals. Admittedly, a conspiracy charge can be brought in any of the federal courts. Even so, Moussaoui's transfers suggest that his final destination was calculated to provide the most favorable environment for prosecutors. He was arrested on immigration violations in Minnesota, was transferred to New York (the Second Circuit) as a material witness, and was suspected of being involved with Flight 93, which crashed in Pennsylvania (the Third Circuit). Even so, the government moved him to Virginia, where he was indicted in the Fourth Circuit.[177] One reporter asked the attorney general about the location of the indictment and trial, given that most of the victims of 9/11 were in New York, and the U.S. attorney's office there had successfully prosecuted other terrorism cases. Ashcroft answered that "this is a national matter," and "the national investigative effort" was focused in Washington, D.C.[178] This reply did not address why the indictment and prosecution were not therefore in the D.C. Circuit.

Another unconventional tactic employed by the government was sending federal marshals to question Moussaoui in his cell without the presence of counsel and without advising him of his right to remain silent. While his remarks could not be used at trial to establish his guilt, the government did plan to use them during the penalty phase of the trial to rebut defense testimony. Arguing against their inclusion, his defense attorneys asserted that federal marshals had taken advantage of Moussaoui, who had been held in isolation for months and would have felt eager to converse.[179]

In addition, Moussaoui's defense attorneys faced a chilling realization that, should they win, he probably would be declared an enemy combatant and transferred to military custody. Administration officials made that possibility explicit on numerous occasions.[180] A subsequent military tribunal would provide him with fewer procedural protections. The government's threat to transfer Moussaoui became more credible in mid-2003 after the president declared Ali Saleh al-Marri an enemy combatant just one month before his scheduled trial date.[181] At a certain point, however, the government lost its opportunity to classify Moussaoui an enemy combatant, according to scholar Louis Fisher, because a "multiyear delay in making such a determination would have met with skepticism and incredulity."[182] Even so, the government allegedly made the threat in other cases to have criminal defendants classified as enemy combatants. For example, the defense attorneys in the case of the six defendants from Buffalo, New York, said their clients had been threatened with the enemy combatant designation if they did not plead guilty, a charge that the Justice Department denied.[183] In the end, all six did enter plea agreements with the government and were sentenced for seven to ten years.[184] Many others facing terrorism-related prosecutions also pled guilty, although there were no reports of coercion.

The government action that raised the most civil liberty questions in Moussaoui's case was its refusal to grant him access to potentially exculpatory testimony. Frank Dunham Jr., one of Moussaoui's attorneys, explained that the issues at stake were critical: "The right to a fair trial, the right to present a defense, the right to call witnesses in your own behalf, the right to force the government to produce evidence it has that is favorable to the defense—all of those things are on the table."[185] Ashcroft's continued insistence on the death penalty made the absence of exculpatory material more troubling, according to Fourth Circuit Judge Roger Gregory. He wrote in dissent, "To leave open the possibility of a sentence of death given these constraints on Moussaoui's ability to defend himself would, in my view, subvert the well-established rule that a defendant cannot be sentenced to death if the jury is precluded from considering mitigating evidence."[186]

In many ways, the Moussaoui case illustrates the difficulty of fitting the traditional law enforcement model into the framework of a war against terrorism. Some argued that the case demonstrated "how the system works,"[187] but other observers called the case "simply unmanageable"[188] and an "embarrassing spectacle."[189] The difficulty of trying terror suspects in civilian courts, according to former Reagan Justice official Victoria Toensing, was likened to trying to fit "the stepsister's foot in Cinderella's shoe."[190] Fair judicial process requires disclosure of exculpatory material, but that could compromise intelligence operations. Speed is important in regular trials, while intelligence gathering tends to be slow. And information gathered through intelligence methods includes rumors, speculation, and hearsay, which are much less reliable than evidence gathered for trial by law enforcement officers. The need for a degree of secrecy in terrorism prosecutions led some to argue that military tribunals with established procedures are "the least objectionable solution" to cases like Moussaoui's. Otherwise civilian judges will be asked "to relax the ordinary rules of procedure in light of the intelligence and national security concerns at stake," raising serious constitutional questions.[191] Opponents of this view, however, note that the government will simply move weak criminal cases to military tribunals, effectively creating "an end run around two centuries of constitutional law."[192] One critic explained, "If you can't win in the civilian court, just call them an enemy combatant. It is a slippery slope that would leave no American citizen protected."[193]

Detroit "Terror Cell" Case

The Detroit case in many ways appears to support the contention of some defense attorneys that the Justice Department has been overly aggressive, at the expense of defendants' rights. As the first jury trial on terrorism-related charges after 9/11, it carried symbolic weight. One Detroit journalist observed, "If federal prosecutors lose, Attorney General John Ashcroft and the Justice Department will suffer a humiliating defeat. . . . It could erode public confidence in the administration."[194] Ironically, in the end, the actions of the U.S. attorney's office did more to erode public confidence. Because of credible allegations of prosecutorial misconduct, the Justice Department was forced to request that the three convictions won in the trial, including two on terrorism–related charges, be dismissed.

The story began less than a week after the terrorist strikes. Looking for Al-Marabh, the previous tenant, government agents visited the Detroit apartment of Farouk Ali-Haimoud of Algeria and Ahmed Hannan and Karim Koubriti of Morocco. A search of the apartment uncovered a forged passport and other

documents related to fraud, scores of audiotapes that the government characterized as radical Islamic lectures, and a day planner with crude sketches that appeared to refer to an American air base in Turkey and a military hospital in Jor-
dan, among other suspicious notations.[195] Although the three men claimed their
innocence, they were charged with document fraud and conspiracy to provide
material support for terrorists, along with a fourth man named Abdel-Ilah Elmardoudi. The government's star witness against them was a former roommate
named Youssef Hmimssa, who told investigators that they were planning to recruit and arm terrorists to strike the air base, the hospital, and other targets, and
to give funds to other designated terrorist groups.[196] From the government's
perspective, the men were members of a "sleeper operational combat cell."[197]

Despite the government's confidence in Hmimssa's veracity, his testimony
was suspect. He was in the country illegally, unlike Ali-Haimoud, Hannan,
and Koubriti, and was wanted in three states on credit card fraud charges.
Hiding from these charges, Hmimssa stayed only briefly with the men during
the summer of 2001. He was interested in cooperating with prosecutors in
hopes of securing leniency.[198] The defendants claimed that the fraudulent
documents discovered in the apartment had been his, although it is unclear
why they would have kept them once he had left. The suspicious day planner
had also been left by a previous tenant, a Yemeni immigrant described as
mentally unstable who had committed suicide in March 2001.[199] Regarding
the damning audiotapes, an expert witness called by the defense described
them as "just regular lectures" and not extremist diatribes.[200]

The case went to trial in the spring of 2003 with Assistant U.S. Attorney
Richard Convertino leading the prosecution. During the nine-week trial, the
government called on fifty witnesses and introduced 1,000 exhibits.[201] John
Ashcroft buttressed the public perception that the men were guilty when he
issued a statement soon after Hmimssa's testimony calling him "a critical
tool" in the fight against terrorism.[202] In the end, however, the jury acquitted
Ali-Haimoud of all charges and convicted Hannan only on conspiracy related
to document fraud. Koubriti and Elmardoudi were convicted on the charges
related to terrorism.[203] Ashcroft announced the verdict as a government victory against terrorism, bringing "us closer to our ultimate goal of victory in
the war on terrorism."[204] He said: "Today's convictions send a clear message:
The Department of Justice will work diligently to detect, disrupt and dismantle the activities of terrorist cells in the United States and abroad. We will
commit every resource to preventing terrorist attacks, and sending those who
aid our enemies to jail. Today's verdict reaffirms our commitment to pursuing
aggressively the evidence wherever it may lead."[205]

Within months, however, the Justice Department and FBI began internal investigations into the Detroit prosecution. Convertino was accused of reducing

Hmimssa's fraud sentence without higher-level approval and of asking a pre-trial services officer for confidential information related to a defense witness.[206] He was removed from the case in September 2003. In a December hearing, the new prosecutors went further and said that Convertino had withheld exculpatory evidence that should have been given to defense attorneys, specifically, "a letter from a cellmate of the government's star witness, suggesting that the witness had lied."[207] Convertino explained that the letter had not been shared with the defense because he believed it was not credible, since it also accused President Bush's family of dealing in drugs. He questioned the motives of the author of the letter.[208] The internal investigation continued, uncovering "serious prosecutorial misconduct in the case." At that point, the Justice Department asked Judge Gerald Rosen to dismiss the convictions, and he did. The department decided not to reinstate the charges related to terrorism and to retry Koubriti, Elmardoudi, and Hannan only on the charges related to document fraud.[209]

Meanwhile, Convertino alleged that he was removed from the case not because of any misconduct but because he had testified before a Senate committee about "the lack of support and resources, the micromanaging by Washington and the total lack of cooperation and intense territorial infighting within the department and with other agencies."[210] In February 2004, he brought a lawsuit against the attorney general and the department, charging that his removal was retaliation for his public criticism of Justice.[211]

Prosecuting Material Support of Terrorism

Most of the prosecutions brought in the war against terrorism were tied to the provision of material support rather than the crime of terrorism itself. As Ashcroft was leaving office, at least fifty-two defendants had been charged with violations of the material support law.[212] One charge, brought against a computer science student in Idaho, will be examined in the next chapter because it involved a Patriot Act provision. Under the earliest federal law criminalizing material support of terrorism, passed in 1994, the burden was on the government to show that the material support was connected to an act of terrorism.[213] That changed with the 1996 Antiterrorism and Effective Death Penalty Act, passed after the bombing of the Murrah Federal Building in Oklahoma City. The Antiterrorism Act includes provisions criminalizing material support to terrorists and terrorist groups. They are Section 2339A, Providing Material Support to Terrorists, and Section 2339B, Providing Material Support or Resources to Designated Foreign Terrorist Organizations. Both sections define material support as "currency or monetary instruments or financial securities, financial services, lodging, training, safehouses, false documentation or identification, communication equipment, facilities, weapons, lethal substances, explosives, personnel, transportation, and other physical assets, except medicine or religious materials."[214] The Patriot Act's Section 805 added the provision of "expert advice or assistance."[215]

Unlike traditional complicity laws, Sections 2339A and 2339B criminalize providing support to a criminal (a terrorist or organization), *not* aiding the perpetration of a crime (terrorism). This means that a crime need not have been accomplished for the government to prosecute someone for complicity under the material support law. There are other important differences as well. Traditional complicity laws require that the accomplice have the purpose of advancing a crime; the material support laws accept as mens rea (or guilty mind) the mere knowledge that the support will advance a crime. Legal scholar Norman Abrams speculated that the mens rea of knowledge, without a mens rea of purpose, is what led Congress to list the specific categories of aid that are forbidden, rather than use a more general term, such as "substantial facilitation," which is more common in complicity liability. It was a legislative effort to provide some limits so that the law did not go too far; otherwise, minor employees or a "vendor who supplies materials readily available" on the market could be prosecuted. In this way, material support would be functionally the same as "substantial facilitation."[216] The problem, as Abrams and others have pointed out, is that the categories have been interpreted beyond their ordinary meaning by Justice Department attorneys. For example, in the Lynne Stewart case, to be discussed later, "communication equipment" was stretched to cover her telephone.[217] According to Abrams, the natural reading of forbidden "communication equipment" would be "short wave radios, walkie talkies, and the like—that is, types of electronic apparatus that could be used in terrorist activities."[218] This broad reading of the categories, which some courts have sustained, could criminalize minor, everyday assistance, and do so in a way that an ordinary person would not know that he or she was breaking the law. This is the problem of "vagueness," which led a few federal courts to strike down the inclusion of personnel, communications equipment, and expert advice and assistance among the unlawful categories.[219]

Another problematic element of the material support law is the potential for criminalizing or chilling constitutionally protected speech and association. Law professor David Cole testified to the Senate Judiciary Committee that Section 2339B's ban on providing training, personnel, and expert advice or assistance (which had been added by the Patriot Act) to groups designated by the secretary of state as terrorist could criminalize "virtually all human activity on behalf of such organizations, including a substantial amount of core political speech and advocacy entitled to First Amendment protection."[220] He pointed out that groups like the Humanitarian Law Project could be prosecuted for providing human rights training, giving legal advice, or testifying before Congress in support of a group designated a foreign terrorist organization. The activities themselves are perfectly lawful; however, under the material support provisions, they would be seen as freeing up resources that a group could then use for unlawful purposes.[221] In a case involving the Humanitarian Law Project, the Ninth Circuit Court of Appeals agreed, striking down those provisions.[222]

Prior to the September 11 attacks, the material support provisions were rarely used; prosecutors applied them only three times and never against someone alleged to be supporting al Qaeda.[223] After the attacks, however, the Justice Department aggressively utilized those provisions as part of its preventive campaign against terrorism. Deputy Assistant Attorney General Alice Fisher, who headed the department's counterterrorism efforts, told a House committee in 2003 that material support charges had been brought against sixty-one people in the war against terrorism.[224] Justice spokesman Bryan Sierra portrayed the prosecutions as "part of the effort to choke off the resources used by terrorists, not only money, but people and weapons and anything else. We see the statute as a very valuable tool," he added, "and it's one we'll keep going to if we find cases in which we can use it."[225] Abrams described the Justice Department's reliance on the material support provisions: "These provisions can be used to impose punishment for conduct remote from the commission of criminal harms, often conduct involving minimal and outwardly non-criminal acts. . . . The government is using them as catch-all offenses, that can be invoked in widely varying situations where individuals engage in conduct that may contribute in some way to the commission of terrorist offenses."[226]

Muslim charities in the United States have been particularly susceptible to charges that their donations to Islamic groups overseas helped to support terrorism. The cases of two such groups based in Illinois—Global Relief Foundation (GRF) and Benevolence International Foundation (BIF)—illustrate some of these concerns. Their experiences are described in a case study published by the staff of the 9/11 commission, the National Commission on Terrorist Attacks upon the United States.

The two charities were suspected of channeling some of their humanitarian aid to jihadist fighters in Chechnya and Bosnia-Herzegovina. They had been under FBI investigation since the early 1990s, but their operations had not been disrupted. That changed with 9/11, with the realization that "money potentially earmarked for al Qaeda . . . [could finance] another potential mass casualty attack."[227] Following the terrorist strikes, while the FBI investigation continued, the Office of Foreign Assets Control in the Treasury Department temporarily blocked these foundations' assets under a provision of the International Emergency Economic Powers Act (IEEPA). The temporary block lasted almost a year before each group was formally named a Specially Designated Global Terrorist (SDGT) and its assets were frozen permanently. Both groups denied any tie with terrorist activities.[228]

The government attempted to prosecute BIF's executive director, Enaam Arnaout, for lying on a statement that he had attached to BIF's lawsuit seeking the return of its assets and the lifting of the blocking order. But the judge dismissed the indictment because his statement did not fall under the federal perjury statute.[229] Then the government located documents in Bosnia which established that BIF supported Muslim fighters there and in Chechnya, and that BIF and Arnaout were associated with Osama bin Laden and al Qaeda in the 1980s. With the Bosnia evidence, the government moved to prosecute Arnaout for using charitable donations to support terrorist organizations. BIF attorneys pointed out that al Qaeda was not designated a foreign terrorist organization by the United States until 1999. A grand jury indicted him on seven counts, including "conspiracy to engage in a racketeering enterprise, . . . material support to terrorists, . . . money laundering, . . . mail fraud, and . . . wire fraud."[230] Raising the profile of the case, Attorney General Ashcroft traveled to Chicago to announce the indictment in person, noting that, if convicted, Arnaout could face ninety years in prison. In an impassioned speech, Ashcroft said: "To those who would exploit the generosity of others, break the law, and provide financing to terrorists and other groups engaged in violence, my message is this: we will find the sources of terrorist blood money, we will shut down these sources, and we will ensure that both terrorists and their financiers meet the same, swift, certain justice of the United States of America."[231] The case did not go to trial, however. In February 2003, Arnaout pled guilty to one count of racketeering conspiracy for misleading donors to the charity; he admitted to using their donations to buy boots, uniforms, and tents for Muslim fighters in Bosnia and Chechnya.[232] District judge Suzanne Conlon permitted a sentencing enhancement due to the aggravating factor that Arnaout's fraud hurt the refugees and orphans for whom the funds were intended. However, she denied the government's request to add twenty years to his sentence for the crime of terrorism, since Arnaout had not been convicted of a terrorism offense, nor was there any evidence that he had planned or participated in any act of terrorism. His association with Osama bin Laden occurred during the Afghani war against the Soviet Union, when the United States did not oppose bin Laden's activities. Furthermore, the judge ruled, the government had not established that the fighters in Bosnia and Chechnya were terrorists under U.S. law.[233]

The evidence against GRF was more circumstantial, and no criminal charges were filed against it or its leadership. However, one of the cofounders of the group and a major fund-raiser, Rabih Haddad, was detained by the Immigration and Naturalization Service. He requested asylum, but an immigration judge found he was not eligible because he was "a security danger to the United States." Officials in Washington, D.C., decided to deport him rather than continue a criminal investigation. The Board of Immigration Appeals upheld the deportation. Meanwhile, his detention continued for almost three years; Haddad was finally deported to Lebanon in 2003.[234] Because his initial immigration hearing was closed, he and several press organizations filed a lawsuit. That case will be examined in the chapter on government secrecy. Meanwhile, the charity, GRF, challenged the temporary block on its assets, on the grounds that the freeze was instituted without any formal review process, either judicial or administrative. GRF filed a lawsuit in January 2002 against Ashcroft, the secretaries of state and treasury, and others, seeking an injunction on the freeze. The district court denied the request, a ruling that was upheld on appeal. The Supreme Court did not accept the case for review. In October 2002, the government issued an SDGT designation of GRF, which made the freeze permanent. A few days later, the United Nations listed it as an organization associated with al Qaeda, which shut down GRF's global operations. The group continued to litigate, challenging the basis on which it was classified a terrorist organization.[235]

The Justice Department's handling of these cases was criticized because of the adverse public relations fallout among the Muslim communities in Chicago and Detroit, as noted in the 9/11 commission's report. Some senior FBI agents in Chicago argued that a public trial of Arnaout would have been preferable to a plea bargain because the government would have had an opportunity to lay out its evidence. That would have helped convince the Muslim community that the government was not "picking on a poor guy," but that Arnaout and BIF were indeed culpable.[236] Likewise in Haddad's case, supporters "considered his detention in solitary confinement on what appeared to be a minor visa violation as a prime example of discrimination against Muslims and an overzealous government response to 9/11, in violation of basic civil rights."[237] His subsequent deportation elicited sympathy as well; the government's failure to indict him was cited as evidence of his innocence. Despite the department's continued assertions that Haddad "was a substantial threat to the United States," and that the decision to prosecute is based on many factors, not simply a person's guilt, the perception of discrimination continued.[238]

Some of the key civil liberty questions posed by these two cases also were explored in the 9/11 staff report. First, the report found the application of the IEEPA to a domestic organization or U.S. citizen to be "potentially dangerous," since the decision to freeze assets and shut down an organization while an investigation is pending can be made without any formal hearing, much less a determination of guilt. In fact, the action only "requires a single piece of paper, signed by a midlevel government official." In addition, the temporary freezes in these two cases—of ten and eleven months—were hardly temporary. The 9/11 monograph recommended "placing a strict and short limit on the duration of such a temporary blocking." Second, a permanent freeze and SDGT designation can be made on the basis of evidence usually not considered reliable and therefore not admissible in court, for example, hearsay such as news stories. The government also can rely on classified evidence not available to the defense and therefore beyond its refutation or explanation. An appeal of the designation can be raised in court, but the presumption favors the government.[239] These factors mean that the process of classifying a group as terrorist—which has serious consequences for people affiliated with the group, including donors—is fraught with subjectivity and lack of independent review.

The 9/11 staff report did find troubling links between the groups and terrorists.[240] Yet, the report concluded, "despite unprecedented access to the U.S. and foreign records of these organizations, one of the world's most experienced and best terrorist prosecutors has not been able to make any criminal case against GRF and resolved the investigation of BIF without a conviction for support of terrorism."[241] In other words, the cases illustrated the difficulty posed for law enforcement investigating allegations of possible terrorist fund-raising: the difference between troubling links and compelling evidence.[242] The first was sufficient for an intelligence investigation but could not serve as a reliable basis for a criminal prosecution, even when the standard for criminality is set at a level below that for all other crimes.

Individuals as well as organizations were subject to the material support charge when a more direct case alleging terrorism was not viable. In at least one instance, Justice Department prosecutors claimed that the violation of special administrative measures could constitute material support of terrorism. That case, involving New York attorney Lynne Stewart, dramatizes how administrative rule violations, which do not in themselves constitute a crime, could be conflated with material support of a terrorist or terrorist organization, and thus be elevated to the level of a major criminal offense.

As noted, SAMs applied to many of those in prison on terrorism charges, including Stewart's client, Sheik Omar Abdel Rahman. Rahman was convicted in 1995 of conspiracy in the World Trade Center bombing of 1993 and in a plan to blow up several Manhattan bridges and tunnels. His access to telephone, mail, and visitors was limited, and he was barred from speaking to the media. Stewart was obliged to sign an agreement to abide by the SAMs before she was permitted to visit him.[243] In 2000, she broke the agreement, first by speaking in English during a prison visit, which distracted guards from noticing an Arabic conversation between Rahman and his translator, and second by issuing a press release to Reuters with the news that the sheik no longer supported a cease-fire by his supporters in Egypt. The Clinton administration protested her violation of the rules. Stewart admitted her fault and then signed another SAM agreement. From that moment, she was unwittingly subjected to a wiretap authorized by the Foreign Intelligence Surveillance Court, which covered her prison visits to Rahman. After September 11, federal prosecutors decided to charge her with fraud for signing the agreement with the intent of violating it, making false statements, conspiracy, and providing material support to a foreign terrorist organization. In April 2002, John Ashcroft personally announced the indictment against her.[244] The two most serious counts were based on Section 2339B, providing "communications equipment" and "personnel" to a foreign terrorist organization. The government alleged that she herself was the "personnel" provided to advance the terrorist organization and that her cell phone was the "communications equipment." She pleaded not guilty and argued that the two serious counts were unconstitutionally vague and overbroad. The federal district judge agreed with Stewart and dismissed them.[245] Instead of appealing, the government brought a second superseding indictment that charged Stewart and the others under Section 2339A, altering its strategy to argue the defendants had facilitated Rahman's communication with terrorists on the outside and thereby "provided" Rahman—the personnel—to those confederates. It was, as Norman Abrams noted, "an awkward fit between the facts alleged and the definition of material support."[246] Even so, the judge accepted it. Following a jury trial in February 2005, Stewart was convicted. No evidence was presented that either her press release or other communications led to any act of terrorism or violence.[247] In October 2005, a district judge rejected her argument for a retrial on the grounds that some jurors were biased against her. Stewart was scheduled to be sentenced in March 2006.[248]

Law professor David Cole noted that Stewart "crossed the line from zealous advocacy to wrongful conduct," but that her violation of the administrative agreement merited no more than disciplinary charges against her and not a likely prison sentence of twenty to thirty years.[249] A Justice Department spokesman defended the application of SAMs to defense counsel: "Even the most honorable of individuals might become the inadvertent, unknowing and unwitting conduit for the transmission of nefarious messages, even when there is a good-faith belief that such communications are being made in pursuit of a client's defense."[250]

Stewart's successful prosecution could have a chilling effect on the willingness of attorneys to represent certain clients. Stewart considered this one of the government's intentions in prosecuting her. "I think the government has an interest in deterring lawyers from representing political people," she said in a 2003 interview, "an even greater interest, perhaps, in deterring lawyers from representing Moslem defendants." [251]

The Legal Limbo of Enemy Combatants

The category of enemy combatants is new in domestic law. Until the war on terrorism was declared, criminals and enemy soldiers were conceptually distinct, subject to different handling by the state. The first fell under regular criminal law, including the protection of criminal procedural rights, the second, under international laws and the law of war. Now, however, the line has blurred.

During his first term in office, Bush classified three men as enemy combatants and confined them in a military brig without charges or access to counsel. The basis for the president's classification was an affidavit called the Mobbs Declaration filed by an undersecretary in the Defense Department; the affidavit—which purported to present the factual record—was based on hearsay collected in interrogations of captured enemy soldiers and al Qaeda leaders. Two of the men, Yaser Hamdi and José Padilla, are U.S. citizens; Ali Al Marri is from Qatar. Al Marri and Padilla were picked up in the United States initially on material witness warrants; Al Marri's case was progressing through the criminal justice system at the time he was designated an enemy combatant. Hamdi was captured in Afghanistan, as was John Walker Lindh, another U.S. citizen.

Unlike the others, Lindh was not classified an enemy combatant, and his case was handled by a regular civilian court. Initially, though, different rules were applied in Lindh's case as well. His family alleged that neither they nor his attorney had been permitted to see him, and that he had been denied medical care until he agreed to answer questions.[252] Meanwhile, he was interrogated first by the military and later by an FBI agent in Afghanistan, neither time with counsel present, even though the Justice Department had informed the FBI that questioning could not continue without counsel. Under interrogation, Lindh confessed, and that confession served as the basis for the ten-count indictment against him.[253] The possibility that that confession would be ruled inadmissible led government attorneys to offer him a plea agreement on the charge of violating the U.S. economic sanctions against the Taliban. He was sentenced to a twenty-year prison term.[254]

The cases of Lindh, Hamdi, Al Marri, and Padilla, as well as those of Moussaoui and Reid, were handled so differently by the government that constitutional scholar Louis Fisher observed, "The Justice Department has not adopted consistent or even understandable principles in its prosecution of 'terrorist' suspects."[255] The enemy combatant designation seems particularly susceptible to subjective determinations. When asked to describe the criteria by which the government made its "enemy combatant" determinations, the solicitor general, Theodore Olson, said, "There will be judgments and instincts and evaluations and implementations that have to be made by the executive that are probably going to be different from day to day, depending on the circumstances."[256] The arbitrary, open-ended quality of the criteria appears to conflict with the principles of due process.

The "enemy combatant" designation provides the government with the opportunity to remove a suspected terrorist from the criminal justice system and detain him for an indefinite time, without counsel or contact with the outside world. The primary argument justifying this suspension of constitutional rights is national security, particularly the benefits to be gained through interrogation. In its legal brief seeking reconsideration of the district court's ruling that Padilla had to be given limited access to counsel, the Justice Department claimed that "interrogations of detained enemy combatants [had] produced vital intelligence and helped to thwart an estimated 100 or more attacks against the United States and its interests since Sept. 11, 2001."[257] Access to an attorney, even for a brief period and limited purpose, would inhibit the psychological dependence that interrogators seek to build with suspects.

Most of those falling under the enemy combatant designation are foreign nationals captured during the war in Afghanistan and held at the U.S. naval base in Guantánamo Bay, Cuba. However, the possibility remains that additional U.S. citizens and legal aliens in the United States will be classified in this manner. In 2002, government officials reported that a plan was under consideration to create a panel that could designate others in the United States as enemy combatants.[258] The status of that plan was not known at the time of this writing.

The fundamental civil liberty issue pertaining to enemy combatants is their right to a neutral review of the factual basis for their classification as enemy combatants in the first place. Even in a wartime context where there may not be a presumption of innocence, prisoners within the jurisdiction of federal courts have the right to raise a habeas corpus challenge of the grounds for their detention. Sometimes called the Great Writ, habeas corpus dates back 800 years. A Latin phrase meaning "you have the body," a writ of habeas corpus is issued by a judge to compel the government to produce a person held in custody, to determine if the detention is lawful.[259] Legal scholar Eric Freedman called it "perhaps the most cherished remedy in Anglo-American jurisprudence."[260] It is guaranteed in the body of the U.S. Constitution itself: "The privilege of the writ of habeas corpus shall not be suspended, unless when in cases of rebellion or invasion the public safety may require it."[261] Because this provision is placed within Article I, which deals with congressional powers and limits, only Congress constitutionally can suspend the writ, although Abraham Lincoln did so in the early days of the Civil War, when Congress was not in session. Congress later affirmed the suspension. This institutional arrangement was intended to prevent abuse, according to constitutional scholar Laurence Tribe.[262]

The constitutional guarantee is not self-executing, however, and legislation is needed. The U.S. Code currently recognizes that "the Supreme Court, any justice thereof, the district courts and any circuit court judge within their respective jurisdictions" have the authority to grant writs.[263] Congress may alter its application. For example, the Antiterrorism and Effective Death Penalty Act of 1996 made it more difficult for prisoners to succeed in filing federal habeas petitions, by putting the burden on them to show that a state court made a mistake in their cases—either in its factual findings or in its application of federal law. In addition, the 1996 law bars petitions from advancing new claims unless a change of law or facts necessitates it.[264]

The habeas petition, long the province of death penalty and immigration cases, gained greater visibility as the federal government rounded up foreign nationals in the weeks following the attacks and later detained captured enemy combatants from Afghanistan and elsewhere at Guantánamo Bay. By December 2001, government lawyers worried that a federal district court might accept a petition for a writ of habeas corpus filed by a prisoner detained at Guantánamo. In a memorandum to the Defense Department's general counsel, two attorneys in the Justice Department Office of Legal Counsel provided a legal rationale for why such a petition should be dismissed by a federal court for lack of jurisdiction. Parsing language and selectively citing precedent,[265] the two deputy assistant attorneys general wrote on December 28, 2001, "Federal courts lack jurisdiction over habeas petitions filed by alien detainees held outside the sovereign territory of the United States," which included Guantánamo Bay.[266] They supported this assertion by quoting from the 1903 lease agreement with Cuba, by which "the United States recognizes the continuance of the ultimate sovereignty of the Republic of Cuba" over the lands and waters of Guantánamo, although the United States would "exercise complete jurisdiction and control over and within" the leased territory. The OLC attorneys argued that the terms "sovereignty" and "territorial jurisdiction" were interchangeable, meaning that the precedent they relied on—*Johnson v. Eisentrager,* discussed in the previous chapter—applied to Guantánamo as well as to post–World War II Germany.[267] Because of that, they added, Guantánamo fell within no federal court's jurisdiction,[268] thus placing the naval base beyond the scope of the habeas corpus authority provided in the

U.S. Code. The OLC attorneys then conceded, "There remains some litigation risk that a district court might reach the opposite result."[269] Interestingly, the March 2002 OLC memo involving torture argued the opposite, that any torture committed at Guantánamo Bay would not violate the federal antitorture law because the statute applied only to actions outside of U.S. jurisdiction.[270]

In the cases of Shafiq Rasul and Yaser Hamdi, the Supreme Court addressed the habeas issue directly. The first, *Rasul v. Bush* and a companion case, involved a habeas petition brought by fourteen prisoners at Guantánamo. The petitioners, although captured in Afghanistan and Pakistan by non-U.S. forces, denied they were either terrorists or combatants against the United States. The U.S. District Court, construing their claims as habeas corpus petitions, dismissed for want of jurisdiction, since the men were aliens held in territory not under U.S. sovereignty. The court of appeals affirmed,[271] but in a 6 to 3 ruling, the Supreme Court reversed. The federal courts did have jurisdiction, because the Guantánamo base was not outside of U.S. control. Under the lease agreement and a 1934 treaty, the United States exercised "plenary and exclusive authority" over the territory, despite formal Cuban sovereignty.[272] The justices then emphasized the role that the writ of habeas corpus plays in restraining executive power. Writing for the majority,[273] Justice John Paul Stevens quoted former justice Robert Jackson's comment that "the historic purpose of the writ has been to relieve detention by executive authorities without judicial trial."[274]

The case of *Hamdi v. Rumsfeld* raised the issues of habeas corpus and the right to counsel, in addition to a separation of powers argument discussed in chapter 5. After Hamdi's transfer to custody in the United States, a federal district judge granted him brief access to a federal public defender without military personnel present.[275] The government quickly appealed to the Fourth Circuit, which agreed to block further access to counsel. Because Hamdi himself could not file the petition, due to the conditions of his confinement, his public defender and a man not related to him did so in the capacity of "next friend." The district court accepted the petition, but the Fourth Circuit rejected it, because these individuals had no prior relationship with him and therefore could not serve as his "next friend."[276] Then Hamdi's father filed a habeas petition as his "next friend," and the district court again ordered that the military provide him access to his court-appointed public defender. The Fourth Circuit, on appeal, reversed the order and remanded the case, instructing the district court to reconsider the case in light of the earlier appellate ruling and new evidence (the Mobbs Declaration, discussed earlier) presented by the government. The district court, however, found that evidence insufficient and sought additional documents for in camera or secret review. The government appealed the order to produce more material, and the

Fourth Circuit again reversed the district court. Hamdi's attorney and father appealed to the Supreme Court, which granted certiorari.[277]

In their brief, government attorneys argued that Hamdi, like thousands of others captured in Afghanistan, had received an adequate review of the facts justifying his detention, sufficient for the demands of due process. He had gone through "a multi-step screening process to determine if their continued detention is necessary . . . , i.e., whether the individual 'was part of or supporting forces hostile to the United States or coalition partners, and engaged in an armed conflict against the United States.'"[278] Prosecutors also argued that enemy combatants had no "automatic right of access to counsel" because that "would interfere with the military's compelling interest in gathering intelligence to further the war effort."[279] Perhaps to render the issue of counsel moot, however, the Defense Department announced just before the Supreme Court's consideration of the case that it would permit "an enemy combatant who is a presumed citizen and detained in the United States" to have access to an attorney once the interrogation stage was past, security was in place, and the Pentagon determined that national security would not be compromised.[280] Citing this policy in their brief, Justice Department attorneys informed the court that Hamdi had already met with counsel the previous February and March, the latter without military monitors present. They suggested that the justices reserve the issue of counsel for another day and another case.[281]

On several of these key points, however, the Supreme Court did not agree. In June 2004, the justices reversed and remanded the appeals court decision. Setting aside the larger question of the executive's authority to detain, six justices found that a citizen designated an enemy combatant still had to receive a "meaningful opportunity" to challenge the factual basis for his or her detention, which meant both a neutral decision maker and access to counsel for the limited purpose of assisting in this process.[282] The review that Hamdi had received after capture did not meet the minimum requirements of due process. For the Court, Justice Sandra Day O'Connor explained, "An interrogation by one's captor, however effective an intelligence-gathering tool, hardly constitutes a constitutionally adequate fact-finding before a neutral decision maker." As noted in chapter 5, the majority opinion did not extend traditional criminal procedural rights to Hamdi; for example, it shifted the burden of proof from the government to the alleged enemy combatant, and it did not guarantee access to counsel throughout the process. Two of the three dissenters would have gone further than the majority in protecting the habeas right. Antonin Scalia and John Paul Stevens wrote that, under the Constitution, the government had to charge Hamdi with a crime or release him. There was no third option, as asserted by the government.[283]

As of mid-2005, the Supreme Court rulings in *Hamdi* and *Rasul* had not resulted in the release of any detainees held at Guantánamo Bay. Despite the decision that they had a right to neutral review, "the prisoners' fate hinges on myriad procedural considerations, especially such issues as exactly whom the prisoners may sue for their freedom and which judge or judges will ultimately rule on their pleas."[284] A key question related to venue, that is, in which jurisdictions the detainees could file. Multiple habeas corpus petitions were filed following the *Rasul* decision, but a Defense Department spokesman said the government had not yet determined how it would respond. He said, "The Department of Defense, the Justice Department and the administration are still working together to determine how we're going to comply with the Supreme Court direction."[285] By November 2004, the Defense Department had established a Combatant Status Review Tribunal to resolve preliminary questions in the case of one Guantánamo prisoner, Australian David Hicks, but the initial hearing was plagued by the lack of legal knowledge of two of the three judges. One critical observer, the senior legal adviser for Human Rights Watch, characterized the hearings as "an introductory law school class," because basic concepts in constitutional and international law had to be explained to the two military officers who served as judges.[286]

The authority claimed by the White House to classify U.S. persons—citizens and legal residents—as enemy combatants represents an unprecedented exercise of unilateral power. From the administration's perspective, neither Congress nor the courts need to confirm that authority, and neither branch can check it. "The avoidance of separation of powers constraints in the domestic war on terrorism," wrote scholar Kim Lane Scheppele, "has reached its height with the claimed presidential power to label suspect individuals as enemy combatants who are immune from legal process altogether."[287] The direct question about the constitutionality of this power claim has yet to be resolved by the Supreme Court.

Conclusion

The Justice Department under Ashcroft did successfully investigate and prosecute terrorism-related cases. Ashcroft made the decision to try Richard Reid in a federal court rather than have him transferred to a military tribunal, and Reid was convicted on multiple terrorism-related charges and sentenced to life in prison.[288] Truck driver Iyman Faris pleaded guilty and was sentenced to twenty years for assisting al Qaeda by delivering cell phones and money, and investigating the possibility of blowing up the Brooklyn Bridge.[289] Also pleading guilty was James Ujaama, for "conspiring to provide goods and services to the Taliban in violation of the International Emergency Economic Powers Act." He was sentenced to two years.[290] Others pleaded guilty for providing material support. The defendants in the Buffalo Six case pleaded guilty to attending a terrorist training camp in Afghanistan, as did the six defendants in custody in the so-called Portland terror cell case. As Ashcroft and others noted, there were no other attacks after 9/11. One senior prosecutor defended the department's record: "I don't understand the criticism, truly. We didn't break any laws and we protected the nation. It was the Justice Department's finest hour."[291]

As the sunsetted provisions of the Patriot Act were being debated in Congress in the summer of 2005, Bush announced that—due to the Patriot Act—charges had been brought against more than 400 suspects, with more than 200 terrorists convicted.[292] The veracity of these figures remains unclear, however. One case-by-case analysis of the records revealed that "39 people—not 200, as officials have implied—were convicted of crimes related to terrorism or national security." The majority were convicted of relatively minor crimes.[293] The Executive Office of U.S. Attorneys (EOUSA) also documented an increase in antiterrorism convictions from an average of 35 per year for the preceding five years to approximately 160 in 2002. According to the Government Accountability Office, however, the increase was due not only to the new Justice priority placed on fighting terrorism but also to a new classification system that captured terrorism-related hoaxes and financing. Responding to allegations that the Justice Department was inflating its terrorism-related conviction statistics in its performance reports, the GAO also found problems of overclassification in figures reported by the U.S. attorneys offices: "At least 132 of the 288 USAO cases (about 46 percent) were misclassified as terrorism-related" in fiscal year 2002, and the "overall accuracy of the remaining 156 convictions is questionable."[294] The cause, according to the GAO, was the Justice Department's failure to provide "sufficient management oversight and internal controls" to ensure the accuracy and reliability of its terrorism-related conviction statistics. Another problem facing the government in classifying the cases is the lack of a "single, uniform definition of terrorism." A case could be categorized as terrorism-related even if it does not "involve force or violence," if there are "acts in preparation of terrorist activities," such as money laundering and document fraud.[295]

While there were not as many court victories as the administration claimed in the war against terrorism, there were some genuine successes. In the process of winning them, however, civil rights and liberties were weakened, particularly for Muslims. Muslims were singled out in the FBI's initial investigation of 9/11, the discretionary application of immigration and material witness laws, and the mandatory registration program instituted under the

Patriot Act. Noting how those detained and interrogated were overwhelmingly Muslim, attorney Randall Hamud, who represented three material witnesses, referred to the resulting hesitation of the Muslim community to assist government's antiterrorist efforts: "It's very difficult for this community to cooperate in 9/11 investigations and search for terrorists when it has been terrorized by the Department of Justice."[296]

Rosenzweig's statement that no actual abuse of civil liberties occurred is not supported by the record, which chronicles long and harsh imprisonment of people later deemed innocent and troubling prosecution tactics, including the overhanging threat of a transfer to military custody. These elements of the domestic war against terrorism reveal a disregard for—even a distrust of—the legal limitations established by the Bill of Rights on executive and legislative action, at least among some who served in the Ashcroft Justice Department.

The attorney general's comments about ordered liberty are worth remembering. A robust legal system and the rule of law are not contrary to civil liberties. Rule of law does preserve liberty not only because it restrains citizens but because it also restrains government. This broader understanding of ordered liberty was missing in the attorney general's remarks. Rule of law applies to rulers as well as the ruled. Government actors must be limited in what they can do, even when they are in pursuit of just and important aims.

Some of the defendants—particularly Zacarias Moussaoui, with his abusive rants, and Richard Reid, unrepentant and uncooperative—are not sympathetic in the least. Yet, as legal commentator Michael Dorf notes, "Important civil liberties cases rarely involve genuine heroes. Klan members and pornographers test the limits of freedom of speech, drug dealers and robbers challenge overzealous searches and seizures, and terrorists call into question our commitment to the presumption of innocence." He adds, "One need not sympathize with any of these unsavory characters to recognize that the issues they raise have consequences for everyone."[297]

Fighting terrorism in the courtroom does not require suspension of the normal rules that guide criminal prosecution. District judge William Young's handling of the Richard Reid case demonstrated this. By accepting as valid a search warrant that did not provide exact words and phrases, he ensured that the government's investigatory tools were not unduly circumscribed. At the same time, he rejected government efforts to limit Reid's contact with counsel, and he chastised prosecutors for releasing a prejudicial and misleading videotape of a bomb exploding on a plane. Asserting that "all of this war talk is way out of line," Young refused to dignify Reid with the title of soldier or enemy combatant. He treated Reid as a criminal defendant facing justice. In the end, Reid was convicted. Legal commentator Juliette Kayyem noted that the trial "provides sound guidelines for how terrorism trials can work—and why military tribunals may well be unnecessary."[298] This approach to confronting terrorism at home, however, was largely eschewed by the chief law officer of the nation.

Popular concerns with government power and civil liberties have centered primarily on the USA Patriot Act, which will be addressed next.

7 Surveillance, Privacy, and the Patriot Act

Six days after September 11, George W. Bush urged John Ashcroft to move ahead with the legislative package that was to become the USA Patriot Act, to provide the FBI with the power "to track, wiretap and stop terrorists."[1] The antiterrorism bill that resulted was heavily identified with Ashcroft. For many it became "a symbol of . . . Ashcroft's legal excesses."[2] President Bush let his attorney general take the lead and the heat in promoting the measure. In contrast to Ashcroft's active role, Bush made only one public plea for the bill in a speech at FBI headquarters.[3]

The Justice Department already had been developing a draft of a mammoth antiterrorism measure, incorporating some powers that the government had unsuccessfully sought earlier. Abner Mikva, who had served as White House counsel in the Clinton administration, said he recognized the resurrection of some of the worst ideas rejected in the 1995 antiterrorism law; they were, he said, "just dumped wholesale into the Patriot Act."[4] Ashcroft may have wanted to push the boundaries even further than the administration. Reportedly, the administration's version did not go as far as he wanted, due to opposition of some senior GOP legislators.[5]

The attorney general brought the draft to Congress on September 19, 2001, and urged passage within the week. He appeared twice more on Capitol Hill during the next week to repeat the message of urgency.[6] "The American people do not have the luxury of unlimited time in erecting the necessary defenses to future terrorist acts," he told the House Committee on the Judiciary.[7] He lobbied Congress hard to get the chambers to vote on a measure that greatly expanded law enforcement authorities.

Legislators did not, at first, comply. By late September, there was skepticism that the bill could pass by the end of October because many leaders in both chambers resisted an expedited process that bypassed committee hearings. Opposition also grew over certain portions of the bill, some of which were eliminated and others revised. One that was dropped completely would have permitted the government to utilize material collected by foreign government wiretaps of U.S. citizens.[8] The legislative process was unorthodox. The House Judiciary Committee held one hearing and a markup, accepted amendments, and issued a favorable committee report that was approved by a vote of 36 to 0. The full House, however, moved to bar all amendments, except one that replaced the House bill with a new version that was closer to what the attorney general wanted. In the Senate, the Democratic leadership also fought against amendments, and no committee hearings were held. In the end, the bill that passed as the USA Patriot Act had not been read by the vast majority of members.[9] Representative Ron Paul (R-Tex.) described the process this way: "When the Patriot Act was passed, it was in the passions following 9/11, and that bill should never have been passed. It was brought up carelessly, casually, in a rapid manner. The bill that had been discussed in the Committee on the Judiciary was removed during the night before we voted. The full text of this bill is very difficult to find. I am convinced that very few members were able to review this bill before voting."[10]

A House colleague, David Obey (D-Wisc.), said he voted "present" and not "yes" on the Patriot Act because "we were asked to vote blind. . . . I did not feel that I knew enough about the contents of that bill to vote for it." He later voted yes when the bill returned from conference committee, because "I assumed the Justice Department would exercise those authorities with restraint. I was wrong."[11] Those worried about expanded government power may have felt placated by the attachment of expiration dates, called sunset provisions, to sixteen sections of the Patriot Act. The sunsets required Congress to reauthorize those sections by December 2005; otherwise they would expire. Ashcroft opposed such limits on the bill.[12] The bill passed Congress by a vote of 98 to 1 in the Senate and 357 to 66 in the House of Representatives. Bush signed it into law October 26, 2001.

Much of the Patriot Act was noncontroversial and widely supported, but the rush to passage began to seem reckless to some in Congress and led to a growing discontent. The administration soon realized that civil libertarians in both parties were concerned with some of the powers granted through the act. The White House liaison to Congress explained why he was watching congressional reaction to the law: "The left meets the right on those issues, so you always have to be concerned about them."[13] In time, opposition to the Patriot Act brought together such diverse groups as the American Civil Liberties Union, the American Conservative Union (ACU), and the Eagle Forum.[14] The ACLU and ACU later formed a coalition called Patriots to Restore Checks and Balances, headed by former Republican congressman Bob Barr, a critic of the act's broad surveillance powers.[15] Other Republican lawmakers joined Democrats in expressing concern about the new powers and their own oversight abilities. Representative Charles Eberle of Idaho warned against undercutting checks and balances: "People out here in the West are used to taking care of themselves. We don't like the government intruding on our constitutional rights."[16] The House of Representatives, led by a conservative named Butch Otter (R-Idaho), voted in July 2003, to defund the provision in the Patriot Act that permitted delayed notification searches; the vote was 309 to 118, with 113 Republicans in favor.[17] But congressional leaders kept the amendment out of the omnibus spending bill then going through Congress, effectively killing it. One former aide to Senator Strom Thurmond admonished that "we shouldn't be making suspects out of 280 million Americans."[18]

A common misconception is that the administration's most aggressive and controversial antiterrorism actions can be credited to the Patriot Act. In fact, as noted in the previous chapter, a number of them were undertaken through executive authority alone, particularly policy changes made by Ashcroft. In addition, other statutes, such as the Homeland Security Act, include provisions that could invite abuse.[19] Even so, the Patriot Act is worth examining because it and related rule changes enhance the centralization of authority in the White House, particularly those pertaining to domestic surveillance. The attorney general played a major role in framing and promoting the act.

Ashcroft Promoting the Patriot Act

Greater law enforcement powers, according to Ashcroft, were critical weapons in the fight against terrorism.[20] The Patriot Act, he declared, provides "tools to prevent terrorists from unleashing more death and destruction on our soil."[21] The department's preventive mission to stop a terrorist attack amplified the need for greater surveillance authority. Ashcroft explained: "The best friend of prevention is information. If you have the right information, you can prevent. Without that information, you can't."[22]

One of the Justice attorneys who helped to draft the criminal provisions in the Patriot Act explained the government's need for the new authorities: "Without understanding the challenge we face, one cannot understand the need for the measures law enforcement has employed. In the aftermath of September 11, we have an obligation to try to prevent future terrorist attacks. Our fundamental duty to protect America and its people requires no less. Yet it is equally important to emphasize that the investigative techniques the government is currently employing are all legal under the Constitution and applicable federal law as it existed both before and after September 11th."[23] The message of legality and restraint was advanced repeatedly by the Department of Justice. Even so, criticism grew.

Challenging the act's opponents, Ashcroft took the offensive, first establishing a Web site linked to the Justice Department home page, which posted a point-by-point rebuttal of "myths" that opponents had spread about the Patriot Act.[24] He also instructed U.S. attorneys to help build support for the law by writing opinion pieces for local newspapers and holding town hall meetings.[25] Then he took his message on the road in August and September 2003, telling audiences in eighteen cities that curtailing Patriot Act powers would "disconnect the dots; risk American lives; sacrifice liberty; and reject September 11th's lessons. . . . To abandon these tools would senselessly imperil American lives and American liberty."[26] It was a theme he continued throughout his monthlong tour around the country. "Make no mistake: our strategy, our tactics, are working. Our tools are effective," he told an audience in Philadelphia.[27]

The states on his itinerary may have been chosen in part because they were considered important to the president's reelection strategy the following year, particularly Pennsylvania, Ohio, and Michigan.[28] The tour appeared to be timed to undercut the growing grassroots movement to get municipal, county, and state governments to pass resolutions opposed to the act.[29] In addition, there was an increasing threat that Congress might curtail some of the act's powers.

Ashcroft's public appearances were carefully orchestrated. The events were by invitation only, closed to the general public. U.S. attorneys were encouraged to recruit uniformed police officers to attend and sit behind Ashcroft. That way, television cameras broadcasting his speeches would capture the image of the attorney general flanked by law enforcement forces.[30] But beyond the range of the cameras in every city were hundreds of protesters.[31] In Boston, for example, Ashcroft's audience of 150 was far outmatched by 1,200 protesters outside of Faneuil Hall.[32] Nor did his tour stop criticism. Representative Butch Otter admonished, "Instead of hitting the campaign trail, the attorney general should be listening to the concerns that many Americans have about some portions of the act."[33] The *New York Times* suggested that Ashcroft was engaging in a charm offensive to "spin-doctor" the problem of the Patriot Act. Instead, "Mr. Ashcroft should work with the law's critics to develop a law that respects Americans' fundamental rights."[34] The *Christian Science Monitor* also advocated a "more thoughtful, reasonable discussion of how the act can be adjusted to better balance security and liberty."[35]

Although the tour generated a lot of news coverage, it did not convince the doubters. In fact, it raised an additional question about the propriety of using government funds for what was—in effect—a public relations tour. Government officials since 1919 have been barred by law from using public funds for propaganda or lobbying the public unless authorized by Congress.[36] Representative John Conyers Jr. (D-Mich.) wrote a letter to the attorney general asking that he either explain how his actions—and those of the U.S. attorneys who participated—did not violate those restrictions or else "desist from further speaking engagements." Ashcroft's spokesperson, Barbara Comstock, replied that the tour had been reviewed and approved by department lawyers.[37] While Conyers's charge that U.S. attorneys illegally engaged in grassroots lobbying may justify further examination, Ashcroft's public speeches would be permissible under the law.[38] Regardless, the issue of unlawful lobbying diverted attention from his main message about the Patriot Act.

Ashcroft's efforts to sway public opinion may have had the opposite effect, by increasing public debate about the Patriot Act's substantial expansion of government powers. Just before the start of Ashcroft's campaign in mid-August, for example, 142 cities and counties, along with three states, had passed resolutions objecting to parts of the Patriot Act.[39] Less than a week later, the number of communities passing resolutions had increased to 150,[40] and by September 8, the number had grown to 160, including Durham, North Carolina, which held its vote after Ashcroft's visit.[41] By November, the Gallup polls also revealed a mounting public concern that restrictions on civil liberties had gone too far.[42]

The ACLU: Phantoms of Lost Liberty?

One of the most active opponents in the public arena, as well as in the courtroom, was the American Civil Liberties Union. The ACLU, extending beyond its traditional interest group strategy of litigation, developed an advertising campaign, sent letters to the attorney general, launched a Web site called "Safe and Free," issued press releases, filed Freedom of Information Act requests, organized coalitions with like-minded groups, and lobbied both the House and the Senate to reject the Patriot Act and later to amend it.[43] Ashcroft considered the ACLU one of the groups scaring "peace-loving people with phantoms of lost liberty,"[44] and Justice Department spokesman Mark Corallo accused it of fomenting fear.[45] Ashcroft clashed with the ACLU on other issues as well, including abortion, Internet censorship, and the death penalty. But the big battle between them was over the Patriot Act and other antiterrorism measures. The ACLU focused its public campaign on Sections 213, 215, and 505.

The first provision, Section 213, deals with delayed notification searches, also called "sneak and peek," because the subject is not notified until well after the search. Delayed notification is authorized when a court finds that there is "reasonable cause to believe that providing immediate notification of the execution of the warrant may have an adverse result." Applying to evidence of any criminal offense, this provision does not set deadlines for eventual notification; instead, it requires notification of a search warrant "within a reasonable period of its execution," with the possibility of court extensions for good cause.[46] The delay could, conceivably, be indefinite. This provision effectively voids the law enforcement tradition of "knock and announce," which developed not as a courtesy but as a safeguard that a search would be conducted legally; that is, the subject would have the opportunity to contact an attorney, examine the search warrant, and ensure that police officers did not overstep the boundaries of the warrant. The use of delayed notification searches has accelerated in recent years. From October 26, 2001, until April 1, 2003, federal law enforcement used the provision 47 times, or just under 3 times per month; from April 1, 2003, until January 31, 2005, it was used 108 times, an average of almost 5 times per month.[47]

The second Patriot Act provision opposed by the ACLU, Section 215, generated much of the bill's controversy. It permits the FBI to use warrants granted by the secret Foreign Intelligence Surveillance Court (FISA court) to search and seize "any tangible things . . . for an investigation to protect against international terrorism or clandestine intelligence activities." Tangible items could include membership and subscription lists, business and library documents, medical and psychiatric records, even genetic information, according to Ashcroft.[48] Anyone who provides those documents is barred from disclosing that fact to the subject of the search. The Patriot Act also exempts the provider from state privacy laws barring the disclosure of certain records.[49] FISA warrants will be examined in more detail later.

Section 505 also sparked opposition by the ACLU. With the innocuous title "Miscellaneous National Security Authorities," this section authorizes the FBI to use administrative subpoenas, called national security letters (NSLs), to collect certain records for the same purpose outlined in Section 215. In addition, like Section 215, it permanently bars those receiving these subpoenas from disclosing that fact.[50] The subjects of these searches are never informed. Administrative subpoenas do not require authorization by a grand jury, a judge, an administrative law judge, or even the FISA court unless a case goes to court. The standard used is based not on the Fourth Amendment but on "reasonableness." Agencies are bound only by internally promulgated guidelines.[51] The Patriot Act amended the Right to Financial Privacy section of the U.S. Code to read as follows:

Financial institutions, and officers, employees, and agents thereof, shall comply with a request for a customer's or entity's financial records made pursuant to this subsection by the Federal Bureau of Investigation when the Director of the Federal Bureau of Investigation (or the Director's designee in a position not lower than Deputy Assistant Director at Bureau headquarters or a Special Agent in Charge in a Bureau field office designated by the Director) certifies in writing to the financial institution that such records are sought for foreign counter intelligence purposes to protect against international terrorism or clandestine intelligence activities, provided that such an investigation of a United States person is not conducted solely upon the basis of activities protected by the first amendment to the Constitution of the United States.[52]

Searches conducted under this statute are not limited to suspected terrorists or spies, but anyone whose records could be relevant to a national security investigation. NSLs are more narrow in scope than regular warrants. For example, they cannot be used to reveal the actual content of an e-mail message, but they can be used to gather information about a user's screen name, Web sites visited, and other details useful for tracking.[53] Most administrative subpoenas in existence prior to the Patriot Act were limited in their reach, used to investigate fraud in Medicare and similar government programs. Now, NSLs can be requested in 335 different areas.[54] Ashcroft defended the new powers as applied to antiterrorism: "I believe that if those are requestable on the basis of health care fraud and other things, that for terrorism cases we would be well-served to have that same kind of authority."[55]

Citing the war on terrorism, Ashcroft also altered how the mass of data would be used. Under 1995 guidelines, records collected on a U.S. person—a citizen or legal resident—had to be destroyed if they were not relevant to the intelligence purpose of the search. Ashcroft rescinded those limits in 2003, instead authorizing the information to be added to a permanent data bank of public and consumer records accessible to government agencies and certain unspecified private entities. The bank, called the Investigative Data Warehouse, utilizes Oracle technology to mine the data for suspicious activity.[56] The Justice Department maintained secrecy about how often such subpoenas were issued after 9/11; however, in response to a Freedom of Information Act (FOIA) lawsuit brought by the ACLU, the FBI in March 2003 released five redacted pages of logs, suggesting active use.[57] The FBI's heavy reliance on national security letters became clear in November 2005, when the *Washington Post* reported that the agency had issued more than 30,000 of them annually under expanded Patriot Act powers.[58]

Librarians: Baseless Hysteria?

The American Library Association (ALA) has been an outspoken opponent of parts of the Patriot Act as well. The focus of its critique is Section 215, but Sections 214 and 216 also raise questions because they could affect the public access computers at many public libraries; they deal with pen register and with trap and trace authorities, respectively. The ALA Council passed a resolution in January 2002 to reaffirm "the principles of intellectual freedom" that it felt were at risk in the new legislation. The librarians' concern with Section 215 centered on its potential to invade readers' privacy, create a chilling effect on the right to read, and impose a gag on librarians who are barred from telling patrons of FBI searches.[59]

Wanting the aggregate data on the section's implementation, the ALA's legal defense unit, the Freedom to Read Foundation, filed a FOIA request in August 2002. When negotiations with the Justice Department failed to produce the information, the group filed a lawsuit with the ACLU, the American Booksellers Foundation for Free Expression, and the Electronic Privacy Information Center, seeking judicial enforcement of the request.[60] At the ALA's convention in January 2003, the organization passed a resolution denouncing Section 215 and urging its repeal. Two dozen state library associations followed suit in the next few months. While some librarians expressed no concerns with the Patriot Act, others instituted their own resistance measures, posting signs on computer screens and throughout the library warning patrons that the FBI could secretly monitor their reading habits. Some libraries destroyed computer sign-up sheets and circulation records once items were returned, and organized public educational programs.[61] The activism of librarians helped to spur the proliferation of anti–Patriot Act resolutions in communities around the country.[62]

Justice Department officials complained that librarians' fears were unfounded, based on misconceptions and misinformation. Ashcroft pointed out the need for a warrant and added that the FBI's heavy workload precluded agents from monitoring the reading habits of millions of Americans.[63] He and other Justice officials insisted that Section 215 "only gives agents the power to research the library habits of 'agents of a foreign power.'"[64] The attorney general became increasingly frustrated, and his frustration exploded in September 2003, as he finished his Patriot Act tour. He began a speech to the National Restaurant Association by observing, "Washington is involved in a debate where hysteria threatens to obscure the most important issues."[65] With scarcely hidden sarcasm, he elaborated:

> If you were to listen to some in Washington, you might believe the hysteria behind this claim: "Your local library has been surrounded by the FBI."

Agents are working round-the-clock. Like the X-Files, they are dressed in
raincoats, dark suits, and sporting sunglasses. They stop patrons and
librarians and interrogate everyone like Joe Friday. In a dull monotone they
ask every person exiting the library, "Why were you at the library? What
were you reading? Did you see anything suspicious?" According to these
breathless reports and baseless hysteria, some have convinced the American
Library Association that under the bipartisan Patriot Act, the FBI is not
fighting terrorism. Instead, agents are checking how far you have gotten on
the latest Tom Clancy novel. Now you may have thought with all this
hysteria and hyperbole, something had to be wrong. Do we at the Justice
Department really care what you are reading? No. . . . The hysteria is
ridiculous. Our job is not.[66]

The flippant and insulting tone of the speech was not well received by many
in the larger community. Press coverage accused Ashcroft of mocking librarians,[67] and throwing a "temper tantrum."[68] The speech also did not address
the substance of the librarians' concern, such as the extent to which patrons'
records were being accessed by law enforcement. Ashcroft faced mounting
pressure to prove that librarians' concerns were unfounded. He finally agreed
to declassify the data about implementation that he had fought so hard to
keep confidential. A few days after the National Restaurant Association
speech, he made the stunning announcement that Section 215 had been used
"zero times."[69] His announcement served to discredit those who had complained of the section's intrusiveness, enabling him to characterize them as
unnecessarily fearful and hysterical. But his answer raised other questions.
First, if the power had not been used to date, was it needed? Corallo, speaking
for the department, compared that question to arguing "that if a police officer
has never had to fire his weapon in 20 years on the force, we should take his
weapon away."[70] Second, why did Ashcroft's announcement not comport
with figures released elsewhere? For example, Associate Attorney General
Viet Dinh had already testified to Congress that FBI agents had visited about
50 libraries in the conduct of terrorism investigations, some visits at the invitation of suspicious librarians.[71] Ashcroft did not explain the source of the
disparity, but it appears to be the result of his careful phrasing of the announcement, which quietly excluded FBI library visits not conducted under
Section 215. This possibility appears confirmed by surveys conducted by the
ALA itself. One survey reported in 2003 found that of 900 public libraries
that responded, 550 had received requests for patrons' records from local and
federal law enforcement in the previous year.[72] Two years later, another study
reported that more than 200 libraries—of 500 responding—had received law
enforcement inquiries about their patrons since October 2001. The requests

were both formal and informal, made by local as well as federal law officers, probably working through the FBI's joint terrorism task forces. The ALA, which sponsored the study, extrapolated from those figures to estimate a total of 600 formal requests following 9/11. The ALA also noted that the figures could be an undercount, since some librarians who had received FISA warrants could have felt forbidden under the law from disclosing that fact.[73]

Despite Ashcroft's efforts to deflate the opposition, concern about Section 215 did not abate. In fact, its specific application to libraries and bookstores was specifically repudiated by the House of Representatives in June 2005 when an amendment passed 238 to 187 to require the FBI to get regular search warrants in those cases. That amendment—attached to an appropriations bill for Justice, Commerce, and State—was later removed during conference committee.[74] The next month, though, a bipartisan group of House members acted again, attaching a sunset requirement to Section 215 even as the chamber voted to reauthorize the Patriot Act. Of note is that the House did not reenact sunsets in fourteen of the original sixteen Patriot Act provisions that had them.[75]

The role of the Foreign Intelligence Surveillance Court in authorizing Section 215 searches formed a key part of the controversy about the Patriot Act. Proponents focused on the court's oversight function as a check against abuse, and opponents focused on its secrecy and deference to the chief executive. The attorney general's relationship to the court, and his broad interpretation of Section 215 powers, will be examined next.

The Foreign Intelligence Surveillance Court, which predates the Patriot Act by more than twenty years, originated as a check on government surveillance power. But the Patriot Act expanded the court's authority beyond foreign intelligence, which the Ashcroft Justice Department then aggressively applied in its preventive war on terrorism and crime. Composed of eleven semiretired federal district judges who meet in secret in a room in the Justice Department, the FISA court reviews and grants applications for warrants for electronic and physical surveillance for intelligence purposes. The applications are submitted by FBI personnel after they have been approved by either the attorney general or the deputy attorney general and reviewed by the Office of Intelligence Policy and Review (OIPR) in the Justice Department.[76] The OIPR advises the attorney general on national security policy and law, reviews and files all FISA applications with the FISA court, and provides legal advice on intelligence to other government agencies, including the FBI, CIA, and Departments of State and Defense.[77]

The FISA court had a long track record of granting the government's requests. Until 2002 and the case to be discussed here, it had rejected only one request for a warrant since its inception in 1979, and that was due to lack of jurisdiction.[78] In 2003 and 2004, a few more were denied, and a couple were modified and then approved. The court did report making substantive modifications in ninety-four of the applications before approving them in 2004.[79] The high approval rate suggests that the FISA court generally defers to claims of executive necessity. Critics have called the court little more than a rubber stamp, giving the government what it wants.[80] The court itself reported, "It was not uncommon for courts to defer to the expertise of the Executive Branch in matters of foreign intelligence collection."[81] The impression of deference should be tempered, however, because of the gatekeeper role played by the OIPR in some administrations, where it was known to eliminate weak applications before they reached the FISA court. Former attorney general Griffin Bell noted that, during his time at Justice, the person who headed the OIPR "wouldn't put anything before the FISA court unless there were good grounds for granting the request."[82] The OIPR also exercised an oversight role after the warrants were granted, over investigations that involved both foreign intelligence and criminal matters. It regularly attended meetings between the Criminal Division of the Justice Department and the FBI when there was a possibility that criminal and intelligence strands would become entangled. That practice ended with 9/11,[83] which may mean that the OIPR exercised less of this oversight function in the Ashcroft Justice Department.

Under the Fourth Amendment to the Constitution and Title III of the Omnibus Crime Control and Prevention Act of 1968, searches and seizures related to ordinary crime must be reasonable, as established by a judge's approval of a warrant based on probable cause. Although not defined in the Fourth Amendment, probable cause is commonly understood to mean a reasonable belief that a crime has been committed. The warrant also must specify the persons and places to be searched and the persons or things to be seized.[84]

In intelligence matters, the process historically has been less exacting. In fact, prior to passage of the Foreign Intelligence Surveillance Act in 1978, there were few limits. The attorney general could authorize intelligence-related searches with no outside oversight. During the 1950s, 1960s, and early 1970s, however, not just spies but also civil rights activists, antiwar dissidents, and others became the subjects of intrusive government surveillance. Senate hearings held by the Church Committee in 1976 revealed a long pattern of abuse, and pressure built to reform the process. Yet there remained compelling national security reasons not to hold foreign intelligence searches to the same rigorous standards as used in regular criminal investigations. In addition to a concern with national security and secrecy, searches conducted purely for intelligence purposes arguably would not implicate individual rights to the same degree, because the evidence would not be used in prosecutions for ordinary crime. With the backing of Griffin Bell, Jimmy Carter's law officer, the Foreign Intelligence Surveillance Act passed Congress in 1978.[85]

The new law included several constraints on government surveillance. First, the law established a special Foreign Intelligence Surveillance Court to evaluate FBI requests for warrants. The discretion would no longer be left in the hands of a single federal officer, the attorney general. In addition, regular procedures now governed the conduct of foreign intelligence searches. Probable cause still would be needed for a warrant, albeit a different standard, more easily met. Instead of probable cause to believe a crime had been committed, under FISA it meant "probable cause to believe that the [surveillance] technique is directed against a foreign power or an agent of a foreign power."[86] Nor was FISA a blank check for the FBI; agents seeking such warrants must state the facts and circumstances leading them to believe that foreign intelligence would be found on the premises to be searched, including an affirmation that the information sought could not be gathered through normal channels.[87] The law also distinguished between U.S. persons (defined as citizens and permanent legal residents) and all others. For U.S. persons, the intrusiveness of the search had to be minimized. That requirement was instituted because searches authorized under FISA could last for an extensive time period, utilize pervasive and invasive surveillance techniques, and result in secret evidence. If surveillance material pertaining to a U.S. person *could not* be related to foreign intelligence, the government was limited on how it could use that material, including its retention and dissemination to other agencies. In fact, such material was supposed to be discarded, destroyed, and otherwise made nonretrievable. That meant no use in ordinary, non-intelligence-related criminal prosecutions. Of course, the "could not" standard was a presumption still weighing heavily in favor of the government.[88] Finally, FISA erected barriers between agents in law enforcement and intelligence in order to ensure that law enforcement did not use intelligence warrants to create a shortcut around the Fourth Amendment. These "information screening walls" were not impermeable; the FISA court could authorize the sharing of intelligence information with prosecutors, since foreign agents were likely to be violating U.S. laws. However, information sharing was not permitted in the other direction, with law enforcement guiding counterintelligence investigations, because prosecutors could then use intelligence investigations to fish for information useful in ordinary criminal trials.[89] This was the wall on which Ashcroft blamed the intelligence failures behind 9/11.

Bell explained that the idea for the court had originated with Edward Levi, his predecessor at Justice. Both men believed the judiciary had to be involved in the intelligence surveillance review process in order to restore public trust shaken in the 1970s.[90]

Following passage of the act, President Reagan issued Executive Order 12333, which delegated a major responsibility to the attorney general to oversee the conduct of intelligence activities. It is under this order that the attorney general promulgates guidelines for using FISA warrants.[91] There were notable successes; this was the process in place when FISA warrants led to the capture of the 1993 World Trade Center bombers and U.S. spy Aldrich Ames.[92] But when September 11 occurred, questions exploded about intelligence and communication failures.

Ashcroft did not have to wait for new legislation before he could act, even though he implied this in his testimony before the 9/11 commission. Under FISA, he already had the authority to issue emergency intelligence surveillance warrants, which can last for seventy-two hours before being authorized by the FISA court. Ashcroft aggressively utilized emergency warrants. In the first eighteen months after 9/11, he issued more than 170; only 47 had been issued in the two preceding decades.[93] But he also wanted new powers to strengthen intelligence gathering and sharing. The Patriot Act provided them—including Section 215—in Title II, "Enhanced Surveillance Procedures."

One of the fiercest battles in the Senate over the Patriot Act reportedly dealt with proposed changes in the section altering the standard for authorizing a FISA search. FISA permitted surveillance "for the purpose of obtaining foreign intelligence information."[94] Ashcroft and the administration lobbied hard to change "the purpose" to "a purpose"; this language would have permitted a broad application of FISA wiretaps. The Senate balked.[95] In the final bill "the purpose" was replaced with "a significant purpose." The new phrase implies that foreign intelligence gathering remains the FISA court's chief mandate. However, according to Michael Chertoff, assistant attorney general at the time, this language was open enough to give the administration the leeway it sought to wiretap under FISA. In fact, Ashcroft interpreted the change to mean that FISA could now "be used primarily for a law enforcement purpose, so long as a significant foreign intelligence purpose remains."[96]

Ashcroft made this interpretation in guidelines he issued on March 6, 2002. Citing national security needs, he consciously altered earlier policies separating law enforcement and intelligence—the so-called wall. His guidelines expressly authorized information sharing between intelligence agents and criminal investigators and encouraged criminal investigators to offer advice and make recommendations about intelligence investigations.[97] He not only permitted criminal investigators to have routine access to foreign intelligence information but also permitted them to help direct intelligence investigations, with an eye toward prosecution. Such communication would no longer require FISA court approval.[98] The change was necessary, he felt, because the earlier legal interpretation had created "a culture of law enforcement inhibition [that] prevented communication and coordination."[99] He believed the wall was the direct cause of the 9/11 attacks. He told the bipartisan commission investigating September 11: "In 1995, the Justice Department designed a system that was destined to fail. By 2000, the Justice Department was so addicted to the wall it actually opposed legislation to lower the wall. Finally, the USA Patriot Act tore down this wall between our intelligence and law enforcement personnel in 2001."[100] As noted earlier, his department had also endorsed the so-called wall addiction prior to 9/11. The Patriot Act itself did not dismantle the wall, but the change in language provided the avenue for Ashcroft to do so in his March 6 guidelines.

The issue came to a head on May 17, 2002, when the Justice Department brought a request before the FISA court. Breaking from a long history of deference, the FISA court struck down key parts of Ashcroft's guidelines. The FISA judges began with a discussion about the statutory requirement to minimize the impact of surveillance on U.S. persons. Then the court addressed the long-standing use of "information screening walls" in cases where intelligence and criminal investigations overlapped. The court then took note of the Justice Department's confession in September 2000 that there had been misstatements and omissions on seventy-five FBI affidavits filed in support of applications related to major terrorist attacks. The judges blamed those errors on "information sharing and unauthorized disseminations to criminal investigators and prosecutors." The government had also misused the law when, on at least four occasions, intelligence agents had shared intelligence information with prosecutors in New York.[101] Concerned about further misuse, the judges ruled that Ashcroft's guidelines conflicted with the Patriot Act's language and intent because they encouraged information sharing from prosecutors to intelligence.[102] For the court, presiding judge Royce Lamberth wrote:

> Law enforcement officials shall not make recommendations to intelligence officials concerning the initiation, operation, continuation or expansion of FISA searches or surveillances. Additionally, the FBI and the Criminal Division shall ensure that law enforcement officials do not direct or control the use of the FISA procedures to enhance criminal prosecution. . . . The

purpose of minimization procedures as defined in the Act is . . . to protect the privacy of Americans in these highly intrusive surveillances and searches, "consistent with the need of the United States to obtain, produce and disseminate foreign intelligence information."[103]

Ashcroft's guidelines, they concluded, would have to be modified.

The decision was classified, but in August 2002 the presiding judge released the opinion at the request of the Senate Judiciary Committee after the attorney general had refused to do so. It was an unprecedented move, since no prior decisions had ever been released.[104] The Justice Department opposed the release.[105]

Meanwhile, the Justice Department submitted the issue again to the FISA court in July, using guidelines that still had not been modified. When rebuffed again, the department appealed. To hear the appeal, the Foreign Intelligence Surveillance Court of Review met for the first time in September 2002. It was composed of three judges from the Circuit Courts of Appeal, appointed to serve on the panel by Chief Justice William Rehnquist.[106] The review court's proceedings were so secret that two organizations seeking to file friend-of-the-court briefs in opposition—the ACLU and the National Association of Criminal Defense Lawyers—had some initial difficulty discovering the appropriate process. In the end, their briefs were accepted and considered by the appeals court. But the only party to argue before the court was the government. Solicitor General Theodore Olson laid out three points: that prior to the Patriot Act, there was no requirement for a wall to separate foreign intelligence and criminal prosecutions; that, even if there had been, the Patriot Act eliminated it; and that the restrictions imposed by the FISA court "are so intrusive into the operation of the Department of Justice as to exceed the constitutional authority of Article III judges";[107] in other words, the FISA court had violated the separation of powers.

Issuing its ruling on November 18, 2002, the court of review overturned the FISA court. It decided that the 1978 act did not preclude the use of information gathered in a foreign intelligence investigation from a criminal prosecution, although warrants could not be used to gather criminal evidence if the ordinary crime was not "inextricably intertwined with foreign intelligence crimes."[108] Further, analyzing Patriot Act amendments to FISA, the review court found that the FISA court had no basis for limiting contact between prosecutors and intelligence officials. In fact, the court ruled, "the FISA court may well have exceeded the constitutional bounds that restrict an Article III court. The FISA court asserted authority to govern the internal organization and investigative procedures of the Department of Justice which are the province of the Executive Branch and Congress."[109] Finding that FISA warrants were consistent with the Fourth Amendment, the judges provided the government with a complete victory. Under FISA, the decision was not reviewable by the U.S. Supreme Court, where it might have been subject to greater public scrutiny.

The Justice Department applied the new powers with vigor. Ashcroft told senators in March 2003 that government agents had obtained 18,000 subpoenas and search warrants and more than 1,000 national security surveillance warrants to track "hundreds and hundreds" of suspected terrorists.[110] Supporters of a more aggressive application of FISA authority argued that the bureaucracy had been too timid in seeking the power before September 11. They pointed to the case of Zacarias Moussaoui: a cautious FBI failed to seek FISA authorization to search his laptop computer, believing that such a search would breach the "wall" between law enforcement and intelligence.[111] FBI agents themselves reportedly hesitated to bring requests to the FISA court if there was a chance of denial.[112]

Ironically, the dismantling of the wall that separated law enforcement and intelligence agencies may complicate antiterrorism prosecutions, a fact that came to light in the Moussaoui case. If intelligence agents are "actively involved" with a prosecution, defense attorneys may insist that they produce any exculpatory evidence in their files,[113] a claim raised by Moussaoui and his attorneys, as discussed in the previous chapter.

The use of FISA warrants increased in recent years. In the late 1990s, the Reno Justice Department sought and received an average of 820 FISA warrants annually.[114] By 2000, according to Ashcroft, the number had arisen to 1,005,[115] with 932 warrants in 2001.[116] By 2002, the number had increased to 1,228.[117] A significant jump occurred by 2003, with 1,727 applications and 1,724 approvals.[118] In 2004, there were 1,758 applications and 1,754 approvals.[119]

Throughout this time, top Ashcroft aides sought to reassure the Senate and the public that FISA warrants could not be abused, that the authority was limited. Justice spokeswoman Barbara Comstock, chiding *Time* magazine for inaccuracies in its May 12, 2003, coverage of the department's antiterrorism actions, wrote about the government's surveillance and search powers: "If the matter concerns national security, the government obtains this court order from the FISA court after demonstrating, through a showing of probable cause that the subject of the surveillance or search is a foreign power or an agent of a foreign power—e.g. that he 'knowingly engages' in 'sabotage or international terrorism' or is preparing to do so, on behalf of an international terrorist group."[120] Similarly, David Kris, deputy associate attorney general, told the Senate Judiciary Committee that a "United States person—a citizen or green card holder—cannot be an 'agent of a foreign power' under the rubric of terrorism, and therefore cannot be a

FISA target, unless the government shows, and the court finds, probable cause that he is 'knowingly engaged in' or 'preparing' to engage in 'international terrorism' for or on behalf of a foreign power."[121] Kris described the probable cause standard as "probable cause that the person is engaged in clandestine intelligence activities, international terrorism, sabotage, or related activity."[122]

However, both Comstock and Kris misread Section 215's language: searches are not limited to agents of a foreign power, but to "an investigation to protect against international terrorism or clandestine intelligence activities." In other words, the individual under surveillance is not necessarily the target of the investigation. The actual target might be a family member or friend. Furthermore, evidence of criminal wrongdoing collected on a nonterrorist suspect subject to surveillance would no longer be discarded, as it would have under the earlier rules. Comstock and Kris also choose to ignore more troubling elements of Section 215. For example, while investigations of U.S. persons cannot be "conducted solely upon the basis of activities protected by the First Amendment," such as pure speech, that does not deter investigations when other elements are present. Finally, the term "U.S. persons" as used here is very narrow, applying only to citizens and permanent resident aliens. Of note is that the term is more inclusive when used in other government documents, even in executive orders pertaining to terrorism, where it refers to "any U.S. citizen, permanent resident alien, entity organized under the laws of the U.S., or any person in the United States."[123] That definition would include international students and other legal residents who do not have green card status. As applied to FISA warrants, however, these people are vulnerable to sweeping surveillance, sometimes on the basis of scant initial evidence. The Justice Department's investigation and prosecution of Sami al-Hussayen dramatizes how longtime foreign nationals who are in the country legally can become the subject of FISA searches when there are no more than circumstantial or tangential ties to suspicious organizations.

The Idaho Webmaster Case

Sami al-Hussayen was a Saudi graduate student in the United States for almost a decade at the time of his arrest in Idaho in 2003. He was not a permanent resident alien, and therefore not a "U.S. person." Few legal limits restrained the government in his case.

Al-Hussayen was a doctoral candidate in computer science at the University of Idaho when he came to the attention of federal authorities. A bank teller had reported suspicions about an Arab student. Although the bank account in question was not his, investigators continued to focus on him.[124] The government found it suspicious that he volunteered to help various Muslim organizations around the country with their Web sites. To investigate further, the FBI sought and received a FISA warrant because there was insufficient evidence to establish probable cause under the Fourth Amendment. Over the next year, about 20,000 e-mails and 9,000 phone calls of his were monitored.[125]

When al-Hussayen was arrested in February 2003, Ashcroft announced that he was part of a fanatical and fierce threat to Americans, and that his prosecution would reveal how al Qaeda fund-raising was accomplished.[126] The initial indictment, as with many post-9/11 detainees, charged him with two immigration law violations: failure to disclose his connection to one of the Muslim groups he helped—although the group was not listed as having terrorist links—and lying on his visa application when he said that he entered the country solely to study, but then volunteered to work on the Web sites.[127] In a superseding indictment, the government additionally charged him with providing material support for terrorists—"expert advice"—when he set up and operated more than a dozen Web sites, including ones used by two radical Saudi sheikhs.[128] Section 805 of the Patriot Act added "expert advice" to the list of activities considered to be "material support."[129] He was also accused of designing Web sites to funnel donations to groups and charities alleged to have links to terrorism.[130] In addition to eleven immigration charges, he faced three terrorism charges, each carrying possible fifteen-year sentences.[131] Al-Hussayen was the first person charged under this provision of the Patriot Act, and the Justice Department made his case a priority.[132]

The trial lasted seven weeks. Prosecutor Kim Lindquist said, "Al-Hussayen provided the linkage to create the platform and then the content to advocate extreme jihad" through the Web sites. The law, Lindquist argued, did not require al-Hussayen to intentionally aid terrorists, only that he knew that his Web sites brought donations or recruits to terrorist groups.[133] However, according to jurors who reviewed boxes of evidence gathered under the FISA search, nothing established that the Web sites actually resulted in donations or recruits for terrorism, or that al-Hussayen agreed with the messages posted on some of them.[134] Furthermore, even if he had agreed, his beliefs and speech to that effect would be protected under the First Amendment, since there was no evidence of an imminent threat of lawless action, the standard established in the landmark free speech case, *Brandenburg v. Ohio*.[135]

The jury acquitted al-Hussayen of all three terrorism-related charges.[136] One juror afterward called the terrorism charges "a real stretch." While acquitting him of three of the immigration violations, the jury deadlocked on the other eight. In the end, the government permitted him to return to Saudi

Arabia rather than conduct another trial on the eight counts. He had spent about eighteen months in jail.[137]

The material support section of the Patriot Act, which also arose in the Lynne Stewart prosecution, led civil liberties and Muslim groups to call the trial "a confrontation between the First Amendment and the war on terror." The phrase "expert advice" was too vague and could cover constitutionally protected speech.[138]

Idaho's U.S. attorney, Tom Moss, denied that the jury's acquittal was a repudiation of the Patriot Act. "This case had some connection to the Patriot Act, but most of this case could have been prosecuted if the Patriot Act had never happened," he said.[139] However, he did not specify how a search warrant would have been granted or a material support charge established without the Patriot Act.

Fighting Garden-Variety Crime

Ashcroft asserted in 2004 that "Congress intended that the Patriot Act be used to save lives from terrorist attacks."[140] Yet he ensured that the law was immediately put to use to pursue ordinary criminals as well. Several Patriot Act provisions are not limited to terrorism, including the provision for the delayed notification of searches and seizures, which explicitly applies to any criminal investigation.

This led one liberal critic to argue that the Justice Department had "used terrorism as a guise to expand law enforcement powers in areas that are totally unrelated to terrorism."[141] This deception may have been the case prior to the Patriot Act's enactment, but once it was passed, Ashcroft made little attempt to hide what the department was doing. Despite questions about the adverse impact on Fourth Amendment rights in particular, he saw no constitutional difficulty in extending the reach of the new antiterrorism law to ordinary crime. As in so many areas, he was unconvincible and unapologetic: "I believe history will record that in the first decade of the 21st century, the men and women of our nation's Justice community embraced the challenge of defending freedom through the law; and as their responsibilities have increased, so too have their accomplishments. Asked to defend America's freedom from terror, they have given us new freedom from violent crime, drug abuse, gun crime, and corporate crime."[142]

On a number of occasions, Ashcroft reported how the Patriot Act was useful in a wide range of criminal investigations. In a "Report from the Field" issued in 2004, he stated, "The Patriot Act has . . . allowed us to go after violent criminals who would harm the innocent."[143] He then announced various successful investigations. In one, he said, Section 212—"the emergency disclosure of electronic communications to protect life and limb"—had been instrumental in the rescue of a thirteen-year-old girl lured out and abducted by a man she had met online. When an anonymous caller told the FBI that he had chatted online with someone claiming credit for the crime, agents used the Internet service provider to trace the kidnapper. Ashcroft announced that Section 210 had been used to arrest and prosecute a Kentucky couple on child pornography charges. That section deals with "the scope of subpoenas for records of electronic communications." Federal agents received information from the couple's Internet service provider that served as the basis for a search warrant for their house, where the evidence was seized.[144] In the past, such evidence might have been inadmissible in court, since the warrant for the house stemmed from a warrantless search of their Internet account. Ashcroft was vague about the necessity of using Section 210 to conduct the house search; while he noted that the regular Fourth Amendment process was "unlikely" to have permitted a search, he did not rule it out.[145] In sum, "hundreds of non-terrorism cases" had relied on Patriot Act powers, according to a Justice Department report to Congress. Among them were cases against an identity thief, a drug distributor, an investor who bilked millions from clients and then fled to Belize, and a young woman who planted threatening notes on a cruise ship in an effort to get it to turn around so she could be back with her boyfriend.[146] In one memorably named case called Operation G-String, Patriot Act subpoena power was used to access the financial records of two Las Vegas strip club owners suspected of bribing local officials.[147] In another example, expanded Customs authority led to nine money-laundering investigations of Latin American officials.[148] These suspects did not fit the "violent criminals" profile presented by the attorney general. Ordinary procedures may have been adequate in many of these cases, and questions remain about the necessity of bypassing them.

The Patriot Act provision relating to money laundering may be especially susceptible to wider nonterrorist application. Money laundering means using legal cover to hide illicit funds. To follow terrorist funds, the Patriot Act provides broad money-laundering surveillance authority. The FBI can submit a suspect's name to the Treasury Department, which then can order banks and other financial institutions to look for a match in their records. When a suspect is matched to a bank, the government issues a subpoena for those records. Previously, a search warrant could be issued only to a particular bank and only if there was already evidence that a suspect was a customer there.[149] But the authority is not limited to terrorism cases. According to one 2003 report, in at least 4,500 cases with no apparent connection to terrorism, the FBI relied on this process instead of grand jury subpoenas, including Operation

G-String.[150] In all, two-thirds of the searches conducted under that provision had "no apparent terrorism connection," including cases involving tax fraud, postage fraud, food stamp fraud, and counterfeiting.[151]

As noted earlier, even crimes that appear to be disconnected from terrorism on the surface could be perpetrated on behalf of terrorist causes. Generally, such cases are classified as terrorism-related by the Justice Department. But Justice officials do not deny that Patriot Act powers are being applied to fight ordinary crime. Said spokesman Mark Corallo: "There are many provisions in the Patriot Act that can be used in the general criminal law. And I think any reasonable person would agree that we have an obligation to do everything we can to protect the lives and liberties of Americans from attack, whether it's from terrorists or garden-variety criminals."[152] While the war framework was responsible for the creation of these broad new powers, they are extending well beyond the domestic antiterrorism effort. The result has been a change in domestic law enforcement. Noted one news report, "The law and a series of related policies issued by Attorney General John Ashcroft have blurred historic legal differences in the way the government treats suspected terrorists and handles ordinary citizens."[153]

The Administrative Arsenal in the War on Terrorism

Statutory authorities alone did not create the law enforcement mechanisms used to investigate suspected terrorists and criminals. In response to 9/11, Ashcroft initiated new programs and promulgated new rules to increase government authority and ability to act. An attorney general has a substantial range of action here, with no oversight except to the extent that the president, Congress, or the courts hold him or her accountable. Ashcroft, as described elsewhere, issued guidelines for compliance with the Freedom of Information Act,[154] and instructed his chief immigration judge to alter the policy regarding public access to immigration hearings.[155] He also worked with the secretaries of state and homeland security, as well as the FBI and CIA directors, to create the Terrorist Screening Center, to consolidate information about possible terrorists and produce a comprehensive terrorist watch list.[156]

Regarding the practices of the FBI, the attorney general has particular power. No single, overarching statute governs the FBI, giving the attorney general wide latitude to establish guidelines in the areas not fully covered by law. Such guidelines are not subject to the customary publication and public comment procedure followed in administrative rule-making. They rest solely on the attorney general's judgment, within the parameters of the relevant statute. Administratively, Ashcroft reorganized the FBI,[157] and promulgated new guidelines to govern FBI national security investigations and foreign intelligence collection,[158] FBI undercover operations,[159] and FBI domestic investigations.[160]

Edward Levi in the 1970s was the first to issue guidelines governing how the FBI handled domestic investigations, delineating the scope, techniques, and objectives that were permissible when the government turned its surveillance eye on citizens.[161] When Levi entered office, public trust in the executive branch was low, due to revelations about White House use of investigations to harass political opponents. His FBI guidelines were noted for their emphasis on restraint and rights. Subsequent law officers issued guidelines as well; the ones in effect on September 11 had been adopted in 1989.[162]

Immediately after the 9/11 attacks, Ashcroft authorized the FBI to waive the existing investigative guidelines if necessary to stop another terrorist attack. He reported that, while FBI agents did use the authority, "I am disappointed that it was not used more widely."[163] He then instituted a review of the 1989 guidelines and made comprehensive revisions with the goal of getting the bureau to "investigate more vigorously."[164] The new guidelines were unveiled on May 30, 2002.[165] They institutionalized his aggressive preemptive approach to conducting investigations into both terrorism and crime. The goal of the policy change, he said, was to "free the field agents—the brave men and women on the front lines—from the bureaucratic, organizational and operational restrictions and structures that hindered them from doing their jobs effectively."[166]

Ashcroft's guidelines made multiple specific changes. First, they delegated authority to field agents so that they would not have to receive approval from FBI headquarters in order to start an investigation. Second, consistent with prevention, they established stronger investigative authority at earlier stages. For example, the new policy permitted any investigative technique in a preliminary inquiry except opening mail and nonconsensual electronic surveillance. Third, agents could jump to a higher level of investigation immediately—from checking leads to a full investigation—if the threshold standard was met. Under the previous policy, they had to go through a multistep process before commencing a full-scale investigation. Fourth, the threshold for triggering an investigation was lowered. While never required to show probable cause, agents in the past had to show some "objective, factual basis" before they could conduct full investigations. Now full investigations could be started if there was a "reasonable indication" that a criminal act would occur in the future. Fifth, speech, alone, could trigger an investigation if "statements advocate criminal activity or indicate an apparent intent to engage in a crime." The guidelines do admonish that investigations "not be based solely on activities protected by the First Amendment or on the lawful exercise of other rights," but advocacy of unlawful behavior could be investigated unless "there is no prospect of harm."[167] Sixth, to detect or prevent terrorism, agents were permitted to draw on "all lawful sources of information," such as surfing the Internet for suspicious activity, visiting mosques and other meeting places open to the public, attending political rallies, and infiltrating organizations. Seventh, the FBI was empowered to establish a database of information gathered through its preliminary and full investigations, and another database drawing on "pertinent information from any source permitted by law," such as consumer records, FISA intelligence, and commercial databases. In addition to the federal government, those databases are accessible by local, state, and tribal law enforcement officers.[168]

The Justice Department said the new authorities were being used with restraint. Reporting to Congress a year after the adoption of the 2002 guidelines, the department said that "fewer than 10 FBI field offices had visited mosques as part of their investigations." In the same report, Justice said that—with the wall between intelligence and criminal investigations gone—it now could examine 4,500 intelligence files related to terrorism to see if criminal charges were appropriate.[169] A *New York Times* editorial conceded that—even while "the potential for abuse still exists"—"the Justice Department has been relatively restrained in the use of the new terrorism-fighting powers."[170]

The changes in the FBI investigation guidelines raised concerns, however, because they appeared to invite greater government surveillance into private lives and lawful activity. Individuals and groups opposed to government policies could become targets of government investigations. Some evidence supports that allegation. In July 2004, the Justice Department began a criminal investigation into critical Internet postings of the names of the Republican convention delegates.[171] On another occasion, federal officials issued grand jury subpoenas to four Iowa peace activists and a subpoena to Drake University for records about a National Lawyer's Guild conference held there; all were later withdrawn.[172] The FBI has set up files on dozens of political organizations, including the American Indian Movement of Colorado and an antiwar coalition, United for Peace and Justice.[173] In addition, the FBI in recent years compiled files of 1,173 pages on the ACLU and 2,383 pages on the environmental group Greenpeace, according to documents released through a FOIA lawsuit. Officials with the bureau insisted that they were not monitoring "the political activities of any activist groups" and were interested only in monitoring potentially disruptive political protests and criminal activity. But the two groups contested that assertion. The ACLU focuses on litigation, not political action. The executive director,

Anthony Romero, wondered, "Why would the FBI collect almost 1,200 pages on a civil rights organization engaged in lawful activity? What justification could there be, other than political surveillance of lawful First Amendment activities?"[174] Greenpeace executive director John Passacantando said the revelation about the FBI surveillance "suggests they're just attempting to stifle the voices of their critics."[175]

The question of a potential conflict between FBI practices and the First Amendment was examined by the Office of Legal Counsel in 2004, in response to a request by Inspector General Glenn Fine. The OLC evaluated two FBI bulletins that advised law enforcement to watch out for "protest tactics" at a large antiwar rally in late October 2003 and a large free-trade protest one month later. In addition to listing various unlawful activities as "possible indicators of protest activity," the bulletins listed marches, Internet recruitment, fund-raising and coordination, and "intimidation of law enforcement through videotaping," activities that are legal. If they saw any potentially illegal acts, officers were instructed to inform the nearest FBI joint terrorism task force (JTTF), a unit in each FBI district of local and federal officers. After reviewing the bulletins, the OLC concluded that they did not violate free-speech rights. The guidance provided was generic, not linked to the specific content of the speech. Further, "illegal acts and terrorist threats" do not have First Amendment protection, nor do actions conducted in the public sphere have any privacy expectation. Any chilling effect on the willingness of people to participate in the demonstrations would be minimal. Finally, officers were not instructed to stop such activity but simply to inform a JTTF.[176] The OLC opinion, regrettably, did not address the involvement of a joint terrorism task force in monitoring illegal—but not terrorist—political activity. The JTTF's role here feeds concerns raised about the vagueness of the definition of domestic terrorism (see p. 174). Furthermore, the FBI bulletins used the phrases "potentially illegal" and "possible terrorist threat," an adverb and adjective missing from the analysis presented in the OLC memo. Those are important words in terms of assessing a First Amendment chilling effect because whereas a crime might be easy for officers to spot at a protest rally, a "potential" crime involves a judgment call. And that increases the likelihood of an overzealous response and chilled speech.

Conclusion

Until the day he left office, Ashcroft insisted that the Patriot Act had made the nation safer, ensuring that another attack did not occur. The law enforcement powers were not abused, he insisted. Instead of taking concerns seriously,

The Difficulty of Defining "Terrorism"

While federal law presents multiple definitions of terrorism, the one used for domestic terrorism in the Patriot Act is particularly broad. It reads as follows:

The term domestic terrorism means activities that:

    A. involve acts dangerous to human life that are a violation of the criminal laws of the United States or of any State;

    B. appear to be intended

        a. to intimidate or coerce a civilian population

        b. to influence the policy of a government by intimidation or coercion, or

        c. to affect the conduct of a government by mass destruction, assassination, or kidnapping; and

    C. occur primarily within the territorial jurisdiction of the United States.[1]

Any criminal action that threatens human life and that "appears to be intended" to intimidate or coerce civilians could be defined as domestic terrorism. According to some legal observers, this language could elevate ordinary "barroom brawls" or domestic altercations to the level of a national security threat.[2] Furthermore, an organization engaged in political action could be classified terrorist if any of its members engaged in reckless or violent behavior that threatens others. The attorney general alone classifies domestic groups as terrorist, with no effective avenue of judicial appeal.

As of 2002, the list of domestic terrorist groups included not only al Qaeda but "radical animal rights and environmental groups, violent anti-government groups and white Supremacists and threats against the information infrastructure."[3] The groups so defined could change in a different administration. Explaining his concern with the vagueness of the language, Republican congressman Butch Otter observed that antiabortion groups someday could be labeled "domestic terrorists."[4] Even if not a member, any person who advocates or provides support for such a group—including "expert advice"—could be prosecuted on a charge of material support for terrorism.

1. USA Patriot Act, Section 802, PL 107–56, 2001; Terrorism, 18 USCS 2331 (2005).

2. Mindy Finn, "Congress Expands Definition of Terrorism in New Law," *Congressional Quarterly On-line,* Nov. 20, 2001.

3. FY 2002 Performance Report, Strategic Objective 1.1, p. 2 of the annual report. www.usdoj.gov/ag/annualreports/pr2002.

4. Michael Isikoff and Daniel Klaidman, "Ashcroft's Campaign to Shore Up the Patriot Act," *Newsweek,* Aug. 25, 2003, 6.

however, he dismissed them as trivial. He told one audience that they only need fear the Patriot Act "if you are spending a lot of time surveilling nuclear power plants with your al Qaeda pals" or "if you have cave-side dinners with a certain terrorist thug named bin Laden . . . [and] enjoy swapping recipes for chemical weapons from your 'Joy of Jihad' cookbook."[177] Later, he may have realized the ineffectiveness of such ridicule. On leaving office, he said his greatest failure had been not explaining the Patriot Act fully to the public. Even then, he asserted that time would prove he had been right, that the measure was not a threat to the Constitution. Ashcroft and the president regularly pointed to successes—indictments and prosecutions—in the war on terrorism to which the Patriot Act contributed. The attorney general did not mention the other achievement of the Patriot Act, the significant expansion of executive power.

The new antiterrorism authorities created through statute and subsequent administrative actions have enhanced the potential for executive surveillance of political opponents. Many of the standards guiding surveillance are low enough, and subjective enough, that the danger of political spying, so prevalent in the 1960s and early 1970s, has returned. Given the subjective elements in the Patriot Act's definition of domestic terrorism, this risk is compounded. In addition, the guarantees of the Fourth Amendment appear more fragile in an environment where "garden variety" crime is perceived as a danger tantamount to terrorism, and therefore worthy of extraordinary executive measures. Even conceding the administration's assertion that abuse has not occurred and restraint has been exercised, these new law enforcement authorities provide the mechanisms through which a future president—acting under the commander-in-chief powers—could claim a virtually unchecked authority to investigate dissidents.

The Patriot Act does include oversight provisions. Under Section 1001, for example, the Office of Inspector General (OIG) in the Justice Department is charged with investigating complaints regarding civil rights abuses by department employees and issuing a semiannual report to the House and Senate judiciary committees.[178] Five such reports were issued between July 2002 and September 2004. This does not include the explosive report on the treatment of detainees in the wake of 9/11, already discussed in chapter 6.[179] In other sections, Congress is empowered to receive information necessary for oversight. Section 215, for example, charges the attorney general to provide the congressional intelligence and judiciary committees with information pertaining to FISA warrants.[180] The problem for Congress, as noted in chapter 5, is getting the attorney general to comply fully with requests for information, so that genuine oversight can occur.

The next chapter will explore the difficulty of exercising a meaningful check on presidential power when secrecy surrounds so many aspects of the war on terrorism.

8   Secrecy and Accountability

The presidency of George W. Bush has been portrayed as having "a penchant for secrecy" that bypasses that of previous administrations, frustrating journalists, scholars, and a bipartisan group of legislators.[1] It is "an epidemic of official secrecy," said Steven Aftergood of the Federation of American Scientists. "There's just a resistance to disclosure that has characterized this administration."[2] Larry Klayman, the head of the conservative group Judicial Watch, called it "even more secretive than the Nixon administration. They don't believe the American people or Congress have any right to information."[3] Some members of Congress shared the view that government secrecy was on the rise.[4] "It's been a very non-transparent system," said Senator Jeff Bingaman (D-N.M.),[5] which has made congressional oversight difficult. Legislators complained about the administration's tight hold on unclassified as well as classified national security information, "without scrutiny and input from Congress or the public."[6]

White House press secretary Ari Fleischer contested the view that the administration was not transparent: "The president is dedicated to an open government, a responsive government, while he fully exercises the authority of the executive branch."[7] Yet Fleischer's comment is revealing because it frames the issue of transparency within the larger context of presidential authority. The need to protect executive powers from encroachment was the key rationale used when the White House refused to release a pre-9/11 president's daily brief,[8] documents related to the role Enron played on the vice president's energy task force in 2001,[9] and memos sought by the House of Representatives relating to Janet Reno's decision not to request a special prosecutor, which the president claimed executive privilege to shield.[10]

September 11 provided the overt cause for greater secrecy, but the Bush administration's concern with disclosures and confidentiality predated the attacks. From the start, it engaged in an active classification of documents. In the year ending September 30, 2001, for example, 18 percent more documents were classified than in the previous year.[11] The shift toward nondisclosure is evident in the administration's efforts to delay the release of the presidential records of the Reagan administration. Under the 1978 Presidential

Records Act and an executive order issued in 1989, the records—including the papers of Vice President George H. W. Bush—were due for release in January 2001.[12] But the new Bush White House extended the deadline for their release three times, with memos sent to the U.S. archivist in March, June, and August 2001.[13] The delay was formalized after the 9/11 strikes, when Bush revoked the earlier executive order and issued a new one that established much more restrictive procedures for implementing the Presidential Records Act.[14] Historians, archivists, journalists, and civic groups reacted with alarm to the new procedures, asserting that they undermined the law.[15] Public and congressional efforts to challenge the executive order ended when the administration announced in December 2003 that almost all of the 68,000 pages relating to the Reagan administration would be released after all.[16]

Secrecy was driven in part by the administration's passionate dislike of news leaks. President Bush had long fought unauthorized leaks, starting in his father's administration.[17] Capitol Hill, he believed, was particularly leaky. Following the terrorist strikes, he issued a memorandum to limit the number of government officials who could do briefings on classified or law enforcement information and the number of congressmen who could attend. Only the directors of the FBI and CIA and the secretaries of justice, state, treasury, and defense, or their designees, would be permitted to brief Congress, and only the leadership and ranking members of the intelligence committees of the House and Senate—a total of 8 of the 535 members—would be briefed. Members of Congress protested that the president gave no evidence that news leaks originated with them. Furthermore, they argued that many other committees also required access to classified and law enforcement information in order to fulfill their constitutional duties. When the chairmen of the Senate and House intelligence committees reassured the White House that information would be kept confidential, the memo was rescinded.[18] The controversy over news leaks did not diminish, however. The initial White House opposition to an independent 9/11 commission stemmed in part from a concern that sensitive items would be leaked.[19] White House spokesman Fleischer explained, "The selective, inappropriate leaking of snippets of information risks undermining national security."[20] The administration particularly frowned on public airing of internal staff disagreements. For example, when former aide John DiIulio criticized top adviser Karl Rove and others in an e-mail to a magazine writer for trying to "prevent the types of internal policy debates that beget bad press," he was pressured by the White House to recant. In his mea culpa, DiIulio called his remarks "groundless and baseless," virtually the same phrases used earlier by Fleischer to characterize DiIulio's comments.[21]

The securitized environment that followed the terrorist attacks accelerated efforts to restrict the flow of government information. Between 2001 and 2004, the number of documents that were classified almost doubled, up to a record of 15.6 million documents. At the same time, the number of pages declassified annually dropped to 28 million pages in 2004, down from a high of 204 million pages in 1997. Government agencies have also invented new categories of secrecy, such as "sensitive security information," which have no clear classification guidelines. According to some critics, these are "bogus categories" designed to shield from review material that belongs in the public domain.[22]

After 9/11, government Web sites were bleached of information, and CD-ROMs with government data were pulled from libraries or destroyed by librarians at the government's request.[23] Much of the information shielded pertained to highly sensitive matters with national security implications: data on hazardous chemical sites and aviation accident reports, for example.[24] Making these sorts of documents less accessible did not spark particular controversy, but efforts to remove information related to court cases and the implementation of the law engendered more opposition.[25] The Justice Department defended the greater secrecy in both investigations and prosecutions. Speaking for the department, Barbara Comstock explained the rationale, "Giving terrorists a virtual roadmap to our investigation may allow terrorists to map out a potentially deadly detour around our efforts, bringing further tragedy to our nation."[26] Solicitor General Theodore Olson defended the secrecy surrounding certain immigration hearings: "This is an extraordinary case, touching on the nation's very ability to defend itself against the continuing threat of a hostile attack from myriad and unknown sources."[27]

This chapter focuses specifically on the secrecy surrounding the government's domestic war on terrorism. As noted in chapter 4, such a war is not limited or temporary, suggesting that measures enacted to shield government information will not be limited or temporary either. As scholar Mary Graham cautioned, "What are often being couched as temporary emergency orders are in fact what we are going to live with for 20 years. . . . We make policy by crisis, and we particularly make secrecy policy by crisis."[28] The policies that institutionalize greater secrecy—many of them enacted by the attorney general—may represent a permanent change and could complicate the ability of citizens and their representatives in Congress to hold federal officials, including the president, politically accountable.

Secrecy and the Justice Department

While many officials in the Bush administration were credited with the drive to control information, including the vice president and his chief counsel,[29] John Ashcroft was a key player in framing government transparency as a point of vulnerability in the war against terrorism. Several times he averred that openness would aid the terrorist mission, that even "mere tidbits of information" had to be guarded because they could add up to useful intelligence for terrorists.[30] Terrorists, he said, "exploit our openness—not randomly or haphazardly—but by deliberate, premeditated design."[31] The release of government information could enlighten the enemy as much as citizens and Congress.

A captured al Qaeda training manual confirmed his fears. In his words, it advised terrorists "to use the benefits of a free press—newspapers, magazines and broadcasts—to stalk and kill their victims."[32] The framework of a war on terrorism—with its emphasis on "collecting intelligence rather than criminal evidence"—reinforces the ethic of secrecy, according to a former FBI agent who served during Ashcroft's tenure; the intelligence orientation compels secrecy.[33]

Prior to 9/11, Ashcroft did not seem as concerned with secrecy as some others in the administration. For example, a week before the terrorist attacks, he opposed a proposed provision in the intelligence authorization act to criminalize unauthorized leaks of classified information.[34] By that December, however, he was leading an interagency task force to review current law related to leaks and make recommendations to address them.[35] Early in his tenure, he also made regular appearances on television talk shows, particularly as a guest on *Larry King Live,* as documented in chapter 1.

Despite this, Ashcroft was never comfortable with the news media. Instead of an informal weekly session with reporters, as was Janet Reno's practice, Ashcroft appeared before the press only to give formal announcements, answering two or three questions before leaving the room. His political aides, concerned with his public image, controlled the coverage coming out the department's public affairs office and kept their boss largely inaccessible. As a result, "there was no opportunity to fix [Ashcroft's] image after his confirmation, because he never gave access," said a reporter who covered the department, adding, "I think that distancing himself and making everything into sound bites and photo ops were the biggest mistakes his press and political aides made." Another journalist concurred, noting that Ashcroft's sense of humor was not captured in news accounts as a result.[36] His inaccessibility fed the negative stereotypes about the attorney general, which in turn fed the suspicions of Ashcroft and his aides that the media suffered from a liberal bias, resulting in even less access. This cycle became entrenched after September 11, especially as his policies began to engender heated criticism. His office arranged for him to make statements before friendly audiences, such as the Federalist Society, where he was a member, and the Heritage Foundation.[37] In his Patriot Act tour, he met only with television reporters from local stations, giving brief one-on-one interviews. He avoided print reporters entirely, considering them too critical and opinionated.[38] His handling of the press brought a reproving letter from the Society of Professional Journalists, which argued, "Your selective public access policy allows your office to further control the debate and to present a misleading portrayal of the event itself."[39] Ashcroft's aide David Israelite explained, "He's not going on the road to debate the Patriot Act as much as to inform the American public about what it is and what it isn't, because there are a lot of misconceptions out there."[40] A former chairman of the Republican National Committee also defended Ashcroft's strategy of avoiding unfriendly audiences and editorial boards: "He wants to get his message across directly to the voters, and the more he can do that without tangling with folks along the way, the better."[41] This episode led one journalism scholar to call Ashcroft "the supersecretive, supersensitive attorney general."[42]

The Ashcroft Justice Department scaled back the information it released to the public about its internal operations. For example, the Office of Legal Counsel—which issues formal legal opinions to the president and executive agencies—reduced the number of opinions it released to the other branches, the professional bar, and the public from a high of eighteen in 2001 to just three in 2004.[43] Compared with other administrations, this figure was low. In 1992, for example, fifteen opinions were released; that was the earliest year accessible on the OLC's Web site and the last year of the George H. W. Bush administration. During the Reno years, an annual average of thirty opinions was released, from a high of forty-seven in 1996 to a low of twenty-three in 1993.[44]

In some cases, the culture of confidentiality extended to sharing information within the Justice Department itself. A fascinating example is evident in one of the internal e-mails released as a result of a FOIA lawsuit; in the message, dated June 2004, an official in the FBI's Office of General Counsel reported to agency coworkers, "I'm still trolling the Internet in hopes of finding the 2002 DOJ memo re: use of torture." The official had located copies of other Justice Department legal memos that had been leaked to the press but could not locate this one. The official knew about the "use of torture memo" because the attorney general had mentioned it in congressional testimony earlier in the day.[45]

Among the secrets tightly guarded is the FBI's use of national security letters after 9/11, discussed in the previous chapter. A type of administrative subpoena, a national security letter can be used to access credit reports, Internet usage, telephone calls, and financial records. People whose records are searched are not informed, and therefore they cannot raise a complaint in the courts or with the Office of the Inspector General in the Justice Department. People who receive an NSL demanding records are prohibited from discussing that fact, even with their attorneys. In the rare instances when courts have heard challenges raised by those who received an NSL, the Justice Department tried to hide the case's existence and/or heavily redacted all briefs and exhibits. For its part, Congress received little of the information about the scope and approval process of NSLs that it had requested. The Justice Department simply ignored some of the requests.[46]

Heightened secrecy characterized the relations between the Ashcroft Justice Department and other actors within and outside government. The primary tools employed were administrative, including a new legal policy interpreting the Freedom of Information Act (FOIA). Through the power to issue new interpretations of FOIA, an attorney general can exercise an "outsized influence over how open and accountable the federal government will be," according to a former public affairs director under Janet Reno.[47]

New Rules for the Freedom of Information Act

The Freedom of Information Act was passed in 1966 to permit members of the public, corporate and individual, regardless of citizenship, to request non-classified government documents. Until then, those making a request had to establish their basis for needing the information. FOIA, in contrast, presumed public accessibility, shifting the burden to agencies to justify denying a request. Intended to foster greater government accountability, FOIA does recognize nine types of information that can be exempted from the requirement for disclosure, covering such matters as national security, law enforcement, trade secrets, regulation of financial institutions, personal privacy, and internal memos, among others. Agencies are not required to exclude these categories; instead, they have the discretion to restrict access. Those whose requests are denied may appeal to the agency head and, if still denied, may take the question to federal district court.[48] Under the statute, the attorney general is responsible for encouraging compliance with the act. It is the attorney general who receives annual reports from the agencies documenting compliance, the attorney general who makes those reports available electronically, and the attorney general who develops reporting and performance guidelines.[49]

Incoming attorneys general often issue policy memoranda on handling FOIA requests across the government, starting with Griffin Bell in 1977. Janet Reno's policy, issued in October 1993, interpreted the statute broadly, to encourage disclosure in the absence of "foreseeable harm."[50] Replacing the Reno document, John Ashcroft's FOIA memorandum, issued in October 2001, made two important changes.[51] First, the basis on which discretionary disclosures would be made shifted from a policy of "maximum responsible disclosure" under Reno to "careful consideration" under Ashcroft.[52] The second change in the Ashcroft memo involved how the Department of Justice would handle FOIA litigation. Under the Reno policy, the department would defend nondisclosure only if the agency could show that disclosure could produce a "foreseeable harm" to an interest listed among the exemptions. In contrast, under the Ashcroft policy, the department would defend *nondisclosures* "unless they lack a sound legal basis or present an unwarranted risk of adverse impact on the ability of other agencies to protect other important records."[53] This interpretation of FOIA represented an important shift against the presumption of disclosure.

In other ways as well, the Ashcroft memo appeared to dissuade the release of information. It instructed agencies throughout the government that the decision to disclose a document "should be made only after full and deliberate consideration of the institutional, commercial and personal privacy interests that could be implicated."[54] A policy founded on the right to know was transformed into one based on the need to know. One journalist worried that emphasizing privacy interests "sends a heavy message to government officials to use privacy interests more widely."[55] According to the executive director of the Reporters Committee for Freedom of the Press, the personal privacy exemption also was expanded; the mere mention of a person's name in a government document now could be cited as grounds for denying its release.[56]

Although issued after the terrorist strikes, the policy change was in the works prior to 9/11.[57] Some career staff in the Justice Department acknowledged the need for change because they believed the Reno policy had gone too far. For example, C. Madison Brewer, a former head of the Justice Department's Information and Privacy Unit, explained that the earlier FOIA policy had made it difficult to keep confidential even such matters as a prosecutor's home address when it appeared on certain documents, to the detriment of the prosecutor's privacy interests.

Critics charged that the Ashcroft FOIA policy went too far in the other direction, shielding information that many argued belonged in the public domain. The attorney general cited his policy to support his refusal to release the names of those detained after 9/11 and his closure of "special interest" immigration cases. Other information also was kept from the public. By November 2001, according to one news report, "Watchdog groups say that they have already started to see rejections of requests that likely would have been granted before."[58] Government officials were making fewer discretionary disclosures, according to a Justice Department official who explained, "As a matter of policy, we are not advocating the making of discretionary disclosures."[59] Some government agencies reiterated this in their internal FOIA documents; the Department of Defense, for example, explicitly noted and underlined that "discretionary disclosures are no longer encouraged."[60] By early 2003, agencies throughout the government were accused of delaying the release of requested information. One critic compared the Ashcroft memo to putting "molasses or sand in the gears."[61]

The adverse impact of the Ashcroft memorandum on the release of information is not entirely clear, however. Reports from the Government Accountability Office—the nonpartisan investigative arm of the U.S. Congress—offered data that could be interpreted either way. In 2004, the GAO found that, of those requests processed, the "number of FOIA requests denied dropped dramatically between 2000 and 2001, and remained low in 2002." Agencies also reported a decrease in the backlog of processing requests.[62] Some organizations successfully gathered material through FOIA requests that they used to issue reports critical of the government. For example, the Center for Public Integrity used the Freedom of Information Act to collect information for its report criticizing how the government awarded contracts for reconstruction work in Iraq and Afghanistan.[63] But a GAO study in 2003 produced less positive numbers. That study assessed the impact of the attorney general's memo on agency responses to FOIA requests. While documenting little effect on most FOIA officers, the study reported that almost a third of the FOIA officers responding (fifty-seven) reported seeing a decrease in the release of documents, and three out of four of them cited the Ashcroft memo as the reason for the change.[64]

In addition, selected organizations reported problems with their FOIA requests, compelling them to seek court assistance to get compliance. For example, nineteen civil and human rights organizations twice filed a FOIA request for the names of the more than 1,000 people detained in the weeks after September 11; eventually, the organizations sued the Justice Department. That case, *Center for National Security Studies, et al., v. Department of Justice,*[65] will be covered later. Another organization whose FOIA requests often ended up in court was the American Civil Liberties Union. In 2003, it and several other civil liberty organizations sought access to hundreds of internal FBI e-mails and memos critical of the military's interrogation practices at Guantánamo Bay, Cuba. When the Justice Department did not comply, the ACLU sued.[66] One organization that compiles and analyzes government data in order to help monitor government effectiveness encountered particular problems with the new FOIA guidelines. That organization, Transactional Records Access Clearinghouse (TRAC) at Syracuse University, analyzes data that include the number of cases referred to U.S. attorneys by the FBI. Its users include the news media, researchers, public interest groups, and even members of Congress. TRAC had struggled over access to information during Janet Reno's tenure. The struggle intensified following 9/11, particularly after the clearinghouse issued an embarrassing report that many of the indictments counted by the government as terrorism-related did not actually deal with terrorism at all. By late 2002, Justice stopped releasing the data to TRAC. The department justified the greater secrecy as necessary on mosaic theory grounds, arguing that terrorists and criminals could use even innocuous-looking information to track government investigations. In response, critics charged that the data aggregated and assessed by TRAC were too vague to provide insight into specific cases or investigations.[67]

Even when a federal court has agreed that documents must be released pursuant to a FOIA request, the documents may be so redacted that they are meaningless in terms of government accountability. Many of the documents released as a result of the ACLU's successful FOIA lawsuit were heavily redacted by the Justice Department in consultation with the Department of Defense, leaving little more than incomprehensible phrases. One five-page memo contained only a few lines that were not redacted; in fact, only four short sentences had no redactions at all.[68] Another memo of nine paragraphs had four of them completely redacted and partial redactions in the others.[69] Some critics questioned the necessity of the redactions. Three months after their release, Senator Carl Levin (D-Mich.) successfully pressured the Justice Department to disclose some of the redacted material in one memo sent by an FBI agent to a superior in May 2004. Once the redactions were filled in, Senator Levin remarked, "As I suspected, the previously withheld information had nothing to do with protecting intelligence and methods, and everything to do with protecting the DOD from embarrassment."[70] On occasion, the government redacted documents retroactively, if they had been released earlier without redactions. For example, in 1999, the Defense Intelligence Agency released a nonredacted copy of a brief biography on Augusto Pinochet, the former Chilean dictator. Three years later, however, when the National Security Archive at George Washington University sought a copy as part of a FOIA request, redactions had been made, and some of the redactions made little sense. Such sentences as "Gen. Pinochet is conservative in his political thinking" and he likes "fencing, boxing and horseback riding" now were blacked out.[71]

Members of Congress responded to Ashcroft's FOIA policy by introducing legislation. In the 109th Congress, several bills were introduced relating to the Freedom of Information Act. The stated intent of the OPEN Government Act, for example, was to "significantly expand the accessibility, accountability, and openness of the Federal Government."[72] Another measure entitled the Faster FOIA Act of 2005 called for a commission to examine the alleged processing delays in government responses to FOIA requests, with a quarter of the commission's members to be drawn from organizations using FOIA in the past. A third bill expressly addressed the new policy. Called the

Restore Open Government Act of 2005, it was intended to revoke "Bush administration memoranda regarded to encourage the withholding of information, . . . restore public access to presidential records, prohibit use of secret advisory committees and promote the timely declassification of information."[73] One provision of that bill would require Congress to be explicit when making new FOIA exemptions; that would keep legislators from slipping new exemptions into bills covertly. In recent years, such exemptions were unobtrusively passed more than 140 times. One cosponsor, Senator John Cornyn (R-Tex.), declared, "Congress should not establish new secrecy provisions through secret means."[74] A director at the Heritage Foundation, Mark Tapscott, lauded the Senate passage of the Open Government Act of 2005, saying that "conservatives are taking leading roles in making government more transparent." The effort to challenge such secrecy, according to Tapscott, reflects "a growing realization on the right that big government's worst enemy is transparency."[75] None of these measures had become law at the time of this writing.

Secret Detentions

Hundreds of people—INS detainees, criminal suspects, material witnesses, and others—were held in secret in the months following the terrorist attacks. More controversial than their detentions was the fact that their names and locations, as well as the charges against them, were not disclosed, contrary to customary practice in law enforcement. In some cases, even family members and attorneys had difficulty locating individuals in custody, as noted in chapter 6. The attorney general was under increasing pressure to release their names when he announced in November 2001 that he would refuse to release even the numbers of those detained.[76] As a result, the precise number of those held in the aftermath of 9/11 is still not known. The Ashcroft Justice Department also issued a directive barring state and local governments from giving the names of any detainees jailed in their jurisdiction. The issue came to a head because a New Jersey state judge had ordered the government to release the names of those detained in state jails, or he would do so. Because they were federal inmates serving in state jails on a contract basis, the Justice Department's directive prevailed.[77]

Seeking the names and other information about those imprisoned after 9/11, the Center for National Security Studies, the American Civil Liberties Union, Amnesty International, the Electronic Privacy Information Center, and fifteen other civil rights, human rights, and media organizations filed a FOIA request in late October 2001. The basic information sought included their names and locations, the identities of their lawyers, and the courts and legal orders connected with the detainees. The request was filed under Justice Department rules providing for expedited processing when the "information is urgently needed to inform the public concerning some actual or alleged government activity, . . . is of widespread and exceptional media interest, . . . involves possible questions about the government's integrity which affect public confidence," and could prevent "the loss of substantial due process rights," as well as "threats to their physical safety."[78] Denying the request, the Justice Department cited Ashcroft's memo governing FOIA.[79] The groups filed suit under the Freedom of Information Act, the First Amendment, and common law.[80] The district court ruled that the names of the detained and their lawyers had to be released, but the other information could be withheld under the FOIA exemption related to law enforcement proceedings. The government appealed even this level of transparency, filing two affidavits with the Court of Appeals for the District of Columbia Circuit, one from Dale Watson, the FBI's counterterrorism chief, and another by James Reynolds, director of the Justice Department's Terrorism and Violent Crime Section. The court of appeals reversed the district court's order to release the names, saying it deferred to the arguments advanced in the affidavits. The court majority concluded, "We owe deference to the government's judgments contained in its affidavits."[81] Those affidavits were not part of the public record.

The cases most shrouded in secrecy were those involving material witness arrests. Virtually all court proceedings were closed and documents sealed, and gag orders were imposed on family members and defense attorneys. In the majority of cases, no mention of material witness hearings even appeared on court dockets. Some material witnesses were denied access to the government's application for the warrants used to arrest them, and some defense attorneys were not permitted to see the affidavits supporting the warrants against their clients. Congressional requests for information also were largely ignored. Because of the secrecy, according to a report by Human Rights Watch issued in 2005, "Justice Department mistakes were not rectified as quickly as they might have been."[82] In the end, as noted in chapter 6, the government had to apologize to thirteen men held as material witnesses. One of those receiving an apology was Brandon Mayfield. An Oregon attorney, Mayfield was arrested as a material witness after a partial fingerprint seemed to link him to the March 2004 train bombing in Madrid. His case, including his location, was kept secret, with information becoming public only after he was released.[83]

The Justice Department attempted to keep at least one detainee's case invisible. Mohamed Bellanouel, who had worked at a restaurant patronized by two of the September 11 hijackers, was held for five months after the attacks and then was released on an immigration bond in March 2002; he had over-stayed his 1996 student visa. It is important to note that Bellanouel was not charged in a terrorism-related crime. His entire federal habeas corpus case—known only as *M.K.B. v. Warden*—was conducted in secret, even to the identity of the lower federal courts that granted the government's request for a blanket seal. All documents were under seal and kept in a secret filing system. Court dockets made no mention of the case. In fact, the public had no knowledge that the case even existed until it was inadvertently and briefly posted on the public docket of an appeals court in March 2003, where a Miami news reporter saw it.[84] When the case was appealed to the U.S. Supreme Court in July 2003, Bellanouel's petition for a writ of certiorari was partially censored.[85] More notable, the solicitor general declined to file a response, still refusing to concede publicly that the case even existed. On the Supreme Court's insistence, the government filed a brief against the certiorari petition, which the solicitor general asked to be kept secret. He also issued a one-paragraph filing that said, "This matter pertains to information that is required to be kept under seal."[86] The gist of the government's argument, according to administration officials, was that "public records and open court hearings involving terror suspects could provide Al Qaeda a road map of U.S. counterterror efforts."[87] Another justification for the high degree of secrecy appeared to be the government's intent to use defendants like Bellanouel as undercover agents who could infiltrate al Qaeda cells. Secrecy would be essential to maintaining their cover.[88] Bellanouel fought the secrecy surrounding his case. His certiorari petition argued that the secrecy "necessarily remov[ed] Petitioner's legal plight from the public debate."[89] The Reporters Committee for Freedom of the Press filed a brief seeking to be included as a party, more than a friend-of-the-court status, in order to better represent the First Amendment and common-law issues at stake. Representing a coalition of twenty-three news and legal organizations, the Reporters Committee argued against all secrecy in the case except that "truly required for national security purposes."[90] Even though the case raised major issues regarding total secrecy of proceedings in federal courts, the Supreme Court did not accept it for review.[91] The Justice Department's broad secrecy claim—while not affirmed by the Supreme Court—was sustained in this case.

Ashcroft's rationale for enforcing such secrecy in the case of the detainees changed over time. He initially defended it as something he was required to do under the law. But when a reporter asked what specific law prohibited the release of information, Ashcroft replied that no law compelled disclosure and that, therefore, he was upholding the law. He emphasized twice during that exchange that his department was "following the law scrupulously."[92] Later, Ashcroft said the secrecy was needed to protect the privacy of those detained.

He testified before the Senate Judiciary Committee that "all persons being detained have the right to contact their lawyers and their families. Out of respect for their privacy, and concern for saving lives, we will not publicize the names of those detained."[93] On at least one occasion, Justice attorneys argued that releasing the names would violate the right to privacy exemption in the Freedom of Information Act.[94] In other remarks, however, Ashcroft made clear that his primary concern was that information on the detainees could help the terrorists. He explained, "When the United States is at war, I will not share valuable intelligence with our enemies."[95] That argument appeared in the closure of immigration hearings as well.

Closed Immigration Hearings

Among those picked up by the FBI after September 11 were hundreds of foreign nationals, many of whom had overstayed their visas or had other irregularities on their immigration papers. After questioning by the FBI, most were transferred to the custody of the Immigration and Naturalization Service, still within the Justice Department at the time. As with other detainees, their identities and the details of their arrests and custody were kept secret. Because they were determined to be "special interest" in connection with the 9/11 investigation, their subsequent immigration hearings were closed. In 2003, the Justice Department reported that 766 detainees had been classified "special interest," and 611 of them had at least one closed deportation hearing.[96]

The closures occurred pursuant to a memorandum issued by chief immigration judge Michael Creppy. Responding to Ashcroft's stipulation that "special procedures" be used for those picked up in the investigation into 9/11, Creppy issued new instructions for handling "cases requiring additional security,"[97] among them the following:

> Because some of these cases may ultimately involve classified evidence, the cases are to be assigned only to judges who currently hold at least a secret clearance. . . .
>
> Each of these cases is to be heard separately from all other cases on the docket. The courtroom must be closed for these cases—no visitors, no family, and no press.
>
> The Record of Proceeding is not to be released to anyone except an attorney or representative who has an EOIR-28 on file for the case (assuming the file does not contain classified information). . . .
>
> This restriction on information includes confirming or denying whether such a case is on the docket or scheduled for a hearing. . . .

The ANSIR record for the case is to be coded to ensure that information about the case is not provided on the 1-800 number and the case is not listed on the court calendars posted outside the courtrooms. . . .

Finally, you should instruct all courtroom personnel, including both court employees and contract interpreters, that they are not to discuss the case with anyone.[98]

Under the Creppy memo, these cases would not exist on public court dockets or calendars. The news media would receive neither confirmation nor denial of their existence. Attorneys representing detainees would not have access to classified material in their files. Even family members would be barred from attending the hearings.

Creppy did not provide the criteria for determining which cases would be "special interest." Instead, immigration judges would be notified by his office if and when such cases were filed in their courts.[99] More insight was provided by the FBI's executive assistant director for counterterrorism and counterintelligence, who explained that people classified as "special interest" were those who "might have connections with, or possess information pertaining to, terrorist activities against the United States."[100] Yet, as a *Washington Post* study of 361 cases revealed, the "special interest" classification was extended even to detainees who were quickly determined to have no link to terrorism.[101]

Controversy arose because immigration hearings, by long custom, are open.[102] There is a historic presumption in the United States against secret tribunals. Further, defense attorneys were quick to argue that the Sixth Amendment's guarantee of a public trial was violated by the closures. The Justice Department responded that immigration hearings are not covered by the Sixth Amendment because they are administrative and not judicial. The enforcement and adjudication of immigration law and policy rests with the executive, and immigration judges, including Creppy, are employees of the Justice Department. Critics cited a Supreme Court decision in a state sovereign immunity case, where the justices found that "administrative adjudication . . . strongly resembles civil suits,"[103] which implies a right to a public hearing. Others countered that these immigration hearings dealt with national security concerns, so greater deference was due executive decisions to close the hearings.[104] Associate Attorney General Jay Stephens described the department's position this way: "We will continue to defend the principle that the Constitution does not require immigration proceedings to be opened."[105]

Several legal challenges to the closures and the Creppy memo were filed. One case arose in Detroit, involving a Lebanese immigrant named Rabih Haddad who had been detained shortly after September 11. Without notifying

Haddad or his counsel, the immigration judge closed his bond hearing. Subsequent hearings also were closed.[106] Haddad's counsel brought a challenge in federal district court. Local news outlets, which had been barred from covering his hearings, filed separate complaints, as did Congressman John Conyers Jr. (D-Mich.); those cases were consolidated as *Detroit Free Press v. Ashcroft*. The government argued that closed hearings were needed to prevent "public identification of individuals associated with them," protect the investigation's progress, encourage cooperation of the detainees with government interrogators, and ensure detainees were not stigmatized once they were released. Rejecting those arguments, the district court judge, Nancy Edmunds, ruled that blanket closures of deportation hearings were unconstitutional. She granted the injunction and sent the case back to the immigration court for a new bond hearing.[107] Government attorneys appealed, but a three-judge panel of the Sixth Circuit Court of Appeals affirmed the principle that blanket closures of deportation hearings are unconstitutional. Circuit judge Damon Keith conceded that "the political branches of our government enjoy near unrestrained ability to control our borders," and that "neither the Bill of Rights nor the judiciary can second-guess government's choices." But, in ruling for the news media in Haddad's case, Keith wrote, "The only safeguard on this extraordinary governmental power is the public, deputizing the press as the guardians of their liberty. . . . Today, the Executive Branch seeks to take this safeguard away from the public by placing its actions beyond public scrutiny." Keith then provided one of the more widely quoted statements arising in post-9/11 litigation: "Democracies die behind closed doors."[108] The government filed for a rehearing en banc, but it was denied.[109]

Concurrently, a New Jersey challenge to the closure of immigration hearings—*North Jersey Media Group v. Ashcroft*—resulted in a government loss at the district court level but a victory before the Third Circuit Court of Appeals. The district judge issued an order to enjoin the attorney general from denying access to the media plaintiffs.[110] While that decision was appealed to the Third Circuit, the government sought a stay on the temporary injunction, which the Supreme Court granted.[111] The Third Circuit then reversed the district judge. Chief Judge Edward Becker explained that administrative hearings did not have the same tradition of openness as ordinary criminal and civil trials, even if they had procedural similarities. While conceding the policy benefits to be derived from government openness, he wrote, "The primary national policy must be self-preservation." Becker accepted the assertion made in an affidavit filed by Watson of the FBI's counterterrorism unit that the case-by-case assessment advocated by the media plaintiffs would "ineffectively protect the nation's interests." Referring again to the mosaic theory, the Watson declaration asserted that details that seem innocuous and even trivial could be meaningful to terrorists. Deferring to Watson's assessment, Becker discounted the ability of immigration judges to tell the difference: "Immigration judges cannot be expected accurately to assess the harm that might result from disclosing seemingly trivial facts."[112] The Justice Department embraced the appellate decision: "Opening sensitive immigration hearings could compromise the security of our nation and our ongoing investigations, by revealing valuable information to terrorist organizations seeking to harm America."[113] The Supreme Court denied a request by the media plaintiffs to review the case,[114] which left standing the contradictory rulings issued by the Sixth and Third Circuit Courts.

Sibel Edmonds Case

The case of former FBI translator Sibel Edmonds illustrates the Justice Department's aggressive use of the classification authority to keep information out of the public arena, even when it had already been released. The department may have been particularly sensitive about Edmonds's allegations because they included some classified information, and they criticized internal workings at the FBI.

Edmonds worked as a contract linguist with the FBI's Foreign Language Program in the months following the terrorist attacks. She reportedly found incompetent translation work, incomplete translation of material involving acquaintances of one of the translators, and other questionable activities that arguably undermined national security.[115] After she made multiple complaints, however, the FBI determined she was disruptive and terminated her contract. She brought a lawsuit, alleging that she had been fired in retaliation for her complaints. In response, Ashcroft asserted a state secrets privilege, claiming a national security privilege "over information at the heart of that case," and sought dismissal of her lawsuit. Almost two years later, the district court upheld the privilege claim and granted the motion to dismiss.[116]

The secrecy continued. One day before its hearing on the Edmonds appeal, the Court of Appeals for the D.C. Circuit closed the hearing. Only Edmonds, her attorneys, and Justice Department attorneys were permitted. Of note is that all the court briefs on the case already were public.[117] At the hearing itself, after presenting their arguments, Edmonds and her lawyers were ordered from the courtroom while the government presented its side.[118] On May 6, 2005, the appellate court affirmed the dismissal of Edmonds's lawsuit against the Justice Department, citing the "state secrets privilege."[119] Rick Blum, head of a coalition of more than thirty groups opposed to government secrecy, called the closure "one more black hole in a universe of secrecy and it's unclear how this country is safer for it. . . . We have no idea if the system is working or not because it was all in secret."120

Meanwhile, the FBI gave unclassified briefings about Edmonds's allegations to the staff of the Senate Judiciary Committee. Committee members Patrick Leahy and Charles Grassley sent a letter to the Justice Department's inspector general asking him to pursue them, and another letter two months later to the attorney general. In another two months, Grassley sent a letter to FBI director Robert Mueller asking about Edmonds's allegations. These letters were posted on their Web sites and disseminated electronically, including to an independent government watchdog group called the Project on Government Oversight (POGO). Almost two years after the Senate briefings, the FBI put the Senate Judiciary staff on notice that the bureau "now considers some of the information contained in two Judiciary Committee briefings to be classified," including the posted letters. The FBI implied that the classification was necessary due to civil litigation brought by some families of the 9/11 victims against the government.121 Edmonds had been asked to testify on behalf of the families.122 The attorney general, however, provided a different rationale for the classification; he told the Senate Judiciary Committee that he made the decision to reclassify because "the national interests of the United States would be seriously impaired if information provided in one briefing to the Congress were to be made generally available."123 About this time, the inspector general's report on Edmonds's allegations was completed, but it was classified as well.

POGO brought a lawsuit against Ashcroft seeking to have the retroactive classification deemed unlawful for violating the requirements for reclassification, and unconstitutional as a prior restraint on the group's free speech rights.124 The organization said it "faced the threat of prosecution if it disseminated the information" that it had earlier retrieved from the senators' Web sites.125 The Justice Department responded that the complaint should be dismissed because POGO had no standing and no private right of action.126 In February 2005, just as a hearing before a federal district judge was scheduled, a trial attorney in the Justice Department's Civil Division issued a letter explicitly releasing the contested documents. The role that the new attorney general, Alberto Gonzales, may have played in that decision remains unclear.127

The month before, an unclassified summary of the inspector general's investigation was released. The summary supported some of Edmonds's contentions: "Had the FBI performed a more careful investigation of Edmonds's allegations, it would have discovered evidence of significant omissions and inaccuracies by the co-worker related to these allegations." Although the inspector general did not uncover evidence that Edmonds's coworker was engaged in espionage, as she had implied, the summary report did conclude that "the FBI should have investigated the allegations more thoroughly," particularly in light of the espionage case then building against FBI counterintelligence agent Robert Hanssen.[128] The critical conclusions drawn in the unclassified summary lend credence to allegations that the Justice Department shrouded Edmonds's case in secrecy to avoid embarrassment as well as accountability for the FBI's superficial investigation into her fairly serious charges.

Questions about the Release of Information

Secrecy in Ashcroft's Justice Department appeared to be used selectively, treated as an imperative much of the time but bypassed when the attorney general wanted to comment. Critics charged the selectivity was motivated by political considerations, to discredit opponents, or to avoid embarrassment or blame. Some pointed to the department's handling of an announcement on its Web site that a grants program for first responders would be delayed. The announcement made a brief appearance before being excised from the site just as the press picked up the story. Democrats in Congress protested what they viewed as a politically motivated deletion of bad news. The Justice Department countered that the deletion had been due to a computer glitch. The announcement then reappeared.[129]

More significant examples of an inconsistent application of secrecy exist. One often-cited example occurred during Ashcroft's testimony before the commission investigating the September 11 attacks. When he charged that the Clinton administration was responsible for not stopping the terrorist attacks on New York and Washington, he blamed a 1995 Justice Department legal memo explaining the need to separate law enforcement and intelligence-gathering activities. The memo was authored by a former deputy attorney general, Jamie Gorelick, at the time a member of the 9/11 commission.[130] Immediately following his testimony, Ashcroft declassified the 1995 memo and posted it on the Justice Department's Web site. Critics accused him of selective declassification to suit his political purposes.[131] As noted in chapter 3, the negative fallout from his action reportedly triggered a rebuke from the president.[132]

Some defense attorneys also alleged that the government engaged in selectively leaking confidential information in ways that hurt their clients, in a context where a defendant would not be able to respond.[133] Selective leaking may have occurred in the high-profile prosecution of Zacarias Moussaoui. On a number of occasions, details about him or the case appeared in the press despite the fact that documents were under seal and a judicial gag order was in place. The details generally disadvantaged the defense, suggesting that they originated from someone sympathetic with the government side.[134] Brandon Mayfield's experience also demonstrated how secrecy could contribute to the perception of guilt. Despite sealed records and gag orders, the government leaked the news that Mayfield's fingerprint was an "absolutely incontrovertible match" to one connected with the Madrid train bombing.[135] The secrecy surrounding his case not only made the leak more newsworthy and therefore more likely to be published but also disadvantaged Mayfield, since he was unable to respond to the government's false assertion due to the gag order. A similar issue was raised in the case of José Padilla when the deputy attorney general, James Comey, told the press that Padilla had been sent by al Qaeda "to set off natural gas explosions in U.S. apartment buildings," and that he planned to wrap the explosives in uranium.[136] Comey's statement could not be rebutted by the defense. One of Padilla's defense attorneys said, "We are in the same position we've been in for two years, where the government says bad things about Mr. Padilla and there's no forum for him to defend himself."[137] Another defense attorney, Donna Newman, who met with Padilla in March 2004 for the first time since the enemy combatant designation, said that her conversations with her client were classified, so that she could not even report if he disputed the allegations. "Everything my client says to me is classified. I can't offer any defense," she said.[138]

The government's handling of Padilla's case also raised a question about the timing of the release of information. For two years, Justice attorneys had fought to maintain the highest level of secrecy surrounding his detention. Then, just weeks before the Supreme Court was expected to announce its ruling in *Rumsfeld v. Padilla,* Comey released newly declassified Pentagon documents to the press and contended that the intelligence could not have been gathered had Padilla been granted access to counsel: "He would very likely have followed his lawyer's advice and said nothing, which would have been his constitutional right. He would likely have ended up a free man, with our only hope being to try to follow him 24 hours a day."[139] The declassified information was not directly relevant to the question before the justices, which focused on the president's authority to declare a citizen an enemy combatant. Yet it could have influenced their perception of the need for such an executive power. Comey said the timing of the release was coincidental with the Supreme Court decision. He explained that his announcement was aimed not at the justices but at the general public, to quell its concerns about the government's actions.[140] Even if not intended to sway the justices, however, the public release of such prejudicial material while a related matter is before the high court is troubling.

Ashcroft's warning in late May 2004 that a terrorist strike was "almost ready" also brought charges that he manipulated the timing of his warning for political ends. Some Bush opponents, including firefighter and police union leaders working with John Kerry's presidential campaign, asserted that Ashcroft's remarks seemed designed to influence the president's declining poll numbers and distract attention from the Iraqi insurgency. Sidestepping the question about timing, the attorney general said, "We believe the public, like all of us, needs a reminder."[141]

Implications for Democratic Accountability

The concerns expressed by the attorney general—national security, law enforcement, and privacy needs—support a degree of secrecy in the nation's legal business. Many public officials agreed with Ashcroft about the imperative for heightened secrecy after the 9/11 strikes. William Barr, former attorney general in the first Bush administration, told the Senate Judiciary Committee, "Information about who is presently detained by the government, when and where they were arrested, their citizenship, and like information could be of great value to criminal associates who remain free."[142] A similar observation was made by Senator Daniel Inouye (D-Hawaii), who worried that release of information about those detained would work "right into the hands of the organization we are trying to combat: al Qaeda."[143] An executive branch cloaked in secrecy can operate with much greater freedom in pursuit of terrorists, without a concern with intrusive oversight or compromised military and intelligence secrets.

Yet heightened secrecy would not have made the nation safer on September 10, 2001. Former New Jersey governor Thomas Kean, who led the 9/11 commission, observed that the terrorist attacks were caused not by leaks of sensitive information but by the FBI's misunderstanding about the legal barriers to information sharing. Kean argued, "We're better off with openness. The best ally we have in protecting ourselves against terrorism is an informed public."[144] Others shared this view that "there are very few examples of terrorists actually using public records to glean sensitive information."[145] In addition, too much secrecy itself poses a danger because other political actors will not know enough to hold abusers accountable. One former FBI official said, "Perhaps the government has some incredibly incriminating piece of information and saved us from a terrible act of violence; it would make everybody feel better to know it. Conversely, if they did something wrong, the public needs to know that."[146] Official secrecy undermines democratic oversight, either by Congress or by the public through the press. The certiorari petition for Bellanouel noted the importance of access to information for the general public. Citing a classic First Amendment case, *Grosjean v. American Press Co.,*[147] it argued, "An informed public is the most potent of all restraints on misgovernment."[148]

9   General Ashcroft at Justice

How does one assess the tenure of Attorney General John Ashcroft? His four-year stewardship of the Justice Department generated intense debate and visceral emotions. His public style—abrasive, unyielding, intolerant of opposition—arguably hurt his ability to do his job. Speaking off the record, a number of people who had worked with him—including supporters—noted that he sometimes was his own worst enemy, by engaging in personal attacks against opponents and refusing to share information with allies in Congress. Critics had an easy task of characterizing him as an extremist.

Yet Ashcroft's record as a culture warrior was not extreme, despite the fears of the left at the time of his nomination. Although moving public policy toward the right in a number of areas such as gun regulation, he fulfilled his confirmation pledge to follow the law, notably in matters related to abortion. Admittedly, no case came to the Supreme Court that would have given him an opportunity to argue for overturning *Roe v. Wade;* nor did he have the opportunity to advance a pro-life nominee to the high court. But his department did prosecute violations of the Freedom of Access to Clinic Entrances Act and filed friend-of-the-court briefs in some lawsuits against antiabortion protesters, as noted in chapter 3. In addition, he promoted federal efforts to fight violence against women, human trafficking, and sexual servitude.

Ashcroft's tenure was consumed less with fighting the culture wars and more with fighting the war on terrorism, and it was this record that he wanted remembered. Stepping down from office, he trumpeted the lack of an attack within the United States as evidence of his success.[1] He said, "The world is not absent terror. But the United States has been absent terror."[2] His supporters made similar claims about his legacy. Senator Orrin Hatch (R-Utah) said, "The liberal media have got to admit that John Ashcroft and President Bush and others have done a terrific job in making our country safer."[3] While not as effusive as Hatch, Paul Rosenzweig of the Heritage Foundation predicted, "Because of September 11, Ashcroft will be remembered as the first Attorney General to confront terrorism seriously. And though his critics have not been kind and his efforts have not been completely free of missteps, when history looks back on Ashcroft's efforts, it will treat him quite well."[4] Such an assessment would please Ashcroft. His longtime aide David Israelite characterized his attitude at the end of his term as being "more concerned about the judgment of history than the judgment of how he's portrayed in the press or by opportunists on either side."[5] Yet, as attorney general, he did not take the long view of history and stay above the fray; his heightened sensitivity about how he was portrayed is evident in his active public relations campaigns and his overreaction to criticism throughout his tenure.

Will history treat him well? He certainly worked long hours and exhibited a passionate commitment to the struggle against the terrorist threat. But can Ashcroft's term in office be defined as a success? The criterion used by the administration—that no new domestic attacks occurred on his watch—is impossible to evaluate. We cannot know what terrorist plans were *not* developed due to Ashcroft's intervention, nor do we know if an alternative approach would have had a similar outcome. Further, the information released by the administration about possible terrorist conspiracies in Buffalo and Portland is too incomplete and inconclusive to provide persuasive evidence of success. Both of those cases resulted in plea agreements, not trials where at least some of the evidence would have been public. In addition, many Justice Department detentions have been shrouded in secrecy, particularly those involving material witnesses. Although plea bargains and secrecy may be justified on national security grounds in some cases, they do complicate an independent evaluation of the administration's record of achievement.

In contrast, multiple examples tend to undercut Ashcroft's claim of effectiveness. As noted in chapter 6, the Detroit terrorist convictions were voided and reprosecution on those charges was abandoned, and the material support prosecution of the head of the Global Relief Foundation was downgraded to a guilty plea for conspiracy to mislead the charity's donors. Furthermore, as chapter 7 documents, jurors were not always convinced of the government's case, as in the acquittal of the Idaho webmaster charged with providing material support to terrorists, even though the attorney general had used hyperbolic terms about the importance of the prosecution. Ashcroft's claim of success is also tarnished by allegations that the Justice Department threatened to classify criminal suspects as enemy combatants and transfer them to the military if they did not plead guilty. The government confirmed this threat in the case of Zacarias Moussaoui, and defense attorneys in the Buffalo cell case made the same charge. Such a threat could undermine the veracity of guilty pleas in some other terrorism-related cases. Finally, according to the Government Accountability Office, the Justice Department inflated its antiterrorism record by including in its tally numerous cases cleared of any link to terrorism. Another study, conducted by Syracuse University and reported in chapter 6, found that the same number of people faced sentences of five or more years in connection with terrorism in the two years *following* September 11 as in the two years *prior* to the strikes. This suggests that the antiterrorism prosecution record of the Ashcroft Justice Department was not substantially different from that of his predecessor in office, Janet Reno. These pieces of the puzzle raise some doubt about the picture Ashcroft and allies have presented of a record of achievement in the war on terrorism.

Furthermore, defining Ashcroft's success solely in terms of advancing the president's antiterrorism agenda ignores the other dimensions of the office. As explained in chapter 2, the attorney general has obligations to the people as well as the president, and obligations to the law as well as to the administration's agenda. As Orrin Hatch, an Ashcroft supporter, described the office, the attorney general "does owe allegiance to the president, but he owes a greater allegiance to the American people and the Constitution."[6] This study takes the latter role seriously and evaluates Ashcroft's years at the Justice Department by that standard—his impact on the American public and on the constitutional framework that checks the concentration and abuse of power. The record here is not positive.

Regarding his allegiance to the American people, Ashcroft's general response to criticism damaged the dialogue between citizen and state so essential in a democracy. Even as he claimed to value "open, honest debate,"[7] he engaged in four rhetorical tactics fundamentally at odds with self-governance.

First, he and supporters questioned the motives of opponents, putting them on the defensive. He initially charged critics with partisanship or ideological bias, but that charge rang hollow as more and more criticism came from fellow Republicans and conservatives, as well as from Democrats and liberals who might be expected to oppose his policies. By the end, his aide David Israelite was calling opponents "opportunists," although it is not clear what opportunity they were exploiting.

Second, Ashcroft browbeat critics, accusing them either of scaring people and thereby helping the terrorist cause, or of obstructing the effort to stop a future attack, particularly if Patriot Act powers were scaled back. The most famous example occurred in his December 6, 2001, Senate testimony, when he accused those who made "misstatements" about his policies of aiding terrorists and giving "ammunition to America's enemies."[8]

Third, Ashcroft discredited legitimate concerns by setting them up as "straw men," portrayed in such exaggerated terms that they were easy to ridicule and dismiss. He accused librarians of imagining FBI agents "in raincoats, dark suits, and sporting sunglasses," interrogating library patrons about reading Tom Clancy novels.[9] He set up a false choice in another speech, saying that his critics wanted to return to business as usual in the fight against terrorism, but that "history instructs us that reticence and complacency are not defenses of freedom."[10] He used a similar framework to admonish senators to follow the president's lead: "Since those first terrible hours of September 11, America has faced a choice that is as stark as the images that linger of that morning. One option is to call September 11 a fluke, to believe it could never happen again, and to live in a dream world that requires us to do nothing differently. The other option is to fight back, to summon all our strength and all our resources and devote ourselves to better ways to identify, disrupt and dismantle terrorist networks."[11]

Finally, Ashcroft denied there were any grounds for debate or disagreement, which removed those issues from public discussion. The administration's antiterrorism response did not affect civil liberties, Ashcroft said repeatedly and with growing impatience. And the doctrine of separation of powers, far from being threatened by the president, was under assault by Congress and the courts when they intervened in his core executive powers. President Bush followed the same course of denial; even in his farewell thank-you to Ashcroft, where he noted the transformation of the Justice Department, the president insisted that "the rights of Americans are respected and protected."[12]

In addition to his practice of dissuading and marginalizing dissent and thereby disserving the American public, Ashcroft failed to fulfill the constitutional obligation of his office, to assist the president to take care that the laws are faithfully executed. Previous chapters have documented how the attorney general's antiterrorism actions contributed to the erosion of separation of powers, civil liberties, and government accountability. Based on the totality of the record, his tenure cannot be classified a success because he failed to fulfill the special obligations of his office to the law.

Ashcroft himself did not see his policies as a conscious trade-off between the Constitution and presidential power to fight the war on terror, despite his occasional disparaging remarks about lawyers and courts in fighting terrorism. He often advanced the notion that "principled republican . . . government demands adherence to the text and original intent of the Constitution,"[13] and his comments about the Constitution appear to be sincere. Following 9/11, though, he came to believe that waging war on terrorism was among the "core executive powers" secured in the Constitution, with secondary congressional and judicial roles. He promoted that view in testimony before the Senate Judiciary Committee on December 6, 2001: "As Attorney General, it is my responsibility—at the direction of the President—to exercise those core executive powers the Constitution so designates. The law enforcement initiatives undertaken by the Department of Justice, those individuals we arrest, detain or seek to interview, fall under these core executive powers."[14] In his view, neither

Congress nor the courts had authority to define or oversee law enforcement efforts to detain and interrogate suspects. His statement that day captures the misconception that the presidency alone dictates in wartime: "In accordance with over two hundred years of historical and legal precedent, the executive branch is now exercising its core Constitutional powers in the interest of saving the lives of Americans. I trust that Congress will respect the proper limits of Executive Branch consultation that I am duty-bound to uphold. I trust, as well, that Congress will respect this President's authority to wage war on terrorism and defend our nation and its citizens with all the power vested in him by the Constitution and entrusted to him by the American people."[15]

This view is not reflected in his earlier explanations of constitutional power when, as a senator, he resisted broad claims of executive authority during the Clinton years. Yet Ashcroft's embrace of expansive presidential authority was not cynical and opportunistic, as some critics might believe, but the result of the prism through which he saw 9/11 and the fight against terrorism. It was a struggle of good versus evil, and good needed all the tools available in order to prevail. He shared this perspective with the president. When faced with the complex, uncertain, and evolving situation in the days after the tragic event, both men adopted the cognitive frame of evil to make sense of the catastrophe and prepare for the future. The frame was simplistic, black and white. And it had consequences for the constitutional system. In a struggle so profound, there can be no disunity; in a war against evil, there is no middle ground. With Congress and the courts in supporting roles, the president would dominate the action—the heroic leader, with "God and the good squarely on the American side."[16] To fight successfully, the president had to be unfettered. Ironically, it was the nation's top law officer who was charged with loosening those legal constraints.

Leading the phalanx of federal law enforcement, Ashcroft utilized the formal and informal powers of his office to follow the president's lead. He fought in the federal courts, Congress, and the court of public opinion, staking out legal positions that made unprecedented claims about the president's power in relation to the other branches of government. Congress, he argued, could not obstruct and the courts could not second-guess the executive's core powers. The laws and policies instituted on his watch provided the executive with vast subjective and undefined authority to determine what individual or group was suspicious or illegal, with few established criteria or procedures, and little opportunity for meaningful outside review. At the Justice Department, he inaugurated a preemptive approach and all that it entails: a shift from gathering criminal evidence to gathering intelligence, a shift from presumption of innocence to presumption of guilt, the increasing use of preventive detention, the policy of "hold until cleared."

Ashcroft's approach to international law reflected a similarly suspicious attitude toward legal constraints. Instead of restricting the administration's actions, he and his department provided legal justifications for the position that coercive interrogations were permissible; that the Geneva Conventions did not apply; that the men detained at Guantánamo Bay were neither prisoners of war under international law nor ordinary prisoners with habeas corpus rights.

Three calculations appear to be at work in his thinking, linking his actions to the goal of winning the war against terrorism. First, success in war required unity, which required deference to the White House; it was the president alone who could define the threat and fashion the response, in the domestic as well as the international arena. Second, success in war required flexibility, which meant few restraints on executive action vis-à-vis suspicious individuals or groups; the president needed a free hand to deal with possible enemies at home and abroad. Third, an effective campaign against terror necessitated good intelligence, which in turn necessitated less privacy for the individual. "Information is the best friend of prevention," he observed.[17] The focus on intelligence also drove Ashcroft's commitment to greater government secrecy. For the sake of national security, he believed that the private sphere would have to be transparent, but the public sphere would not.

For inconsistencies between the administration's actions and the law (and there were many), Ashcroft simply interpreted them away. Constitutional history was twisted to bolster his claim that the framers intended a preeminent president, as is clear in his Federalist Society speech discussed in chapter 5. He also mischaracterized history and precedent to support the contention that the president has unilateral authority to create military tribunals, a position that has been debunked repeatedly and effectively by separation of powers scholar Louis Fisher.[18] Ashcroft reinterpreted the constitutional guarantees of the writ of habeas corpus and due process, and the right of access to counsel and a speedy and public trial, to bring them in line with executive practices. In the same way, his Office of Legal Counsel reinterpreted international and federal laws to accord with the administration's actions at Guantánamo Bay. The Freedom of Information Act, material witness statute, Presidential Records Act, Posse Comitatus Act, Immigration and Nationality Act, and other laws were reinterpreted by Ashcroft and the OLC in ways that expanded executive power but broke with customary understandings.

The impact that Ashcroft had on the office is not moot simply because he is gone. His mark on the Justice Department remains visible after his departure. While the new attorney general's style may have insulated him from some of the heat Ashcroft engendered, Alberto Gonzales continues to promote the same antiterrorism programs and policies as his predecessor, including advocacy of an expanded Patriot Act.[19] On matters of substance, there is little indication that the new attorney general disagrees with the old. In fact, the Justice Department, with the exception of some internal reorganization, has shown "no signs of major policy shifts in law enforcement or counterterrorism" since Ashcroft's departure.[20] After Gonzales, future law officers and future presidents may continue to find the enhanced power of the presidency seductive. Even Ashcroft's critics, once in office, could feel tempted to maintain the structures he instituted, in the service of their own policies and agendas. His legacy, in other words, may last much longer than adversaries or advocates imagine.

It is this normalization of unilateral executive power that has so profoundly altered the constitutional system since 9/11, and much of the transformation has occurred without public discussion or even public knowledge. The chief champion of these changes in the domestic arena was John David Ashcroft, the attorney general of the United States, a man with a missionary zeal and faith in the president.

Appendix I
Organization of Department of Justice during Ashcroft Tenure

Attorney General
   Deputy Attorney General
      Associate Attorney General
         Office of Justice Programs
         Community Oriented Policing Services (COPS)
         Executive Office for U.S. Trustees
         Office of Information and Privacy
         Office of Dispute Resolution
         Foreign Claims Settlement Commission of the United States
         Office on Violence against Women
         Civil Rights Division
         Civil Division
         Antitrust Division
         Environment and Natural Resources Division
         Tax Division
         Community Relations Service
      Solicitor General
      Office of Legal Policy
      Office of Public Affairs
      Office of Legislative Affairs
      Office of Legal Counsel
      Office of Intergovernmental and Public Liaison
      Federal Bureau of Investigation
      Criminal Division
      Drug Enforcement Administration
      Federal Bureau of Prisons
      Executive Office for U.S. Attorneys
      U.S. Marshals Service
      Bureau of Alcohol, Tobacco, Firearms, and Explosives
      U.S. National Central Bureau-INTERPOL
      U.S. Attorneys
      Office of the Detention Trustee
      Office of the Inspector General
      Office of Professional Responsibility
      Office of Intelligence Policy and Review
      Office of the Pardon Attorney
      Justice Management Division
      U.S. Parole Commission

Executive Office for Immigration Review
National Drug Intelligence Center
Professional Responsibility Advisory Office

Source: U.S. Department of Justice, accessed April 1, 2004, available at www.usdoj.gov/02organizations/02_2.html.

Appendix II
A Brief History of the Office

For eighty years after the formation of the Office of Attorney General, there were few administrative duties and no Justice Department. In fact, until the inauguration of Franklin Pierce in 1853, the position was part-time; the attorney general received half the salary of the other cabinet secretaries with the expectation that he would continue his private law practice.

Jealous of state sovereignty, many early Americans resisted nationalizing the law. It is worth noting that the Articles of Confederation provided for neither a national attorney general nor a federal judiciary. Cases involving the new nation had to be addressed in state courts. The suspicion of centralized legal power continued for a number of years after ratification of the U.S. Constitution. In fact, this suspicion slowed passage of the Judiciary Act. Even though it was the first Senate bill proposed in the first session of Congress, it was not passed until after the three less controversial executive offices of State, War, and Treasury were formed, thus making the attorney general's post the fourth executive office to be created.

For several more decades, the nation's legal business remained poorly institutionalized and fragmented. For example, when President Andrew Jackson sought legislation to expand the attorney general's duties in 1829, Senator Daniel Webster blasted the proposal. He argued that the attorney general should focus on the Supreme Court and leave domestic affairs to a home department. Webster's alternative bill—creating the post of solicitor in the Treasury Department—was enacted instead of Jackson's. This began a long process of fragmentation in national legal affairs, with Congress subsequently creating law posts in the Departments of Internal Revenue, War, Navy, and the Post Office. President James Polk's recommendation of a law department was ignored. Only when federal litigation exploded in the wake of the Civil War did Congress agree to the formation of the Justice Department in 1870, largely as a cost-saving measure so that outside counsel would not be needed to represent the government in court.

Legal fragmentation has continued to a degree. Other agencies and departments maintain their own legal staffs that develop expertise in those areas of the law. On rare occasions, agency legal staffs have staked out different litigation positions from Justice. Further, with the appointment of a White House counsel starting in the Franklin Roosevelt administration, the attorney general's role as the president's legal adviser has been eclipsed.

Even so, the twentieth century brought dramatic changes to the national government, extending the reach of federal law into more and more areas. This development greatly expanded the authority of the attorney general and the Justice Department. Today, the attorney general's office commands a higher profile than most other cabinet positions. In large measure, this could be due to the Justice Department's jurisdiction over several hotly contested policy areas, particularly its leadership role in the wars against drugs and terrorism.

Source: Nancy V. Baker, *Conflicting Loyalties: Law and Politics in the Attorney General's Office, 1789–1990* (Lawrence: University Press of Kansas, 1992).

Appendix III
Attorney General Senate
Confirmation Votes, 1790–2005

Law Officer	Year Confirmed	Senate Vote	Law Officer	Year Confirmed	Senate Vote
Alberto Gonzales	2005	60–36	James McReynolds	1913	NR
John Ashcroft	2001	58–42	George Wickersham	1909	NR
Janet Reno	1993	98–0	Charles Bonaparte	1906	NR
William Barr	1991	Voice vote	William Moody	1904	NR
Richard Thornburgh	1988	85–0	Philander Knox	1901	NR
Edwin Meese III	1985	63–31–6	John Griggs	1898	NR
William French Smith	1981	96–1	Joseph McKenna	1897	NR
Benjamin Civiletti	1980	94–1	Judson Harmon	1895	NR
Griffin Bell	1977	75–21	Richard Olney	1893	NR
Edward Levi	1975	NR	William Miller	1889	NR
William Saxbe	1974	75–10–14	Augustus Garland	1885	NR
Elliot Richardson	1973	82–3–15	Benjamin Brewster	1881	NR
Richard Kleindienst	1972	64–19–16	Wayne MacVeagh	1881	NR
John Mitchell	1969	NR	Charles Devens	1877	NR
Ramsey Clark	1967	NR	Alphonso Taft	1876	NR
Nicholas Katzenbach	1965	NR	Edwards Pierrepont	1875	NR
Robert Kennedy	1961	NR	George Williams	1872	NR
William Rogers	1957	NR	Amos Ackerman	1870	NR
Herbert Brownell Jr.	1953	NR	Ebenezer Hoar	1869	NR
James McGranery	1952	52–18–26	William Evarts	1868	27–7
Howard McGrath	1949	NR	Henry Stanberry	1866	NR
Tom Clark	1945	NR	James Speed	1864	NR
Francis Biddle	1941	NR	Edward Bates	1861	40–5
Robert Jackson	1940	NR	Edwin Stanton	1860	NR
Frank Murphy	1939	78–7	Jeremiah Black	1857	NR
Homer Cummings	1933	NR	Caleb Cushing	1853	NR
William Mitchell	1929	NR	John Crittenden	1850	NR
John Sargent	1925	NR	Reverdy Johnson	1849	NR
Harlan F. Stone	1924	NR	Isaac Toucey	1848	NR
Harry Daugherty	1921	NR	Nathan Clifford	1846	NR
A. Mitchell Palmer	1919	NR	John Mason	1845	NR
Thomas Gregory	1914	NR	John Nelson	1843	NR

Law Officer	Year Confirmed	Senate Vote	Law Officer	Year Confirmed	Senate Vote
Hugh Legare	1841	NR	Richard Rush	1814	23–6
John Crittenden	1841	NR	William Pickney	1811	NR
Henry Gilpin	1840	NR	Caesar Rodney	1807	NR
Felix Grundy	1838	NR	John Breckenridge	1805	NR
Benjamin Butler	1833	NR	Levi Lincoln	1801	NR
Roger Taney	1831	NR	Charles Lee	1795	NR
John Berrien	1829	NR	William Bradford	1794	NR
William Wirt	1817	NR	Edmund Randolph	1790	NR

NR: Not recorded

Sources: Congressional Research Service "Department of Justice. Table 11. Attorneys General 1789–1985," CRS-15, CRS-16, CRS-17, Library of Congress, 1985. Author's tabulations from 1988 to 2005.

Notes

Introduction

1. Michael Herz, "Washington, Patton, Schwarzkopf and . . . Ashcroft?" *Constitutional Commentary* 19 (Winter 2002): 663. Herz documented that Fleischer used the term once before September 11, then thirteen times between that date and December 17, 2001, and not at all in the following six months.

2. White House, "press briefing by Attorney General, Secretary of HHS, Secretary of Transportation, and FEMA Director," Sept. 11, 2001, available at www.whitehouse.gov/news/releases/2001/09.

3. U.S. House of Representatives, Committee on the Judiciary, "Oversight of the Justice Department: Testimony of Attorney General John Ashcroft," Federal Document Clearing House, June 5, 2003. The members of Congress were John Carter (R-Tex.), Bob Goodlatte (R-Va.), Mark Green (R-Wisc.), John Hostettler (R-Ind.), Tammy Baldwin (D-Wisc.), and Anthony Weiner (D-N.Y.).

4. 9/11 Commission Hearing, Transcript of Hearings with Attorney General John Ashcroft, National Commission on Terrorist Attacks upon the United States, FDCH E-Media, Apr. 13, 2004, available at www.washingtonpost.com/wp-dyn/articles/A9088-2004Apr13.html#ashcroft.

5. *Larry King Live,* interviews with John Ashcroft, CNN, Feb. 7, 2001, Nov. 9, 2001, Jan. 21, 2002, May 31, 2002, Dec. 17, 2002, and Sept. 11, 2003, available at http://www.cnn.com/TRANSCRIPTS.

6. Herz, "Washington, Patton, Schwarzkopf."

7. David G. Savage and Eric Lichtblau, "Ashcroft Deals with Daunting Responsibilities," *Los Angeles Times,* Oct. 28, 2001.

Chapter 1: A Controversial Law Officer

1. Jack Lessenberry, "Ashcroft vs. Constitution," *Metro Times,* Nov. 28, 2001, available at www.metrotimes.com/editorial/story.asp?id=2714; Haroon Siddiqui, "Ayatollah Ashcroft's Law," *Toronto Star,* June 12, 2003, available at http://www.commondreams.org/cgi-bin/print.cgi?file=/views03/0612-07.htm; Ali Moayedian, "Letter from Ayatollah Ashcroft to His CounterPart Ayatollah Shahroudi of Iran," *CounterPunch,* Nov. 21, 2002, available at www.counter punch.org/moayedian1121.html.

2. Dick Meyer, "John Ashcroft: Minister of Fear," Against the Grain Commentary, CBSNews.com. June 12, 2002, available at www.cbsnews.com/stories/2002.

3. *Economist,* "Steamroller Ashcroft," U.S. Edition, May 3, 2003.

4. Jeffrey Toobin, "Profiles: Ashcroft's Ascent," *New Yorker,* Apr. 15, 2002, 52.

5. David Cole, "The Course of Least Resistance: Repeating History in the War on Terrorism," in Cynthia Brown, ed., *Lost Liberties: Ashcroft and the Assault on Personal Freedom* (New York: New Press, 2003), 13–32.

6. Stanley Coben, *A. Mitchell Palmer: Politician* (New York: Columbia University Press, 1963), vii.

7. Pat Holt, "Driving Dangerously with the Patriot Act," *Christian Science Monitor,* Oct. 2, 2003, available at www.csmonitor.com/2003/1002. Holt is the former chief of staff of the Senate Foreign Relations Committee.

8. Marianne Means, "John Ashcroft Will Not Be Missed," *Seattle Post-Intelligencer,* Nov. 11, 2004, available at seattlepi.nwsource.com/opinion/199080_means11.html.

9. Paul Krugman, "Travesty of Justice," *New York Times,* June 15, 2004, available at www.nytimes.com/2004/06/15/opinion; Dan Eggen and Jim VandeHei, "Ashcroft Taking Fire from GOP Stalwarts," *Washington Post,* Aug. 29, 2003, A1.

10. Byron York, "Democrats Need John Ashcroft to Kick Around," *The Hill,* Oct. 8, 2003, available through Lexis-Nexis Congressional Universe. Blasting the attorney general is an old campaign strategy; candidate Richard Nixon in the 1968 election made a similar promise to fire Lyndon Johnson's attorney general, Ramsey Clark.

11. Linda Feldmann, "John Edwards's Quest to Sway a Bigger Jury," *Christian Science Monitor,* Oct. 29, 2003, available at www.csmonitor.com/2003/1029.

12. Adam Nagourney, "For Democrats Challenging Bush, Ashcroft Is Exhibit A," *New York Times,* July 13, 2003, sec. 1, 14; Chitra Ragavan, "Ashcroft's Way," *U.S. News & World Report,* Jan. 26, 2004, available at www.usnews.com/usnews/news/articles/040126ashcroft.htm.

13. Julie Koszczuk, "Ashcroft Drawing Criticism from Both Sides of the Aisle," *Congressional Quarterly,* Sept. 7, 2002, 2287.

14. Joel Mowbray, "The Trouble with Ashcroft," Townhall.com. Dec. 20, 2001, available at http://www.townhall.com/columnists/joelmowbray/jm20011220.shtml.

15. William Safire, "Rights of Terror Suspects," *New York Times,* July 5, 2004, available at www.nytimes.com/2004/07/05/opinion. Safire initially published this opinion in a Nov. 15, 2001, column.

16. Bret Stephens, "Um, You're Right. (Not Really)," *Wall Street Journal,* Nov. 12, 2001, available at www.opinionjournal.com/taste/?id=110005886.

17. Walter B. Jones, "Congressman Jones Continues to Fight for Senator Ashcroft's Nomination for U.S. Attorney General," press release, Jan. 25, 2001, available at jones.house.gov/html/12501.html.

18. U.S. Senate, Remarks of Sen. Bob Smith, Committee on the Judiciary, Confirmation Hearing on the Nomination of John Ashcroft to be Attorney General of the United States, 107th Cong., 1st sess., S. Hrg. 107-196. Jan. 16–19, 2001.

19. Ibid., testimony of Kay Cole James.

20. Albert Hunt, "The Unaccountable Attorney General," *Wall Street Journal,* June 6, 2002, A15.

21. Dana Milbank, "Soaring Mightily into Retirement," *Washington Post,* Jan. 25, 2005, A 13, available at www.washingtonpost.com/wp-dyn/articles/A33675-2005Jan24.html.

22. Orrin Hatch, U.S. senator, Utah, interview with author, Washington, D.C., May 10, 2005.

23. See, for example, Ben Shapiro, "Liars, Manipulators and the Great John Ashcroft," *Town Hall,* Nov. 27, 2003, available at www.townhall.com/columnists/benshapiro/bs20030227.shtml.

24. Morton Kondracke, "Ashcroft-Bashing Could End Up Hurting Democrats," *Roll Call,* Sept. 11, 2003, available through Lexis-Nexis Congressional Universe.

25. Ragavan, "Ashcroft's Way."

26. Wendy Simmons, "Ashcroft Receives Mixed Review from the Public," Gallup Organization, Jan. 18, 2001, available at www.gallup.com.

27. *Late Show with David Letterman,* "Ashcroft to Appear on Letterman," Apr. 6, 2002, available at www.allstarz.org/davidletterman.

28. *Larry King Live,* CNN, available at www.cnn.com/TRANSCRIPTS. The broadcast dates are Feb. 7, 2001; Nov. 9, 2001; Jan. 21, 2002; May 31, 2002; Dec. 17, 2002; and Sept. 11, 2003. The Bob Jones University story aired on Jan. 12, 2001. Transcripts accessed Mar. 31, 2004.

29. Ibid. Transportation Secretary Norman Mineta and Homeland Security Secretary Tom Ridge twice appeared, and Education Secretary Spencer Abraham and Health and Human Services head Tommy Thompson each appeared once.

30. Vanderbilt Television News Index and Abstracts, Vanderbilt University. Archives, Dec. 31, 2004, available at tvnews.vanderbilt.edu/TV-NewsSearch. Search of archive for "John Ashcroft." These figures were compiled from a review of the titles and abstracts of evening news and special news programs from the announcement of Ashcroft's selection on December 22, 2000, to December 31, 2004.

31. Ibid. Searches of archive for "Patriot Act" and "terrorism," cross-referenced with "John Ashcroft" on Mar. 15, 2004. News coverage after this date increasingly focused on the presidential election.

32. *Washington Post,* archives of the "War on Terror Special Report," Apr. 8, 2004, available at www.washingtonpost.com. Search for "John Ashcroft."

33. Vanderbilt Television, search of archive for "John Ashcroft" on Dec. 31, 2004.

34. Ibid. Search of archive for "Janet Reno," "William French Smith," and "Griffin Bell" on Mar. 15. Reno's relevant dates are Feb. 11, 1993, to Dec. 30, 1996. Smith's are Dec. 11, 1980, to Dec. 31, 1984. Bell's are Dec. 20, 1976, to Aug. 15, 1979. Other recent attorneys general served briefer tenures.

35. Richard Ellis, *Presidential Lightning Rods: The Politics of Blame Avoidance* (Lawrence: University Press of Kansas, 1994), 174. Ellis relied on the same Vanderbilt Television News Index and Abstracts for his compilation.

36. Vanderbilt Television News Index and Abstracts, Vanderbilt University. Archives, Apr. 7, 2005, available at tvnews.vanderbilt.edu/TV-NewsSearch.

37. Kay Nordlinger, "Ashcroft with Horns," *National Review,* May 24, 2002, available at http://www.nationalreview.com/flashback/flashback-nordlinger.

38. *MAD* magazine, Jan. 2003, 43.

39. About.com, Political Humor, accessed Mar. 17, 2004, available at politicalhumor.about.com.

40. About.com. Political Humor, accessed Mar. 17, 2004, available at politicalhumor.mingco.com.

41. TrixiePix Graphics, accessed Mar. 17, 2004, available at www.trixiepixgraphics.com/books/ashcroft-constitution.

42. Bush House of Cards, accessed Mar. 17, 2004, available at www.bushhouseofcards.com.

43. Bongo News, accessed Mar. 17, 2004, available at www.bongonews.com.

44. Axis of Logic, accessed Mar. 17, 2004, available at www.axisoflogic.com. Jackson exposed her breast during the televised halftime show at the 2004 Super Bowl.

45. nbc17news.com, accessed Mar. 17, 2004, available at www.comand-post.org.

46. Boot Newt Sing Along Page, available at bootnewt.tripod.com/ashsongs, accessed Mar. 17, 2004. As of this date, this site alone had seventy Ashcroft song parodies.

47. See, for example, the comic strip "La Cucaracha," Dec. 25, 2003, with a cartoon Ashcroft sending Santa's reindeer to Guantánamo Bay because of their "fruity" names, and a chart in the on-line satire newspaper *The Onion* with his photograph next to a satirical listing of

"The Patriot Act's Problem Parts," including "Section 222, which revokes the Constitution," accessed Dec. 26, 2003, available at www.theonion.com.

48. Milbank, "Soaring Mightily into Retirement."

49. Julian Borger, "Staff Cry Poetic Injustice as Singing Ashcroft Introduces Patriot Games," *Guardian,* Mar. 4, 2002, available at www.guardian.co.uk.

50. Maureen Dowd, "A Blue Burka for Justice," *New York Times,* Jan. 30, 2002, A27; Richard Willing, "John Ashcroft to Teach Class at Va. College," *USA Today,* Mar. 16, 2005, available at www.usatoday.com/news/nation/2005-03-16-ashcroft-teach_x.htm.

51. Ragavan, "Ashcroft's Way."

52. Dan Eggen, "Sculpted Bodies and a Strip Act at Justice Dept.," *Washington Post,* June 25, 2005, A2, available at www.washingtonpost.com/wp-dyn/content/article/2005/06/24/AR2005062401797_pf.html. Ashcroft appeared in April 2002.

53. Ibid.

54. Dowd, "A Blue Burka for Justice."

55. Lloyd Grove, "Why Cher Is Steamed at John Ashcroft," *Washington Post,* Feb. 26, 2002, C3, available at www.washingtonpost.com/ac2/wp-dyn. Also see Borger, "Staff Cry Poetic Injustice."

56. Eggen, "Sculpted Bodies."

57. See Shirley Anne Warshaw, *Powersharing: White House–Cabinet Relations in the Modern Presidency* (Albany: State University of New York Press, 1996).

58. Toobin, "Profiles," 52.

59. Eric Lichtblau and Adam Liptak, "On Terror and Spying, Ashcroft Expands Reach," *New York Times,* Mar. 15, 2003, A1.

60. U.S. Department of Justice, "Department of Justice Success: The Past 4 Years," Nov. 9, 2004, available at www.usdoj.gov/ag/speeches/2004/ag_successes_110904.htm. One of Ashcroft's last public documents, this report trumpeted in boldfaced and underlined text: "There have been no major terrorist attacks on American soil since 9/11." Also see the opening remarks of Representatives Howard Coble, J. Randy Forbes, and John Hostettler in U.S. House of Representatives, Committee on the Judiciary, "Oversight of the Justice Department: Testimony of Attorney General John Ashcroft," Federal Document Clearing House, June 5, 2003. At the same hearing, Ashcroft added to that impression by concluding his recitation of the department's antiterrorism actions with the observation that "no major terror attack has occurred on American soil since September 11th." Also see United Press International, "Analysis: Ashcroft Trips but Carries On," Dec. 17, 2003, available through infotrac.galegroup.com.

61. See, for example, the title of *Lost Liberties: Ashcroft and the Assault on Personal Freedom,* edited by Cynthia Brown. Yet included in the book are essays on areas outside of the attorney general's control, such as military commissions, Guantánamo Bay prisoners, and international policies. Also see Nat Hentoff, *The War on the Bill of Rights and the Gathering Resistance* (New York: Seven Stories Press, 2003).

62. White House, "Fact Sheet: Counter-terrorism; The White House's Position on Terrorism," Office of the Press Secretary, 1995, available at nsi.org/Library/Terrorism/policy/html. Quoting Clinton's address at the State Fair Arena, Oklahoma City, Oklahoma, Apr. 23, 1995.

63. Antiterrorism and Effective Death Penalty Act of 1996, P.L.104-132, 110 Stat.1214.

64. James X. Dempsey and David Cole, *Terrorism and the Constitution,* 2nd ed. (Washington, D.C.: First Amendment Foundation, 2002), 3; Dan Eggen and Steve Fainaru, "For Prosecutors, 1996 Law Is Key Part of Anti-terror Strategy," *Washington Post,* Oct. 15, 2002, A2, available at www.washingtonpost.com/ac2/wp-dyn/A25838-2002Oct14.

65. 9/11 Commission Hearing, Transcript of Hearings with Attorney General John Ashcroft, National Commission on Terrorist Attacks upon the United States, FDCH E-Media, Apr.

13, 2004, available at www.washingtonpost.com/wp-dyn/articles/A9088-2004Apr13.html #ashcroft.

66. Vanessa Blum, "Why Bush Won't Let Go," *Legal Times,* Feb. 4, 2002, 1; Dana Milbank, "In War, It's Power to the President," *Washington Post,* Nov. 20, 2001, A1, available at www .washingtonpost.com/wp-dyn; David Sanger, "When Goals Meet Reality: Bush's Reversal on 9/11 Testimony," *New York Times,* Mar. 31, 2004, available at www.nytimes.com/2004/03/31/ politics.

67. Robert Kaiser, "That Giant Hissing Sound: What You Hear Is Congress Giving Up Its Clout," *Washington Post National Weekly Edition,* Mar. 22–28, 2004. 22.

68. Dana Milbank, "In Cheney's Shadow, Counsel Pushes the Conservative Cause," *Washington Post,* Oct. 11, 2004, A21, available at www.washingtonpost.com/ac2/wp-dyn/A2265-2004 Oct10.

69. Mark Rozell, "Executive Privilege and the Bush Administration: Essay: Executive Privilege Revived? Secrecy and Conflict during the Bush Presidency," *Duke Law Journal* 52 (Nov. 2002): 403.

70. Bob Woodward, "Cheney Upholds Power of the Presidency," *Washington Post,* Jan. 20, 2005, A7, available at www.washingtonpost.com/wp-dyn/articles/A22190-2205Jan19.html.

71. James Pfiffner, "Introduction," in Gary Gregg and Mark Rozell, eds., *Considering the Bush Presidency* (New York: Oxford University Press, 2004).

72. U.S. Department of Justice, press release, "Attorney General Ashcroft Announces Citizen Corps' Volunteers in Police Service Initiative." May 30, 2002, available at www.usdoj .gov/opa/pr/2002/May/02.

73. David Corn, "The Fundamental John Ashcroft," *Mother Jones,* Mar. 2002, available at www.motherjones.com/magazine/MA02.

74. Kevin Johnson and Toni Locy, "Patriot Act at Heart of Ashcroft's Influence," *USA Today,* Sept. 15, 2003, available at /www.usatoday.com/news/washington/2003-09-15.

75. Editorial, "The Ashcroft Years," *St. Louis Post-Dispatch,* Dec. 20, 2004, 6B.

Chapter 2: The Singular Office of Attorney General

1. U.S. Senate, Committee on the Judiciary, "Confirmation Hearing on the Nomination of John Ashcroft to Be Attorney General of the United States," 107th Cong., 1st sess., S. Hrg. 107-196, Jan. 16–19, 2001, Opening remarks by Senator Patrick Leahy.

2. Among the close presidential advisers in the past fifty years were Robert Kennedy, John Mitchell, and Edwin Meese III. Former attorneys general who joined the Court were Roger Taney, Nathan Clifford, James McReynolds, Harlan Fiske Stone, Frank Murphy, Robert Jackson, and Tom Clark. At least two other nominations of former attorneys general—Ebenezer Hoar and Caleb Cushing—were not successful. The attorney general who hoped to use his tenure to become president was A. Mitchell Palmer in 1920. Somewhat ironically, Palmer's actions as attorney general—particularly the 1919–1920 Palmer raids on suspected anarchists and Reds—undid his ambitions.

3. Ann Blackman et al., "The Fight for Justice," *Time,* Jan. 22, 2001, 20.

4. U.S. Senate, "Confirmation Hearing on John Ashcroft."

5. Barack Obama, Nomination of Alberto R. Gonzales to Be Attorney General of the United States, Senate, 109th Cong., 1st sess., Feb. 3, 2005, 151 *Congressional Record* S923, 928.

6. Edwin Meese, "Introductory Remarks to True Faith and Allegiance by the Honorable John Ashcroft," Heritage Foundation Lecture no. 865, Feb. 11, 2005, available at www.heritage .org/Research/LegalIssues/hl865.cfm. He was quoting his predecessor, William French Smith.

7. Richard Thornburgh, U.S. attorney general, 1988–1991, interview with author, Washington, D.C., May 12, 2005.

8. Ibid.

9. U.S. Senate, "Confirmation Hearing on John Ashcroft."

10. Bert Brandenburg, "Open Government in the Ashcroft Era: What Went Wrong and How to Make It Right," Watching Justice: An Eye on the Department of Justice, 2005, 3, available at www.watching justice.org/reports/article.php?docID=663.

11. U.S. Constitution, Article II, Section 2.

12. Nancy V. Baker, Conflicting Loyalties: Law and Politics in the Attorney General's Office, 1789–1990 (Lawrence: University Press of Kansas, 1992).

13. Charles Warren, "New Light on the History of the Federal Judiciary Act of 1789," Harvard Law Review 37 (Nov. 1932): 109.

14. Judiciary Act of 1789, Chapter 20 § 35, 1 Stat. 73.

15. Rebecca Mae Salokar, The Solicitor General: The Politics of Law (Philadelphia: Temple University Press, 1992), 29, 30.

16. Baker, Conflicting Loyalties.

17. Dee Ashley Akers, "The Advisory Opinion Function of the Attorney General," Kentucky Law Journal 38 (1950): 561.

18. Peter Heiser Jr., "The Opinion Writing Function of Attorneys General," Idaho Law Review 18 (1982): 41.

19. Edward Levi, An Introduction to Legal Reasoning (Chicago: University of Chicago Press, 1949), 6.

20. Martin Sheffer, "The Attorney General and Presidential Power," Presidential Studies Quarterly 12 (1982): 54–65.

21. Nancy V. Baker, "Guarding the Parchment Barrier: The Attorney General and Presidential Power in Wartime," in Lori Cox-Han and Michael Genovese, eds., The Presidency and the Challenge of Democracy (New York: Palgrave/Macmillan, 2006).

22. Baker, Conflicting Loyalties.

23. This phenomenon has long been noted by scholars in critical legal studies; they argue that judges and attorneys can utilize legal interpretation to "advance their ideologies through legal argument and still sincerely claim to be upholding the rule of law." See, for example, Jack M. Balkin, "Bush v. Gore and the Boundary between Law and Politics," Yale Law Journal 110 (2001): 1407.

24. U.S. Senate, "Confirmation Hearing on John Ashcroft."

25. Vanessa Blum, "Curtains Raised for Change at DOJ?" Legal Times. Mar. 8, 2005, available at www.law.com/jsp.

26. Michael Paris, "Legal Mobilization and the Politics of Reform: Lessons from School Finance Litigation in Kentucky, 1984–1995," Law and Social Inquiry 26 (2001): 631.

27. Patricia Ewick and Susan S. Silbey, The Common Place of Law: Stories from Everyday Life (Chicago: University of Chicago Press, 1998). Also see Sally Engel Merry, Getting Justice and Getting Even: Legal Consciousness among Working-Class Americans (Chicago: University of Chicago Press, 1990); and Austin Sarat, "The Law Is All Over: Power, Resistance and the Legal Consciousness of the Welfare Poor," Yale Journal of Law and the Humanities 2 (1990): 343–379.

28. Alexis de Tocqueville, Democracy in America, trans. and ed. Harvey Mansfield and Delba Winthrop (Chicago: University of Chicago Press, 2000), vol. 1, pt. 2, chap. 8, p. 257.

29. Quoted in Mike Allen, Martha Sawyer, and Graydon Royce, "Defining the Common Good," Minneapolis Star-Tribune, Feb. 9, 2002, 7B, available through Lexis-Nexis Academic Universe.

30. There is much literature in sociology on the potency of certain symbols of civil religion in the United States, among them the anthem "God Bless America" and historic battlefields like Gettysburg. See Robert Bellah, "Religion and Legitimation in the American Republic," *Society* 35 (Jan./Feb. 1998): 193; Brian Lowe, "Soviet and American Civil Religion: A Comparison," *Journal of Interdisciplinary Studies* 13 (2001): 73; Stephen Scott, "In the U.S., Symbols of a Civil Religion Are Plentiful," *St. Paul Pioneer Press,* Oct. 25, 2001, available through Lexis-Nexis Academic Universe; "Some Inaugural Speeches Serve as Sermons," *St. Paul Pioneer Press,* Oct. 25, 2001, available through Lexis-Nexis Academic Universe.

31. Daniel Meador, *The President, the Attorney General and the Department of Justice* (Charlottesville, Va.: White Burkett Miller Center of Public Affairs, University of Virginia, 1980), 26.

32. U.S. Senate, "Confirmation Hearing on John Ashcroft."

33. Baker, *Conflicting Loyalties,* 32–33.

34. Ibid.

35. Ibid.

36. Donald McCoy, *Calvin Coolidge: The Quiet President* (New York: Macmillan, 1967). Eventually, he selected someone else, who was then confirmed unanimously.

37. Baker, *Conflicting Loyalties.* Senate debates were held in 1870, 1924, 1953, and 1974.

38. Gerald Ford, memorandum, "President's talking points at the swearing in ceremony of Edward Levi," Feb. 7, 1975, Folder FG 17/A 8/9/74-2/10/75, Box 88, FG 17/A-Department of Justice, Gerald R. Ford Library.

39. Baker, *Conflicting Loyalties.*

40. Ibid.

41. Ibid., 27.

42. Homer Cummings, *Liberty under Law and Administration* (New York: Scribner's, 1934), 114, 119.

43. Elizabeth Mensch, "The History of Mainstream Legal Thought," in David Kairys, ed., *The Politics of Law* 3rd ed. (New York: Basic Books, 1998), 23–53.

44. David Kairys, "Introduction," in David Kairys, ed., *The Politics of Law,* 3rd ed. (New York: Basic Books, 1998), 1–20.

45. James Pfiffner, "Introduction," in Gary Gregg and Mark Rozell, eds., *Considering the Bush Presidency* (New York: Oxford University Press, 2004), 15.

46. *Larry King Live,* "Interview with John Ashcroft and Ted Olson," CNN, Dec. 17, 2002, available at www.cnn.com/TRANSCRIPTS/0212/17.

47. J. Guadalupe Carney, 2001. "How Bush Chose Ashcroft," *Time,* Jan. 22, 2001, 27.

48. Blackman et al., "The Fight for Justice," 20.

49. U.S. Senate, "Confirmation Hearing on John Ashcroft," remarks of Senator Strom Thurmond.

50. Elisabeth Bumiller and Eric Lichtblau, "Debating a Leak: Attorney General Is Closely Linked to Inquiry Figures," *New York Times,* Oct. 2, 2003, 1A.

51. Ibid.

52. David Johnston and Neil Lewis, "Religious Right Made Big Push to Put Ashcroft in Justice Dept.," *New York Times,* Jan. 7, 2001, sec. 1, p. 1.

53. *Larry King Live,* "John Ashcroft Discusses His New Job as Attorney General," CNN, Feb. 7, 2001, available at www.cnn.com/TRANSCRIPTS/0102/07.

54. Brian Duffy, "Respecting the Client, with Clarity," *U.S. News & World Report,* Jan. 26, 2004, 32.

55. Carney, "How Bush Chose Ashcroft," 27.

56. Jeffrey Toobin, "Profiles: Ashcroft's Ascent," *New Yorker,* Apr. 15, 2002, 53.

57. People for the American Way, "Ashcroft's Missouri Record Found 'Deeply Disturbing' on Issues of Civil Rights, Reproductive Rights, and Other Fundamental Constitutional Freedoms," *Oppose Ashcroft,* Jan. 13, 2001, available at www.opposeashcroft.com/press.

58. U.S. Senate, "Confirmation Hearing on John Ashcroft."

59. Toobin, "Profiles," 52.

60. John J. Miller, "Mr. Clean: John Ashcroft Has a Sterling Ethical Record and a Socially Conservative Base. But Does He Have What It Takes to Win?" *National Review,* Mar. 23, 1998, 36; Blackman et al., "The Fight for Justice," 2001.

61. U.S. Senate, "Confirmation Hearing on John Ashcroft."

62. Ibid., "Statement by Sam Brownback."

63. Ibid., "Statement by Joseph Biden."

64. Joshua Green, "How Ashcroft Happened," *American Prospect,* Feb. 26, 2001, 16–17.

65. People for the American Way, "Ashcroft's Missouri Record."

66. Betsy McCaughey, "Ashcroft, Man of Principle: His Quest for a Restrained Judiciary," *National Review,* Jan. 8, 2001, available at www.nationalreview.com/comment.

67. U.S. Senate, "Confirmation Hearing on John Ashcroft."

68. Mary Anne Borrelli, *The President's Cabinet: Gender, Power and Representation* (Boulder, Colo.: Lynne Rienner, 2002), 178.

69. U.S. Senate, "Confirmation Hearing on John Ashcroft."

70. Borrelli, *The President's Cabinet,* 183.

71. U.S. Senate, "Confirmation Hearing on John Ashcroft."

72. As noted in chapter 3, John Tower's failure to be confirmed as head of the Defense Department was only the second time that the Senate had rejected a former senator for a cabinet position.

73. U.S. Senate, "Confirmation Hearing on John Ashcroft."

74. Borrelli, *The President's Cabinet,* 182.

75. U.S. Senate, "Confirmation Hearing on John Ashcroft."

76. Ibid.

77. Ibid. *Roe v. Wade* (1973) and *Planned Parenthood v. Casey* (1994) are Supreme Court decisions recognizing a woman's right to choose an abortion.

78. U.S. Department of Justice, statement of Senator John Ashcroft, "Upon His Confirmation as Attorney General," Feb. 1, 2001, available at www.usdoj.gov/ag/speeches/2001.

79. Duffy, "Respecting the Client," 32.

80. Blum, "Curtains Raised for Change at DOJ?"

81. Vanessa Blum, "Point Man: Paul Clement Leads the Charge in Defending the Administration's Tactics in the War on Terror," *Legal Times,* Jan. 16, 2004, available at www .law.com/jsp/article.jsp?id=1073944820670.

82. Toobin, "Profiles," 54.

83. David Vise and Dan Eggen, "Ashcroft Names Key Aides to Senior Posts at Justice," *Washington Post,* Feb. 3, 2001, A4.

84. Blum, "Point Man: Paul Clement."

85. U.S. Department of Justice, "Personnel Announcement," Mar. 1, 2001, available at www .whitehouse.gov/news/releases/2001/03/20010301-3.html.

86. Toobin, "Profiles," 54.

87. Dan Eggen, "Liberals Need Not Apply?" *Washington Post National Weekly Edition,* Jan. 20–26, 2003, 14.

88. C. Madison (Brick) Brewer, telephone interview with author, May 24, 2005; Eggen, "Liberals Need Not Apply?"

89. Brandenburg, "Open Government in the Ashcroft Era."

90. Griffin Bell, interview with author, Atlanta, Georgia, May 16, 2005.

91. Brewer, telephone interview.

92. See, for example, U.S. Attorney General Remarks, "Attorney General Transcript: News Conference Regarding Zacarias Moussaoui," Dec. 11, 2001, available at www.usdoj.gov/archive/ag/speeches/2001/agcrisisremarks12_11.htm; U.S. Attorney General Remarks, "Attorney General Ashcroft Announces Indictment of Alleged Terrorist Financier," Chicago, Illinois, Oct. 9, 2002, available at www.usdoj.gov/archive/ag/speeches/2002/100902agremarksbifindictment.htm; U.S. Attorney General Remarks, "Implementation of NSEERS," Nov. 7, available at www.usdoj.gov/ag/speeches/2002; U.S. Attorney General Remarks, "Islamic Group Indictment/SAMS," Apr. 9, available at www.usdoj.gov/ag/speeches/2002; U.S. Attorney General Remarks, "National Security Entry-Exit Registration System," June 6, available at www.usdoj.gov/ag/speeches/2002; U.S. Attorney General Remarks, "The Transfer of Abdullah Al Muhajir (Born José Padilla) to the Department of Defense as an Enemy Combatant," June 10, available at www.usdoj.gov/ag/speeches/2002; and U.S. Attorney General Remarks, "Operation E-Con Press Conference," May 16, 2003, available at www.usdoj.gov/ag/speeches/2003.

93. Marianne Means, "John Ashcroft Will Not Be Missed," *Seattle Post-Intelligencer,* Nov. 11, 2004, available at seattlepi.nwsource.com/opinion/199080_means11.html.

94. Republican Policy Committee, "John Ashcroft: The Most Experienced Attorney General Nominee—in U.S. History," U.S. Senate, Jan. 18, 2001, available at www.senate.gov/~rpc/releases/1999/jd011801.htm.

95. Green, "How Ashcroft Happened"; Elisabeth Bumiller, "Evangelicals Sway White House on Human Rights Issues Abroad," *New York Times,* Oct. 26, 2003, available at www.nytimes.com/2003/10/26/politics; Alicia Montgomery, "Conservatives Flex Muscles over Ashcroft," *Salon,* Jan. 11, 2001, available at salon.com/politics/feature/2001/01/11/conservatives.

96. Borrelli, *The President's Cabinet,* 1.

97. Brian Doherty, "John Ashcroft's Power Grab," *Reason On-line,* June 2002, available at reason.com/0206.

98. Walter E. Dellinger et al., Memorandum to Attorney General John Ashcroft, Judge Alberto Gonzales and Acting Assistant Attorney General Daniel B. Levin, "Attached Principles to Guide the Office of Legal Counsel," Dec. 21, 2004, available at leahy.senate.gov/press/200412/122204a.html.

99. Louis Henkin, *Foreign Affairs and the Constitution* (New York: Norton, 1975), 40.

100. U.S. Department of Justice, Office of Legal Counsel, Memorandum for William J. Haynes III from John Yoo and Robert Delahunty, "Re: Application of Treaties and Laws to al Qaeda and Taliban Detainees," Jan. 9, 2002, Memo 4 in Karen Greenberg and Joshua Dratel, eds., *The Torture Papers: The Road to Abu Ghraib* (New York: Cambridge University Press, 2005).

101. Ibid.

102. White House, Memorandum from Alberto R. Gonzales to President Bush, "Decision Re: Application of the Geneva Convention on Prisoners of War to the Conflict with al Qaeda and the *Taliban*," Jan. 15, 2002, Memo 7 in Greenberg and Dratel, *The Torture Papers;* Neil Lewis and Eric Schmitt, "Lawyers Decided Bans on Torture Didn't Bind Bush," *New York Times,* June 8, 2004, available at www.nytimes.com/20-04/06/08/politics/08ABUS.html.

103. U.S. Attorney General, Letter to President George Bush from John Ashcroft, Feb. 1, 2002, Memo 9 in Greenberg and Dratel, *The Torture Papers.*

104. Louis Fisher, *Military Tribunals and Presidential Power* (Lawrence: University Press of Kansas, 2005), 198–199.

105. U.S. Department of Justice, Office of Legal Counsel, Memorandum for William J.

Haynes III from Patrick Philbin and John C. Yoo, "Re: Possible Habeas Jurisdiction over Aliens Held at Guantanamo Bay, Cuba," Dec. 28, 2001, Memo 3 in Greenberg and Dratel, *The Torture Papers,* 29, 36.

106. Dana Priest, "Reinterpreting International Law?" *Washington Post National Weekly Edition,* Nov. 1–7, 2004, 16; Fourth Geneva Convention, Article 49.

107. U.S. Department of Justice, Office of Legal Counsel, Memorandum for Alberto Gonzales, Counsel to the President, from Jay S. Bybee, "Re: Standards of Conduct for Interrogation under 18 U.S.C. §§ 2340-2340A," Aug. 1, 2002, Memo 14 in Greenberg and Dratel, *The Torture Papers.*

108. Ibid.

109. Michael Isikoff, "Double Standards?" *Newsweek* Web exclusive, May 25, 2004, available at www.msnbc.com/id/5032094/site/newsweek.

110. Dana Priest, "CIA Puts Harsh Tactics on Hold," *Washington Post,* June 27, 2004, A1, available at www.washingtonpost.com/ac2/wp-dyn/A8534-2004Jun26; Adam Liptak, "Author of '02 Memo on Torture: 'Gentle' Soul for a Harsh Topic," *New York Times,* June 24, 2004, available at www.nytimes.com/2004/06/24/politics.

111. Neil Lewis, "Bush Didn't Order Any Breach of Torture Laws, Ashcroft Says," *New York Times,* June 9, 2004, available at www.nytimes.com/2004/06/09/politics.

112. Dana Priest and R. Jeffrey Smith, "Memo Offered Justification for Use of Torture," *Washington Post,* June 8, 2004, A1, available at www.washingtonpost.com/ac2/wp-dyn/A23373-2004Jun7, quoting Defense Department general counsel William J. Haynes II.

113. Carl Levin, nomination of Alberto R. Gonzales to be Attorney General of the United States, Senate, 109th Cong., 1st sess., Feb. 3, 2005, 151 *Congressional Record* S923, 928.

114. Lewis and Schmitt, "Lawyers Decided Bans on Torture."

115. Associated Press, "New U.S. Memo Backs Off Torture Arguments," *New York Times,* Dec. 31, 2004, available at www.nytimes.com/2004/12/31/politics/html.

116. Fisher, *Military Tribunals and Presidential Power,* 206.

117. The most influential decision was issued in 1939, upholding the federal government's authority to outlaw sawed-off shotguns. Charles Lane, "Guns for All?" *Washington Post National Weekly Edition,* May 13–19, 2002, 32; Matthew Nosanchuk, "The Embarrassing Interpretation of the Second Amendment," *Northern Kentucky Law Review* 29 (2002): 766.

118. Robert J. Spitzer, "Gun Rights for Terrorists? Gun Control and the Bush Presidency," In Jon Kraus, Kevin McMahon, and David Rankin, eds., *Transformed by Crisis: The Presidency of George W. Bush and American Politics* (New York: Palgrave Macmillan, 2004), 154.

119. Lane, "Guns for All?"

120. James Vicini, "Supreme Court Declines Review on Right to Own Guns," Reuters, June 10, 2002, available at news.findlaw.com/new/20020610/courtgunsdc.html.

121. *Emerson v. U.S.* and *Haney v. U.S., 122* S.Ct. 2362 (2002).

122. Spitzer, "Gun Rights for Terrorists?"

123. Chitra Ragavan, "Ashcroft's Way," *U.S. News and World Report,* Jan. 26, 2004, available at www.usnews.com/usnews/news/articles/040126ashcroft.htm.

124. U.S. Department of Justice, Office of Legal Counsel, Memorandum Opinion for the Attorney General, Aug. 24, 2004, available at www.usdoj.gov/olc/secondamendment2.htm.

125. U.S. Attorney General Remarks, U.S. Conference of Mayors, eMediaMillWorks, Oct. 25, 2001, available at www.washingtonpost.com/wp-svr/nation/specials/attacked/transcript/ashcroft.

126. Nat Hentoff, "John Ashcroft v. the Constitution: Giving the FBI a 'Blank Warrant,'" *Village Voice,* Nov. 26, 2001, available at www.villagevoice.com/news/0148,hentoff,30259,6.html.

127. U.S. House of Representatives, Committee on the Judiciary, "Oversight of the Justice Department: Testimony of Attorney General John Ashcroft," June 5, 2003, Federal Document Clearing House.

128. U.S. Senate, Committee on the Judiciary, "Hearings Concerning Oversight of the Department of Justice," witness: Attorney General John Ashcroft, July 25, 2002, available at www.usdoj.gov/ag/testimony/2002.

129. U.S. Attorney General Remarks, "U.S. Attorneys Conference, New York City," Oct. 1, 2002, available at www.usdoj.gov/ag/speeches/2002/1001012agremarkstousattorneysconference.htm.

130. U.S. Attorney General Remarks, "International Association of Chiefs of Police Conference," Oct. 7, 2002, available at www.usdoj.gov/ag/speeches/2002/100702chiefsofpolicemn1.htm.

131. U.S. Attorney General Transcript, News Conference—SEVIS, May 10, 2002, available at www.usdoj.gov/ag/speeches/2002.

132. U.S. Attorney General Remarks, Eighth Circuit Judges Conference, Duluth, Minn., Aug. 7, 2002, available at www.usdoj.gov/ag/speeches/2002.

133. U.S. Attorney General Remarks, "Federalist Society National Convention," Nov. 15, 2003, available at www.usdoj.gov/ag/speeches/2003.

134. U.S. Attorney General Remarks, "The Transfer of Abdullah al Muhajir (Born José Padilla) to the Department of Defense as an Enemy Combatant," June 10, 2002, available at www.usdoj.gov/ag/speeches/2002.

135. Priest and Smith, "Memo Offered Justification."

136. Edward Klein, "We're Not Destroying Rights, We're Protecting Rights," *Parade Magazine,* May 19, 2002, 4.

137. U.S. Attorney General Remarks, Eastern District of Virginia/Interview Projects Results Announcement, Mar. 20, 2002, available at www.usdoj.gov/ag/speeches/2002.

138. U.S. Attorney General Remarks, "Attorney General Guidelines," May 30, 2002, available at www.usdoj.gov/ag/speeches/2005/53002agpreparedremarks.htm.

139. *Larry King Live,* "Interview with John Ashcroft," CNN, Jan. 21, 2002, available at www.cnn.com/TRANSCRIPTS/0201/21.

140. Curt Anderson, "Ashcroft: Nuke Threat the Largest Danger," Associated Press, Jan. 27, 2005, available at news.findlaw.com/ap_stories/a/w/1152/1-27/2005/20050.

141. R. Jeffrey Smith and Dan Eggen, "Gonzales Helped Set the Course for Detainees," *Washington Post,* Jan. 5, 2005, A1, available at www.washingtonpost.com/ac2/wp-dyn/A48446-2.

Chapter 3: Understanding Ashcroft

1. *Law for Business,* published by West Publishing, is in its fourteenth edition (July 2001).

2. John Ashcroft, *Lessons from a Father to His Son* (Nashville, Tenn.: Thomas Nelson, 1998).

3. Margaret M. Poloma, "Charisma and Structure in the Assemblies of God: Revisiting O'Dea's Five Dilemmas," prepared for the Organizing Religious Work Project, Feb. 6, 2002, available at www3.uakron.edu/sociology/poloma.htm.

4. Ashcroft, *Lessons from a Father.*

5. Ibid.; Member Profile Report Archive, "Senator John Ashcroft," 106th Congress, Congressional Information Service database, available through Lexis-Nexis Congressional Universe; Nancy Baker, "John Ashcroft," in Roger Newman, ed., *Yale Biographical Dictionary of American Law* (New Haven, Conn.: Yale University Press, 2006).

6. *State of Missouri v. National Organization for Women,* 620 F. 2d 1301 (1980); 1980 U.S. App. LEXIS 19133.

7. *Planned Parenthood Association of Kansas City, Missouri v. Ashcroft,* 462 U.S. 476; 103 S.Ct. 2517 (1983); 1983 U.S. LEXIS 64.

8. Ann Blackman et al., "The Fight for Justice," *Time,* Jan. 22, 2001, 20. Ashcroft's critics argued that he doubled the actual cost of the desegregation plans.

9. Jason Zengerle, "The Gospel According to John: Senator Ashcroft's Longshot Presidential Bid," *New Republic,* Dec. 22, 1997, 18, available at www.tnr.com/archive/12/122297/zengerle 122297.html.

10. Blackman et al., "The Fight for Justice," 20.

11. Chitra Ragavan and Sheila Kaplan, "Is Ashcroft Unsinkable?" *U.S. News & World Report,* Jan. 8, 2001, 13.

12. U.S. Senate, Committee on the Judiciary, "Confirmation Hearing on the Nomination of John Ashcroft to Be Attorney General of the United States," 107th Cong., 1st sess., S. Hrg. 107-196. Jan. 16–19, 2001.

13. Blackman et al., "The Fight for Justice."

14. Virginia Young, "Ashcroft Backs Fight against Moving Patient," *St. Louis Post-Dispatch,* Feb. 12, 1991, 7A; David Aguillard, "The State Does Battle Anonymously," *St. Louis Post-Dispatch,* Dec. 12, 1991, 1C.

15. Brian Doherty, "John Ashcroft's Power Grab," *Reason On-line,* June 2002, available at reason.com/0206.

16. U.S. Senate, "Confirmation Hearing on John Ashcroft," presentation by Christopher Bond.

17. Ibid., Senator Orrin Hatch Statement.

18. Blackman et al., "The Fight for Justice."

19. Ibid.

20. Zengerle, "The Gospel," 18.

21. Blackman et al., "The Fight for Justice."

22. Jim Mosley and Kathryn Rogers, "Ashcroft Takes Office, Urges Fight on Drugs, Porn," *St. Louis Post-Dispatch,* Jan. 10, 1989, 1A.

23. Member Profile Report Archive, "Senator John Ashcroft," 1998.

24. U.S. Senate, "Confirmation Hearing on John Ashcroft," Senator Orrin Hatch Statement.

25. National Association of Attorneys General, "Resolution: Congratulating Gale Norton and John Ashcroft," adopted Mar. 14, 2001, Washington, D.C., available at http://www.naag .org/naag/resolutions/res-spr01-norton_ashcroft.php.

26. Republican Policy Committee, "John Ashcroft: The Most Experienced Attorney General Nominee—in U.S. History," U.S. Senate, Jan. 18, 2001, available at www.senate.gov/ ~rpc/releases/1999/jd011801.htm. Italics in original.

27. Chitra Ragavan, "Ashcroft's Way," *U.S. News & World Report,* Jan. 26, 2004, available at www.usnews.com/usnews/news/articles/040126ashcroft.htm, quoting his deputy at Justice, James Comey, and his oldest friend, Dick Foth.

28. Doherty, "John Ashcroft's Power Grab."

29. Member Profile Report Archive.

30. Ibid.

31. John Ashcroft, "A Guide to Charitable Choice: The Rules of Section 104 of the 1996 Federal Welfare Law Governing State Cooperation with Faith-Based Social Service Providers," the Center for Public Justice, Washington, D.C., and the Christian Legal Society's Center for Law and Religious Freedom, Jan. 1997, available at the Christian Legal Society's Web site, www.clsnet.org.

32. John Ashcroft, "Statement on the Articles of Impeachment against President Clinton,"

Congressional Record, Feb. 12, 1999, available at www.australianpolitics.com/usa/clinton/trial/statements/ashcroft.shtml.

33. Ibid.

34. Human Life Act of 1998, S 2135.

35. David Johnston and Neil Lewis, "Religious Right Made Big Push to Put Ashcroft in Justice Dept.," *New York Times,* Jan. 7, 2001, sec. 1, p. 1.

36. Senate Joint Resolution, SJ Res. 49, 1998.

37. *Congressional Quarterly,* "Ashcroft Backed Genetic Privacy Bill, Opposed New Gun Show Restrictions, Voted to Curb Abortion and Cloning," Jan. 6, 2001, 29; 1997–1998 Legislative Chronology, "Assisted Suicide," and "Judicial Activism," in *Congress and the Nation, 1997–2001,* vol. 10 (Washington, D.C.: CQ Press, 2002).

38. Howard Gleckman, "John Ashcroft's Holy War," *Business Week Online,* Apr. 23, 2002, available at www.businessweek.com/bwdaily/dnflash/apr2002.

39. United Press International, "Analysis: Senate May Go Easy on Ashcroft," Dec. 22, 2000, P1008357u7573.

40. *Congressional Quarterly,* "Ashcroft Backed"; 1997–1998 Legislative Chronology, 2002.

41. Jack White, "The Wrong Choice for Justice," *Time,* Jan 8, 2001, 30.

42. U.S. Senate, "Confirmation Hearing on John Ashcroft"; Randall Kennedy, "In Extremis," *American Prospect,* Feb. 26, 2001, 14. Judge White had supported a retrial on the grounds that effective counsel was needed to ensure a fair trial in a capital case.

43. *Congressional Quarterly,* "Ashcroft Backed."

44. Ibid., 29.

45. Johnston and Lewis, "Religious Right."

46. William Raspberry, "No!" *Washington Post,* Dec. 29, 2000, A33.

47. *Congressional Quarterly,* "Ashcroft Backed."

48. Jeff Bingaman, U.S. senator, New Mexico, interview with author, Las Cruces, New Mexico, Mar. 31, 2005.

49. Bill Lambrecht and Patrick Wilson, "Abortion Activists Vow to Stress Moral Issues," *St. Louis Post-Dispatch,* Jan. 23, 1998, 4A.

50. Doherty, "John Ashcroft's Power Grab"; Johnston and Lewis, "Religious Right." Out of 2.3 million votes, Ashcroft lost by fewer than 49,000.

51. Thomas B. Edsall, "Christian Right Lifts Ashcroft," *Washington Post,* Apr. 14, 1998, A1. Reportedly, Robertson had considered Ashcroft as a possible attorney general nominee when he was running for the White House in 1988.

52. Jon Sawyer and Lia Dean, "Durbin, Ashcroft Let Others Pick Up the Tab for Travels," *St. Louis Post-Dispatch,* Aug. 3, 1998, 1A.

53. Reuters, "Ashcroft Wins South Carolina Presidential Poll," May 17, 1998.

54. John J. Miller, "Mr. Clean: John Ashcroft Has a Sterling Ethical Record and a Socially Conservative Base. But Does He Have What It Takes to Win?" *National Review,* Mar. 23, 1998, 36.

55. *Church & State,* "Ashcroft Bails Out of Presidential Race," Feb. 1999, 15.

56. Miller, "Mr. Clean."

57. Zengerle, "The Gospel."

58. Ibid.; Miller, "Mr. Clean."

59. Doherty, "John Ashcroft's Power Grab"; Johnston and Lewis, "Religious Right"; *Economist,* "Dead Man Winning," U.S. edition, Nov. 11, 2000, 41.

60. U.S. Senate, "Confirmation Hearing on John Ashcroft," quoted in opening remarks of Senator Orrin Hatch.

61. Doherty, "John Ashcroft's Power Grab"; Johnston and Lewis, "Religious Right"; *The Economist,* "Dead Man Winning," U.S. edition.

62. Joshua Green, "How Ashcroft Happened," *American Prospect,* Feb. 26, 2001, 16–17.

63. United Press International, "Analysis."

64. Green, "How Ashcroft Happened"; J. Guadalupe Carney, "How Bush Chose Ashcroft," *Time,* Jan. 22, 2001, 27; *Weekly Standard,* "How Ashcroft Won," Jan. 1–8, 2001, 2.

65. United Press International, "Analysis."

66. Michael Isikoff, "Why Keating Didn't Cut It," *Newsweek,* Jan. 15, 2001, 28.

67. *Larry King Live,* "John Ashcroft Discusses His New Job as Attorney General," CNN, Feb. 7, 2001, available at http://www.cnn.com/TRANSCRIPTS/0102/07.

68. Johnston and Lewis, "Religious Right."

69. Carney, "How Bush Chose Ashcroft," 27.

70. United Press International, "Analysis."

71. Blackman et al., "The Fight for Justice," 20.

72. Mary Anne Borrelli, *The President's Cabinet: Gender, Power and Representation* (Boulder, Colo.: Lynne Rienner, 2002), 6.

73. John C. Green, Mark Rozell, and Clyde Wilcox, "The Christian Right's Long Political March," and Danielle Vinson and James Guth, "Advance and Retreat in the Palmetto State: Assessing the Christian Right in South Carolina," in John C. Green, Mark Rozell, and Clyde Wilcox, eds., *The Christian Right in American Politics* (Washington, D.C.: Georgetown University Press, 2003).

74. Ragavan and Kaplan, "Is Ashcroft Unsinkable?" 13.

75. Johnston and Lewis, "Religious Right," 1.

76. James Lamare, Jerry Polinard, and Robert Wrinkle, "Texas: Religion and Politics in God's Country," in Green, Rozell, and Wilcox, eds., *The Christian Right in American Politics.* Maintaining his influence with the White House, Barton reportedly talked to President Bush on a weekly basis.

77. Johnston and Lewis, "Religious Right."

78. Thomas Fitton, "From the Desk of Judicial Watch President Tom Fitton," Judicial Watch, Nov. 11, 2004, available at www.judicialwatch.org/jwnews/111104.htm.

79. Ragavan and Kaplan, "Is Ashcroft Unsinkable?" 13.

80. Albert Hunt, "The Unaccountable Attorney General," *Wall Street Journal,* June 6, 2002, A15.

81. Bingaman, interview with author.

82. Jeffrey Toobin, "Profiles: Ashcroft's Ascent" *New Yorker,* Apr. 15, 2002, 52.

83. Online NewsHour, "Attorney General-Designate John Ashcroft," Dec. 22, 2000, available at www.pbs.org/newshour/inauguration/transition.

84. Nicholas D. Kristof, "The 2000 Campaign: The Decision; For Bush, His Toughest Call Was the Choice to Run at All," *New York Times,* Oct. 29, 2000, 1.

85. Paul Bedard et al., "Judge Ashcroft," *U.S. News & World Report,* Jan. 22, 2001, 6.

86. White, "The Wrong Choice," 30.

87. Ragavan and Kaplan, "Is Ashcroft Unsinkable?" 13.

88. Blackman et al., "The Fight for Justice."

89. CBSNews.com, "Poll: Undecided on Ashcroft," Jan. 18, 2001, available at www.-cbsnews.com/stories/2001/01/18/politics.

90. Wendy Simmons, "Ashcroft Receives Mixed Review from the Public," Gallup Organization, Jan. 18, 2001, available at www.gallup.com.

91. CBSNews.com, "Poll: Undecided on Ashcroft." Overall, 58 percent of the public

approved the cabinet selections with 19 percent disapproving, with even liberals and Democrats being more likely to approve than disapprove.

92. Editorial, "Mr. Bush's Justice Department," *Washington Post,* Feb. 2, 2001, A22. Also see White, "The Wrong Choice," 30; Blackman et al., "The Fight for Justice."

93. David Canon and Katherine Cramer Walsh, "George W. Bush and the Politics of Gender and Race," in Colin Campbell and Bert Rockman, eds., *The George W. Bush Presidency: Appraisals and Prospects* (Washington, D.C.: CQ Press, 2004), 265–297.

94. Dan Eggen, and Helen Dewar, "Ashcroft Wins Confirmation," *Washington Post,* Feb. 2, 2001, A1, available at www.washingtonpost.com/ac2/wp-dyn/A16007-2001Feb1.

95. People for the American Way, "A Record of Extremism," Jan. 2001, available at www.opposeashcroft.com.

96. Walter B. Jones, "Congressman Jones Continues to Fight for Senator Ashcroft's Nomination for U.S. Attorney General," press release, Jan. 25, 2001, available at jones.house.gov/html/12501.html.

97. Johnston and Lewis, "Religious Right."

98. Blackman et al., "The Fight for Justice."

99. Chavez was controversial with labor leaders because of her vocal opposition to affirmative action, but she withdrew her name from consideration when news surfaced that she had employed an illegal immigrant as a housekeeper.

100. Jonah Goldberg, "Ashcroft on My Mind," *National Review Online,* Jan. 17, 2001, available at www.nationalreview.com/goldberg.

101. Elizabeth Arens, "Republican Futures," *Policy Review,* Heritage Foundation, Apr. 2001, 13.

102. Linda Feldmann, "Ashcroft's Lightning Rod Role," *Christian Science Monitor,* Sept. 24, 2003, available at www.csmonitor.com/2003/0924.

103. U.S. Senate, "Confirmation Hearing on John Ashcroft."

104. Ibid.

105. Ibid.

106. Eric Lichtblau and Alissa Rubin, "Gay Issue Adds to Ashcroft Dispute," *Sun-Sentinel,* Jan. 26, 2001, available at sns.sunsentinel.com/news/national.

107. U.S. Senate, "Confirmation Hearing on John Ashcroft," Senator Edward Kennedy statement.

108. Kennedy, "In Extremis," 14.

109. U.S. Senate, "Confirmation Hearing on John Ashcroft," John Ashcroft statement.

110. Ibid.

111. Kennedy, "In Extremis," 14.

112. Borrelli, *The President's Cabinet,* 7.

113. Online NewsHour, "Confirmation Update," Jan. 24, 2001, available at www.pbs.org/newshour/bb/politics/jan-june01/ashcroft_01-24.html.

114. Orrin Hatch, interview with author, Washington, D.C., May 10, 2005.

115. Eggen and Dewar, "Ashcroft Wins Confirmation."

116. Congressional Research Service, "Department of Justice. Table 11. Attorneys General 1789–1985," CRS-15, CRS-16, CRS-17, Library of Congress, 1985. Only seventeen Senate confirmation votes have been recorded.

117. David Van Biema, "Son of a Preacher, Quiet Pentecostal," *Time,* Jan. 22,.2001, 24+.

118. Johnston and Lewis, "Religious Right," 1.

119. David Corn, "The Fundamental John Ashcroft," *Mother Jones,* Mar. 2002, available at www.motherjones.com/magazine/MA02.

120. Eric Lichtblau and Adam Liptak, "On Terror and Spying, Ashcroft Expands Reach," *New York Times,* Mar. 15, 2003, A1.

121. Kevin Johnson and Toni Locy, "Patriot Act at Heart of Ashcroft's Influence," *USA Today,* Sept. 15, 2003, available at www.usatoday.com/news/washington/2003-09-15. Also see Lichtblau and Liptak, "On Terror and Spying," A1.

122. *Larry King Live,* "John Ashcroft Discusses His New Job as Attorney General."

123. Diana R. Gordon, "Ashcroft Justice," *Nation,* July 23–30, 2001, 20.

124. Griffin Bell, interview with author, Atlanta, Georgia, May 16, 2005.

125. Sheldon Goldman, "Judicial Confirmation Wars: Ideology and the Battle for the Federal Courts," *University of Richmond Law Review* 39 (Mar. 2005): 889.

126. Ibid.

127. Paul Bedard, Chitra Ragavan, and Kevin Whitelaw, "Homesick," *U.S. News & World Report,* May 21, 2001, 8.

128. Ragavan, "Ashcroft's Way."

129. Paul Bedard, Kevin Whitelaw, and Mark Mazzetti, "Get the Ritalin," *U.S. News & World Report,* July 9, 2001, 10.

130. Vanessa Blum, "Curtains Raised for Change at DOJ?" *Legal Times,* Mar. 8, 2005, available at www.law.com/jsp.

131. Ragavan, "Ashcroft's Way."

132. Blum, "Curtains Raised for Change at DOJ?"

133. Jonathan Kaplan, "Ashcroft Joins K Street Legions," *The Hill,* May 1, 2005, available at www.hillnews.com/thehill/export/TheHill/News/Frontpage/042805/ashcroft.html.

134. Political MoneyLine, "Two New Lobbyists," Oct. 20, 2005, available at www.fecinfo.com. Oracle hired Ashcroft to lobby on antitrust matters; ChoicePoint on matters related to law enforcement.

135. Corn, "The Fundamental John Ashcroft," 52–54.

136. Bedard, Ragavan, and Whitelaw, "Homesick," 8.

137. 9/11 Commission Hearing. Transcript of Hearings with Thomas Pickard, National Commission on Terrorist Attacks upon the United States, FDCH E-Media, Apr. 13, 2004, available at www.washingtonpost.com/wp-dyn/articles/A9088-2004Apr13.html#pickard.

138. Charles Walcott and Karen Hult, "The Bush Staff and Cabinet System," in Gary Gregg and Mark Rozell, eds., *Considering the Bush Presidency* (New York: Oxford University Press, 2004), 58–59.

139. James Pfiffner, "Introduction," in Gary Gregg and Mark Rozell, eds., *Considering the Bush Presidency* (New York: Oxford University Press, 2004), 7.

140. John Burke, "The Bush Transition," in Gary Gregg and Mark Rozell, eds., *Considering the Bush Presidency* (New York: Oxford University Press, 2004), 43.

141. Johnson and Locy, "Patriot Act at Heart of Ashcroft's Influence."

142. U.S. Attorney General Remarks, "Attorney General Guidelines," May 30, 2002, available at www.usdoj.gov/ag/speeches/2002/53002agpreparedremarks.htm.

143. Joel C. Rosenberg, "Flashtraffic: Ashcroft Bulks Up Anti-terror Forces," *World Magazine,* Apr. 5, 2003, available at Lexis-Nexis Academic Universe; David Johnston and Richard Stevenson, "Threats and Responses: Washington Memo; Ashcroft, Deft at Taking Political Heat, Hits a Rocky Patch," *New York Times,* June 30, 2004, A14.

144. *Larry King Live,* "Secretary Rumsfeld Interview with Larry King," Dec. 5, 2001, CNN, available at http://www.cnn.com/TRANSCRIPTS/0112/05.

145. Reprinted by conservative and liberal outlets. Media Research Center CyberAlert, "Walters Pressed Bush from Left," Jan. 18, 2001, available at 63.66.59.27/news/cyberalert/

2001/cyb200101118.asp#1; David Corn, *The Lies of George W. Bush: Mastering the Politics of Deception* (New York: Crown, 2003), 67.

146. Richard Ellis, *Presidential Lightning Rods: The Politics of Blame Avoidance* (Lawrence: University Press of Kansas, 1994), 7.

147. Jay Nordlinger, "Ashcroft with Horns," *National Review,* May 24, 2002, available at www.nationalreview.com/flashback/flashback-nordlinger.

148. Lichtblau and Liptak, "On Terror and Spying," A1.

149. Johnston and Stevenson, "Ashcroft, Deft at Taking Political Heat," A14.

150. Pfiffner, "Introduction," 7.

151. Adriel Bettelheim, "Congress Changing Tone of Homeland Security Debate," *Congressional Quarterly,* Aug. 31, 2002, 2222.

152. Feldmann, "Ashcroft's Lightning Rod Role."

153. Richard Dunham, "How Much Heat Can Ashcroft Take?" *Business Week,* June 17, 2002, 41.

154. Charles Lewis and Adam Mayle, "Justice Dept. Drafts Sweeping Expansion of Anti-Terrorism Act," Center for Public Integrity, Feb. 20, 2003, available at www.publicintegrity.org; Nat Hentoff, "Ashcroft's America," *Editor and Publisher,* Apr. 7, 2003, 46.

155. ACLU Press Release, "ACLU Says New Ashcroft Anti-terror Proposal Undermines Checks and Balances," Feb. 7, 2003, available at www.aclu.org/SafeandFree.

156. American Conservative Union Press Release, "ACU Analysis of the Domestic Security Enhancement Act of 2003, also Known as Patriot Act II," Public Memorandum to Conservative Leaders and Activists, Feb. 26, 2003, available at www.conservative.org/pressroom/030226.

157. U.S. Senate, Committee on the Judiciary, "Hearings on the War against Terrorism," witnesses: U.S. Attorney General John Ashcroft; Homeland Security Secretary Tom Ridge; FBI Director Robert Mueller, Federal News Service, Mar. 4, 2003.

158. Hentoff, "Ashcroft's America."

159. See, for example, Hentoff, "Ashcroft's America"; ACU, "ACU Analysis of the Domestic Security Act"; ACLU, "ACLU Says New Ashcroft Anti-terror Proposal."

160. Jack Balkin, "Ashcroft Readies New Assault on Civil Rights," *Los Angeles Times,* Feb. 13, 2003, B23.

161. Lewis and Mayle, "Justice Dept. Drafts."

162. U.S. Department of Justice, Office of the Inspector General, "The September 11 Detainees: A Review of the Treatment of Aliens Held on Immigration Charges in Connection with the Investigation of the September 11 Attacks," Apr. 2003, available at www.usdoj.gov/oig/special/0306/full.pdf.

163. Eric Lichtblau, "Ashcroft Defends Detentions as Immigrants Recount Toll," *New York Times,* June 5, 2003, available at www.nytimes.com/2003/06/05/national.

164. Anita Ramasastry, "A Flawed Report Card: How DOJ Mishandled the Post–September 11 Detention Process," FindLaw's Writ Legal Commentary, Aug. 1, 2003, available at writ.news.findlaw.com.

165. Adam Liptak, "The Pursuit of Immigrants in America after Sept. 11," *New York Times,* June 8, 2003, available at www.nytimes.com/2003/06/08/weekinreview.

166. U.S. Senate, "Confirmation Hearing on John Ashcroft," remarks of Senator Herbert Kohl.

167. Kennedy, "In Extremis," 14.

168. White House, "Press Conference by the President," Mar. 31, 2002, available at www.whitehouse.gov/news/releases/2002/03/20020313-8.html.

169. John Mintz and Susan Schmidt, "Ashcroft Assailed on Terror Warning," *Washington Post,* May 28, 2004, A4, available at www.washingtonpost.com/ac2/wp-dyn/A61742-

2004May27; John Mintz and Susan Schmidt, "Ridge, Ashcroft Issue Statement on Threat," *Washington Post,* May 29, 2004, A2, available at www.washingtonpost.com/ac2/wp-dyn/A64374-2004May28.

170. Michael Duffy and John Dickerson, "Cooling on Ashcroft," *Time,* June 7, 2004, 20.

171. Eric Lichtblau, "Threats and Responses: The Attorney General; White House Criticizes Justice Dept. over Papers," *New York Times,* Apr. 30, 2004, A24, available at www.nytimes.com/2004/04/30/national.

172. John Burke, "The Bush Transition," in Gary Gregg and Mark Rozell, eds., *Considering the Bush Presidency* (New York: Oxford University Press, 2004), 48.

173. David Moore, "Public Little Concerned about Patriot Act," CNN/USA Today/Gallup poll, Sept. 9, 2003, available at www.gallup.com.

174. Darren Carlson, "Far Enough? Public Wary of Restricted Liberties," Gallup poll, Jan. 20, 2004, available at www.gallup.com.

175. Ponemon Institute Report, "Privacy Trust Survey of the United States Government: Executive Summary Presented by Ponemon Institute and the CIO Institute of Carnegie Mellon University," Jan. 31, 2004, available through www.ponemon.org/privacy-trust-survey.

176. Duffy and Dickerson, "Cooling on Ashcroft," 20; Mike Allen, "Staying or Going? Some Possibilities If Bush Wins," *Washington Post,* Oct. 22, 2004, A23, available at www.washingtonpost.com/ac2/wp-dyn/A52687-2004Oct21.

177. Johnston and Stevenson, "Ashcroft, Deft at Taking Political Heat," A14.

178. Ibid.

179. Ashcroft was hospitalized with a severe case of gallstone pancreatitis in the spring of 2004. Eric Lichtblau and Lawrence Altman, "Ashcroft in Hospital with Pancreatic Ailment," *New York Times,* Mar. 6, 2004, available at www.nytimes.com/2004/03/06/politics.

180. Ibid.

181. Ibid., A14.

182. Ragavan, "Ashcroft's Way."

183. Deborah Mathis, "Religion—But Not Religious Groups—Drive Ashcroft," Gannett News Service, July 17, 1996.

184. Ashcroft, *Lessons from a Father,* 209.

185. Liz Szabo, "Senator Focuses on Themes of Faith, Family and Politics," *Virginia-Pilot & Ledger Star,* May 10, 1998, B1.

186. Ashcroft, *Lessons from a Father,* 198–199.

187. Julian Borger, "Staff Cry Poetic Injustice as Singing Ashcroft Introduces Patriot Games," *Guardian,* Mar. 4, 2002, available at www.guardian.co.uk.

188. Regent University, course catalog, Fall 2002, available at www.regent.edu/general/catalog/fall2002/gov/services/html.

189. Melanie Edwards, "Robertson's 75th Birthday Gala Set for Mid-March in Texas," Regent University press release, March 2005, available at www.regent.edu/news/75_release2.html.

190. Richard Willing, "John Ashcroft to Teach Class at Va. College," *USA Today,* Mar. 16, 2005, available at www.usatoday.com/news/nation/2005-03-16-ashcroft-teach_x.htm.

191. "Former Attorney General John Ashcroft to Join Regent University Faculty," Regent University press release, Mar. 18, available at www.regent.edu/news/_press_releases/Mar._2005/ashcroft.cfm.

192. Johnston and Lewis, "Religious Right," 1.

193. John Green, "The Christian Right and the 1996 Elections: An Overview," in Mark Rozell and Clyde Wilcox, eds., *God at the Grass Roots, 1996* (Lanham, Md.: Rowman and Littlefield, 1997), 2.

194. Poloma, "Charisma and Structure in the Assemblies of God," 8–9.

195. Mark Rozell and Clyde Wilcox, "Conclusion: The Christian Right in Campaign '96," in Mark Rozell and Clyde Wilcox, eds., *God at the Grass Roots, 1996* (Lanham, Md.: Rowman and Littlefield, 1997), 264.

196. Ashcroft, *Lessons from a Father,* 191.

197. David Goldstein, "Ashcroft Mixes Religion, Action in Pitch to Christian Coalition," *Kansas City Star,* Sept. 14, 1997, A24.

198. U.S. Senate, "Confirmation Hearing on John Ashcroft," questioning by Senator Patrick Leahy.

199. "Former Attorney General to Join Regent University."

200. Doherty, "John Ashcroft's Power Grab."

201. U.S. Senate, "Confirmation Hearing on John Ashcroft," statement of Harriet Woods.

202. Ragavan, "Ashcroft's Way."

203. Toobin, "Profiles," 52.

204. Ashcroft, *Lessons from a Father,* 35.

205. Blackman et al., "The Fight for Justice."

206. NBC, *Meet the Press,* Apr. 19, 1998.

207. B. Drummond Ayers Jr., "Political Briefing; Conservative's Shift Angers Backers," *New York Times,* Dec. 7, 1998, A22.

208. Ibid.

209. Green, "The Christian Right," 2.

210. Ashcroft, *Lessons from a Father,* 209.

211. Ragavan, "Ashcroft's Way."

212. Nat Hentoff, *The War on the Bill of Rights and the Gathering Resistance* (New York: Seven Stories Press, 2003), 79. Ashcroft was chairman of the Senate Commerce Subcommittee on Consumer Affairs, Foreign Commerce and Tourism at the time.

213. Jim Mosley and Virginia Young, "Missouri Upheld on Cruzan," *St. Louis Post-Dispatch,* June 26, 1990, 1A.

214. Pamela Schaeffer and Roger Signor, "Decision Hailed in Cruzan Case," *St. Louis Post-Dispatch,* Dec. 16, 1990, 1A.

215. Terry Ganey and Virginia Young, "Courts Reject Suits to Save Cruzan's Life," *St. Louis Post-Dispatch,* Dec. 21, 1990, 1A.

216. Virginia Young, "Cruzan Testifies for Bill," *St. Louis Post-Dispatch,* Jan. 22, 1991, 4A.

217. Young, "Ashcroft Backs Fight against Moving Patient."

218. Virginia Young, "Ashcroft Gets Right-to-Die Bill," *St. Louis Post-Dispatch,* May 16, 1991, 1A.

219. Terry Ganey and Virginia Young, "Tax Hike to Go before Voters; Stronger Laws Approved on Ethics, Driving Drunk," *St. Louis Post-Dispatch,* May 18, 1991, 1A.

220. Dan Eggen and Ceci Connolly, "Ashcroft Ruling Blocks Ore. Assisted-Suicide Law," *Washington Post,* Nov. 7, 2001, A1, available at www.washingtonpost.com/wp-dyn/articles/A49218-2001Nov6.html.

221. Ibid.

222. Ibid.; William Booth, "Judge Blocks Sanctions over Assisted Suicide," *Washington Post,* Nov. 9, 2001, A2; *Oregon v. Ashcroft,* U.S. District Court for the District of Oregon, 192 F. Supp. 2d 1077 (2002); 2002 U.S. Dist. LEXIS 6695. The U.S. district judge struck down the federal action as inconsistent with case law, the CSA's legislative history and language, and state regulation of the medical field, in the absence of specific congressional authorization. At the time of this writing, Ashcroft had not yet determined the department's response.

223. Hentoff, *The War on the Bill of Rights.*

224. CBSNews.com, "Ashcroft Interprets 2nd Amendment," May 23, 2001, available at www.cbsnews.com/stories/1002/05/23/politics.

225. U.S. Attorney General Remarks, "Violent Crime Initiative," PSN National Conference, Kansas City, Missouri, June 16, 2004, available at www.usdoj.gov/ag/speeches/2004/agpns061504.htm.

226. Tanya Green, "U.S. Attorney General John Ashcroft Obtains Injunctions against Pro-Lifers," Concerned Women for America, Feb. 5, 2002, available at www.cwfa.org.

227. U.S. Department of Justice, Office of Solicitor General, amicus curiae against certiorari in *American Coalition of Life Activists v. Planned Parenthood of Columbia/Willamette,* No. 02-563, 2002, available at www.usdoj.gov/osg/briefs/2002/2pet/6invit/2002-0563.pet.ami.inv.html.

228. U.S. Department of Justice, Office of Solicitor General, amicus curiae on merits in *Scheidler v. NOW* and *Operation Rescue v. NOW,* Nos. 01-1118; 01-1119, 2002, available at www.usdoj.gov/osg/briefs/2002/3mer/1mi/2001-1118.mer.ami.html.

229. *Scheidler v. National Organization for Women,* 537 U.S. 393 (2004). The justices were concerned with the implications for political speech in general.

230. Eric Lichtblau, "Ashcroft to Defend Ban on Some Abortion Protests," *New York Times,* Aug. 30, 2003, available at www.nytimes.com/2003/08/30/politics.

231. U.S. Attorney General Remarks, "Regarding Human Trafficking," Jan. 29, 2004, available at www.usdoj.gov/speeches/2004.

232. Debbie Nathan, "Oversexed," *Nation,* Aug. 29–Sept. 5, 2005, 28.

233. White House, "Remarks Via Satellite by the President to the National Association of Evangelicals Convention," Office of the Press Secretary, Mar. 11, 2004, available at www.whitehouse.gov/news/releases/2004/03.

234. U.S. Justice Department, "Justice Department Files Motion to Intervene in Title IX Sexual Harassment Case against Rhinebeck Central School District," Mar. 18, 2004, available at www.usdoj.gov/opa/pr/2004/March. The case is *AB et al. v. Rhinebeck Central School District and Thomas Mawhinney.*

235. U.S. Justice Department, "Justice Department Files Complaint against Oklahoma School District Seeking to Protect Student's Right to Wear Headscarf to Public School," Mar. 30, 2004, available at www.usdoj.gov/opa/pr/2004/March. The case is *Hearn et al. v. Muskogee Public School District 020.*

236. U.S. Attorney General Remarks, Violence against Women Act Symposium, Tenth Anniversary, Sept. 13, 2004, available at www.usdoj.gov/ag/speeches/2004/ag091304_ovw.htm.

237. Partial Birth Abortion Ban Act, PL 108-105.

238. Eric Lichtblau, "Justice Dept. Seeks Hospitals' Records of Some Abortions," *New York Times,* Feb. 12, 2004, available at www.nytimes.com/2004/02/12/politics; Robert Pear and Eric Lichtblau, "Administration Sets Forth a Limited View on Privacy," *New York Times,* Mar. 6, 2004, available at www.nytimes.com/2004/03/06/politics; Eric Lichtblau, "Justice Dept. Backs Off Its Demand for Abortion Records," *New York Times,* Mar. 23, 2004, available at www.nytimes.com.2004/03/23/politics.

239. *Northwestern Memorial Hospital v. Ashcroft,* Seventh Circuit Court of Appeals, No. 04-1379, Mar. 26, 2004.

240. David G. Savage and Eric Lichtblau, "Ashcroft Deals with Daunting Responsibilities," *Los Angeles Times,* Oct. 28, 2001, available at www.latimes.com/news/nationworld/nation/la-000085817oct28.story.

241. U.S. Attorney General Remarks, "Reorganization and Mobilization of the Nation's

Justice and Law Enforcement Resources," Nov. 8, 2001, available at www.usdoj.gov/ag/speeches/2001agcrisisremarks.

242. U.S. House of Representatives, Committee on the Judiciary, "Oversight of the Justice Department: Testimony of Attorney General John Ashcroft," June 5, 2003, Federal Document Clearing House, available at www.usdoj.gov/ag/testimony/2003/060503aghouseremarks.htm.

243. Nina Easton, "A Life of Faith" *Washington Post,* Nov. 4, 2001, F1.

244. John Ashcroft, U.S. Attorney General Remarks, "Commencement Address for the University of Missouri Columbia School of Law," U.S. Department of Justice, May 18, 2002, available at www.usdoj.gov/ag/speeches/2002.

245. Savage and Lichtblau, "Ashcroft Deals with Daunting Responsibilities."

246. George W. Bush, "State of the Union Address," Jan. 29, 2002, available at www.whitehouse.gov/news/releases/2002/01/20020129.

247. White House, "Remarks via Satellite by the President."

248. Bob Woodward, *Plan of Attack* (New York: Simon and Schuster, 2004); William Hamilton, "Bush Began to Plan War Three Months after 9/11," *Washington Post,* Apr. 16, 2004, available at www.washingtonpost.com/wp-dyn/articles/A17347-2004Apr16.html.

Chapter 4: Framing 9/11 as a War on Terrorism

1. Bob Woodward, *Bush at War* (New York: Simon and Schuster, 2002), 17, 45.

2. U.S. House of Representatives, Committee on the Judiciary, "Oversight of the Justice Department: Testimony of Attorney General John Ashcroft," Federal Document Clearing House, June 5, 2003.

3. Laurence Tribe, *American Constitutional Law,* 3rd ed., vol. 1 (New York: Foundation Press, 2000), 670–671.

4. *Youngstown Sheet and Tube Co. v. Sawyer,* 343 U.S. 579 (1952).

5. Ibid., 644.

6. Terry M. Moe and William G. Howell, "Unilateral Action and Presidential Power: A Theory," *Presidential Studies Quarterly* 29 (1999): 850–872.

7. Louis Fisher, *American Constitutional Law,* 6th ed. (Durham, N.C.: Carolina Academic Press, 2005), 170; Tribe, *American Constitutional Law,* 634–635.

8. *Curtiss Wright Export Corp. v. U.S.,* 299 U.S. 304, 57 S.Ct. 216 (1936).

9. *Dames & Moore v. Regan,* 453 U.S. 654 (1981).

10. Aaron Wildavsky, "The Two Presidencies," *Trans-Action,* 4, no. 2 (1966); reprinted in Aaron Wildavsky, ed., *Perspectives on the Presidency* (Boston: Little, Brown, 1975), 448.

11. Steven A. Shull, ed., *The Two Presidencies: A Quarter-Century Assessment* (Chicago: Nelson Hall, 1991). He uses the term "intermestic" to characterize policies that overlap the domestic and international.

12. See, for example, the positive assessments of his post-9/11 growth in office in David Frum, *The Right Man* (London: Weidenfeld and Nicolson, 2003), and Woodward, *Bush at War.*

13. Jon Roper, "George W. Bush and the Myth of Heroic Presidential Leadership," *Presidential Studies Quarterly* 34, no. 1 (Mar. 2004): 132–142.

14. Nancy Kassop, "The War Power and Its Limits," *Presidential Studies Quarterly* 33, no. 3 (Sept. 2003): 510–511.

15. Executive Order 12958, Designation under Executive Order 12958, Order of Sept. 26, 2002, *Federal Register* 67, no. 189 (Sept. 20, 2002): 61463; and Executive Order 12958, Designation under Executive Order 12958, Order of Sept. 17, 2003, *Federal Register* 68, no. 184 (Sept. 23, 2003): 55257, available at www.fas.org/sgp/bush/ostp.html.

16. White House, press release, "On the Executive Order to Establish a Presidential Task Force on Citizen Preparedness in the War on Terrorism," Office of the Press Secretary, Nov. 9, 2001, available at www.whitehouse.gov/news/releases/2001/11. The Executive Order is 13234. The other offices were the Office of the Vice President, the Office of Science and Technology Policy, Office of Management and Budget, the Environmental Protection Agency, the Federal Emergency Management Agency, and the Corporation for National and Community Service.

17. Ivo Daalder and James Lindsay, *America Unbound* (Washington, D.C.: Brookings Institution Press, 2003). Also see *The Bubble of American Supremacy* by George Soros, *Superpower Syndrome* by Robert Jay Lifton, and *After the Empire* by Emmanuel Todd.

18. Daalder and Lindsay, *America Unbound,* 2.

19. Reuters, transcript from Bush's television interview with *Meet the Press, New York Times,* Feb. 8, 2004, available at www.nytimes.com/2004/02/08/politics.

20. George W. Bush, "Radio Address of the President to the Nation," Sept. 29, 2001, Office of the Press Secretary, available at www.whitehouse.gov/news/releases/2001/09/20010929.html.

21. George W. Bush, "Transcript: President Bush Delivers Remarks on Homeland Security," *New York Times,* Sept. 10, 2003, available at www.nytimes.com/2003/09/10/politics.

22. CNN, "Bush Speaks at Justice Department," Paula Zahn, CNN anchor, Feb. 14, 2003, transcript #021404CN.V54.

23. George W. Bush, "State of the Union Address," Jan. 20, 2004, available at www.whitehouse.gov/news/releases/2004/01/20040120.

24. Richard Cheney, "Vice President's Remarks on War on Terror at American Enterprise Institute," Federal Document Clearing House, July 24, 2003.

25. Elisabeth Bumiller and Richard Stevenson, "In Speech, President Casts Himself as a Steady Commander in Chief," *New York Times,* Jan. 21, 2004, available at www.nytimes.com/2004/01/21/politics.

26. Todd Purdum, "Bush Uses Speech to Nation to Get in Position for '04 Race," *New York Times,* Jan. 21, 2004, available at www.nytimes.com/2004/01/21/politics.

27. U.S. Senate, Committee on the Judiciary, "Hearings on the War against Terrorism," remarks of U.S. Senator Saxby Chambliss (R-Ga.), witnesses: U.S. Attorney General John Ashcroft; Homeland Security Secretary Tom Ridge; Federal Bureau of Investigation Director Robert Mueller, Federal News Service, Mar. 4, 2003.

28. U.S. Senate, Committee on the Judiciary, "Department of Justice Oversight: Preserving Our Freedoms While Defending against Terrorism," witness: Attorney General John Ashcroft, Dec. 6, 2001, 107th Cong., 1st sess., Federal News Service, available at web.lexis-nexis.com/congcomp/document.

29. Ibid. Ashcroft was responding to questioning by Senator Kennedy.

30. The meaning of the commander-in-chief phrase has long been debated, a discussion that is beyond the scope of this book. For an insightful overview, see Louis Fisher, *Constitutional Conflicts between Congress and the President,* 4th ed. (Lawrence: University Press of Kansas, 1997).

31. Alexander Hamilton, "The Real Character of the Executive," *The Federalist* No. 69. Mar. 14, 1788, available at www.constitution.org/fed/federa69/htm.

32. Arthur M. Schlesinger Jr., *The Imperial Presidency* (Boston: Houghton Mifflin, 1973), 188.

33. Kim Lane Scheppele, "Law in a Time of Emergency: States of Exception and the Temptations of 9/11," *University of Pennsylvania Journal of Constitutional Law* 6 (May 2004): 1023.

34. White House, Memorandum from Bill Clinton to the Vice President, Secretary of State, et al., subject: U.S. Policy on Counterterrorism, June 21, 1995, available at www.fas.org/irp/offdocs/pdd39.htm.

35. Harold Hongju Koh, "We Have the Right Courts for Bin Laden," *New York Times,* Nov. 23, 2001, A39; Harold Hongju Koh, "Against Military Tribunals," *Dissent* 49, no. 4 (Fall 2002); 58.

36. White House, press briefing by Attorney General, Secretary of HHS, Secretary of Transportation, and FEMA Director, Sept. 11, 2001, available at www.whitehouse.gov/news/releases/2001/09.

37. *Larry King Live,* "Secretary Powell on CNN's Larry King Live," CNN, Nov. 27, 2001, available at http://www.cnn.com/TRANSCRIPTS/0111/27.

38. Woodward, *Bush at War,* 96.

39. George W. Bush, "State of the Union Address," 2004.

40. George W. Bush, "Remarks by the President at Bush-Cheney 2004 Reception, the Shrine Auditorium, Los Angeles, California," Office of the Press Secretary, Mar. 3, 2004, available at www.whitehouse.gov/news/releases/2004/03/print/20040303-16html.

41. U.S. Senate, "Preserving Our Freedoms."

42. 9/11 Commission Hearing, Transcript of Hearings with Attorney General John Ashcroft, National Commission on Terrorist Attacks upon the United States, FDCH E-Media, Apr. 13, 2004, available at www.washingtonpost.com/wp-dyn/articles/A9088-2004Apr13.html #ashcroft.

43. Woodward, *Bush at War;* Peter Feaver, "The Clinton Mind-Set," *Washington Post National Weekly Edition,* Mar. 29–Apr. 4, 2004, 26.

44. White House, "President Addresses the Nation in Prime Time Press Conference," Office of the Press Secretary, Apr. 13, 2004, available at www.whitehouse.go/news/releases/2004/04.

45. T. D. Gill, *The 11th of September and the International Law of Military Operations* (Amsterdam: Vossiuspers UvA, 2002).

46. Jack Beard, "Military Action against Terrorists under International Law," *Harvard Journal of Law and Public Policy* 25 (Spring 2002): 559.

47. Scheppele, "Law in a Time of Emergency."

48. 9/11 Commission Hearings, Transcript: National Security Adviser Condoleezza Rice, National Commission on Terrorist Attacks upon the United States, FDCH E-Media, Apr. 8, 2004, available at www.washingtonpost.com/wp-dyn/articles/A61252-2004Apr8.html.

49. Glenn Frankel, "Europe, U.S. Diverge on How to Fight Terrorism," *Washington Post,* Mar. 28, 2004, A15, available at www.washingtonpost.com/ac2/wp-dyn.

50. Howard LaFranchi, "U.S. vs. Europe: Two Views of Terror," *Christian Science Monitor,* Mar. 18, 2004, available at www.csmonitor.com/2004/0318.

51. Frankel, "Europe, U.S. Diverge," A15.

52. Scheppele, "Law in a Time of Emergency," 1004.

53. Grenville Byford, "The Wrong War," *Foreign Affairs,* July/Aug. 2002, 34.

54. Gary Gregg and Mark Rozell, eds., *Considering the Bush Presidency* (New York: Oxford University Press, 2004), quoting Cheney on NBC's *Meet the Press,* interview with Tim Russert on Sept. 16, 2001.

55. 9/11 Commission Hearings, Transcript: Rice.

56. Eric Schmitt and Thom Shanker, "U.S. Officials Retool Slogan in Terror War," *New York Times,* July 26, 2005, available at /www.nytimes.com/2005/07/26/politics/26strategy.html?ex=1123214400&en=44a1e10bf887024d&ei=5070&emc=eta1.

57. White House, press release, "President Addresses Military Families, Discusses War on Terror," Office of the Press Secretary, Aug. 24, 2005, available at www.whitehouse.gov/news/releases/2005/08/29959824.html.

58. Noah Feldman, "Choices of Law, Choices of War," *Harvard Journal of Law and Public Policy* 25 (Spring 2002): 477. He argues that neither paradigm is well suited for addressing mass terror.

59. David Luban, "The War on Terrorism and the End of Human Rights," *Philosophy and Public Policy Quarterly* 22, no. 3 (Summer 2002): 9–14. Also see the U.S. government's defense in David Brunnstrom, "U.S. Says Raid Killing Afghan Children Was Legitimate," Reuters, Mar. 10, 2004, available at news.findlaw.com.

60. Third Geneva Convention, 1949; Feldman, "Choices of Law," 458, 477.

61. Feldman, "Choices of Law," 458, 477.

62. Jeffrey Shaffer, "Commentary: Iraq Blurs the Line between Crime and War," *Christian Science Monitor,* Apr. 16, 2004, available at www.csmonitor.com/2004/0416.

63. *The 9/11 Commission Report,* final report of the National Commission on Terrorist Attacks upon the United States (New York: Norton, 2004), 348.

64. Neil Lewis and Eric Schmitt, "Cuban Detentions May Last Years," *New York Times,* Feb. 13, 2004, available at www.nytimes.com/2004/02/13/politics.

65. White House, Memorandum from George W. Bush, "Humane Treatment of al Qaeda and Taliban Detainees," Feb. 7, 2002, Memo 11 in Karen Greenberg and Joshua Dratel, eds., *The Torture Papers: The Road to Abu Ghraib* (New York: Cambridge University Press, 2005). For the legal advice leading up to this presidential decision, see U.S. Department of Justice, Office of Legal Counsel, Memorandum for Alberto Gonzales, Counsel to the President, from Jay S. Bybee, "Application of Treaties and Laws to al Qaeda and Taliban Detainees," Jan. 22, 2002, Memo 6; and White House, Memorandum from Alberto R. Gonzales to President Bush, "Decision Re: Application of the Geneva Convention on Prisoners of War to the Conflict with al Qaeda and the Taliban," Jan. 15, 2002, Memo 7, both in Greenberg and Dratel, *The Torture Papers.*

66. Bush, "Transcript: President Bush Delivers Remarks on Homeland Security."

67. Craig Trebilcock, "The Myth of Posse Comitatus," *Journal of Homeland Security,* Oct. 2000, available at www.homelandsecurity.org/journal/articles/Trebilcock.htm.

68. Memorandum to Alberto Gonzales and William Haynes, from John Yoo and Robert Delahunty, "Re: Authority for the Use of Military Force to Combat Terrorist Activities within the United States. Oct. 23," Memo 13, Greenberg and Dratel, *The Torture Papers.*

69. Robert Block and Gary Fields, "Is Military Creeping into Domestic Law Enforcement?" *Wall Street Journal,* Mar. 9, 2004, available at www.commondreams.org/headlines04/0309-02.htm.

70. Robert O'Harrow Jr., "The Pentagon Teams Up with Computer Sleuths," *Washington Post National Weekly Edition,* Nov. 18–24, 2002, 29–30.

71. Carl Hulse, "Congress Shuts Pentagon Unit over Privacy," *New York Times,* Sept. 26, 2003, available at www.nytimes.com/2003/09/26/national.

72. Robert O'Harrow Jr., "In Age of Security, Firm Mines Wealth of Personal Data," *Washington Post,* Jan. 20, 2005, A1, available at www.washingtonpost.com/ac2/wp-dyn/A22269-2005Jan19.

73. Kassop, "The War Power," 510.

74. Luban, "The War on Terrorism," 13.

75. Woodward, *Bush at War,* 97.

76. U.S. Senate, "Preserving Our Freedoms."

77. U.S. House of Representatives, Committee on the Judiciary, "Testimony of Attorney General John Ashcroft on the USA Patriot Act," Sept. 24, 2001, available at www.usdoj.gov/ag/testimony/2001/agcrisisremarks9_24.htm.

78. Michael Powell and Michelle Garcia, "Amid Praise, Doubts about Nominee's Post 9/11 Role," *Washington Post,* Jan. 31, 2005, A1, available at www.washingtonpost.com/ac2/wp-dyn/A49950-2005Jan30.

79. U.S. Attorney General Remarks, "Reorganization and Mobilization of the Nation's Justice and Law Enforcement Resources," Nov. 8, 2001, available at www.usdoj.gov/ag/speeches/2001agcrisisremarks.

80. 9/11 Commission Hearing, Transcript: John Ashcroft, Apr. 13, 2004, available at www.washingtonpost.com/wp-dyn/articles/A9088-2004Apr13.html#ashcroft.

81. U.S. Attorney General Remarks, "Attorney General Ashcroft Speaks about the Patriot Act, Boise, Idaho," Aug. 25, 2003, available at www.lifeandliberty.gov/subs/speeches/patriot actroadspeech_boise.

82. U.S. House of Representatives, Judiciary Committee Hearings, "Oversight of the Justice Department," witness Attorney General John Ashcroft, June 5, 2003, Federal Document Clearing House.

83. Woodward, *Bush at War,* 42.

84. Barton Gellman and Susan Schmidt, "U.S., Pakistan Intensify the Search for Bin Laden," *Washington Post,* Mar. 7, 2003, A1, available at www.washingtonpost.com/ac2/wp-dyn.

85. Jerry Markon, "Post 9/11 Probe Revived Stolen-Cereal Incident," *Washington Post,* June 12, 2005, A19, available at www.washingtonpost.com/wp-dyn/content/article/2005/06/11/AR2005061100380_2.html.

86. U.S. Department of Justice, statement of Barbara Comstock, Director of Public Affairs, "Regarding the Third Circuit Argument in North Jersey Media Group v. Ashcroft Today," Sept. 17, 2002, available at www.usdoj.gov/opa/pr/2002/September.

87. U.S. Attorney General Remarks, "Press Conference," Oct. 18, 2001, available at www.usdoj.gov/ag/speeches/2001/agcrisisremarks.

88. U.S. Attorney General Remarks, "Report from the Field: The USA Patriot Act at Work," July 13, 2004, available at www.usdoj.gov/ag/speeches/2004/071304_patriot_report_remarks.htm.

89. U.S. House of Representatives, "Oversight of the Justice Department."

90. U.S. Attorney General Remarks, "Reorganization and Mobilization."

91. U.S. Attorney General Remarks, "Speak for Israel Meeting," Apr. 2, 2003, available at www.usdoj.gov/ag/speeches/2003.

92. U.S. Senate, "Preserving Our Freedoms."

93. Dan Eggen, "Ashcroft Plans to Reorganize Justice, Curtail Programs," *Washington Post,* Nov. 9, 2001, A17.

94. Gara LaMarche, "Welcome to Watching Justice," Apr. 14, 2004, available at www.watchingjustice.org/reports/article.php?docId=179.

95. U.S. Attorney General Remarks, "Reorganization and Mobilization."

96. C. Madison (Brick) Brewer, retired career attorney with Justice Department, including service with the Executive Office of the U.S. Attorneys and the Information and Privacy Unit, telephone interview with author, May 24, 2005.

97. "President Bars 5 DOJ Agencies from Unionizing," *Federal Human Resources Week,* Jan. 21, 2002.

98. Dana Priest and Dan Eggen, "Are We Ready to Thwart Attacks?" *Washington Post National Weekly Edition,* Nov. 18–24, 2002, 29.

99. National Academy of Public Administration, *Transforming the FBI: Progress and Challenges* (Washington, D.C.: National Academy of Public Administration, Jan. 2005).

100. U.S. Attorney General Remarks, "FBI Reorganization," May 29, 2002, available at www.usdoj.gov/ag/speeches/2002.

101. Priest and Eggen, "Are We Ready?"

102. Toni Locy and Kevin Johnson, "How the U.S. Watches Suspects of Terrorism," *USA Today,* Feb. 12, 2003.

103. Nina Bernstein, "Questions, Bitterness and Exile for Queens Girl in Terror Case," *New York Times,* June 17, 2005, available at www.nytimes.com/2005/06/17/nyregion/17suicide.html?th&emc=th.

104. Tim Golden, "Threats and Responses: Tough Justice; Administration Officials Split over Stalled Military Tribunals," *New York Times,* Oct. 25, 2004, A1.

105. Ibid.

106. Ibid.

107. Ibid.

Chapter 5: Presidential Action and Separation of Powers

1. James Madison, "The Particular Structure of the New Government and the Distribution of Power among Its Different Parts," *The Federalist* No. 47, Jan. 30, 1788, available at www.constitution.org/fed/federa47.htm.

2. James Madison, "These Departments Should Not Be So Far Separated as to Have No Constitutional Control over Each Other," *The Federalist* No. 48, Feb. 1, 1788, available at www.constitution.org/fed/federa48.htm.

3. James Madison, "The Structure of the Government Must Furnish the Proper Checks and Balances between the Different Departments," *The Federalist* No. 51, Feb. 6, 1788, available at www.constitution.org/fed/federa51.htm.

4. Arthur M. Schlesinger Jr., *The Imperial Presidency* (Boston: Houghton Mifflin, 1973), 331.

5. Ibid., 207.

6. Harold Hongju Koh, *The National Security Constitution* (New Haven, Conn.: Yale University Press, 1990), 39.

7. Ibid., 42.

8. Kim Lane Scheppele, "Law in a Time of Emergency: States of Exception and the Temptations of 9/11," *University of Pennsylvania Journal of Constitutional Law* 6 (2004): 1022.

9. White House, "Press Conference by the President," Mar. 31, 2002, available at www.whitehouse.gov/news/releases/2002/03/20020313-8.html.

10. Carl Levin, "Use of Force Authority by the President," U.S. Senate, *Congressional Record,* Oct. 1, 2001, S9951, available at thomas.loc.gov/home/r107query.html.

11. Adriel Bettelheim, "Congress Changing Tone on Homeland Security Debate," *Congressional Quarterly,* Aug. 31, 2002, 2222.

12. Authorization for Use of Military Force, Senate Joint Resolution 23/House Joint Resolution 64, Sept. 14, 2001, Public Law 107-40, 115 Stat. 224. It was signed by President Bush on September 18.

13. Ibid.

14. Peter DeFazio, "Authorizing Use of Military Force in Response to Terrorist Attacks," House of Representatives, *Congressional Record,* Sept. 14, 2001, H5632, available at thomas.loc.gov/home/r107query.html.

15. David Rosenbaum, "A Nation Challenged: The Lawmakers; Congressional Leaders

Offer Strong Endorsement of Attack," *New York Times,* Oct. 8, 2001, B11.

16. George W. Bush, statement by the President, "President Signs Authorization for Use of Military Force Bill," Sept. 18, 2001, available at www.whitehouse.gov/news/releases/2001/09/20010918-10.html.

17. Ibid.

18. George W. Bush, "Military Order: Detention, Treatment and Trial of Certain Non-citizens in the War against Terrorism," *Federal Register* 66 (Nov. 13, 2001): 222, available at www.gpoaccess.gov/fr/.

19. White House, Office of the Press Secretary, "Joint Resolution to Authorize the Use of United States Armed Forces against Iraq," Oct. 2, 2002, available at www.whitehouse.gov/news/releases/2002/10/20021002-2.html.

20. Ibid.

21. Brief for the respondents, *Hamdi v. Rumsfeld,* no. 03-6996, filed with the U.S. Supreme Court, Mar. 2004, available at www.usdoj.gov/osg/briefs/2003/3mer/2mer/toc3index.html; Brief for Petitioner, *Rumsfeld v. Padilla,* no. 03-1027, filed with U.S. Supreme Court, Mar. 2004, available at www.usdoj.gov/osg/briefs/2003/3mer/2mer/toc3index.html.

22. Jennifer Dlouhy, and Elizabeth Palmer, "New Assertions of Executive Power Anger, Frustrate Some on Hill," *Congressional Quarterly,* Nov. 24, 2001, 2784.

23. Vanessa Blum, "When the Pentagon Controls the Courtroom," *Recorder,* Nov. 27, 2001.

24. U.S. Attorney General Remarks, "Press Conference." Oct. 18, 2001, available at www.usdoj.gov/ag/speeches/2001/agcrisisremarks.

25. Dlouhy and Palmer, "New Assertions of Executive Power," 2784.

26. Jackie Koszczuk, "Lawmakers Struggle to Keep an Eye on Patriot Act," *Congressional Quarterly,* Sept. 7, 2002, 2284.

27. Mike McIntire, "Terror Lesson Fading for Some, Ashcroft Says in Manhattan," *New York Times,* Sept. 10, 2003, available at www.nytimes.com/2003/09/10/nyregion/10ASHC.html.

28. U.S. Senate, Committee on the Judiciary, "Ashcroft Comments on Anti-Terror Policy," June 8, 2004, FDCH E-Media, available at www.washingtonpost.com/wp-dyn/articles/A25211-2004Jun8.html.

29. Eric Lichtblau and Janet Hook, "White House Angered by Leaks on Intelligence," *Los Angeles Times,* June 21, 2002, A15.

30. U.S. Senate, Committee on the Judiciary, "Department of Justice Oversight: Preserving Our Freedoms While Defending against Terrorism," witness: Attorney General John Ashcroft, Dec. 6. 2001, 107th Cong., 1st sess., Federal News Service, available at web.lexis-nexis.com/congcomp/document.

31. White House, Office of the Press Secretary, "Remarks by President Bush and Chancellor Schroeder of Germany in Press Availability," May 23, 2002, available at www.fas.org/sgp/news/2002/05/gwb052302.htm.

32. White House, Office of the Press Secretary, press briefing by Ari Fleischer, Jan. 17, 2002, available at www.whitehouse.gov/news/releases/2002/01/20020117-8.html.

33. The GAO was formerly named the General Accounting Office.

34. U.S. Department of Justice, press release, statement of Barbara Comstock, Director of Public Affairs, May 22, 2002, available at www.usdoj.gov/opa/pr/2002/May.

35. *Walker v. Cheney,* 230 F. Supp. 2d 51; 2002 U.S. Dist. LEXIS 23385, decided Dec. 9, 2002.

36. Dana Milbank, "GAO Backs Off Cheney Lawsuit," *Washington Post,* Feb. 7, 2003, available at www.washingtonpost.com/ac2/wp-dyn/A40562-2003Feb7. The case was *Walker v. Cheney.*

37. The conversations, which were not translated until September 12, 2001, make vague references to what could be the next day's attacks.

38. Faye Bowers and Gail Russell Chaddock, "Major Battle Brewing over Leaks in Senate," *Christian Science Monitor,* Aug. 29, 2002, available at www.csmonitor.com/2002/0829/p01s02-uspo.htm.

39. Ibid.

40. Ibid.; Christopher Newton, "FBI Probes Lawmakers for Leak," Associated Press, Aug. 2, 2002, available at news.findlaw.com.

41. Associated Press, "Daschle, Lott Oppose Polygraphs," Aug. 5, available at news.findlaw.com/ap_stories.20020805050022_05.htm.

42. U.S. Senate, "Ashcroft Comments on Anti-terror Policy."

43. U.S. Senate, "Preserving Our Freedoms."

44. Ibid.

45. U.S. Department of Justice, Speeches, statements and testimony, "Speeches by the Attorney General. 2003 Speeches," available at www.usdoj.gov/ag/speeches.html.

46. The Senate hearings were held on October 21, 2003.

47. U.S. Department of Justice, speeches, statements, and testimony, "Speeches by the Attorney General. 2004 Speeches," n.d., available at www.usdoj.gov/ag/speeches.html.

48. Emily Pierce, "Ashcroft Rapped over Oversight," *Roll Call,* June 9, 2003, available through Lexis-Nexis Congressional Universe.

49. Damon Chappie, "9/11 Report Shows Hill Investigator Got Snubbed," *Roll Call,* July 28, 2003, available through Lexis-Nexis Congressional Universe. The FBI and the committee finally agreed to send the informant a list of written questions, but the informant's legal counsel advised that he not comply unless he was granted immunity.

50. Jeff Bingaman, Speech on the floor of the U.S. Senate, "Administrative Detentions and Right to Due Process," July 14, 2003, available at www.cq.com/cqonline/docs/html/crtext/108/crtext108-000000763112.html; Jeff Bingaman, interview with author, Las Cruces, New Mexico, Mar. 31, 2005.

51. USA Patriot Act, Section 502, "Congressional Oversight." PL 107-56, 2001.

52. Bettelheim, "Congress Changing Tone," 2222.

53. *Washington Post,* "Transcript: Ashcroft on Terror Probe Suspects," On Politics, Nov. 27, 2001, available at www.washingtonpost/com/ac2/wp-dyn.

54. Dan Eggen, "Ashcroft Assailed on Policy Review," *Washington Post,* Aug. 21, 2002, A2, available at www.washingtonpost.com/ac2/wp-dyn/A41859-2002Aug20.

55. Bettelheim, "Congress Changing Tone," 2222.

56. Koszczuk, "Lawmakers Struggle to Keep," 2284.

57. U.S. House of Representatives, Committee on the Judiciary, "News Advisory: Sensenbrenner/Conyers Release Justice Department Oversight Answers Regarding USA Patriot Act and War on Terrorism," May 20, 2003, available at www.house.gov/judiciary/news052003.htm.

58. Ibid.

59. Eggen, "Ashcroft Assailed n Policy Review."

60. Koszczuk, "Lawmakers Struggle to Keep," 2284.

61. Eggen, "Ashcroft Assailed on Policy Review."

62. Jackie Koszczuk, "Ashcroft Drawing Criticism from Both Sides of the Aisle," *Congressional Quarterly,* Sept. 7, 2002, 2287.

63. U.S. Senate, "Ashcroft Comments on Anti-terror Policy."

64. Ibid.

65. George W. Bush, memorandum for the attorney general, "Subject: Congressional Subpoena for Executive Branch Documents," Dec. 12, 2001, available at www.whitehouse.gov/news/releases/2001/12/20011213-1.html.

66. Ralph Ranalli, "Lawmakers Scold Justice Dept. over Shielded FBI Documents," *Boston Globe* Feb. 7, 2002, A21; J. M. Lawrence, "Justice Dept. Won't Turn Over Memo in Salvati Case," *Boston Herald,* Feb. 12, 2002, 016.

67. Koszczuk, "Lawmakers Struggle to Keep," 2284.

68. Pierce, "Ashcroft Rapped over Oversight."

69. Ibid.

70. Ibid.

71. Eggen, "Ashcroft Assailed on Policy Review."

72. Bush, "Military Order, Detention, Treatment and Trial."

73. U.S. Constitution, Article III, Section 1.

74. Bush, "Military Order, Detention, Treatment and Trial."

75. U.S. Senate, "Preserving Our Freedoms," witness: Michael Chertoff, Nov. 28, 2001, 107th Cong., 1st sess., available at www.frwebgate.access.gpo.gov/cgi-bin/getdoc.cgi?dbname= 107_senate_hearings&docid=f:81998.wais.

76. Jim Oliphant, "Justice during Wartime: Order on Military Trials Final Piece of Sept. 11 Response," *Legal Times,* Nov. 19, 2001, 1.

77. U.S. Senate, "Preserving Our Freedoms," Nov. 28, 2001.

78. Ibid.

79. U.S. Senate, Committee on the Judiciary, "Department of Justice Oversight: Preserving Our Freedoms While Defending against Terrorism," witness: Attorney General John Ashcroft, Dec. 6., 2001, 107th Cong., 1st sess., Federal News Service, available at web.lexis-nexis.com/ congcomp/document.

80. Ibid. Also see Reuters, "Ashcroft Defends Actions to Congress," Dec. 6, 2001, FindLaw .com. Available at news/findlaw.com.

81. U.S. Senate, "Preserving Our Freedoms," Dec. 6, 2001.

82. Bush, "Military Order: Detention, Treatment and Trial."

83. *New York Times,* "White House Push on Security Steps Bypasses Congress," Nov. 15, 2001, A1, available at www.nytimes.com/2001/11/15.

84. Louis Fisher, *Military Tribunals and Presidential Power* (Lawrence: University Press of Kansas, 2005); Louis Fisher, *Nazi Saboteurs on Trial* (Lawrence: University Press of Kansas, 2003). Due to his expertise in the field, he also wrote a friend-of-the-court brief in *Hamdan v. Rumsfeld.* Louis Fisher, "Brief Amicus Curiae of Louis Fisher in Support of Petitioner-Appellee Urging Affirmance," *Hamdan v. Rumsfeld,* United States Courts of Appeal for the District of Columbia Circuit, No. 04-5393, Dec. 29, 2004.

85. Ibid.

86. *Morrison v. Olson,* 487 U.S. 654, 108 S. Ct. 2597 (1988).

87. Among the cases where these clauses have been debated are *Bas v. Tingy,* 4 U.S. 37 (1800); *Little v. Barreme,* 6 U.S. 170 (1804); *The Prize Cases,* 67 U.S. 635 (1862); and *Youngstown Sheet and Tube Co. v. Sawyer,* 343 U.S. 579 (1952).

88. See, for example, Fisher, *Nazi Saboteurs on Trial;* Stephen Dycus, Arthur Berney, William Banks, and Peter Raven-Hansen, *National Security Law* (Boston: Little, Brown, 1990); Louis Henkin, *Foreign Affairs and the Constitution* (New York: Norton, 1975); Laurence H. Tribe, *American Constitutional Law,* 3rd ed., vol. 1 (New York: Foundation Press, 2000).

89. Alexander Hamilton, "The Real Character of the Executive," *The Federalist* No. 69, Mar. 14, 1788, available at www.constitution.org/fed/federa69/htm.

90. Nicholas Kulish, "Ashcroft Seeks More Antiterrorism Provisions," *Wall Street Journal,* June 6, 2003, B2.

91. Koszczuk, "Ashcroft Drawing Criticism," 2286.

92. Pierce, "Ashcroft Rapped over Oversight."

93. Joseph Pika, John Anthony Maltese, and Norman C. Thomas, *The Politics of the Presidency,* 5th ed. (Washington, D.C.: CQ Press, 2002), 378.

94. Bettelheim, "Congress Changing Tone," 2222.

95. David Nather and Jill Barshay, "Hill Warning: Respect Level from White House Too Low," *Congressional Quarterly,* Mar. 9, 2002, 630.

96. Editorial, "Stakes for Liberty," *Washington Post National Weekly Edition,* Jan. 6–12, 2003, 25.

97. Alexander Hamilton, "The Judiciary Department," *The Federalist* No. 78, June 14, 1788, available at www.constitution.org/fed/federa78.htm.

98. Tribe, *American Constitutional Law,* 366.

99. Louis Fisher, "Judicial Review of the War Power," *Presidential Studies Quarterly,* 35, no. 3 (Sept. 2005): 466–495.

100. U.S. Bureau of Prisons, "National Security; Prevention of Acts of Violence and Terrorism; Final Rule," 28 CFR Parts 500 and 501, effective date, Oct. 31, 2001, available at www .washingtonpost.com/ac2/wp-dyn/A64096-2001Nov8.

101. Reuters, "U.S. to Listen In on Some Inmate-Lawyer Talks," Nov. 11, 2001, available from Find Law Legal News and Commentary, news.findlaw.com.

102. Thannasis Cambanis, "Judge Eases U.S. Limits on Reid; Justice Dept. Hoped to Restrict His Contact," *Boston Globe,* Mar. 26, 2002, B1.

103. Elizabeth Amon, "Courts to Decide Access to Terror Suspects," *Fulton County Daily Report,* June 12, 2002, available through Lexis-Nexis Academic Universe.

104. Ibid. Reid was later convicted and sentenced to life.

105. U.S. Department of Justice, Office of Legal Counsel, Memorandum for William J. Haynes III from Patrick Philbin and John C. Yoo, "Re: Possible Habeas Jurisdiction over Aliens Held at Guantanamo Bay, Cuba," Dec. 28, 2001, Memo 3 in Greenberg and Dratel, *The Torture Papers,* 29.

106. Warren Richey, "How Evidence Stacks Up on Military Tribunals," *Christian Science Monitor,* Mar. 22, 2002, 3, available at www.csmonitor.com/2002/0322; Katherine Seelye, "A Nation Challenged: Military Tribunals," *New York Times,* Mar. 21, 2002, A1.

107. U.S. Department of Justice, Office of Legal Counsel, Memorandum for William J. Haynes III from John Yoo and Robert Delahunty, "Re: Application of Treaties and Laws to al Qaeda and Taliban Detainees," Memo 4 in Greenberg and Dratel, *The Torture Papers.*

108. John Ashcroft, "Prepared Remarks of Attorney General John Ashcroft to the Federalist Society," Nov. 12, 2004, available at www.usdoj.gov/ag/speeches/2004/111204federalist .htm.

109. Amon, "Courts to Decide Access."

110. Memorandum opinion and order, *Khalid v. Bush; Boumediene v. Bush,* U.S. District Court for the District of Columbia, Civil Case No. 1:04-1142 and 1:04-1166, Jan. 19, 2005, 30.

111. Memorandum opinion and order, *Khalid v. Bush,* 32.

112. *In re Guantanamo Detainees Case,* 355 F.Supp.2d 443 (2005); 2005 U.S. Dist. LEXIS 1236.

113. *Hamdan v. Rumsfeld,* memorandum opinion, U.S. District Court for the District of Columbia, 2004, Civil Action No. 04-1519 (JR), 16.

114. Ibid., 18.

115. Ibid.

116. *Hamdan v. Rumsfeld,* U.S. Court of Appeals for the District of Columbia Circuit, July

18, 2005, No. 04-5393, p. 15. Joining him in the majority was circuit judge John Roberts, nominated by the president to the Supreme Court the next day.

117. Brief, June 2002, *Hamdi v. Donald Rumsfeld,* respondents-appellants, U.S. Court of Appeals for the Fourth Circuit, No. 02-6895, 12, available at news.findlaw.com/hdocs/docs/hamdi/hamdirums61902gbrf.pdf.

118. Ibid., 12.

119. *Hamdi v. Rumsfeld,* U.S. Court of Appeals for the Fourth Circuit, 2002 U.S. App. LEXIS 12547, June 26, 2002. Fourth Circuit did not resolve the remaining issues at that time.

120. *Hamdi v. Rumsfeld,* 316 F. 3d 450 (2003); 2003 U.S. App. LEXIS 198. Jan. 8.

121. *Hamdi v. Rumsfeld,* 542 U.S. 507; 124 S.Ct. 2633 (2004).

122. Ibid., at 2650.

123. Ibid.

124. Ibid.

125. *Washington Post,* "Federal Prosecutors Defend Charges against Lindh," June 6, 2002, A12, available at www.washingtonpost.com/ac2/wp-dyn.

126. John Mintz, "Al Qaeda Suspect Enters Legal Limbo: Few Precedents Available for Case, Experts Say," *Washington Post,* June 11, 2002, A10.

127. White House, memorandum from George W. Bush to Secretary of Defense on the transfer of Jose Padilla as an enemy combatant, June 9, 2002; Mobbs Declaration on Jose Padilla, "Declaration of Michael H. Mobbs, Special Advisor to the Undersecretary of Defense for Policy," Aug. 27, 2002, available at findlaw.com.

128. Mintz, "Al Qaeda Suspect Enters Legal Limbo."

129. Mobbs Declaration on Jose Padilla.

130. Motion to Dismiss, "Respondents' Reply in Support of Motion to Dismiss the Amended Petition for a Writ of Habeas Corpus," *Padilla ex rel. Newman v. Bush, Rumsfeld, Ashcroft, Marr.,* U.S. District Court for Southern District of New York, 02 Civ. 4445 (2002).

131. *Padilla ex rel. Newman v. Bush,* U.S. District Court for the Southern District of New York, 233 F. Supp. 2d 564, Dec. 4, 2002.

132. *Padilla v. Rumsfeld,* U.S. Court of Appeals for the Second Circuit, U.S. App. LEXIS 25616, Dec. 18, 2003, No. 032235.

133. Brief for Petitioner, *Rumsfeld v. Padilla.*

134. *Rumsfeld v. Padilla,* 542 U.S. 426; 124 S.Ct. 2711 (2004).

135. U.S. Attorney General Remarks, "The Transfer of Abdullah Al Muhajir (Born José Padilla) to the Department of Defense as an Enemy Combatant," June 10, 2002, available at www.usdoj.gov/ag/speeches/2002.

136. Ibid.

137. Newton, "FBI Probes Lawmakers for Leak"; Tom Hays, "Attorney Says Alleged Terror Suspect Held Unconstitutionally," *Washington Post,* June 11, 2002, available at www.washingtonpost.com/ac2/wp-dyn/A32435-2002Jun11; Michael Isikoff, "And Justice for All," *Newsweek* online, Aug. 12, 2002, available at www.msnbc.com/news/792462.asp.

138. U.S. Attorney General Remarks, "The Transfer of Abdullah Al Muhajir."

139. Charles Hanley, "Scientists Say Dirty Bomb Would Be a Dud," Associated Press, June 9, 2002, available at customwire.ap.org/dynamic/stories/D/DIRTY_BOMB_DUD; Christopher Newton, "U.S.: Terror Suspect Is 'Small Fish,'" Associated Press, Aug. 14, 2002, available at news/findlaw.com.

140. Editorial, "Detaining Justice," *Christian Science Monitor,* June 20, 2002, available at www.csmonitor.com/2002/0620/p08.01-comv.html.

141. *Rasul, et al., v. Bush,* 525 U.S. 466; 124 S.Ct. 2686 (2004).

142. Ibid.

143. Ibid. Kennedy concurrence. Kennedy also noted here *Ex parte Milligan* (1866).

144. Ibid.

145. *Johnson v. Eisentrager,* 339 U. S. 763; 70 S.Ct. 936 (1950).

146. *Rasul, et al., v. Bush.* Scalia dissent.

147. Mintz, "Al Qaeda Suspect Enters Legal Limbo."

148. Bettelheim, "Congress Changing Tone," 2222.

149. Ibid.

150. Richard Schmitt, "Patriot Act Author Has Concerns," *Los Angeles Times,* Nov. 30, 2003, available at www.latimes.com/news/nationworld/nation/la-na-justice30nov30,1, 5074199.story.

151. John Ashcroft, *Lessons from a Father to His Son* (Nashville, Tenn.: Thomas Nelson, 1998), 43.

152. *Congress and the Nation, 1997–2001,* "Judiciary Activism, 1997–1998 Legislative Chronology," vol. 10 (Washington, D.C.: CQ Press, 2002), retrieved 10/17/03 from CQ Electronic Library, CQ Public Affairs Collection: catn97-97-6354-325744.

153. Betsy McCaughey, "Ashcroft, Man of Principle: His Quest for a Restrained Judiciary," *National Review,* Jan. 8, 2001, available at www.nationalreview.com/comment.

154. U.S. House of Representatives, Committee on the Judiciary, "Oversight of the Justice Department: Testimony of Attorney General John Ashcroft," Federal Document Clearing House, June 5, 2003.

155. Ashcroft, "Prepared Remarks to the Federalist Society."

156. Michael C. Dorf, "The Nation's Second-Highest Court Upholds Military Commissions," FindLaw's Writ Legal Commentary, July 20, 2005, available at writ.news.findlaw.com/dorf/20050720.html

157. Nancy V. Baker and Peter Gregware, "Citizens, Professionals or the Executive: Who Owns the Courts?" in G. Larry Mays and Peter R. Gregware, eds., *Courts and Justice,* 3rd ed. (Prospect Heights, Ill.: Waveland Press, 2004).

158. Ashcroft, "Prepared Remarks to the Federalist Society."

159. James Madison, "Notes on the Confederacy" (1787), in Philip R. Fendall, ed., *Letters and Other Writings of James Madison,* published by order of Congress (Philadelphia: Lippincott, 1865).

160. Edmund Randolph, letter to the Speaker of the House of Delegates, Oct. 10, 1787, reprinted in Paul Ford, ed., *Pamphlets on the Constitution of the United States* (Brooklyn, 1888), 262–264.

161. Ashcroft, "Prepared Remarks to the Federalist Society."

162. Tribe, *American Constitutional Law,* 122.

163. William B. Gwyn, *The Meaning of the Separation of Powers* (New Orleans: Tulane Studies in Political Science, 1964); William B. Gwyn, "The Indeterminacy of the Separation of Powers in the Age of the Framers," *William and Mary Law Review* 30 (Winter 1989): 263; William B. Gwyn, "The Indeterminacy of the Separation of Powers and the Federal Courts," *George Washington Law Review* 57 (Jan. 1989): 474.

164. Madison, *The Federalist* No. 48.

Chapter 6: Security and Liberty

1. See, for example, Charles Lane, "Fighting Terror vs. Defending Liberties: A New Debate Has Crystallized since Sept. 11," *Washington Post National Weekly Edition,* Sept. 9–15, 2002,

30; National Public Radio, "Liberty vs. Security: An NPR Special Report," Dec. 6, 2001; Abdon Pallasch, "Does Patriot Act Keep Us Safe or Go Too Far?" *Chicago Sun-Times,* Sept. 15, 2004, available at www.suntimes.com; William Safire, "Security with Liberty," *New York Times,* May 17, 2004, available at www.nytimes.com/2004/05/17/opinion; Editorial, "Terrorism and Liberty," *New York Times,* Dec. 23, 2003, available at www.nytimes.com/2003/12/23/opinion/23TUE3.html.

2. See, for example, Lee Epstein et al., "The Supreme Court during Crisis: How War Affects Only Non-war Cases," *New York University Law Review* 80, no. 1 (Apr. 2005): 1–116; Samuel Issacharoff and Richard Pildes, "Between Civil Libertarianism and Executive Unilateralism: An Institutional Process Approach to Rights during Wartime," *Theoretical Inquiries in Law* 5 (Jan. 2004): 2–44; Jeffrey Rosen, "Symposium on Security, Technology and Individual Rights," *Georgetown Journal of Law and Public Policy* 2, no. 17 (Winter 2004); Nancy V. Baker, "National Security versus Civil Liberties," *Presidential Studies Quarterly* 33 (Sept. 2003): 547–567.

3. Paul Rosenzweig, "Aiding Terrorists—An Examination of the Material Support Statute," Heritage Foundation, May 5, 2004, available at www.heritage.org/Research/LegalIssues/tst050504a.cfm.

4. Ibid.

5. Chitra Ragavan, "Ashcroft's Way," *U.S. News and World Report,* Jan. 26, 2004, available at www.usnews.com/usnews/news/articles/040126ashcroft.htm.

6. U.S. Senate, Committee on the Judiciary, "Department of Justice Oversight: Preserving Our Freedoms While Defending against Terrorism," witness: Attorney General John Ashcroft, Dec. 6, 2001, 107th Cong., 1st sess., Federal News Service, available at web.lexis-nexis.com/congcomp/document.

7. U.S. Attorney General Remarks, International Association of Chiefs of Police Conference, Oct. 7, 2002, available at www.usdoj.gov/ag/speeches/2002.

8. Shannon McCaffrey, "Ashcroft Opens PR Push for Patriot Act," *Philadelphia Inquirer,* Aug. 20, 2003, available at philly.com/mld/inquirer/news/nation.

9. U.S. Attorney General Remarks, "Attorney General Ashcroft Speaks about the Patriot Act, Boise, Idaho," Aug. 25, 2003, available at www.lifeandliberty.gov/subs/speeches/patriotactroadspeech_boise.

10. U.S. Department of Justice, Web site, "Preserving Life and Liberty," Sept. 11, 2003, available at www.lifeandliberty.gov.

11. Vanessa Blum, "Ashcroft: Looking Back, Looking Forward," *Legal Times,* Jan. 31, 2005, available at www.law.com.

12. John Ashcroft, "True Faith and Allegiance," Heritage Foundation Lecture no. 865, Feb. 11, 2005, available at www.heritage.org/Research/LegalIssues/hl865.cfm.

13. U.S. Senate, Committee on the Judiciary, "Ashcroft Comments on Anti-terror Policy," June 8, 2004, FDCH E-Media, available at www.washingtonpost.com/wp-dyn/articles/A25211-2004Jun8.html. Of note is that the hearings where he recounted the case focused on the department's complicity in the controversial memorandum that apparently sanctioned torture.

14. Philip Shenon, "Report on USA Patriot Act Alleges Civil Rights Violations," *New York Times,* July 21, 2003, available at www.nytimes.com/2003/07/21/politics21JUST.html.

15. Ibid.

16. *Larry King Live,* "Secretary Powell on CNN's Larry King Live," CNN. Nov. 27, 2001, available at http://www.cnn.com/TRANSCRIPTS/0111/27.

17. Jeff Bingaman, speech on the floor of the U.S. Senate, "Administrative Detentions and Right to Due Process," July 14, 2003, available at www.cq.com/cqonline/docs/html/crtext/108/crtext108-000000763112.html.

18. Kevin Johnson and Toni Locy, "Patriot Act at Heart of Ashcroft's Influence," *USA Today,* Sept. 15, 2003, available at /www.usatoday.com/news/washington/2003-09-15.

19. Jackie Koszczuk, "Ashcroft Drawing Criticism from Both Sides of the Aisle," *Congressional Quarterly,* Sept. 7, 2002, 2287.

20. Ibid.

21. *Congressional Record,* "Departments of Commerce, Justice, and State, the Judiciary and Related Agencies Appropriations Act, 2004," House of Representatives, 108th Cong., July 22, 2003, pp. H7291–H7293, available at thomas.loc.gov.

22. Richard Thornburgh, U.S. attorney general, 1988–1991, interview with author, Washington, D.C., May 12, 2005.

23. U.S. Attorney General Remarks, "Ashcroft Speaks about the Patriot Act, Boise, Idaho."

24. *Washington Post,* "Transcript: Ashcroft on Terror Probe Suspects," On Politics, Nov. 27, 2001, Available at www.washingtonpost/com/ac2/wp-dyn.

25. Editorial, "Deportation behind Closed Doors," *New York Times,* May 30, 2003, available at ww.nytimes.com/2003/05/30/opinion/30FRI2.html.

26. U.S. Attorney General Remarks, U.S. Conference of Mayors, eMediaMillWorks, Oct. 25, 2001, available at www.washingtonpost.com/wp-svr/nation/specials/attacked/transcript/ashcroft.

27. Charles Lane, "A Second Tier of Justice: A Parallel Legal System—without Constitutional Protections—Is in the Works for Terror Suspects," *Washington Post National Weekly Edition,* Dec. 9–15, 2002, 30.

28. Dan Eggen and Julie Tate, "U.S. Campaign Produces Few Convictions on Terrorism Charges," *Washington Post,* June 12, 2005, A1, available at www.washingtonpost.com/wp-dyn/content/article/2005/06/11/AR2005061100381.html.

29. Mary Beth Sheridan, "Immigration Law as Anti-terrorism Tool," *Washington Post,* June 13, 2005, A1, available at www.washingtonpost.com/wp-dyn/content/article/2005/06/12/AR2005061201441.html.

30. Maureen O'Hagan, "A Terrorism Case That Went Awry," *Seattle Times,* Nov. 22, 2004, A1.

31. Ibid.

32. *New York Times,* "Ashcroft Is Criticized for Remarks about Witness in Terror-Cell Case," Apr. 19, 2003, available at www.nytimes.com/2003/04/19/international.

33. U.S. Attorney General Remarks, "Attorney General Transcript: News Conference Regarding Zacarias Moussaoui," Dec. 11, 2001, available at www.usdoj.gov/archive/ag/speeches/2001/agcrisisremarks12_11.htm.

34. Seymour Hersh, *Chain of Command* (New York: HarperCollins, 2004), 109.

35. *New York Times.* "Ashcroft Is Criticized."

36. David Runk, "Ashcroft Remarks 'Distress' Federal Judge," Associated Press, Apr. 18, 2003, available at news.findlaw.com. The judge did not declare a mistrial, however, because jurors reported being unaware of Ashcroft's remark. Of note is that this prosecution witness, Youssef Hmimssa, had a long record of fraud and had testified against others in order to get a reduced sentence. His testimony was later discredited.

37. Associated Press, "Ashcroft Is Rebuked for Terror Remarks," *New York Times,* Dec. 17, 2003, available at www.nytimes.com/2003/12/17.

38. Ragavan, "Ashcroft's Way."

39. Adam Liptak, "For Post 9/11 Material Witness, It Is a Terror of a Different Kind," *New York Times,* Aug. 19, 2004, available nytimes.com/2004/08/19/politics/19witness.html.

40. Ibid.

41. Amy Goldstein, "A Deliberate Strategy of Disruption: Massive, Secret Detention Effort Aimed Mainly at Preventing More Terror," *Washington Post,* Nov. 4. 2001, A1.

42. Nat Hentoff, "Why Should We Care? It's Only the Constitution," *Progressive,* Dec. 2001, 27; quoting Rabbis David Saperstein and Eric Yoffie.

43. *North Jersey Media Group v. Ashcroft,* 308 F. 3d 198. 2002 U.S. App. LEXIS 21032 (2002).

44. *Center for National Security Studies, et al. v. Department of Justice,* 2003 U.S. App. LEXIS 11910 (2003).

45. Eric Lichtblau, "U.S. Will Tighten Rules on Holding Terror Suspects," *New York Times,* June 13, 2003, available at www.nytimes.com/2003/06/13/national/13TERR.html.

46. Jim McGee, "The Dragnet's Downside," *Washington Post National Weekly Edition,* Dec. 3, 2001, 8.

47. David G. Savage and Eric Lichtblau, "Ashcroft Deals with Daunting Responsibilities," *Los Angeles Times,* Oct. 28, 2001.

48. Goldstein, "A Deliberate Strategy"; Savage and Lichtblau, "Ashcroft Deals with Daunting Responsibilities"; Steve Fainaru, "U.S. Bans the Release of Detainees' Names," *Washington Post,* Apr. 19, 2002, A10, available at www.washingtonpost.com/wp-dyn/articles/A12012-2002Apr18.html.

49. Michael Janofsky, "9/11 Panel Calls Policies on Immigration Ineffective," *New York Times,* Apr. 17, 2004, available at www.nytimes.com/2004/04/17/national/17IMMI.html.

50. David Cole, "We've Aimed, Detained and Missed Before," *Washington Post National Weekly Edition,* June 16–22, 2003, 21.

51. Ibid.

52. Matthew Rothschild, "The Ashcroft Raids," *Progressive,* Apr. 25, 2003, available at www.progressive.org.

53. Jim Oliphant, "Justice during Wartime: Order on Military Trials Final Piece of Sept. 11 Response," *Legal Times,* Nov. 19, 2001, 1.

54. Daniel B. Wood, "Registration for Arabs Draws Fire," *Christian Science Monitor,* Feb. 6, 2003, available at news.findlaw.com; Rothschild, "The Ashcroft Raids"; Eric Schmitt, "New Rules Are Proposed for Appeals of Immigrants," *New York Times,* Feb. 2, 2002, A9.

55. Goldstein, "A Deliberate Strategy."

56. USA Patriot Act, HR 3162,PL 107-56, 2001, Sec. 412, Mandatory Detention of Suspected Terrorists; Habeas Corpus; Judicial Review.

57. Immigration and Nationality Act, 8 U.S.C. 1231 (a) (2000).

58. *Zadvydas v. Davis,* 533 U.S. 678; 2001 U.S. LEXIS 4912 (2001).

59. Michael Powell and Michelle Garcia, "Amid Praise, Doubts about Nominee's Post 9/11 Role," *Washington Post,* Jan. 31, 2005, A1, available at www.washingtonpost.com/ac2/wp-dyn/A49950-2005Jan30, quoting Andrew McCarthy, senior federal prosecutor in New York.

60. Patrick Philbin, "Limitations on the Detention Authority of the Immigration and Naturalization Service," Office of Legal Counsel, U.S. Department of Justice, Feb. 20, 2003, available at www.usdoj.gov/olc/INSDetention.htm.

61. U.S. Department of Justice, Office of the Inspector General, "The September 11 Detainees: A Review of the Treatment of Aliens Held on Immigration Charges in Connection with the Investigation of the September 11 Attacks," Apr. 2003, available at www.usdoj.gov/oig/special/0306/full.pdf.

62. Ibid.

63. Ibid.

64. Ibid.

65. Ibid.

66. U.S. House of Representatives, Committee on the Judiciary, "Oversight of the Justice Department: Testimony of Attorney General John Ashcroft," Federal Document Clearing House, June 5, 2003.

67. U.S. Department of Justice, statement of Barbara Comstock, Director of Public Affairs, "Regarding the IG's Report on 9/11 Detainees," June 2, 2003, available at www.usdoj.gov/opa/pr/2003/June.

68. Edward Walsh, "Treatment of Detainees Defended," *Washington Post,* June 25, 2003, available at www.washingtonpost.com/ac2/wp-dyn/admin/A33233-2003Jun 25.

69. Blum, "Ashcroft: Looking Back."

70. Eric Lichtblau, "Treatment of Detained Immigrants Is under Investigation," *New York Times,* June 26, 2003, available at www.nytimes.com/2003/06/26/national/26DETA.html.

71. Ibid.

72. Lichtblau, "U.S. Will Tighten Rules."

73. Shenon, "Report on USA Patriot Act"; Susan Schmidt, "IG Probes Patriot Act Charges," *Washington Post,* July 22, 2003, A15, available at www.washingtonpost.com/ac2/wp-dyn/A25296-2003Jul21.

74. Dan Eggen, "Tapes Show Abuse of 9/11 Detainees," *Washington Post,* Dec.19, 2003, A1, available at www.washingtonpost.com/ac2/wp-dyn/A13497-2003Dec18.

75. Curt Anderson, "Improvement Seen at 9/11 Detainee Prison," Associated Press, Mar. 19, 2004, available at news.findlaw.com.

76. John Mintz, "New Rules Shorten Holding Time for Detained Immigrants," *Washington Post,* Apr. 14, 2004, available at www.washingtonpost.com/wp-dyn/articles/A9311-2004Aprl13.html.

77. U.S. Department of Justice, Office of the Inspector General, "Report to Congress on Implementation of Section 1001 of the USA Patriot Act," Mar. 11, 2005, 6, available at http://www.usdoj.gov/oig/special/0503/final.pdf.

78. *Turkmen et al. v. Ashcroft et al.,* 2004 U.S. Dist. LEXIS 14537 (2004).

79. *Elmaghraby and Iqbal v. Ashcroft, et al.,* 2005 U.S. Dist. LEXIS 21434 (2005), 60.

80. Steve Fainaru, "A Denial or a Forfeit of Rights?" *Washington Post National Weekly Edition,* June 17–23, 2002, 30.

81. Steve Fainaru and Margot Williams, "Is the Law Being Bent? The Material Witness Statute Keeps Detainees in Jail, but Many Have Never Testified," *Washington Post National Weekly Edition,* Dec 2–8, 2002, 29–30.

82. Fainaru, "A Denial or a Forfeit of Rights?" 30.

83. Ibid.

84. Runk, "Ashcroft Remarks 'Distress' Federal Judge."

85. Fainaru, "A Denial or a Forfeit of Rights?" 30.

86. Curt Anderson, "Study: Terror-Related Cases Often Fizzle," Associated Press, Dec. 8. 2003, available at news.findlaw.com; Sheridan, "Immigration Law as Anti-terrorism Tool."

87. Janofsky, "9/11 Panel Calls Policies."

88. U.S. Department of Justice, letter of Barbara Comstock, Director of Public Affairs, to the editor of *Time* Magazine, May 13, 2003, available at www.usdoj.gov/opa/pr/2003/May/03_opa_292.htm.

89. Janofsky, "9/11 Panel Calls Policies."

90. Warren Richey, "A Legal Tool Emerges in Terror War," *Christian Science Monitor,* June 19, 2002, available at www.csmonitor.com/2002/0619.

91. Liptak, "For Post 9/11 Material Witness."

92. Human Rights Watch, "Witness to Abuse: Human Rights Abuses under the Material Witness Law since September 11," 17, no. 2 (June 2005): 2, 15.

93. Material Witness Statute, 18 U.S.C. § 3144 (1984).

94. Human Rights Watch, "Witness to Abuse."

95. *Barry v. United States ex relatione Cunningham,* 279 U.S. 597, 618.

96. Liptak, "For Post 9/11 Material Witness."

97. Ibid.

98. Human Rights Watch, "Witness to Abuse."

99. Liptak, "For Post 9/11 Material Witness."

100. Human Rights Watch, "Witness to Abuse."

101. *U.S. v. Awadallah,* U.S. District Court for the Southern District of New York, 2002 U.S. Dist. LEXIS 7536, Apr. 30, 2002.

102. Liptak, "For Post 9/11 Material Witness."

103. Ibid.

104. Fainaru and Williams, "Is the Law Being Bent?" 29.

105. Liptak, "For Post 9/11 Material Witness."

106. Human Rights Watch, "Witness to Abuse."

107. *In re application of the United States for material witness warrant,* 214 F. Supp. 2d. 356, 2002 U.S. Dist. LEXIS 14355 (2002); *Higazy v. Millennium Hotel,* 2004. 346 F. Supp. 2d. 430; 2004 U.S. Dist. LEXIS 19605 (2004).

108. *Higazy v. Millennium Hotel.*

109. *In re application for material witness warrant.*

110. *U.S. v. Awadallah,* 2002; *U.S. v. Awadallah,* 349 F. 3d 42, U.S. App. LEXIS 22879 (2003).

111. *U.S. v. Awadallah,* 2002, 22

112. Ibid.; *U.S. v. Awadallah,* 2003.

113. *U.S. v. Awadallah,* 2003.

114. Liptak, "For Post 9/11 Material Witness."

115. Ibid.

116. Ibid.

117. Fainaru and Williams, "Is the Law Being Bent?"

118. Indictment, *U.S. v. Ujaama,* U.S. District Court, Western District of Washington at Seattle, Aug. 28, 2002, available at http://news.findlaw.com/hdocs/docs/terrorism/usujaama 82802ind.pdf.

119. Andrew Kramer, "Software Engineer Admits Aiding Taliban," Associated Press, Aug. 6, 2003, available at www.news.findlaw.com.

120. Fainaru and Williams, "Is the Law Being Bent?" 29–30.

121. Human Rights Watch, "Witness to Abuse," 2.

122. Fainaru and Williams, "Is the Law Being Bent?" 29–30.

123. Human Rights Watch, "Witness to Abuse," 2.

124. Fainaru and Williams, "Is the Law Being Bent?" 29–30.

125. Liptak, "For Post 9/11 Material Witness."

126. Eric Lichtblau, "U.S. Uses Terror Law to Pursue Crimes from Drugs to Swindling," *New York Times,* Sept. 27, 2003, available at www.nytimes.com/2003/09/27/politics.

127. Government Accountability Office, "Justice Department: Better Management Oversight and Internal Controls Needed to Ensure Accuracy of Terrorism-Related Statistics," Jan. 17, 2003, available at www.gao.gov/cgi-bin/getrpt?GAO-03-266.

128. Ibid., 7.

129. Anderson, "Terror-Related Cases Often Fizzle"; Ragavan, "Ashcroft's Way."

130. Findlaw.com, Special Coverage: War on Terrorism, "Civil and Criminal Terror Cases Homepage," accessed July 8, 2005, available at news.findlaw.com/legalnews/us/terrorism/cases/index.html.

131. U.S. Bureau of Prisons, "National Security; Prevention of Acts of Violence and Terrorism; Final Rule," 28 CFR Parts 500 and 501, effective date, Oct. 31, 2001, available at www.washingtonpost.com/ac2/wp-dyn/A64096-2001Nov8; Reuters, "U.S. to Listen In on Some Inmate-Lawyer Talks," Find Law Legal News and Commentary, Nov. 11, 2001, available at news.findlaw.com.

132. U.S. Bureau of Prisons, "National Security."

133. Ibid.

134. U.S. Senate, "Preserving Our Freedoms."

135. U.S. Bureau of Prisons, "National Security."

136. U.S. Senate, "Preserving Our Freedoms."

137. Brief for the United States, *U.S. v. Moussaoui,* U.S. Court of Appeals for the Fourth Circuit, on Appeal from the U.S. District Court for the Eastern District of Virginia, No. 03-4792, Oct. 24, 2003, 10, available at news.findlaw.com/hdocs/docs/Moussaoui/usmouss102403gbrf.pdf. He was charged with conspiracy to commit international terrorism, commit aircraft piracy, destroy aircraft, use weapons of mass destruction, murder U.S. government employees, and destroy property.

138. U.S. Attorney General Remarks, "Zacarias Moussaoui."

139. Ibid.

140. See, for example, Stuart Taylor Jr., "Let's Not Allow a Fiat to Undermine the Bill of Rights," *Atlantic* online, July 23, 2002, available at www.theatlantic.com/politics/nj/taylor2002-07-23.htm; Philip Shenon, "Prosecution Says Qaeda Member Was to Pilot 5th Sept. 11 Jet," *New York Times,* Apr. 16, 2003, B6.

141. Brief for the United States, *U.S. v. Moussaoui.*

142. Larry Margasak, "Moussaoui Seeks Access to Gov't Documents," Associated Press, Apr. 23, 2003, available at news.findlaw.com/ap_stories/other/1110/4-23-2003. As noted, some CIA and FBI agents shared that view, in part due to comments by the 9/11 hijackers themselves prior to the strikes, captured in electronic intercepts. Hersh, *Chain of Command,* 104.

143. Government's Position on Competency and Defendant's Self Representation, *U.S. v. Moussaoui,* U.S. Court of Appeals for the Fourth Circuit, on Appeal from the U.S. District Court for the Eastern District of Virginia, No. 03-4792, June 7, 2002, available at news.findlaw.com/hdocs/docs/Moussaoui/usmouss60702gcomp.pdf.

144. *U.S. v. Moussaoui,* Order, U.S. District Court for the Eastern District of Virginia, Alexandria Division, No. 01:01cr455, Apr. 20, 2005, available at news.findlaw.com/hdocs/docs/moussaoui/usmouss42005ord.html.

145. Associated Press, "Moussaoui Banned from Closed Hearing," Apr. 10, available at news.findlaw.com/ap/o/1110/4-10-2003/20030410; Jerry Markon, "Moussaoui Barred from Hearing," *Washington Post,* May 3, 2003, A9, available at www.washingtonpost.com/ac2/wp-dyn/A7582-2003May2.

146. Hersh, *Chain of Command,* 111–112, 116–117.

147. Ibid., 111–112, 117.

148. Jerry Markon, "Moussaoui Is Spinning a Legal Web," *Washington Post,* May 26, 2003, available at www.washingtonpost.com/wp-dyn/articles; Margasak, "Moussaoui Seeks Access"; Larry Margasak, "Judge: Moussaoui Case Fate Lies in Access," Associated Press, Aug. 8, avail-

able at news.findlaw.com; Larry Margasak, "Moussaoui Worried on Self-Representation," Associated Press, Aug. 22, 2003, available at news.findlaw.com; Associated Press, "Judge Weighs Moussaoui's 9/11 Guilty Plea," Apr. 20, 2005, available at www.nytimes.com/aponline/national/AP-Moussaoui.html.

149. Andrew Kent, "Justice for Terrorists," *Commentary,* June 2004, 40–41.

150. Jerry Markon, "U.S. Tries to Block Access to Witness for Terror Trial," *Washington Post,* Apr. 2, 2003, A7, available at www.washingtonpost.com/ac2/wp-dyn/A6605-2003Aprl.

151. Philip Shenon, "Judge Rules U.S. Must Provide Statements from Qaeda Leaders," *New York Times,* Apr. 23, 2003, available at www.nytimes.com/2003/04/23/international/worldspecial/23USP.html.

152. Philip Shenon, "Moussaoui Case May Have to Shift from U.S. Court to Tribunal," *New York Times,* Feb. 7, available at www.nytimes.com/2003/02/07/politics/07TERR.html.

153. Larry Margasak, "U.S. Seeks to Block Moussaoui Request," *Washington Post,* June 3, 2003, available at www.washingtonpost.com/wp-dyn/articles.

154. Markon, "Moussaoui Is Spinning."

155. Philip Shenon, "Justice Dept. Warns of Risk to Prosecution and Security," *New York Times,* June 4, 2003, A21.

156. Warren Richey, "In Moussaoui Tangle, Glimpse of Terror's Legal Tug of War," *Christian Science Monitor,* July 18, available at www.csmonitor.com/2003/0718/p04s02-usju.html.

157. Ibid.; Jerry Markon, "Major Issues in Moussaoui Appeal," *Washington Post,* Nov. 30, 2003, A19, available at www.washingtonpost.com.

158. Philip Shenon, "Justice Department Will Appeal Ruling in Trial Linked to 9/11," *New York Times,* Feb. 8, 2003, available at www.nytimes.com/2003/02/08/politics; Shenon, "Moussaoui Case May Have to Shift."

159. Richey, "In Moussaoui Tangle"; Larry Margasak, "Moussaoui Makes Plea for Live Testimony," Associated Press, July 24, 2003, available at news.findlaw.com.

160. Brief for the United States, *U.S. v. Moussaoui,* 2003.

161. Associated Press, "Suspect's Lawyers Say Statement Was Distorted," *New York Times,* June 5, 2003, available at www.nytimes.com/2003/06/05/politics/05USP.html.

162. *U.S. v. Moussaoui,* order, U.S. District Court for the Eastern District of Virginia, Alexandria Division, Criminal No. 01-455-A, Oct. 2, 2003, available at news.findlaw.com/hdocs/docs/Moussaoui/usmouss100203.ord.pdf.

163. Jerry Markon, "Judge Bars Death Penalty for Moussaoui," *Washington Post,* Oct. 2, 2003, available at www.washingtonpost.com/ac2/wp-dyn?A34536-2003Oct2.

164. James Vicini, "U.S. Says Error in Barring Moussaoui Death Penalty," Reuters, Oct. 31, 2003, available at news.findlaw.com.

165. Markon, "Major Issues in Moussaoui Appeal."

166. Philip Shenon, "Federal Appeals Court Restores Sept. 11 Prosecution," *New York Times,* Apr. 23, 2004, available at www.nytimes.com/2004/04/23/politics/23 TERR.html.

167. *U.S. v. Moussaoui,* 2004. U.S. Court of Appeals for the Fourth Circuit. No. 03-4792, decided Sept. 13, 2004, p. 37, available at news/findlaw.com/hdocs/docs/Moussaoui/usmouss91304opn.pdf.

168. William Branigin, "Justices Decline to Hear Moussaoui Appeal," *Washington Post,* Mar. 21, 2005, available at www.washingtonpost.com/ac2/wp-dyn/A53515-2005Mar21.

169. Jerry Markon, "Moussaoui Planning to Admit 9/11 Role," *Washington Post,* Apr. 19, 2005, A1, available at www.washingtonpost.com/wp-dyn/articles/A64195-2005Apr18.html; Eric Lichtblau, "Sept. 11 Suspect May Be Set to Admit Guilt," *New York Times,* Apr. 20, available at www.nytimes.com/2005/04/20/national/20moussaoui.html.

170. U.S. Attorney General Remarks, "Zacarias Moussaoui."

171. Hersh, *Chain of Command,* 110.

172. Markon, "U.S. Tries to Block Access," A7; Philip Shenon, "Hearing to Affect Government's Ability to Try Terror Suspects in Civilian Courts," *New York Times,* June 2, 2003, available at www.nytimes.com/2003/06/02/politics/02USP.html; Larry Margasak, "Judge: Tribunal for Moussaoui Case?" Associated Press, June 3, available at news.findlaw .com.

173. U.S. Attorney General Remarks, "Zacarias Moussaoui."

174. Notice of Intent to Seek a Sentence of Death, *U.S. v. Moussaoui,* Criminal No. 01-455-A, filed in the U.S. District Court for the Eastern District of Virginia, Mar. 28, 2002, available at news.findlaw.com/hdocs/docs/moussaoui/usmoussaoui032802ntc.html.

175. Hersh, *Chain of Command,* 104–105, 118.

176. The insistence on the death penalty in other cases also complicated the government's prosecution, when defendants were in the custody of countries that ban capital punishment. Only by promising to forgo an attempt to win a death penalty could the United States secure access to those defendants.

177. Hersh, *Chain of Command,* 107. This was virtually identical to the path taken by the government in the case of José Padilla.

178. U.S. Attorney General Remarks, "Zacarias Moussaoui."

179. Margasak, "Judge: Moussaoui Case Fate Lies in Access."

180. See, for example, Shenon, "Moussaoui Case May Have to Shift"; Shenon, "Hearing to Affect Government's Ability"; and Vicini, "U.S. Says Error in Barring Moussaoui Death Penalty."

181. Eric Lichtblau, "Enemy Combatant Decision Marks Change, Officials Say," *New York Times,* June 25, 2003, available at www.nytimes.com/2003/06/25/politics/25TERR.html.

182. Louis Fisher, *Military Tribunals and Presidential Power* (Lawrence: University Press of Kansas, 2005), 52.

183. Lichtblau, "Enemy Combatant Decision."

184. CNN.com, "Buffalo Terror Suspect Admits Al Qaeda Training," May 20, 2003, available at www.cnn.com/2003/LAW/05/20/buffalo.terror/.

185. Shenon, "Hearing to Affect Government's Ability."

186. Circuit Judge Gregory, concurring in part and dissenting in part. *U.S. v. Moussaoui,* 2004, 80.

187. Markon, "Moussaoui Is Spinning," quoting John Martin, a former government prosecutor in terrorism cases.

188. Ibid., quoting Eric Holder Jr., former top official in the Clinton Justice Department.

189. Editorial, "A Sept. 11 Plea?" *Washington Post,* Apr. 20, 2005, A24, available at www .washingtonpost.com/wp-dyn/articles/A3013-2005Apr19.html.

190. Markon, "Moussaoui Is Spinning," quoting Victoria Toensing of the Reagan Justice Department.

191. Kent, "Justice for Terrorists," 39, 42; Margasak, "U.S. Seeks to Block Moussaoui Request."

192. *New York Times,* "The Trial of Zacarias Moussaoui," July 28, 2003, available at www .nytimes.com/2003/07/28/opionion/28MON1.html. Also see Markon, "U.S. Tries to Block Access."

193. Richey, "In Moussaoui Tangle," quoting I. Dean Ahmad, president of the Minaret Freedom Institute.

194. David Ashenfelter, "Terrorists or Harmless Immigrants? Detroit Trial Could Strike

Blow against Terrorism or Be a Huge Embarrassment," *Detroit Free Press,* Mar. 11, 2003, available at www.freep.com/news/locway/terr11_20030311.htm.

195. Ibid.

196. Ibid.

197. Dan Eggen and Steve Fainaru, "For Prosecutors, 1996 Law Is Key Part of Anti-terror Strategy," *Washington Post,* Oct. 15, 2002, A2, available at www.washingtonpost.com/ac2/wp-dyn/A25838-2002Oct14.

198. Ashenfelter, "Terrorists or Harmless Immigrants?"

199. Ibid.

200. Danny Hakim, "Man Acquitted in Terror Case Says Co-defendants Will Be Cleared," *New York Times,* June 6, 2003, available at www.nytimes.com/2003/06/06/national/06 DETR.html.

201. *Convertino v. Justice Department, Ashcroft, et al.,* complaint, U.S. District Court for the District of Columbia, Feb. 13, 2004, available at www.findlaw.com.

202. Runk, "Ashcroft Remarks 'Distress.'"

203. Hakim, "Man Acquitted in Terror Case."

204. U.S. Department of Justice, statement of Attorney General John Ashcroft, "On Detroit Verdict," June 3, 2003, available at www.usdoj.gov/opa/pr/2003/June/03_ag_331.htm.

205. Ibid.

206. Danny Hakim, "Inquiries Begun into Handling of Detroit Terror Cases," *New York Times,* Jan. 29, 2004, available at www.nytimes.com/2004/01/29/national/29TRIA.html.

207. Ibid.

208. Ibid.

209. Allan Lengel and Susan Schmidt, "U.S. to Seek Dismissal of Terrorism Convictions," *Washington Post,* Sept. 1, 2004, A2, available at www.washingtonpost.com/ac2/wp-dyn/A50698-2004Aug31.

210. Hakim, "Inquiries Begun."

211. Pete Yost, "Federal Prosecutor Sues Ashcroft," *Washington Post,* Feb. 17, 2004, available at www.washingtonpost.com/ac2/wp-dyn/A47812-2004Feb17.

212. O'Hagan, "A Terrorism Case," A1.

213. Ibid.

214. Title 18 of the U.S. Code, Sec. 2339A.

215. USA Patriot Act, HR 3162, PL 107-56, 2001, Section 805, "Material Support for Terrorism."

216. Norman Abrams, "The Material Support of Terrorism Offenses: Perspectives Derived from the (Early) Model Penal Code," *Journal of National Security Law and Policy* 1, no. 5 (2005): 6–7, 18.

217. Indictment, *U.S. v. Sattar,* U.S. District Court, Southern District of New York, Apr. 9, 2002, p. 11, available at news.findlaw.com/hdocs/docs/terrorism/ussattar040902ind.pdf.

218. Abrams, "The Material Support," 19.

219. *Humanitarian Law Project v. Reno,* 205 F. 3d 1130 (2000); *Humanitarian Law Project v. U.S. Department of Justice,* 352 F. 3d 382 (2003); *Humanitarian Law Project v. Ashcroft,* 309 F. Supp. 2d 1185 (2004); and *U.S. v. Sattar, Al-Sirri, Stewart and Yousry,* opinion and order. 02 Cr. 395 (JGK). U.S. District Court for the Southern District of New York, July 22, 2003.

220. David Cole, "Constitutional Implications of Statutes Penalizing Material Support to Terrorist Organizations" testimony before the United States Senate Committee on the Judiciary, May 5, 2004, available at www.bordc.org/resources/cole-materialsupport.php.

221. Ibid.

222. *Humanitarian Law Project v. U.S. Department of Justice;* Eric Lichtblau, "Appeals Court Casts Doubt on Parts of Key Antiterrorism Law," *New York Times,* Dec. 4, 2003, available at www.nytimes.com/2003/12/04/national/04USP.html.

223. Eggen and Fainaru, "For Prosecutors, 1996 Law."

224. U.S. House of Representatives, Subcommittee on Oversight and Investigations, House Committee on Financial Services, testimony of Alice Fisher, 108th Cong., 1st sess., Mar. 11, 2003, available at financialservices.house.gov/media/pdf/031103af.pdf.

225. Eggen and Fainaru, "For Prosecutors, 1996 Law."

226. Abrams, "The Material Support," 6–7.

227. 9/11 Commission Hearing, "Chapter 6: The Illinois Charities Case Study," *Terrorist Financing Staff Monograph,* National Commission on Terrorist Attacks upon the United States, 2004, available at www.9-11commission.gov/staff_statements/911_TerrFin_Ch6.pdf, p. 111.

228. Ibid.

229. *U.S. v. Benevolence International Foundation and Arnaout,* opinion and order, U.S. District Court for the Northern District of Illinois, Eastern Division, No. 02:cr414, Sept. 12, 2002, available at news.findlaw.com/hdocs/docs/terrorism/usbif91302opn.pdf.

230. U.S. Attorney General Remarks, "Attorney General Ashcroft Announces Indictment of Alleged Terrorist Financier," Chicago, Illinois, Oct. 9, 2002, available at www.usdoj.gov/archive/ag/speeches/2002/100902agremarksbifindictment.htm.

231. Ibid.

232. *U.S. v. Arnaout,* plea agreement, U.S. District Court for the Northern District of Illinois, Eastern Division, Feb. 10. 2003, No. 02 CR 892, available at news.findlaw.com/hdocs/docs/bif/usarnaout203plea.pdf.

233. John Mintz, "Head of Muslim Charity Sentenced," *Washington Post,* Aug. 19, 2003, A2; 9/11 Commission Hearing, "Chapter 6."

234. 9/11 Commission Hearing, "Chapter 6," 110, n.123.

235. Ibid.

236. Ibid., 112.

237. Ibid.

238. Ibid., 110, n.123.

239. Ibid., 112.

240. Ibid.

241. Ibid., 111.

242. Ibid., 110.

243. David Cole, "The Lynne Stewart Trial," *Nation,* Mar. 7, 2005, 6.

244. Michael Wilson, "Judge Dismisses Terror Charges against Lawyer," *New York Times,* July 23, 2003, available at www.nytimes.com/2003/07/23/nyregion; Susie Day, "Counter-Intelligent: The Surveillance and Indictment of Lynne Stewart," *Monthly Review,* Nov. 2002, 24–33; Larry Neumeister, "2 Terrorism Charges against Lawyer Tossed," Associated Press, July 23, 2003, available at news.findlaw.com.

245. *U.S. v. Sattar, et al.,* opinion and order.

246. Abrams, "The Material Support," 16.

247. Mark Hamblett, "N.Y. Lawyer Lynne Stewart Convicted of Helping Terrorists," *New York Law Journal,* Feb. 11, 2005, available at www.law.com.

248. Larry Neumeister, "Verdict vs. Lawyer in Terror Case Upheld," SFGate.com. Oct. 25, 2005, available at sfgate.com/cgi-bin/article.cgi?f=/n/a/2005/10/25/national/a203219D99 .DTL.

249. Cole, "The Lynne Stewart Trial," 6.

250. Elizabeth Amon, "Courts to Decide Access to Terror Suspects," *Fulton County Daily Report,* June 12, 2002, available through Lexis-Nexis Academic Universe.

251. Day, "Counter-Intelligent," 33.

252. Reuters, "Ashcroft Says Walker Waived Right to Attorney," Jan. 16, 2002, available at news.findlaw.com; Charles Lane, "Unanswered Questions," *Washington Post National Weekly Edition,* July 22–28, 2002, 9.

253. *Newsweek,* "The Lindh E-Mails," June 24, 2002, available at msnbc.com/news/767536.asp.

254. Jane Mayer, "Beyond Belief," *Washington Post National Weekly Edition,* Sept. 29–Oct. 5, 2003, 33; Lane, "Unanswered Questions."

255. Louis Fisher, "Who's Minding the Courts on Rights?" *Los Angeles Times,* Feb. 23, 2003, M2.

256. Lane, "A Second Tier of Justice," 30.

257. Benjamin Weiser, "U.S. Asks Judge to Deny Terror Suspect Access to Lawyer, Saying It Could Harm Interrogation," *New York Times,* Jan. 10, 2003, available at www.nytimes.com/2003/01/10.

258. Michael Isikoff, "And Justice for All," *Newsweek* online, Aug. 12, 2002, available at msnbc.com/news/792462.asp.

259. Eric M. Freedman, "Milestones in Habeas Corpus: Part I: Just Because John Marshall Said It, Doesn't Make It So: Ex Parte Bollman and the Illusory Prohibition on the Federal Writ of Habeas Corpus for State Prisoners in the Judiciary Act of 1789," *Alabama Law Review* 51 (Winter 2000): 531.

260. Eric M. Freedman, "Hamdi and the Case of the Five Knights," *Legal Times,* Feb. 3, 2003.

261. Article I, Section 9, clause 2.

262. Laurence Tribe, *American Constitutional Law,* 3rd ed., vol. 1 (New York: Foundation Press, 2000), 65.

263. U.S. Code. Title 28, Sec. 2241: Power to grant writ.

264. Antiterrorism and Effective Death Penalty Act of 1996, P.L. 104-132, 110 Stat. 1214.

265. *Johnson v. Eisentrager,* 339 U.S. 763 (1950), and *Vermilya-Brown Co. v. Connell,* 335 U.S. 377 (1948). While in the latter case, all nine justices held that Bermuda was not subject to U.S. sovereignty, five justices did uphold the application of a federal law to the U.S. military base there, suggesting that they might not have summarily rejected an extraterritorial habeas claim.

266. U.S. Department of Justice, Office of Legal Counsel, Memorandum for William J. Haynes III, General Counsel, Department of Defense, from Patrick Philbin and John C. Yoo. "Re: Possible Habeas Jurisdiction over Aliens Held at Guantanamo Bay, Cuba," Dec. 28, 2001, in Karen Greenberg and Joshua Dratel, eds., *The Torture Papers: The Road to Abu Ghraib* (New York: Cambridge University Press, 2005), 29.

267. Ibid., 31.

268. Ibid., 33.

269. Ibid., 29.

270. Neil Lewis and Eric Schmitt, "Lawyers Decided Bans on Torture Didn't Bind Bush," *New York Times,* June 8, 2004, available at www.nytimes.com/2004/06/08/politics/08ABUS.html.

271. *Rasul, et al., v. Bush,* 525 U.S. 466; 124 S.Ct. 2686 (2004).

272. Ibid.

273. Ibid.

274. *Brown v. Allen,* 344 U.S. 443, 533 (1953).

275. Tom Jackman and Dan Eggen, "'Combatants' Lack Rights, U.S. Argues," *Washington Post,* June 20, 2002, A1.

276. *Hamdi v. Rumsfeld,* 294 F.3d 598 (2002).

277. *Hamdi v. Rumsfeld,* 542 U.S. 507; 124 S.Ct. 2633 (2004).

278. Brief for the respondents, *Hamdi v. Rumsfeld,* 2003, No. 03-6996, available at www .gov/osg/briefs/2003/3mer/2mer/toc3index.html, quoting Department of Defense, Fact Sheet: Guantanamo Detainees, available at www.defenselink.mil/news/ Feb2004/d20040220det.pdf.

279. Ibid.

280. Ibid.

281. Ibid.

282. *Hamdi v. Rumsfeld,* 124 S.Ct. 2633 (2004), 14–15.

283. Ibid.

284. Charles Lane, "Justices Move to Define Detainees' Court Access," *Washington Post,* July 1, 2004, A7, available at www.washingtonpost.com/ac2/wp-dyn.

285. Carol Leonnig, "Lawyers Seek Relief for 5 Detainees," *Washington Post,* July 3, 2004, A20, available at http://www.washingtonpost.com/ac2/wp-dyn.

286. Human Rights Watch, "U.S.: Guantanamo Tribunal Lacks Basic Knowledge of Law," Nov. 6, 2004, available at hrw.org/English/docs/2004/11/05/usdom9615_txt.htm.

287. Kim Lane Scheppele, "Law in a Time of Emergency: States of Exception and the Temptations of 9/11," *University of Pennsylvania Journal of Constitutional Law* 6 (May 2004): 1053.

288. Juliette Kayyem, "The Sentencing of 'Shoe Bomber' Richard Reid," FindLaw's Writ Legal Commentary, Feb. 3, 2003, available at writ.findlaw.com/commentary/20030203_ kayyem.

289. Eric Lichtblau, "Trucker Sentenced to 20 Years in Plot against Brooklyn Bridge," *New York Times,* Oct. 29, 2003, available at www.nytimes.com/2003/10/29/national/29TERR.html.

290. U.S. Department of Justice, "Earnest James Ujaama Sentenced for Conspiring to Supply Goods and Services to the Taliban," Feb. 13, available at www.usdoj.gov/opa/pr/ 2004/February/04_crm_086.htm

291. Powell and Garcia, "Amid Praise, Doubts about Nominee's Post 9/11 Role."

292. Nedra Pickler, "Bush: Patriot Act Helped to Nab Terrorists," *San Francisco Chronicle,* June 9, 2005, available at SFGate.comhttp://www.sfgate.com/cgi-bin/article.cgi?f=/n/a/2005/ 06/09/national/w092105D91.DTL.

293. Eggen and Tate, "U.S. Campaign Produces Few Convictions."

294. General Accounting Office, "Better Management Oversight," 2003, 6, 11.

295. Ibid., 3, 7.

296. Liptak, "For Post 9/11 Material Witness."

297. Michael C. Dorf, "The Nation's Second-Highest Court Upholds Military Commissions," FindLaw's Writ Legal Commentary, July 20, 2005, available at writ.news.findlaw.com/ dorf/20050720.html.

298. Kayyem, "The Sentencing of 'Shoe Bomber.'"

Chapter 7: Surveillance, Privacy, and the Patriot Act

1. Bob Woodward, *Bush at War* (New York: Simon and Schuster, 2002), 97.

2. Chitra Ragavan, "Ashcroft's Way." *U.S. News and World Report,* Jan. 26, 2004, available at www.usnews.com/usnews/news/articles/040126ashcroft.htm.

3. Elizabeth A. Palmer, "Committees Taking a Critical Look at Ashcroft's Request for

Broad New Powers," *CQ Weekly,* Sept. 29, 2001, 2263–2265, available at CQ Electronic Library, CQ Public Affairs Collection: weeklyreport107-000000316148.

4. Tom Regan, "Ashcroft Slams Critics as Patriot Act Backlash Grows." *Christian Science Monitor,* Sept. 16, 2003, available at www.csmonitor.com.

5. Ibid.

6. Palmer, "Committees Taking a Critical Look."

7. U.S. House of Representatives, Committee on the Judiciary. "Testimony of Attorney General John Ashcroft on the USA PATRIOT Act," Sept. 24, 2001, available at www.usdoj .gov/ag/testimony/2001/agcrisisremarks9_24.htm.

8. Palmer, "Committees Taking a Critical Look," 2263–2265.

9. Louis Fisher, "Challenges to Civil Liberties in a Time of War," in Richard Conley, ed., *Transforming the American Polity: The Presidency of George W. Bush and the War on Terrorism.* Upper Saddle River, N.J.: Pearson Prentice Hall, 2005.

10. *Congressional Record,* "Departments of Commerce, Justice, and State, the Judiciary and Related Agencies Appropriations Act, 2004," House of Representatives, 108th Cong., July 22, 2003, p. H7291, available at thomas.loc.gov.

11. Ibid.

12. Palmer, "Committees Taking a Critical Look," 2263–2265.

13. Jackie Koszczuk, "Lawmakers Struggle to Keep an Eye on Patriot Act," *Congressional Quarterly,* Sept. 7, 2002, 2284.

14. Michael Isikoff and Daniel Klaidman, "Ashcroft's Campaign to Shore Up the Patriot Act," *Newsweek,* Aug. 25, 2003, 6.

15. Bloomberg News, "Groups Urge Partial Lapse of Patriot Act," *Washington Post,* Mar. 23, 2005, A6, available at www.washingtonpost.com/ac2/wp-dyn/A58068-2005Mar22.

16. Dan Eggen and Jim VandeHei, "Ashcroft Taking Fire from GOP Stalwarts," Washington Post, Aug. 29, 2003, A1.

17. *Congressional Record,* "Departments of Commerce, Justice, and State."

18. Eric Lichtblau, "Ashcroft's Tour Rallies Supporters and Detractors," *New York Times,* Sept. 8, 2003, available at www.nytimes.com/2003/09/08/politics.

19. Gail Russell Chaddock, "Security Act to Pervade Daily Lives," *Christian Science Monitor,* Nov. 21, 2002, available at www.csmonitor.com/2002/1121/p01s03-usju.html.

20. Mike McIntire, "Terror Lesson Fading for Some, Ashcroft Says in Manhattan," *New York Times,* Sept. 10, 2003, available at www.nytimes.com/2003/09/10/nyregion/10ASHC.html.

21. U.S. Attorney General Remarks, "Attorney General Ashcroft Speaks about the Patriot Act, Boise, Idaho," Aug. 25, 2003, available at www.lifeandliberty.gov/subs/speeches/patriot actroadspeech_boise.

22. U.S. Senate, Committee on the Judiciary, "Ashcroft Comments on Anti-terror Policy," June 8, 2004, FDCH E-Media, available at www.washingtonpost.com/wp-dyn/articles/ A25211-2004Jun8.html.

23. John P. Elwood, "Prosecuting the War on Terrorism," *Criminal Justice Magazine,* 17, no. 2 (Summer 2002), available at www.abanet.org/crimjust/cjmag/17-2/prosecuting.html.

24. U.S. Department of Justice, Web site, "Dispelling the Myths," Sept. 11, 2003, available at www.lifeandliberty.gov/subs/u_myths.

25. Isikoff and Klaidman, "Ashcroft's Campaign to Shore Up the Patriot Act," 6.

26. Dan Eggen, "Ashcroft Defends Anti-terrorism Law," *Washington Post,* Aug. 20, 2003, A10.

27. Thomas Ginsberg and Bob Moran, "Ashcroft: Anti-terror Laws Are Working," *Philadelphia Inquirer,* Aug. 20, 2003, available at philly.com/mld/inquirer/news/nation.

28. Curt Anderson, "Ashcroft Mounting Defense of Patriot Act," Associated Press, Aug. 18, 2003, available at news.findlaw.com.

29. Lichtblau, "Ashcroft's Tour Rallies Supporters and Detractors."

30. Ibid.

31. McIntire, "Terror Lesson Fading for Some."

32. Regan, "Ashcroft Slams Critics."

33. Eggen and VandeHei, "Ashcroft Taking Fire," A1.

34. Editorial, "An Unpatriotic Act," *New York Times,* Aug. 25, 2003, available at www .nytimes.com/2003/08/25/opinion

35. Commentary, "Ashcroft's Whistle-Stops," *Christian Science Monitor,* Aug. 21, 2003, available at www.csmonitor.com/2003/0821/p08s01-comv.html.

36. U.S. Department of Justice, Office of Legal Counsel, Guidelines of 18 U.S.C. § 1913, Anti-Lobbying Act, 1995, available at www.amc.army.mil/amc/command_counsel/resources/ documents/newsletter97-6/enc118.pdf.

37. Eric Lichtblau, "Ashcroft Criticized for Talks on Terror," *New York Times,* Aug. 22, 2003, available at www.nytimes.com/2003/08/22/politics.

38. U.S. Department of Justice, Guidelines, Anti-Lobbying Act.

39. Dan Eggen, "Ashcroft Planning Trip to Defend Patriot Act," *Washington Post,* Aug. 13, 2003, A2, available at www.washingtonpost.com/ac2/wp-dyn/A51538-2003Aug12.

40. David B. Caruso, "Ashcroft Begins Patriot Act Tour," Associated Press, Aug. 20, 2003, available at news.findlaw.com/ap_stories.

41. Lichtblau, "Ashcroft's Tour Rallies Supporters and Detractors."

42. Darren Carlson, "Far Enough? Public Wary of Restricted Liberties," Gallup poll, Jan. 20, 2004, available at www.gallup.com.

43. American Civil Liberties Union, "Keep America Safe and Free," n.d., Web site, available at www.aclu.org/SafeandFree/SafeAndFreeMain.cfm.

44. U.S. Senate, Committee on the Judiciary, "Department of Justice Oversight: Preserving Our Freedoms While Defending against Terrorism," witness: Attorney General John Ashcroft, Dec. 6, 2001, 107th Cong., 1st sess., Federal News Service, available at web.lexis-nexis.com/ congcomp/document.

45. Nat Ives, "Celebrities Line Up to Criticize Bush in A.C.L.U. Campaign," *New York Times,* Sept. 12, 2003 available at www.nytimes.com/2003/09/12/business/media.

46. USA Patriot Act, HR 3162, PL 107-56, 2001, Section 213, Authority for Delaying Notice of the Execution of a Warrant.

47. U.S. Department of Justice, "Department of Justice Releases New Numbers on Section 213 of the Patriot Act," Apr. 4, 2005, available at www.usdoj/gov/opa/pr/2005/Apr./05_opa_ 160.htm.

48. U.S. House of Representatives, Committee on the Judiciary, "Oversight of the Justice Department: Testimony of Attorney General John Ashcroft," Federal Document Clearing House, June 5, 2003.

49. USA Patriot Act, Section 215. Access to records and other items under the Foreign Intelligence Surveillance Act.

50. USA Patriot Act, Section 505. Miscellaneous National Security Authorities.

51. U.S. Department of Justice, Office of Legal Policy, "Report to Congress on the Use of Administrative Subpoena Authorities by Executive Branch Agencies and Entities, Pursuant to Public Law 106-544," n.d., available at www.usdoj.gov/olp/intro.pdf.

52. Right to Financial Privacy, 12 USCS § 3414 (2005); USA Patriot Act, Section 805.

53. Dan Eggen, "ACLU Was Forced to Revise Release on Patriot Act Suit," *Washington Post,* May 13, 2004, A27, available at www.washingtonpost.com/ac2/wp-dynA22404-2004 May 12; Julia Preston, "Judge Allows Peek into Challenge to Antiterrorism Law," *New York Times,* May 13, 2004, available at www.nytimes.com/2004/05/13/politics/13suit.html.

54. U.S. Senate, "Ashcroft Comments on Anti-terror Policy."

55. Ibid.

56. Barton Gellman, "The FBI's Secret Scrutiny," *Washington Post,* Nov. 6, 2005, A1, A10, A11.

57. Dan Eggen and Robert O'Harrow Jr., "U.S. Steps Up Secret Surveillance," *Washington Post,* 2003, Mar. 24, 2003, A1, available at www.washingtonpost.com/wp-dyn/articles/A16287-2003Mar23.html.

58. Gellman, "The FBI's Secret Scrutiny," A1.

59. American Library Association Resolution, "The USA Patriot Act in the Library," adopted by the ALA Council Jan. 23, 2002, available at www.ala.org/alaorg/oif/usapatriotlibrary .html.

60. American Library Association News Release, "Freedom to Read Foundation Seeks Justice Department Response," Nov. 15, 2002, available at www.ftrf.org/foiapressrelease.

61. Rene Sanchez, "Librarians Make Some Noise over Patriot Act," *Washington Post,* Apr. 9, 2003, available at www.washingtonpost.com/wp-dyn/articles/A1481-2003Apr9.html; John Berry, "High Profile, Strong Image: If We Didn't Have Attorney General Ashcroft, We Would Have to Invent Him," *Library Journal,* 128, no. 20 (Dec. 2003): 8.

62. Eric Lichtblau, "Government Says It Has Yet to Use New Power to Check Library Records," *New York Times,* Sept. 19, 2003, available at www.nytimes.com/2003/09/19/national.

63. Curt Anderson, "Ashcroft Denounces Patriot Act 'Hysteria,'" Associated Press, Sept. 15, 2003, available at news.findlaw.com.

64. David B. Caruso, "New Monitoring Law Concerns Librarians," Associated Press, Jan. 27, 2003, available at www.news.findlaw.com/ap_stories/ht/1700/1-27-2003/20030127.

65. U.S. Attorney General Remarks, "The Proven Tactics in the Fight against Crime," Sept. 15, 2003, available at www.usdoj.gov/ag/speeches/2003.

66. Ibid.

67. Eric Lichtblau, "Ashcroft Mocks Librarians and Others Who Oppose Parts of Counterterrorism Law," *New York Times,* Sept. 16, 2003, available at www.nytimes.2003/09/16/politics.

68. Editorial, "Mr. Ashcroft's Tantrum," *Washington Post National Weekly Edition,* Sept. 29–Oct. 5, 2003, 25.

69. Eric Lichtblau, "In a Reversal, Ashcroft Lifts Secrecy of Data," *New York Times,* Sept. 18, 2003, available at www.nytimes.2003/09/18/politics; Lichtblau, "Government Says It Has Yet to Use."

70. Lichtblau, "Government Says It Has Yet to Use."

71. Eric Lichtblau, "Justice Dept. Lists Use of New Power to Fight Terror," *New York Times,* May 21, 2003, available at www.nytimes.com/2003/05/21/international/worldspecial/21PATR.html.

72. Sanchez, "Librarians Make Some Noise"; Leigh Estabrook, "Public Libraries and Civil Liberties: A Profession Divided," Library Research Center, University of Illinois at Urbana-Champaign, Jan. 2003, available at alexia.lis.uiuc.edu/gslis/research/civil_liberties.html.

73. Eric Lichtblau, "Libraries Say Yes, Officials Do Quiz Them about Users," *New York Times,* June 20, 2005, available at www.nytimes.com/2005/06/20/politics/20patriot.html.

74. Mike Allen, "House Votes to Limit Patriot Act," *Washington Post,* June 19, 2005, A3, available at www.washingtonpost.com/ac2/w-dyn.

75. Glen Johnson, "House Votes to Extend Patriot Act," *Washington Post,* July 22, 2005, available at www.washingtonpost.com/wp-dyn/content/articles/2005/07/21/AR2005072100711 .html. The other provision was Section 206, dealing with roving wiretap authority.

76. Edmund Sanders, "The Court That Wields the Wiretaps," *Los Angeles Times,* Sept. 30, 2001, available at www.latimes.com/news/nationworld/nation/la-09001fisa.story; U.S. Department

of Justice, Office of Legal Counsel, Memorandum Opinion for the Associate Deputy Attorney General, 2001 OLC LEXIS 3, Nov. 5, 2001.

77. U.S. Department of Justice, Office of Intelligence Policy and Review, home page, accessed June 4, 2004, available at www.usdoj.gov/oipr.

78. Dan Eggen and Susan Schmidt, "Secret Court Rebuffs Ashcroft," *Washington Post,* Aug. 23, 2002, A1, available at www.washingtonpost.com/ac2/wp-dyn/A51220-2002Aug22; Sanders, "The Court That Wields the Wiretaps."

79. FISA Letter 2004, Assistant Attorney General William Moschella to Ralph Mecham, Administrative Office of the United States Courts, Apr. 1, 2005, U.S. Department of Justice, Office of Intelligence Policy and Review, FOIA Reading Room Records, available at www .usdoj.gov/oipr/reading room.

80. Eggen and Schmidt, "Secret Court Rebuffs Ashcroft."

81. *In re: All Matters Submitted to the Foreign Intelligence Surveillance Court,* 218 F.Supp.2d 661 (2002).

82. Griffin Bell, U.S. attorney general, 1977–1980, interview with author, Atlanta, Georgia, May 16, 2005.

83. *In re: All Matters Submitted to the Foreign Intelligence Surveillance Court.*

84. U.S. Constitution, Fourth Amendment; Nancy V. Baker and Peter Gregware, "Citizens, Professionals or the Executive: Who Owns the Courts?" in G. Larry Mays and Peter R. Gregware, eds., *Courts and Justice,* 3rd ed. (Prospect Heights, Ill.: Waveland Press, 2004).

85. Reg Murphy, *Uncommon Sense* (Atlanta: Longstreet Press, 1999).

86. Executive Order 12333, 3 C.F.R. 200, 1981, Section 2.5.

87. Electronic Surveillance, 50 USCS §1804, 2005.

88. *In re: All Matters Submitted to the Foreign Intelligence Surveillance Court.*

89. Ibid.

90. Bell, interview with author.

91. Executive Order 12333, 3 C.F.R. 200, Section 2.5 (1981 Comp.).

92. Sanders, "The Court That Wields the Wiretaps."

93. Tom Brune, "Ashcroft: U.S. Is Beating Terror," *Newsday,* Mar. 5, 2003, A5, available through Lexis-Nexis Academic Universe.

94. *In re: All Matters Submitted to the Foreign Intelligence Surveillance Court,* 2.

95. Sanders, "The Court That Wields the Wiretaps."

96. U.S. Department of Justice, Memorandum to Director of FBI, Assistant Attorney General Criminal Division, Counsel for Intelligence Policy, United States Attorneys, from the Attorney General, Subject: Intelligence Sharing Procedures for Foreign Intelligence and Foreign Counterintelligence Investigations Conducted by the FBI, Mar. 6, 2002, available at www.fas .org/irp/agency/doj/fisa/ag030602.html.

97. *In re: All Matters Submitted to the Foreign Intelligence Surveillance Court.*

98. Eggen and Schmidt, "Secret Court Rebuffs Ashcroft."

99. U.S. Attorney General Remarks, "Ashcroft Speaks about the Patriot Act."

100. 9/11 Commission Hearing, Transcript of Hearings with Attorney General John Ashcroft, National Commission on Terrorist Attacks upon the United States, FDCH E-Media, Apr. 13, 2004, available at www.washingtonpost.com/wp-dyn/articles/A9088-2004Apr13.html# ashcroft.

101. *In re: All Matters Submitted to the Foreign Intelligence Surveillance Court.*

102. Ibid., 19–20.

103. Ibid., 26–27.

104. Deborah Charles, "Feds Appeal Secret Court Ruling on Wiretaps," Reuters, Aug. 23, 2002, available at news.findlaw.com.

105. Eggen and Schmidt, "Secret Court Rebuffs Ashcroft."

106. Neil Lewis, "Court Overturns Limits on Wiretaps to Combat Terror," *New York Times,* Nov. 19, 2002, available at www.nytimes.com/2002/11/19/national/19COUR.html.

107. *In re: Sealed Case no. 02-001, consolidated with 02-002,* U.S. Foreign Intelligence Surveillance Court of Review, Attachments, 310 F3d. 717 (2002).

108. Ibid.

109. Ibid.

110. Brune, "Ashcroft: U.S. Is Beating Terror."

111. Eggen and Schmidt, "Secret Court Rebuffs Ashcroft."

112. Ibid.

113. Andrew Kent, "Justice for Terrorists," *Commentary,* June 2004, 40–41.

114. FISA Letters, Attorney General Janet Reno to Ralph Mecham, Administrative Office of the United States Courts, Apr. 18, 1997, Apr. 29, 1998, Apr. 29, 1999, Apr. 27, 2000, U.S. Department of Justice, Office of Intelligence Policy and Review, FOIA Reading Room Records, 1996–1999, available at www.usdoj.gov/oipr/reading room. The figure for 1996 was 839; 1997, 749; 1998, 796; 1999, 886.

115. FISA Letter 2000, Attorney General John Ashcroft to Ralph Mecham, Administrative Office of the United States Courts, Apr. 27, 2001, U.S. Department of Justice, Office of Intelligence Policy and Review, FOIA Reading Room Records, available at www.usdoj.gov/oipr/reading room.

116. FISA Letter 2001, Acting Attorney General Larry Thompson to Ralph Mecham, Administrative Office of the United States Courts, Apr. 29, 2002, U.S. Department of Justice, Office of Intelligence Policy and Review, FOIA Reading Room Records, available at www.usdoj.gov/oipr/reading room.

117. FISA Letter 2002, Attorney General John Ashcroft to Ralph Mecham, Administrative Office of the United States Courts, Apr. 29, 2003, U.S. Department of Justice, Office of Intelligence Policy and Review, FOIA Reading Room Records, available at www.usdoj.gov/oipr/reading room. This figure includes two that had been approved as modified by the FISA court in its partial rejection of the Ashcroft guidelines, but after the appeals court ruling were approved as they were.

118. FISA Letter 2003, Assistant Attorney General William Moschella to Ralph Mecham, Administrative Office of the United States Courts, Apr. 30, 2004, U.S. Department of Justice, Office of Intelligence Policy and Review, FOIA Reading Room Records, available at www.usdoj.gov/oipr/reading room.

119. FISA Letter 2004, William Moschella to Ralph Mecham, Administrative Office of the United States Courts, Apr. 1, 2005, U.S. Department of Justice, Office of Intelligence Policy and Review, FOIA Reading Room Records, available at www.usdoj.gov/oipr/reading room.

120. U.S. Department of Justice, letter of Barbara Comstock, Director of Public Affairs, to the editor of *Time* magazine, May 13, 2003, available at www.usdoj.gov/opa/pr/2003/May/03_opa_292.htm.

121. U.S. Department of Justice, Statement of Associate Deputy Attorney General David S. Kris before the Senate Judiciary Committee Concerning the Foreign Intelligence Surveillance Act, Sept. 10, 2002, available at www.usdoj.gov/dag/testimony/2002/kirssenjud091002.htm.

122. Ibid.

123. Executive Order 13372, "Prohibiting transactions with terrorists who threaten to disrupt the Middle East peace process," Feb. 16, 2005, 50 U.S. Code 1701 (2005); Executive Order 13224, "Blocking property and prohibiting transactions with persons who commit, threaten or support terrorism," Sept. 23, 2001, available at news.findlaw.com/hdocs/docs/dotreas/terroristsanctions110701.html.

124. Maureen O'Hagan, "A Terrorism Case That Went Awry," *Seattle Times,* Nov. 22, 2004, A1.

125. Ibid.

126. Associated Press, "No Conviction for Student in Terror Case," *New York Times,* June 11, 2004, available at www.nytimes.com/2004/06/11/national/11boise.html.

127. Todd Wilkinson, "Boise Terror Case Tests Patriot Act's Reach," *Christian Science Monitor,* Apr. 22, 2004, available at www.csmonitor.com/2004/0422/p03s01-usju.htm; O'Hagan, "A Terrorism Case."

128. Wilkinson, "Boise Terror Case"; Terry Frieden, "Saudi Grad Student Cleared of Terror Charges; Mistrial Declared on Lesser Charges," CNN, June 15, 2004, available at www.cnn.com/2004/LAW/06/11/computer.terrorism/index/html.

129. USA Patriot Act, Section 805, Material Support for Terrorism.

130. O'Hagan, "A Terrorism Case."

131. Associated Press, "No Conviction for Student."

132. O'Hagan, "A Terrorism Case."

133. Ibid.

134. Ibid.

135. *Brandenburg v. Ohio,* 395 U.S. 444 (1969).

136. Associated Press, "No Conviction for Student"; Frieden, "Saudi Grad Student Cleared."

137. O'Hagan, "A Terrorism Case."

138. Bob Fick, "Trial Merges Terror Charges, Free Speech," Associated Press, May 28, 2004, available at news.findlaw.com; Frieden, "Saudi Grad Student Cleared."

139. Fick, "Trial Merges Terror Charges."

140. U.S. Attorney General Remarks, "Report from the Field: The USA Patriot Act at Work," July 13, 2004, available at www.usdoj.gov/ag/speeches/2004/071304_patriot_report_remarks.htm.

141. Eric Lichtblau, "U.S. Uses Terror Law to Pursue Crimes from Drugs to Swindling," *New York Times,* Sept. 27, 2003, available at www.nytimes.com/2003/09/27/politics.

142. John Ashcroft, "True Faith and Allegiance," Heritage Foundation Lecture No. 865, Feb. 11, 2005, available at www.heritage.org/Research/LegalIssues/hl865.cfm.

143. U.S. Attorney General Remarks, "Report from the Field."

144. Ibid.

145. Ibid.

146. Lichtblau, "U.S. Uses Terror Law."

147. Michael Isikoff, "Show Me the Money: Patriot Act Helps the Feds in Cases with No Tie to Terror," *Newsweek,* Dec. 1, 2003, available at www.msnbc.com/news; Kelley Beaucar, "Critics: Patriot Act Warnings Come to Fruition," Fox News, Nov. 22, 2003, available at www.foxnews.com.

148. Lichtblau, "U.S. Uses Terror Law."

149. Isikoff, "Show Me the Money."

150. Ibid.; *Newsweek/MSNBC.* "Common Sense: Resistance to the Patriot Act Is Growing in the American Heartland," Nov. 20, 2003, Web exclusive, available at www.msnbc.com/news.

151. Isikoff, "Show Me the Money."

152. Lichtblau, "U.S. Uses Terror Law."

153. Koszczuk, "Lawmakers Struggle to Keep," 2284.

154. U.S. Department of Justice, John Ashcroft Memorandum to Heads of All Federal Departments and Agencies, "Subject: The Freedom of Information Act," Oct. 12, 2001.

155. U.S. Immigration and Naturalization Service, Office of the Chief Immigration Judge,

Interim Operating Policies and Procedures Memorandum, "Protective Orders and the Sealing of Records in Immigration Proceedings," July 16, 2002.

156. U.S. Department of Justice, "Fact Sheet: The Terrorist Screening Center," Sept. 3, 2003, available at www.usdoj.gov/opa/pr/2003/September.

157. U.S. Attorney General Remarks, "FBI Reorganization," May 29, available at www.usdoj.gov/ag/speeches/2002.

158. U.S. Attorney General, Guidelines, "FBI National Security Investigations and Foreign Intelligence Collection," Oct. 31, 2003, available at www.usdoj.gov/olp/nsiguidelines.pdf.

159. U.S. Attorney General, Guidelines, "Federal Bureau of Investigation Undercover Operations," May 30, 2002, available at www.usdoj.gov/olp/fbiundercover.pdf.

160. U.S. Attorney General, Guidelines, "General Crimes, Racketeering Enterprise and Terrorism Enterprise Investigations," May 30, 2002, available at www.usdoj.gov/olp/generalcrimes2.pdf.

161. U.S. Attorney General Remarks, "Attorney General Guidelines," May 30, 2002, available at www.usdoj.gov/ag/speeches/2002/53002agpreparedremarks.htm.

162. U.S. Attorney General, Guidelines, "General Crimes, Racketeering."

163. U.S. Attorney General Remarks, "Attorney General Guidelines."

164. Ibid.

165. U.S. Attorney General, Guidelines, "General Crimes, Racketeering."

166. Ibid.

167. U.S. Attorney General, Guidelines, "General Crimes, Racketeering," 7.

168. Ibid.

169. Lichtblau, "Justice Dept. Lists Use of New Power."

170. Editorial, "In the Aftermath of Sept. 11," *New York Times,* May 23, 2003, available at www.nytimes.com/2003/05/23/opinion/23FRI1.html.

171. Eric Lichtblau, "Large Volume of F.B.I. Files Alarms U.S. Activist Groups," *New York Times,* July 18, 2005, A12.

172. Jeff Eckhoff and Mark Siebert, "Group Fights Anti-war Inquiry," *Des Moines Register,* Feb. 7, 2004, available at desmoinesregister.com/news/stories/c4788993/23473647.html; Monica Davey, "Subpoenas on Antiwar Protest Are Dropped," *New York Times,* Feb. 11, 2004, available at www.nytimes.com/2004/02/11/national/11PROT.html.

173. Lichtblau, "Large Volume of F.B.I. Files," A12.

174. Ibid.

175. Ibid.

176. U.S. Department of Justice, Office of Legal Counsel. Memorandum Opinion, to Glenn A. Fine, Inspector General, from Jack Goldsmith, Apr. 5. 2004, available at www.aclu.org/SafeandFree/SafeandFree.cfm?ID=16253&c=282.

177. U.S. Attorney General Remarks, "Protecting Life and Liberty, Memphis, Tennessee," Sept. 18, 2003, available at www.usdoj.gov/ag/speeches/2003/0918.

178. USA Patriot Act, Section 1001, Review of the Department of Justice.

179. U.S. Department of Justice, Office of Inspector General, Special Reports, Accessed June 20, 2005, available at www.usdoj.gov/oig/igspecr1.htm.

180. USA Patriot Act, Section 215.

Chapter 8: Secrecy and Accountability

1. Adam Clymer, "Government Openness at Issue as Bush Holds On to Records," *New York Times,* Jan. 3, 2003, available at www.nytimes.com/2003/01/03/politics/03SECR.html.

2. Deb Reichmann, "U.S. More Tightlipped since Sept. 11," Associated Press, Nov. 15, 2001, available at news.findlaw.com.

3. Alan Elsner, "Bush Expands Government Secrecy, Arouses Critics," Reuters, Sept. 3, 2002, available at news.findlaw.com/politics/s/200209/bushsecrecydc.htm.

4. Clymer, "Government Openness."

5. Jeff Bingaman, interview with author, Las Cruces, New Mexico, Mar. 31, 2005.

6. Eric Lichtblau and Janet Hook, "White House Angered by Leaks on Intelligence," *Los Angeles Times,* June 21, 2002, A15.

7. Clymer, "Government Openness."

8. White House, Office of the Press Secretary, press briefing by Ari Fleischer, May 21, 2002, available at www.whitehouse.gov/news/releases/2002/05/20020521-9.html.

9. White House, Office of the Press Secretary, press briefing by Ari Fleischer, Jan. 17, 2002, available at www.whitehouse.gov/news/releases/2002/01/20020117-8.html.

10. White House, Office of the Press Secretary, press briefing by Ari Fleischer, Dec. 13, 2001, available at www.whitehouse.gov/news/releases/2001/12/20011213-7.html.

11. Clymer, "Government Openness."

12. Presidential Records Act, U.S. Code, Title 44, Chapter 22, Section 2204; Executive Order 12667 issued by Ronald Reagan on January 16, 1989.

13. White House Counsel's Office, letters from Alberto R. Gonzales to John W. Carlin, Archivist of the United States, National Archives and Records Administration, Mar. 23, June 6, and August 31, 2001. Gonzales relied on Section 2(b) of Executive Order 12667 that requires the archivist to extend the time for release at the instruction of the current president.

14. Executive Order 13233, "Further Implementation of the Presidential Records Act," issued by George W. Bush, Nov. 1, 2001. The new procedures require that a specific request be made for access before a document is reviewed for possible release, with release granted only with the concurrence of the current president and the former president. The national archivist can no longer challenge a claim of privilege made by a former president, as had been the case under the earlier order.

15. Francine Kiefer, "A Fight Brews over Ex-President's Papers," *Christian Science Monitor,* Nov. 6, 2001, available at www.csmonitor.com/2001/1106; Emily Eakin, "Presidential Papers as Smoking Guns," *New York Times,* Apr. 13, 2002, available at www.nytimes.com/2002/04/13; Steven L. Hensen, "The President's Papers Are the People's Business," *Washington Post,* Dec. 16, 2001, B1.

16. Clymer, "Government Openness."

17. Francine Kiefer, "Backlash Grows against White House Secrecy," *Christian Science Monitor,* Mar. 25, 2002, 3.

18. Dana Milbank, "In War, It's Power to the President," *Washington Post,* Nov. 20, 2001, A1, available at www.washingtonpost.com/ac2/wp-dyn; Christopher Newton, "FBI Probes Lawmakers for Leak," Associated Press, Aug. 2, 2002, available at news.findlaw.com.

19. Newton, "FBI Probes Lawmakers for Leak."

20. Ibid.

21. Dana Milbank, "DiIulio Saga Highlights Primacy Placed on Secrecy," *Washington Post,* Dec. 10, 2002, A27, available at www.washingtonpost.com/ac2/wp-dyn/A32951-2002Dec9.

22. Scott Shane, "Increase in the Number of Documents Classified by the Government," *New York Times,* July 3, 2005, available at www.nytimes.com/2005/07/03/politics/03 secrecy.html.

23. Eric Lichtblau, "Rising Fears That What We Do Know Can Hurt Us," *Los Angeles Times,* Nov. 18, 2001, available at www.latimes.com.

24. Ariana Eunjung Cha, "Risks Prompt U.S. to Limit Access to Data," *Washington Post,* Feb. 24, 2002, A1, available at www.washingtonpost.com/ac2/wp-dyn/A58430-2002Feb.

25. Clymer, "Government Openness."

26. U.S. Department of Justice, press release, statement of Barbara Comstock, Director of Public Affairs, "Regarding the Oral Argument in National Center for Security Studies v. Department of Justice," Nov. 18, 2002, available at www.usdoj.gov/opa/pr/2002/November.

27. Steve Fainaru, "Immigration Hearings Case Goes to High Court," *Washington Post,* June 22, 2002, A11, available at www.washingtonpost.com/wp-dyn/A26081-2002Jun21.

28. Clymer, "Government Openness."

29. Adriel Bettelheim, "Congress Changing Tone of Homeland Security Debate," *Congressional Quarterly,* Aug. 31, 2002, 2222; Dana Milbank, "In Cheney's Shadow, Counsel Pushes the Conservative Cause," *Washington Post,* Oct. 11, 2004, A21, available at www.washington post.com/ac2/wp-dyn/A2265-2004Oct10.

30. Warren Richey, "Secret 9/11 Case before High Court," *Christian Science Monitor,* Oct. 30, 2003, available at www.csmonitor.com/2003/1030.

31. U.S. Senate, Committee on the Judiciary, "Department of Justice Oversight: Preserving Our Freedoms While Defending against Terrorism," witness: Attorney General John Ashcroft, Dec. 6, 2001, 107th Cong., 1st sess., Federal News Service, available at web.lexis-nexis.com/congcomp/document.

32. Ibid.

33. Nina Bernstein, "Questions, Bitterness and Exile for Queens Girl in Terror Case," *New York Times,* June 17, 2005, available at www.nytimes.com/2005/06/17/nyregion/17suicide .html?th&emc=th, quoting Mike German.

34. *Congressional Weekly,* "Leaking Classified Information," Sept. 6, 2001, 2081.

35. U.S. Department of Justice, "Attorney General Ashcroft Announces Interagency Task Force to Review Ways to Combat Leaks of Classified Information," Dec. 14, 2001, available at www.usdoj.gov/opa/pr/2001.

36. Bert Brandenburg, "Open Government in the Ashcroft Era: What Went Wrong and How to Make It Right," Watching Justice: An Eye on the Department of Justice, 2005, 6, available at www.watchingjustice.org/reports/article/php?docID=663.

37. Ibid.

38. Eric Lichtblau, "Ashcroft's Tour Rallies Supporters and Detractors," *New York Times,* Sept. 8, 2003, available at www.nytimes.com/2003/09/08/politics; Jay Rosen, "John Ashcroft: National Explainer," *Press Think,* Sept. 16, 2003, available at journalism.nyu.edu/pubzone/weblogs/pressthink/2003/09/16-ashcroft_rationale.html.

39. Society of Professional Journalists, "Ashcroft Speeches Should Be More Accessible to the Public and Media," Sept. 18, 2003, AScribe Law News Service, available at web5.infotract .galegroup.com/itw/infomark/72/15/51032787w5/purl=rcl_EAIM_0_A107.

40. Lichtblau, "Ashcroft's Tour Rallies Supporters and Detractors."

41. Ibid., quoting Rich Bond.

42. Walter Brasch, *America's Unpatriotic Acts* (New York: Peter Lang, 2005), 166–167.

43. U.S. Department of Justice, Office of Legal Counsel, "Memoranda and Opinions by Year," accessed Apr. 5, 2005, available at www.usdoj.gov.olc.opinions.htm.

44. Ibid. The annual average during Ashcroft's tenure was ten.

45. FBI e-mail, from [redacted] to Marion Bowman, Valerie Caproni and John Curran, FBI Office of General Counsel, Subject: DOJ 2002 "torture" memo, June 8, 2004, available at www.aclu.org/torturefoia/released/FBI_4931.pdf.

46. Barton Gellman, "The FBI's Secret Scrutiny," *Washington Post,* Nov. 6, 2005, A10–A11.

47. Brandenburg, "Open Government in the Ashcroft Era," 3.

48. Harold Relyea, "Freedom of Information Act (FOIA) Amendments: 109th Congress," Congressional Research Service, CRS Report to Congress, RL32780, updated May 16, 2005, available at www.fas.org/sgp/crs/secrecy/RL32780.pdf.

49. 5 U.S.C. § 552 (2003).

50. U.S. Department of Justice, "New Attorney General FOIA Memorandum Issued," Oct. 16, 2001, available at www.usdoj.gov/opa/pr/2001.

51. U.S. Department of Justice, John Ashcroft Memorandum to Heads of All Federal Departments and Agencies, "Subject: The Freedom of Information Act," Oct. 12, 2001.

52. Linda Koontz, Letter from the Director, Information Management Issues, to Sen. Patrick Leahy, Sept. 3, 2003, General Accounting Office, GAO-03-981, available at www.fas.org/sgp/foia/gao-03-981.pdf.

53. U.S. Department of Justice, John Ashcroft FOIA memorandum.

54. Ibid.

55. Martin Halstuk, "In Review: The Threat to Freedom of Information," *Columbia Journalism Review* 40, no. 5 (Jan./Feb. 2002): 8, available at www.cjr.org, quoting Rose Ciotta, *Philadelphia Inquirer.*

56. Ibid.

57. Clymer, "Government Openness."

58. Lichtblau, "Rising Fears That What We Do Know."

59. Clymer, "Government Openness."

60. H. I. McIntyre, Memorandum from the Director, Directorate for Freedom of Information and Security Review, "Subject: DoD Guidance on Attorney General Freedom of Information Act (FOIA) Memorandum," Department of Defense, Nov. 19, 2001, available at www.fas.org/sgp/foia/dod111901.pdf.

61. Clymer, "Government Openness."

62. General Accounting Office, "Update on Freedom of Information Act Implementation Status," A Report to the Ranking Minority Member, Committee on the Judiciary, U.S. Senate, Feb. 2004, GAO-04-257, available at www.gao.gov/cgi-bin/getrpt?GAO-04-257.

63. Edmund Andrews and Elizabeth Becker, "Bush Got $500,000 from Companies That Got Contracts, Study Finds," *New York Times,* Oct. 31, available at www.nytimes.com/2003/10/31/politics.

64. General Accounting Office, "Freedom of Information Act: Agency Views on Changes Resulting from New Administration Policy," Report to the Ranking Minority Member, Committee on the Judiciary, U.S. Senate, Sept. 2003, GAO-03-981, available at www.gao.gov/cgi-bin/getrpt?GAO-03-981. Of the 183 responses from FOIA officers, 88 (48 percent) reported that they had seen no change in terms of their agencies being more or less likely to make discretionary disclosures under the Freedom of Information Act, while 12 (6.6 percent) reported an increased likelihood of disclosure.

65. Complaint for Injunctive Relief, *Center for National Security Studies, American Civil Liberties Union, Electronic Privacy Information Center, et al., v. Department of Justice,* U.S. District Court for the District of Columbia, Dec. 5, 2001.

66. ACLU press release, "FBI E-Mail Refers to Presidential Order Authorizing Inhumane Interrogation Techniques," Dec. 20, 2004, available at www.aclu.org/SafeandFree/SafeandFree.cfm?IC=17216&c=206.

67. James V. Grimaldi, "At Justice, Freedom Not to Release Information," *Washington Post,* Dec. 2, 2002, E1, available at www.washingtonpost.com/ac2/wp-dyn/A58419-2002Nov30.

68. FBI Memo, Memo To: Washington Field, From: Criminal Investigative. Re: Special Jurisdiction Crimes, [redacted], Crime on Government Reservation, Crime of Violence, July 22, 2004, released to ACLU Dec. 15, 2004, available at www.aclu.org/torturefoia/released/FBI_4368_4372.pdf.

69. FBI Memo. Memo To: [redacted], From: [redacted]. Subject: Current Events, May 13, 2004, released to ACLU Dec. 15, 2004, available at www.aclu.org/torturefoia/released/FBI_ 4140.pdf.

70. R. Jeffrey Smith, "Justice Redacted Memo on Detainees," *Washington Post,* Mar. 22, 2005, A3, available at www.washingtonpost.com/wp-dyn/articles/A55136-2005Mar21.html.

71. Shane, "Increase in the Number of Documents Classified."

72. Relyea, "Freedom of Information Act Amendments."

73. Ibid.

74. Mark Tapscott, "More on the Right Get FOIA Right," *Dallas Morning News,* July 2, 2005, 35A. Tapscott is the director of the Center for Media and Public Policy at the Heritage Foundation.

75. Ibid.

76. Amy Goldstein and Dan Eggen, "U.S. to Stop Issuing Detention Tallies," *Washington Post,* Nov. 9, 2001, A16; Karen Gullo, "Ashcroft Won't Name Detainees," *El Paso Times,* Nov. 27, 2001, 4A.

77. U.S. Immigration and Naturalization Service, "Release of Information Regarding Immigration and Naturalization Service Detainees in Non-federal Facilities," *Federal Register,* Apr. 22, 2002; Steve Fainaru, "U.S. Bans the Release of Detainees' Names," *Washington Post,* Apr. 19, 2002, A10, available at www.washingtonpost.com/wp-dyn/articles/A12012-2002 Apr18.html.

78. Complaint for Injunctive Relief, *Center for National Security Studies.*

79. U.S. Immigration and Naturalization Service, "Release of Information Regarding Immigration and Naturalization Service Detainees," 19508.

80. Complaint for Injunctive Relief, *Center for National Security Studies.*

81. *Center for National Security Studies, et al., v. Department of Justice,* 2003 U.S. App. LEXIS 11910 (2003).

82. Human Rights Watch, "Witness to Abuse: Human Rights Abuses under the Material Witness Law since September 11," June 2005, 2.

83. Anjana Malhotra, "Material Witness Law Is Being Abused," Human Rights Watch, May 27, 2004, originally published in the *Oregonian,* May 27, 2004, available at hrw.org/english/ docs/20-04/05/27/usdom8631_txt.htm.

84. Linda Greenhouse, "News Groups Seek to Open Secret Case," *New York Times,* Jan. 5, 2004, available at www.nytimes.com/2004/01/05/national; Warren Richey, "Supreme Court Asks for More Input on Secret Sept. 11 Case," *Christian Science Monitor,* Nov. 7, 2003, available at www.csmonitor.com/2003/1107.

85. Brief for petitioner, *M.K.B. v. Warden,* On Petition for Writ of Certiorari to the United States Court of Appeals for the [redacted] Circuit, Supreme Court of the United States, No. 03-6747, July 2003, available at www.findlaw.com.

86. Gina Holland, "White House Seeks Secrecy on Detainee," Associated Press, Jan. 5. 2004, available at news.findlaw.com.

87. Warren Richey, "Supreme Court Decision May Limit Access to Terror Cases," *Christian Science Monitor,* Feb. 24, 2004, available at www.csmonitor.com/2004/0224.

88. Richey, "Secret 9/11 Case before High Court."

89. Brief for petitioner, *M.K.B. v. Warden.*

90. Greenhouse, "News Groups Seek."

91. *M.K.B. v. Warden,* 124 S.Ct. 1405 (2004).

92. *Washington Post,* "Transcript: Ashcroft on Terror Probe Suspects," On Politics, Nov. 27, 2001, available at www.washingtonpost.com/ac2/wp-dyn.

93. U.S. Senate, Committee on the Judiciary, "Department of Justice Oversight: Preserving Our Freedoms While Defending against Terrorism," witness: Attorney General John Ashcroft, Dec. 6, 2001, 107th Cong., 1st sess., Federal News Service, available at web.lexis-nexis.com/congcomp/document.

94. Clymer, "Government Openness."

95. "Transcript: Ashcroft on Terror Probe Suspects."

96. Edward Walsh, "High Court Stays Out of Secrecy Fray," *Washington Post,* May 28, 2003, A4, available at www.washingtonpost.com/ac2/wp-dyn/A46103-2003May27.

97. U.S. Immigration and Naturalization Service, Office of Chief Immigration Judge, Michael Creppy Memorandum to All Immigration Judges and Court Administrators, "Subject: Cases requiring special procedures," Sept. 21, 2001, available at news.findlaw.com/hdocs/docs/aclu/creppy092101memo.pdf.

98. Ibid.

99. Ibid.

100. *North Jersey Media Group v. Ashcroft,* 308 F. 3d 198. 2002 U.S. App. LEXIS 21032 (2002), quoting the Dale Watson Declaration.

101. Dan Eggen and Julie Tate, "U.S. Campaign Produces Few Convictions on Terrorism Charges," *Washington Post,* June 12, 2005, A1, available at www.washingtonpost.com/wp-dyn/content/article/2005/06/11/AR2005061100381.html; Jerry Markon, "The Terrorism Case That Wasn't—and Still Is," *Washington Post,* June 12, 2005, A19, available at www.washingtonpost.com/wp-dyn/content/article/2005/06/11/AR2005061100379.html.

102. Steve Fainaru, "Judge Rejects Rule Closing Immigration Hearing," *Washington Post,* Apr. 4, 2002, A1; Clymer, "Government Openness."

103. *FMC v. South Carolina State Ports Authority,* 535 U.S. 743, 122 S.Ct. 1864 (2002).

104. This was the position of the Third Circuit in *North Jersey Media Group v. Ashcroft,* to be discussed.

105. U.S. Department of Justice, Statement of Associate Attorney General Jay Stephens "Regarding the Sixth Circuit Decision in the Haddad Case," Apr. 19, 2002, available at www.usdoj.gov/opa/pr/2002/Apr.

106. 9/11 Commission Hearing, "Chapter 6: The Illinois Charities Case Study," in *Terrorist Financing Staff Monograph,* National Commission on Terrorist Attacks upon the United States, 2004, available at www.9-11commission.gov/staff_statements/911_TerrFin_Ch6.pdf.

107. *Detroit Free Press, et al., v. John Ashcroft, et al.,* 195 F. Supp. 2d 937; 2002 U.S. Dist. LEXIS 5839 (2002); Fainaru, "Judge Rejects Rule."

108. *Detroit Free Press, et al., v. John Ashcroft, et al.,* 303 F. 3d 681; 2002 U.S. App. LEXIS 17646 (2002).

109. *Detroit Free Press, et al., v. John Ashcroft, et al.,* 2003 U.S. App. LEXIS 1278 (2003).

110. *North Jersey Media Group v. Ashcroft,* 205 F. Supp. 2d 288; 2002 U.S. Dist. LEXIS 10136 (2002).

111. *Ashcroft v. North Jersey Media Group,* 536 U.S. 954; 122 S. Ct. 2655 (2002).

112. *North Jersey Media Group v. Ashcroft,* 308 F. 3d 198. 2002 U.S. App. LEXIS 21032 (2002).

113. U.S. Department of Justice, statement of Barbara Comstock, Director of Public Affairs, "Regarding the Third Circuit Argument in North Jersey Media Group v. Ashcroft Today," Sept. 17, 2002, available at www.usdoj.gov/opa/pr/2002/September.

114. *North Jersey Media Group v. Ashcroft,* 538 U.S. 1056; 123 S.Ct. 2215 (2003); Walsh, "High Court Stays Out of Secrecy Fray," A4.

115. Eric Lichtblau, "Whistle-Blowing Said to Be Factor in F.B.I. Firing," *New York Times,* July 29, 2001, available at www.nytimes.com/2004/07/29/politics/29fbi.final.

116. Defendants' memorandum in support of motion to dismiss, *Project on Government Oversight v. Ashcroft and U.S. Department of Justice,* U.S. District Court for the District of Columbia, C.A. No. 1:04CV01032, Sept. 3, 2004, available at www.pogo.org/m/gp/a/Govt%20Motion%20Dismiss%2009%2003%2004.pdf.

117. Rebecca Carr, "Court of Appeals Abruptly Closes Hearing to the Public," Cox News Service, Apr. 20, 2005, available at Lexis-Nexis Academic Universe.

118. Rebecca Carr, "Court Closes Hearing and Meets in Secret," Cox News Service, Apr. 21, 2005, available at Lexis-Nexis Academic Universe.

119. *Edmonds v. Department of Justice,* U.S. Court of Appeals for the D.C. Circuit, 2005 U.S. App LEXIS 8116 (2005).

120. Carr, "Court Closes Hearing."

121. Complaint for declaratory and injunctive relief, *Project on Government Oversight v. Ashcroft and U.S. Department of Justice,* U.S. District Court for the District of Columbia, June 23, 2004, available at www.pogo.org/m/gp/a/Complaint.pdf.

122. R. Jeffrey Smith, "Access to Memos Is Affirmed," *Washington Post,* Feb. 23, 2005, A17.

123. Complaint for declaratory and injunctive relief, *Project on Government Oversight v. Ashcroft.*

124. Ibid.

125. Project on Government Oversight Press Release, "Justice Department Caves In: Allows Publication of Retroactively Classified Information," Feb. 22, 2005, available at www.pogo.org/p/government/ga-050202-Classification.html.

126. Defendants; Memorandum, *Project on Government Oversight v. Ashcroft.*

127. Smith, "Access to Memos Is Affirmed"; U.S. Department of Justice, letter from Vesper Mei to Michael Kirkpatrick, Public Citizen Litigation Group, Re: POGO v. Ashcroft, et al. 04-CV-1032 (JDB). Feb. 18, 2005, available at www.pogo.org/m/gp/gp-02182005-JusticeDept Letter.pdf.

128. U.S. Department of Justice, Office of the Inspector General, "A Review of the FBI's Actions in Connection with Allegations Raised by Contract Linguist Sibel Edmonds," Jan. 2005, available at http://www.usdoj.gov/oig/special/0501/index.htm.

129. Milbank, "DiIulio Saga Highlights Primacy."

130. U.S. Department of Justice, "Instructions on Separation of Certain Foreign Counterintelligence and Criminal Investigations," memorandum from Jamie S. Gorelick, Deputy Attorney General, to Mary Jo White, Louis Freeh, Richard Scruggs, and Jo Ann Harris. It was declassified by the counsel for Intelligence Policy at the U.S. Department of Justice on Apr. 10, 2004; available at www.usdoj.gov.

131. See, for example, remarks by Senator Leahy, U.S. Senate, Committee on the Judiciary, "Ashcroft Comments on Anti-terror Policy," June 8, 2004, FDCH E-Media, available at www.washingtonpost.com/wp-dyn/articles/A25211-2004Jun8.html.

132. Michael Duffy and John Dickerson, "Cooling on Ashcroft," *Time,* June 7, 2004, 20. Ashcroft's comment seemed particularly ill-advised when it became known that his deputy, Larry Thompson, had affirmed the same procedures in August 2001.

133. Jeff Chorney, "Defense Attorneys: Shut Off the Leaks in Probes," *Recorder,* Dec. 6, 2004, available at www.law.com.

134. Jerry Markon, "Moussaoui Planning to Admit 9/11 Role," *Washington Post,* Apr. 19, 2005, A1, available at www.washingtonpost.com/wp-dyn/articles/A64195-2005Apr18.html; Seymour Hersh, *Chain of Command* (New York: HarperCollins, 2004), 111–112, 116–117; Eric Lichtblau, "Sept. 11 Suspect May Be Set to Admit Guilt," *New York Times,* Apr. 20, 2005, available at www.nytimes.com/2005/04/20/national/20moussaoui.html.

135. Malhotra, "Material Witness Law Is Being Abused."

136. Charles Hanley, "Scientists Say Dirty Bomb Would Be a Dud," Associated Press, June 9, 2004, available at customwire.ap.org/dynamic/stories/D/DIRTY_BOMB_DUD; Christopher Newton, "U.S.: Terror Suspect Is 'Small Fish,'" Associated Press, Aug. 14, 2002, available at news/findlaw.com.

137. Anne Gearan, "New Info on Padilla Not Part of Court Case," Associated Press, June 2, 2004, available at news.findlaw.com.

138. Michael Powell, "Padilla Case Puts Lawyers in Limbo, Too," *Washington Post,* June 5, 2004, A3, available at www.washingtonpost.com/ac2/wp-dyn/A16691-2004Jun4; Editorial, "No Defense Possible," *Washington Post,* June 4, 2004, A22, available at www.washingtonpost.com/ac2/wp-dyn/A14252-2004June3.

139. Eric Lichtblau, "U.S. Spells Out Dangers Posed by Plot Suspect," *New York Times,* June 2, 2004, available at www.nytimes.com/2004/06/02/politics.

140. Jonathan Turley, "You Have Rights—If Bush Says You Do," *Los Angeles Times,* June 3, 2004, available at www.latimes.com/news/opinion/commentary.

141. Richard Stevenson and Eric Lichtblau, "As Ashcroft Warns of Attack, Some Question Threat and Its Timing," *New York Times,* May 27, 2004, available at www.nytimes.com/2004/05/27/politics.

142. Brad Knickerbocker, "Security Concerns Drive Rise in Secrecy," *Christian Science Monitor,* Dec. 3, 2001, available at www.csmonitor.com/2001/1203.

143. "National Defense Authorization Act for Fiscal Year 2004," Senate, 108th Cong., 1st sess., July 16, 2003, 149 *Congressional Record* S9448, 9453.

144. Shane, "Increase in the Number of Documents Classified."

145. Lichtblau, "Rising Fears That What We Do Know."

146. Bernstein, "Questions, Bitterness and Exile."

147. 297 U.S. 233, 250 (1936).

148. Brief for petitioner, *M.K.B. v. Warden.*

Chapter 9: General Ashcroft at Justice

1. U.S. Department of Justice, "Department of Justice Success: The Past 4 Years," Nov. 9, 2004, available at www.usdoj.gov/ag/speeches/2004/ag_successes_110904.htm.

2. Curt Anderson, "Ashcroft: Nuke Threat the Largest Danger," Associated Press, Jan. 27, 2005, available at news.findlaw.com/ap_stories/a/w/1152/1-27/2005/20050.

3. Orrin Hatch, U.S. senator, Utah, interview with author, Washington, D.C., May 10, 2005.

4. Paul Rosenzweig, "The Ashcroft Legacy: Liberty and Security," Heritage Foundation, Web Memo No. 607, Nov. 10, 2004, available at www.heritage.org/Research/Homeland Defense/wm607.cfm.

5. Dan Eggen and Jim VandeHei, "Ashcroft Taking Fire from GOP Stalwarts," *Washington Post,* Aug. 29, 2003, A1.

6. Hatch, interview with author.

7. U.S. Attorney General Remarks, "U.S. Attorneys Conference, New York City," Oct. 1, 2002, available at www.usdoj.gov/ag/speeches/2002/1001012agremarkstousattorneys conference.htm.

8. U.S. Senate, Committee on the Judiciary, "Department of Justice Oversight: Preserving Our Freedoms While Defending against Terrorism," witness: Attorney General John Ashcroft, Dec. 6, 2001, 107th Cong., 1st sess., Federal News Service, available at web.lexis-nexis.com/congcomp/document.

9. U.S. Attorney General Remarks, "The Proven Tactics in the Fight against Crime," Sept. 15, 2003, available at www.usdoj.gov/ag/speeches/2003.

10. U.S. Attorney General Remarks, "International Association of Chiefs of Police Conference," Oct. 7, 2002, available at www.usdoj.gov/ag/speeches/2002/100702chiefsof policemn1.htm.

11. U.S. Senate, "Preserving Our Freedoms."

12. White House, "President Thanks Attorney General Ashcroft," Office of the Press Secretary, Nov. 9, 2004, available at www.whitehouse.gov/news/releases/2004/11/20041109-18.html.

13. U.S. Attorney General Remarks, "Federalist Society 20th Anniversary Gala," Nov. 14, 2002, available at www.usdoj.gov/ag/speeches/2002.

14. U.S. Senate, "Preserving Our Freedoms."

15. Ibid.

16. Commentary, "Bully Pulpit," *Christian Century,* Mar. 8, 2003, 5. The commentary is critical of this view.

17. U.S. Attorney General Remarks, "U.S. Attorneys Conference, New York City."

18. See, for example, Louis Fisher, *Military Tribunals and Presidential Power* (Lawrence: University Press of Kansas, 2005).

19. Dan Eggen, "Gonzales Earns Praise, Despite Lack of Policy Change," *Washington Post,* May 16, 2005, A4.

20. Ibid. Also see Vanessa Blum, "Curtains Raised for Change at DOJ?" *Legal Times,* Mar. 8, 2005, available at www.law.com/jsp.

Bibliography

Printed Sources

About.com. Political Humor. Accessed Mar. 17, 2004. Available at politicalhumor.about.com.
——— Political Humor. Accessed Mar. 17, 2004. Available at politicalhumor.miningco.com.
Abrams, Norman. "The Material Support of Terrorism Offenses: Perspectives Derived from the (Early) Model Penal Code." *Journal of National Security Law and Policy* 1 (2005): 5–29.
Aguillard, David. "The State Does Battle Anonymously." *St. Louis Post-Dispatch,* Dec. 12, 1991, 1C.
Akers, Dee Ashley. "The Advisory Opinion Function of the Attorney General." *Kentucky Law Journal* 38 (1950): 561.
Allen, Mike. "House Votes to Limit Patriot Act." *Washington Post,* June 19, 2005, A3. Available at www.washingtonpost.com/ac2/w-dyn.
——— "Staying or Going? Some Possibilities If Bush Wins." *Washington Post,* Oct. 22, 2004, A23. Available at www.washingtonpost.com/ac2/wp-dyn/A52687-2004Oct21.
Allen, Mike, and Dana Milbank. "Leaks Probe Is Gathering Momentum." *Washington Post,* Dec. 26, 2004, A1. Available at www.washingtonpost.com/ac2/w-dyn.
Allen, Mike, Martha Sawyer, and Graydon Royce. "Defining the Common Good." *Minneapolis Star-Tribune,* Feb. 9, 2002, 7B. Available through Lexis-Nexis Academic Universe.
American Civil Liberties Union. "Keep America Safe and Free" Web site. N.d. Available at www.aclu.org/SafeandFree/SafeandFreeMain.cfm.
American Civil Liberties Union Press Release. "ACLU Says New Ashcroft Anti-terror Proposal Undermines Checks and Balances." Feb. 7, 2003. Available at www.aclu.org/SafeandFree.
——— "FBI E-Mail Refers to Presidential Order Authorizing Inhumane Interrogation Techniques." Dec. 20, 2004. Available at www.aclu.org/SafeandFree/SafeandFree.cfm?ID=17216&c=206.
American Conservative Union Press Release. "ACU Analysis of the Domestic Security Enhancement Act of 2003, also known as Patriot Act II." Public memorandum to conservative leaders and activists. Feb. 26, 2003. Available at www.conservative.org/pressroom/030226.
American Library Association News Release. "Freedom to Read Foundation Seeks Justice Department Response." Nov. 15, 2002. Available at www.ftrf.org/foiapressrelease.
American Library Association Resolution. "The USA Patriot Act in the Library." Adopted by the ALA Council Jan. 23, 2002. Available at www.ala.org/alaorg/oif/usapatriotlibrary.html.
Amon, Elizabeth. "Courts to Decide Access to Terror Suspects." *Fulton County Daily Report,* June 12, 2002. Available through Lexis-Nexis Academic Universe.
Anderson, Curt. "Ashcroft Denounces Patriot Act 'Hysteria.'" Associated Press. Sept. 15, 2003. Available at news.findlaw.com.
——— "Ashcroft Mounting Defense of Patriot Act." Associated Press. Aug. 18, 2003. Available at news.findlaw.com.

———— "Ashcroft: Nuke Threat the Largest Danger." Associated Press. Jan. 27, 2005. Available at news.findlaw.com/ap_stories/a/w/1152/1-27/2005/20050.

———— "Improvement Seen at 9/11 Detainee Prison." Associated Press. Mar. 19, 2004. Available at news.findlaw.com.

———— "Study: Terror-Related Cases Often Fizzle." Associated Press. Dec. 8, 2003. Available at news.findlaw.com.

Andrews, Edmund, and Elizabeth Becker. "Bush Got $500,000 from Companies That Got Contracts, Study Finds." *New York Times,* Oct. 31, 2003. Available at www.nytimes.com/2003/10/31/politics.

Antiterrorism and Effective Death Penalty Act of 1996. P.L.104-132, 110 Stat.1214.

Arens, Elizabeth. "Republican Futures." *Policy Review,* Heritage Foundation, Apr. 2001, 13.

Ashcroft, John. "A Guide to Charitable Choice: The Rules of Section 104 of the 1996 Federal Welfare Law Governing State Cooperation with Faith-Based Social Service Providers." The Center for Public Justice, Washington, D.C., and the Christian Legal Society's Center for Law and Religious Freedom. Jan. 1997. Available at the Christian Legal Society's Web site, www.clsnet.org.

———— *Lessons from a Father to His Son.* Nashville, Tenn.: Thomas Nelson, 1998.

———— "Prepared Remarks of Attorney General John Ashcroft: Report from the Field: The USA Patriot Act at Work." July 13, 2004. Available at www.usdoj.gov/ag/speeches/2004/071304_patriot_report_remarks.htm.

———— Prepared remarks of Attorney General John Ashcroft to the Federalist Society. Nov. 12, 2004. Available at www.usdoj.gov/ag/speeches/2004/111204federalist.htm.

———— "Statement on the Articles of Impeachment against President Clinton." *Congressional Record,* Feb. 12, 1999. Available at www.australianpolitics.com/usa/clinton/trial/statements/ashcroft.shtml.

———— "True Faith and Allegiance." Heritage Foundation Lecture no. 865. Feb. 11, 2005. Available at www.heritage.org/Research/LegalIssues/hl865.cfm.

Ashenfelter, David. "Terrorists or Harmless Immigrants? Detroit Trial Could Strike Blow against Terrorism or Be a Huge Embarrassment." *Detroit Free Press,* Mar. 11, 2003. Available at www.freep.com/news/locway/terr11_20030311.htm.

Associated Press. "Ashcroft Is Rebuked for Terror Remarks." *New York Times,* Dec. 17, 2003. Available at www.nytimes.com/2003/12/17.

———— "Daschle, Lott Oppose Polygraphs." Aug. 5, 2002. Available at news.findlaw.com/ap_stories.20020805050022_05.htm.

———— "Judge Weighs Moussaoui's 9/11 Guilty Plea." Apr. 20, 2005. Available at www.nytimes.com/aponline/national/AP-Moussaoui.html.

———— "Moussaoui Banned from Closed Hearing." Apr. 10, 2003. Available at news.findlaw.com/ap/o/1110/4-10-2003/20030410.

———— "New U.S. Memo Backs Off Torture Arguments." *New York Times,* Dec. 31, 2004. Available at www.nytimes.com/2004/12/31/politics/html.

———— "No Conviction for Student in Terror Case." *New York Times,* June 11, 2004. Available at www.nytimes.com/2004/06/11/national/11boise.html.

———— "Suspect's Lawyers Say Statement Was Distorted." *New York Times,* June 5, 2005. Available at www.nytimes.com/2003/06/05/politics/05USP.html.

Authorization for Use of Military Force. Senate Joint Resolution 23/House Joint Resolution 64. Sept. 14, 2001. *Congressional Record,* p. S9951. Public Law 107-40, 115 Stat. 224.

Axis of Logic. Accessed Mar. 17, 2004. Available at www.axisoflogic.com.

Ayers, B. Drummond Jr. "Political Briefing; Conservative's Shift Angers Backers." *New York Times,* Dec. 7, 1998, A22.

Baker, Nancy V. "The Attorney General as Legal Policy-Maker." In Cornell Clayton, ed., *Government Lawyers: The Federal Legal Bureaucracy and Presidential Politics.* Lawrence: University Press of Kansas, 1995.

——— *Conflicting Loyalties: Law and Politics in the Attorney General's Office, 1789–1990.* Lawrence: University Press of Kansas, 1992.

——— "Guarding the Parchment Barrier: The Attorney General and Presidential Power in Wartime." In Lori Cox-Han and Michael Genovese, eds., *The Presidency and the Challenge of Democracy.* New York: Palgrave/Macmillan, 2006.

——— "The Impact of Antiterrorism Policies on Separation of Powers: Assessing John Ashcroft's Role." *Presidential Studies Quarterly* 32 (Dec. 2002): 765–778.

——— "John Ashcroft." In Roger Newman, ed., *Yale Biographical Dictionary of American Law.* New Haven, Conn.: Yale University Press, 2006.

——— "National Security versus Civil Liberties." *Presidential Studies Quarterly* 33 (Sept. 2003): 547–567.

Baker, Nancy V., and Peter Gregware. "Citizens, Professionals or the Executive: Who Owns the Courts?" In G. Larry Mays and Peter R. Gregware, eds., *Courts and Justice.* 3rd ed. Prospect Heights, Ill.: Waveland Press, 2004.

Balkin, Jack M. "Ashcroft Readies New Assault on Civil Rights." *Los Angeles Times,* Feb. 13, 2003, B23.

——— "Bush v. Gore and the Boundary between Law and Politics." *Yale Law Journal* 110 (2001): 1407.

Barstow, David. "Contesting the Vote: The Florida Legislature; Florida Lawmakers Moving to Bypass Courts for Bush." *New York Times,* Nov. 29, 2000, A1.

Beard, Jack. "Military Action against Terrorists under International Law." *Harvard Journal of Law and Public Policy* 25 (Spring 2002): 559.

Beaucar, Kelley. "Critics: Patriot Act Warnings Come to Fruition." Fox News. Nov. 22, 2003. Available at www.foxnews.com.

Bedard, Paul, Chitra Ragavan, and Kevin Whitelaw. "Homesick." *U.S. News & World Report,* May 21, 2001, 8.

Bedard, Paul, et al. "Judge Ashcroft." *U.S. News & World Report,* Jan 22, 2001, 6.

Bedard, Paul, Kevin Whitelaw, and Mark Mazzetti. "Get the Ritalin." *U.S. News & World Report,* July 9. 2001, 10.

Bellah, Robert. "Religion and Legitimation in the American Republic." *Society* 35 (Jan./Feb. 1998): 193.

Bernstein, Nina. "Questions, Bitterness and Exile for Queens Girl in Terror Case." *New York Times,* June 17, 2005. Available at www.nytimes.com/2005/06/17/nyregion/17suicide.html?th&emc=th.

Berry, John. "High Profile, Strong Image: If We Didn't Have Attorney General Ashcroft, We Would Have to Invent Him." *Library Journal* 128, no. 20 (Dec. 2003): 8.

Bettelheim, Adriel. "Congress Changing Tone of Homeland Security Debate." *Congressional Quarterly,* Aug. 31, 2002, 2222.

Biema, David Van. "Son of a Preacher, Quiet Pentecostal." *Time,* Jan. 22, 2001, 24+.

Bingaman, Jeff. Speech on the floor of the U.S. Senate. "Administrative Detentions and Right to Due Process." July 14, 2003. Washington, D.C. Available at www.cq.com/cqonline/docs/html/crtext/108/crtext108-000000763112.html.

Blackman, Ann, et al. "The Fight for Justice." *Time,* Jan. 22, 2001, 20.

Block, Robert, and Gary Fields. "Is Military Creeping into Domestic Law Enforcement?" *Wall Street Journal,* Mar. 9, 2004. Available at www.commondreams.org/headlines04/0309-02 .htm.

Bloomberg News. "Groups Urge Partial Lapse of Patriot Act." *Washington Post,* Mar. 23, 2005, A6. Available at www.washingtonpost.com/ac2/wp-dyn/A58068-2005Mar22.

Blum, Vanessa. "Ashcroft: Looking Back, Looking Forward." *Legal Times,* Jan. 31, 2005. Available at www.law.com.

——— "Curtains Raised for Change at DOJ?" *Legal Times,* Mar. 8, 2005. Available at www .law.com/jsp.

——— "Point Man: Paul Clement Leads the Charge in Defending the Administration's Tactics in the War on Terror." *Legal Times,* Jan. 16, 2004. Available at www.law.com/jsp/article .jsp?id=1073944820670.

——— "When the Pentagon Controls the Courtroom." *Recorder,* Nov. 27, 2001.

——— "Why Bush Won't Let Go." *Legal Times,* Feb. 4, 2002, 1.

Bongo News. Accessed Mar. 17, 2004. Available at www.bongonews.com.

Boot Newt Sing Along Page. Accessed Mar. 17, 2004. Available at bootnewt.tripod.com/ash .songs.

Booth, William. "Judge Blocks Sanctions over Assisted Suicide." *Washington Post,* Nov. 9, 2001, A2.

Borger, Julian. "Staff Cry Poetic Injustice as Singing Ashcroft Introduces Patriot Games." *Guardian,* Mar. 4, 2002. Available at www.guardian.co.uk.

Borrelli, Mary Anne. *The President's Cabinet: Gender, Power and Representation.* Boulder, Colo.: Lynne Rienner, 2002.

Bowers, Faye, and Gail Russell Chaddock. "Major Battle Brewing over Leaks in Senate." *Christian Science Monitor,* Aug. 29, 2002. Available at www.csmonitor.com/2002/0829/ p01s02-uspo.htm.

Brandenburg, Bert. "Open Government in the Ashcroft Era: What Went Wrong and How to Make It Right." Watching Justice: An Eye on the Department of Justice. 2005. Available at www.watchingjustice.org/reports/article.php?docID=663.

Branigin, William. "Justices Decline to Hear Moussaoui Appeal." *Washington Post,* Mar. 21, 2005. Available at www.washingtonpost.com/ac2/wp-dyn/A53515-2005Mar21.

Brasch, Walter. *America's Unpatriotic Acts.* New York: Peter Lang. 2005.

Bridis, Ted. "Secret U.S. Court Approved 934 Wiretaps, Searches Last Year." Associated Press. Apr. 30, 2002. Available at news.findlaw.com.

Brief for Petitioner. *M.K.B. v. Warden.* On Petition for Writ of Certiorari to the United States Court of Appeals for the [redacted] Circuit. Supreme Court of the United States. No. 03-6747. July 2003. Available at www.findlaw.com.

Brief for Petitioner. *Rumsfeld v. Padilla.* U.S. Supreme Court. No. 03-1027. Mar. 2004. Available at www.usdoj.gov/osg/briefs/2003/3mer/2mer/toc3index.html.

Brief for Respondents-Appellants. *Hamdi v. Rumsfeld.* U.S. Court of Appeals for the Fourth Circuit. No. 02-6895. 2002.

Brief for the Respondents. *Hamdi v. Rumsfeld.* No. 03-6996. 2003. Available at www.gov/osg/ briefs/2003/3mer/2mer/toc3index.html.

Brief for the Respondents. *Hamdi v. Rumsfeld.* U.S. Supreme Court. No. 03-6996. Mar. 2004. Available at www.usdoj.gov/osg/briefs/2003/3mer/2mer/toc3index.html.

Brief for the Respondents in Opposition. *Hamdi v. Rumsfeld.* On Petition for Writ of Certiorari to the United States Court of Appeals for the Fourth Circuit. Supreme Court of the United States. Dec. 2003. Available at www.findlaw.com.

Brief for the United States. *U.S. v. Moussaoui.* U.S. Court of Appeals for the Fourth Circuit. No. 03-4792. Oct. 24, 2003. Available at news.findlaw.com/hdocs/docs/Moussaoui/ usmouss102403gbrf.pdf.

Brief for the United States in Opposition. *Moussaoui v. U.S.* Supreme Court of the United States, on Petition for a Writ of Certiorari to the U.S. Court of Appeals for the Fourth Circuit. No. 04-8385. Feb. 10, 2005. Available at news.findlaw.com/hdocs/docs/Moussaoui/ usmouss21005cert.pdf.

Brown, Cynthia, ed. *Lost Liberties: Ashcroft and the Assault on Personal Freedom.* New York: New Press, 2003.

Brune, Tom. "Ashcroft: U.S. Is Beating Terror." *Newsday,* Mar. 5, 2003, A5. Available through Lexis-Nexis Academic Universe.

Brunnstrom, David. "U.S. Says Raid Killing Afghan Children Was Legitimate." Reuters. Mar. 10, 2004. Available at news.findlaw.com.

Bumiller, Elisabeth. "Evangelicals Sway White House on Human Rights Issues Abroad." *New York Times,* Oct. 26, 2003. Available at www.nytimes.com/2003/10/26/politics.

Bumiller, Elisabeth, and Eric Lichtblau. "Debating a Leak: Attorney General Is Closely Linked to Inquiry Figures." *New York Times,* Oct. 2, 2003, 1A.

Bumiller, Elisabeth, and Richard Stevenson. "In Speech, President Casts Himself as a Steady Commander in Chief." *New York Times,* Jan. 21, 2004. Available at www.nytimes.com/ 2004/01/21/politics.

Bush, George W. Memorandum for the Attorney General. "Subject: Congressional Subpoena for Executive Branch Documents." Dec. 12, 2001. Available at www.whitehouse.gov/news/ releases/2001/12/20011213-1.html.

———— "Military Order: Detention, Treatment and Trial of Certain Non-citizens in the War against Terrorism." *Federal Register* 66 (Nov. 16, 2001): 57833. Available at www.gpoaccess.gov/fr/.

———— "Radio Address of the President to the Nation." Sept. 29, 2001. Office of the Press Secretary. Available at www.whitehouse.gov/news/releases/2001/09/20010929.html.

———— "Remarks by the President at Bush-Cheney 2004 Reception, the Shrine Auditorium, Los Angeles, California." Office of the Press Secretary. Mar. 3, 2004. Available at www .whitehouse.gov/news/releases/2004/03/print/20040303-16.html.

———— "State of the Union Address." Jan. 20, 2004. Available at www.whitehouse.gov/news/ releases/2004/01/20040120.

———— "State of the Union Address." Jan. 29, 2002. Available at www.whitehouse.gov/news/ releases/2002/01/20020129.

———— Statement by the President. "President Signs Authorization for Use of Military Force Bill." Sept. 18, 2001. Available at www.whitehouse.gov/news/releases/2001/09/20010918-10 .html.

———— "Transcript: President Bush Delivers Remarks on Homeland Security." *New York Times,* Sept. 10, 2003. Available at www.nytimes.com/2003/09/10/politics.

Bush House of Cards. Accessed Mar. 17, 2004. Available at www.bushhouseofcards.com.

Butler, Judith. "Guantanamo Limbo." *Nation,* Apr. 1, 2002, 20–30.

Byford, Grenville. "The Wrong War." *Foreign Affairs,* July/Aug. 2002, 34.

Cambanis, Thanassis. "Judge Eases U.S. Limits on Reid; Justice Dept. Hoped to Restrict His Contact." *Boston Globe,* Mar. 26, 2002, B1.

Campbell, Colin, and Bert Rockman, eds. *The George W. Bush Presidency: Appraisals and Prospects.* Washington, D.C.: CQ Press, 2004.

Carlson, Darren. "Far Enough? Public Wary of Restricted Liberties." Gallup poll, Jan. 20, 2004. Available at www.gallup.com.

Carney, J. Guadalupe. "How Bush Chose Ashcroft." *Time,* Jan. 22, 2001, 27.

Carr, Rebecca. "Court of Appeals Abruptly Closes Hearing to the Public." Cox News Service. Apr. 20, 2005. Available at Lexis-Nexis Academic Universe.

——— "Court Closes Hearing and Meets in Secret." Cox News Service. Apr. 21, 2005. Available at Lexis-Nexis Academic Universe.

Caruso, David B. "Ashcroft Begins Patriot Act Tour." Associated Press. Aug. 20, 2003. Available at news.findlaw.com/ap_stories.

——— "New Monitoring Law Concerns Librarians." Associated Press. Jan. 27, 2003. Available at www.news.findlaw.com/ap_stories/ht/1700/1-27-2003/20030127.

CBSNews.com. "Ashcroft Interprets 2nd Amendment." May 23, 2001. Available at www .cbsnews.com/stories/1002/05/23/politics.

——— "Poll: Undecided on Ashcroft." Jan. 18, 2001. Available at www.cbsnews.com/stories/2001/01/18/politics.

Cha, Ariana Eunjung. "Risks Prompt U.S. to Limit Access to Data." *Washington Post,* Feb. 24, 2002, A1. Available at www.washingtonpost.com/ac2/wp-dyn/A58430-2002Feb.

Chaddock, Gail Russell. "Security Act to Pervade Daily Lives." *Christian Science Monitor,* Nov. 21, 2002. Available at www.csmonitor.com/2002/1121/p01s03-usju.html.

Chappie, Damon. "9/11 Report Shows Hill Investigator Got Snubbed." *Roll Call,* July 28, 2003. Available through Lexis-Nexis Congressional Universe.

Charles, Deborah. "Feds Appeal Secret Court Ruling on Wiretaps." Reuters. Aug. 23, 2002. Available at news.findlaw.com.

Cheney, Richard. "Vice President's Remarks on War on Terror at American Enterprise Institute." Federal Document Clearing House. July 24, 2003.

Chorney, Jeff. "Defense Attorneys: Shut Off the Leaks in Probes." *Recorder,* Dec. 6, 2004. Available at www.law.com.

Church & State. "Ashcroft Bails Out of Presidential Race." Feb. 1999, 15.

Clymer, Adam. "Government Openness at Issue as Bush Holds On to Records." *New York Times,* Jan. 3, 2003. Available at www.nytimes.com/2003/01/03/politics/03SECR.html.

CNN. "Bush Speaks at Justice Department." Paula Zahn, CNN anchor. Feb. 14, 2003. Transcript no. 021404CN.V54.

CNN.com. "Buffalo Terror Suspect Admits Al Qaeda Training." May 20, 2003. Available at www.cnn.com/2003/LAW/05/20/buffalo.terror/.

Coben, Stanley. *A. Mitchell Palmer: Politician.* New York: Columbia University Press, 1963.

Cole, David. "Constitutional Implications of Statutes Penalizing Material Support to Terrorist Organizations." Testimony before the United States Senate Committee on the Judiciary. May 5, 2004. Available at www.bordc.org/resources/cole-materialsupport.php.

——— "The Course of Least Resistance: Repeating History in the War on Terrorism." In Cynthia Brown, ed., *Lost Liberties: Ashcroft and the Assault on Personal Freedom,* 13–32. New York: New Press, 2003.

——— "The Lynne Stewart Trial." *Nation,* Mar. 7, 2005, 6.

——— "We've Aimed, Detained and Missed Before." *Washington Post National Weekly Edition,* June 16–22, 2003, 21.

Coll, Steve. "Legal Disputes over Hunt Paralyzed Clinton's Aides." *Washington Post,* Feb. 22, 2004, A17. Available at www.washingtonpost.com/ac2/wpdyn.

Commentary. "Ashcroft's Whistle-Stops." *Christian Science Monitor,* Aug. 21, 2003. Available at www.csmonitor.com/2003/0821/p08s01-comv.html.

——— "Bully Pulpit." *Christian Century,* Mar. 8, 2003, 5.

Complaint. *Convertino v. Justice Department. Ashcroft, et al.* U.S. District Court for the District of Columbia. Feb. 13, 2004. Available at www.findlaw.com.

Complaint—Class Action. *Green, et al., v. Transportation Security Administration, et al.* U.S. District Court for the Western District of Washington at Seattle. Apr. 2004. Available at www.findlaw.com.

Complaint for Declaratory and Injunctive Relief. *Project on Government Oversight v. Ashcroft and U.S. Department of Justice.* U.S. District Court for the District of Columbia. June 23, 2004. Available at www.pogo.org/m/gp/a/Complaint.pdf.

Complaint for Injunctive Relief. *Center for National Security Studies, et al., v. Department of Justice.* U.S. District Court for the District of Columbia. Dec. 5, 2001.

Congress and the Nation, 1997–2001. "Judiciary Activism, 1997–1998 Legislative Chronology." Vol. 10. Washington: CQ Press, 2002. Retrieved Oct. 17, 2003, from CQ Electronic Library. CQ Public Affairs Collection: catn97-97-6354-325744.

Congressional Quarterly. "Ashcroft Backed Genetic Privacy Bill, Opposed New Gun Show Restrictions, Voted to Curb Abortion and Cloning." Jan. 6, 2001, 29.

Congressional Record. "Departments of Commerce, Justice, and State, the Judiciary and Related Agencies Appropriations Act, 2004." House of Representatives. 108th Cong. July 22, 2003, H7291–H7293. Available at thomas.loc.gov.

——— "National Defense Authorization Act for Fiscal Year 2004." Senate. 108th Cong., 1st sess. July 16, 2003. 149 *Congressional Record* S9448.

Congressional Research Service. "Department of Justice. Table 11. Attorneys General 1789–1985." CRS-15, CRS-16, CRS-17. Library of Congress. 1985.

Congressional Weekly. "Leaking Classified Information." Sept. 6, 2001, 2081.

Corn, David. "The Fundamental John Ashcroft." *Mother Jones,* Mar. 2002. Available at www.motherjones.com/magazine/MA02.

——— *The Lies of George W. Bush: Mastering the Politics of Deception.* New York: Crown, 2003.

Council on Foreign Relations. "Terrorism: Q & A." 2002. Available at www.terrorismanswers.com.

Cox, Harvey. "Religion and the War against Evil." *Nation,* Dec. 24, 2001, 29–31.

CQ Press. "Assisted Suicide, 1997–1998 Legislative Chronology." In *Congress and the Nation, 1997–2001.* Vol. 10. Washington, D.C.: CQ Press, 2002. Available at CQ Electronic Library, CQ Public Affairs Collection: catn97-97-6354-325703.

CQ Press. "Judicial Activism, 1997–1998 Legislative Chronology." In *Congress and the Nation, 1997–2001.* Vol. 10. Washington: CQ Press, 2002. Available at CQ Electronic Library, CQ Public Affairs Collection: catn97-97-6354-325744.

Cummings, Homer. *Liberty under Law and Administration.* New York: Scribner's, 1934.

Davey, Monica. "Subpoenas on Antiwar Protest Are Dropped." *New York Times,* Feb. 11, 2004. Available at www.nytimes.com/2004/02/11/national/11PROT.html.

Day, Susie. "Counter-Intelligent: The Surveillance and Indictment of Lynne Stewart." *Monthly Review* 54, no. 6 (Nov. 2002): 24–33.

DeFazio, Peter. "Authorizing Use of Military Force in Response to Terrorist Attacks." House of Representatives. *Congressional Record,* Sept. 14, 2001, H5632. Available at thomas.loc.gov/home/r107query.html.

Defendants' Memorandum in Support of Motion to Dismiss. *Project on Government Oversight v. Ashcroft and U.S. Department of Justice.* U.S. District Court for the District of Columbia. C.A. No. 1:04CV01032. Sept. 3, 2004. Available at www.pogo.org/m/gp/a/Govt%20Motion%20Dismiss%2009%2003%2004.pdf.

Dellinger, Walter E., et al. Memorandum to Attorney General John Ashcroft, Judge Alberto Gonzales, and Acting Assistant Attorney General Daniel B. Levin. "Attached Principles to Guide the Office of Legal Counsel." Dec. 21, 2004. Available at leahy.senate.gov/press/200412/122204a.html.

Dempsey, James X., and David Cole. *Terrorism and the Constitution.* 2nd ed. Washington, D.C.: First Amendment Foundation, 2002.

Dlouhy, Jennifer, and Elizabeth Palmer. "New Assertions of Executive Power Anger, Frustrate Some on Hill." *Congressional Quarterly,* Nov. 24, 2001, 2784.

Doherty, Brian. "John Ashcroft's Power Grab." *Reason On-line,* June 2002. Available at reason.com/0206.

Dorf, Michael C. "The Nation's Second-Highest Court Upholds Military Commissions." FindLaw's Writ Legal Commentary. July 20, 2005. Available at writ.news.findlaw.com/dorf/20050720.html.

Dowd, Maureen. "A Blue Burka for Justice." *New York Times,* Jan. 30, 2002, A27.

Duffy, Brian. "Respecting the Client, with Clarity." *U.S. News & World Report,* Jan. 26, 2004, 32.

Duffy, Michael, and John Dickerson. "Cooling On Ashcroft." *Time,* June 7, 2004, 20.

Dunham, Richard. "How Much Heat Can Ashcroft Take?" *Business Week,* June 17, 2002, 41.

Dycus, Stephen, Arthur Berney, William Banks, and Peter Raven-Hansen. *National Security Law.* Boston: Little, Brown, 1990.

Eakin, Emily. "Presidential Papers as Smoking Guns." *New York Times,* Apr. 13, 2002. Available at www.nytimes.com/2002/04/13.

Easton, Nina. "A Life of Faith." *Washington Post,* Nov. 4, 2001, F1.

Eckhoff, Jeff, and Mark Siebert. "Group Fights Anti-war Inquiry." *Des Moines Register,* Feb. 7, 2004. Available at desmoinesregister.com/news/stories/c4788993/23473647.html.

The Economist. "Dead Man Winning." U.S. edition. Nov. 11, 2000.

———— "Steamroller Ashcroft." U.S. edition. May 3, 2003.

Editorial. "The Ashcroft Years." *St. Louis Post-Dispatch.* Dec. 20, 2004, 6B.

———— "Deportation behind Closed Doors." *New York Times,* May 30, 2003. Available at www.nytimes.com/2003/05/30/opinion/30FRI2.html.

———— "Detaining Justice." *Christian Science Monitor,* June 20, 2002.

———— "In the Aftermath of Sept. 11." *New York Times,* May 23, 2003. Available at www.nytimes.com/2003/05/23/opinion/23FRI1.html.

———— "Mr. Ashcroft's Tantrum." *Washington Post National Weekly Edition,* Sept. 29–Oct. 5, 2003, 25.

———— "Mr. Bush's Justice Department." *Washington Post,* Feb. 2, 2001, A22.

———— "No Defense Possible." *Washington Post,* June 4, 2004, A22. Available at www.washingtonpost.com/ac2/wp-dyn/A14252-2004June3.

———— "A Sept. 11 Plea?" *Washington Post,* Apr. 20, 2005, A24. Available at www.washingtonpost.com/wp-dyn/articles/A3013-2005Apr19.html.

———— "Stakes for Liberty." *Washington Post National Weekly Edition,* Jan. 6–12, 2003, 25.

———— "Terrorism and Liberty." *New York Times,* Dec. 23, 2003. Available at www.nytimes.com/2003/12/23/opinion/23TUE3.html.

———— "An Unpatriotic Act." *New York Times,* August 25, 2003. Available at www.nytimes.com/2003/08/25/opinion.

Edsall, Thomas B. "Christian Right Lifts Ashcroft." *Washington Post,* Apr. 14, 1998, A1.

Edwards, Melanie. "Robertson's 75th Birthday Gala Set for Mid-March in Texas." Regent University press release. Available at www.regent.edu/news/75_release2.html.

Eggen, Dan. "ACLU Was Forced to Revise Release on Patriot Act Suit." *Washington Post,* May 13, 2004, A27. Available at www.washingtonpost.com/ac2/wp-dynA22404-2004 May 12.

——— "Ashcroft Assailed on Policy Review." *Washington Post,* Aug. 21, 2002, A2. Available at www.washingtonpost.com/ac2/wp-dyn/A41859-2002Aug20.

——— "Ashcroft Defends Anti-terrorism Law." *Washington Post,* Aug. 20, 2003, A10.

——— "Ashcroft Planning Trip to Defend Patriot Act." *Washington Post,* Aug. 13, 2003, A2. Available at www.washingtonpost.com/ac2/wp-dyn/A51538-2003Aug12.

——— "Ashcroft Plans to Reorganize Justice, Curtail Programs." *Washington Post,* Nov. 9, 2001, A17.

——— "Gonzales Earns Praise, Despite Lack of Policy Change." *Washington Post,* May 16, 2005, A4.

——— "Liberals Need Not Apply?" *Washington Post National Weekly Edition,* Jan. 20–26, 2003, 14.

——— "Sculpted Bodies and a Strip Act at Justice Dept." *Washington Post,* June 25, 2005, A2. Available at www.washingtonpost.com/wp-dyn/content/article/2005/06/24/AR2005062401797_pf.html.

——— "Tapes Show Abuse of 9/11 Detainees." *Washington Post,* Dec.19, 2003, A1. Available at www.washingtonpost.com/ac2/wp-dyn/A13497-2003Dec18.

Eggen, Dan, and Ceci Connolly. "Ashcroft Ruling Blocks Ore. Assisted-Suicide Law." *Washington Post,* Nov. 7, 2001, A1. Available at www.washingtonpost.com/wp-dyn/articles/A49218-2001Nov6.html.

Eggen, Dan, and Helen Dewar. "Ashcroft Wins Confirmation." *Washington Post,* Feb. 2, 2001, A1. Available at www.washingtonpost.com/ac2/wp-dyn/A16007-2001Feb1.

Eggen, Dan, and Steve Fainaru. "For Prosecutors, 1996 Law Is Key Part of Anti-terror Strategy." *Washington Post,* Oct. 15, 2002, A2. Available at www.washingtonpost.com/ac2/wp-dyn/A25838-2002Oct14.

Eggen, Dan, and Robert O'Harrow Jr. "U.S. Steps Up Secret Surveillance." *Washington Post,* Mar. 24, 2003, A1. Available at www.washingtonpost.com/wp-dyn/articles/A16287-2003Mar23.html.

Eggen, Dan, and Susan Schmidt. "Secret Court Rebuffs Ashcroft." *Washington Post,* Aug. 23, 2002, A1. Available at www.washingtonpost.com/ac2/wp-dyn/A51220-2002Aug22.

Eggen, Dan, and Julie Tate. "U.S. Campaign Produces Few Convictions on Terrorism Charges." *Washington Post,* June 12, 2005, A1. Available at www.washingtonpost.com/wp-dyn/content/article/2005/06/11/AR2005061100381.html.

Eggen, Dan, and Jim VandeHei. "Ashcroft Taking Fire from GOP Stalwarts." *Washington Post,* Aug. 29, 2003, A1.

Electronic Surveillance. 50 USCS §1804. 2005.

Ellis, Richard. *Presidential Lightning Rods: The Politics of Blame Avoidance.* Lawrence: University Press of Kansas, 1994.

Elsner, Alan. "Bush Expands Government Secrecy, Arouses Critics." Reuters, Sept. 3, 2002. Available at news.findlaw.com/politics/s/200209/bushsecrecydc.htm.

Elwood, John P. "Prosecuting the War on Terrorism." *Criminal Justice Magazine* 17, no. 2 (Summer 2002). Available at www.abanet.org/crimjust/cjmag/17-2/prosecuting.html.

Epstein, Lee, Daniel E. Ho, Gary King, and Jeffrey A. Segal. "The Supreme Court During Crisis: How War Affects Only Non-War Cases." *New York University Law Review* 80, no. 1 (April 2005): 1–116.

Estabrook, Leigh. "Public Libraries and Civil Liberties: A Profession Divided." The Library Research Center. University of Illinois at Urbana-Champaign. Jan. 2003. Available at alexia .lis.uiuc.edu/gslis/research/civil_liberties.html.

Ewick, Patricia, and Susan S. Silbey. *The Common Place of Law: Stories from Everyday Life.* Chicago: University of Chicago Press, 1998.

Executive Order 12333. 3 C.F.R. 200, Section 2.5. 1981.

Executive Order 12667. Presidential Records Act, order of Jan. 18, 1989.

Executive Order 12947. 1995.

Executive Order 12958. Designation under Executive Order 12958, order of May 6, 2002. *Federal Register* 67, no. 90 (May 9, 2002): 31109.

Executive Order 12958. Designation under Executive Order 12958, order of Sept. 26, 2002. *Federal Register* 67, no. 189 (Sept. 30, 2002): 61463.

Executive Order 12958. Designation under Executive Order 12958, order of Sept. 17, 2003. *Federal Register* 68, no. 184 (Sept. 23, 2003): 55257.

Executive Order 13099. 1998.

Executive Order 13224. Blocking Property and Prohibiting Transactions with Persons Who Commit, Threaten or Support Terrorism, order of Sept. 23, 2001. *Federal Register* 66, no. 186 (Sept. 25, 2001): 49077.

Executive Order 13233. Further Implementation of the Presidential Records Act, order of Nov. 1, 2001. *Federal Register* 66, no. 214 (Nov. 5, 2001): 56023.

Executive Order 13372. "Prohibiting Transactions with Terrorists Who Threaten to Disrupt the Middle East Peace Process." Feb. 16, 2005. 50 U.S. Code 1701 (2005).

Fainaru, Steve. "A Denial or a Forfeit of Rights?" *Washington Post National Weekly Edition.* June 17–23, 2002, 30.

——— "Immigration Hearings Case Goes to High Court." *Washington Post,* June 22, 2002, A11. Available at www.washingtonpost.com/wp-dyn/A26081-2002Jun21.

——— "Judge Rejects Rule Closing Immigration Hearing." *Washington Post,* Apr. 4, 2002, A1. Available at www.washingtonpost.com/wp-dyn/articles/A58187-2002Apr3 .html.

——— "Justice Dept. Report Faults Post-9/11 Detention Practice." *Washington Post,* June 2, 2003. Available at www.washingtonpost.com/ac2/wp-dyn.

——— "U.S. Bans the Release of Detainees' Names." *Washington Post,* Apr. 19, 2002, A10. Available at www.washingtonpost.com/wp-dyn/articles/A12012-2002Apr18.html.

Fainaru, Steve, and Margot Williams. "Is the Law Being Bent? The Material Witness Statute Keeps Detainees in Jail, but Many Have Never Testified." *Washington Post National Weekly Edition,* Dec 2–8, 2002, 29–30.

FBI e-mail. From [redacted] to Marion Bowman, Valerie Caproni, and John Curran, FBI Office of General Counsel. Subject: DOJ 2002 "torture" memo. June 8, 2004. Available at www.aclu.org/torturefoia/released/FBI_4931.pdf.

FBI memo. Memo To: Washington Field, From: Criminal Investigative. Re: Special Jurisdiction Crimes, [redacted], Crime on Government Reservation, Crime of Violence. July 22, 2004. Released to ACLU Dec. 15, 2004. Available at www.aclu.org/torturefoia/released/ FBI_4368_4372.pdf.

FBI memo. Memo To: [redacted], From: [redacted]. Subject: current events. May 13, 2004. Released to ACLU Dec. 15, 2004. Available at www.aclu.org/torturefoia/released/FBI_ 4140.pdf.

Feaver, Peter. "The Clinton Mind-Set." *Washington Post National Weekly Edition,* Mar. 29–Apr. 4, 2004, 26.

Feldman, Noah. "Choices of Law, Choices of War." *Harvard Journal of Law and Public Policy* 25, no. 2 (Spring 2002): 457–485.

Feldmann, Linda. "Ashcroft's Lightning Rod Role." *Christian Science Monitor,* Sept. 24, 2003. Available at www.csmonitor.com/2003/0924.

———— "John Edwards's Quest to Sway a Bigger Jury." *Christian Science Monitor,* Oct. 29, 2003. Available at www.csmonitor.com/2003/1029.

Fick, Bob. "Trial Merges Terror Charges, Free Speech." Associated Press. May 28, 2004. Available at news.findlaw.com.

Findlaw.com. Special Coverage: War on Terrorism. "Civil and Criminal Terror Cases Home-page." Accessed July 8, 2005. Available at news.findlaw.com/legalnews/us/terrorism/cases/index.html.

Finn, Mindy. "Congress Expands Definition of Terrorism in New Law." *Congressional Quarterly On-line,* Nov. 20, 2001.

FISA Letter 2000. Attorney General John Ashcroft to Ralph Mecham, Administrative Office of the United States Courts. Apr. 27, 2001. U.S. Department of Justice. Office of Intelligence Policy and Review. FOIA Reading Room Records. Available at www.usdoj.gov/oipr/reading room.

FISA Letter 2001. Acting Attorney General Larry Thompson to Ralph Mecham, Administrative Office of the United States Courts. Apr. 29, 2002. U.S. Department of Justice. Office of Intelligence Policy and Review. FOIA Reading Room Records. Available at www.usdoj.gov/oipr/reading room.

FISA Letter 2002. Attorney General John Ashcroft to Ralph Mecham, Administrative Office of the United States Courts. Apr. 29, 2003. U.S. Department of Justice. Office of Intelligence Policy and Review. FOIA Reading Room Records. Available at www.usdoj.gov/oipr/reading room.

FISA Letter 2003. Assistant Attorney General William Moschella to Ralph Mecham, Administrative Office of the United States Courts. Apr. 30, 2004. U.S. Department of Justice. Office of Intelligence Policy and Review. FOIA Reading Room Records. Available at www.usdoj.gov/oipr/reading room.

FISA Letter 2004. Assistant Attorney General William Moschella to Ralph Mecham, Administrative Office of the United States Courts. Apr. 1, 2005. U.S. Department of Justice. Office of Intelligence Policy and Review. FOIA Reading Room Records. Available at www.usdoj.gov/oipr/reading room.

FISA Letters. Attorney General Janet Reno to Ralph Mecham, Administrative Office of the United States Courts. Apr. 18, 1997, Apr. 29, 1998, Apr. 29, 1999, Apr. 27, 2000. U.S. Department of Justice, Office of Intelligence Policy and Review, FOIA Reading Room Records. Available at www.usdoj.gov/oipr/readingroom.

Fisher, Louis. *American Constitutional Law,* 6th ed. Durham, N.C.: Carolina Academic Press.

———— "Brief Amicus Curiae of Louis Fisher in Support of Petitioner-Appellee Urging Affirmance." *Hamdan v. Rumsfeld.* United States Courts of Appeal for the District of Columbia Circuit. No. 04-5393. Dec. 29, 2004.

———— "Challenges to Civil Liberties in a Time of War." In Richard Conley, ed. *Transforming the American Polity: The Presidency of George W. Bush and the War on Terrorism.* Upper Saddle River, N.J.: Pearson Prentice Hall, 2005..

———— *Constitutional Conflicts between Congress and the President.* 4th ed. Lawrence: University Press of Kansas, 1997.

———— "Judicial Review of the War Power." *Presidential Studies Quarterly* 3, no. 3 (Sept. 2005): 466–495.

———— *Military Tribunals and Presidential Power.* Lawrence: University Press of Kansas, 2005.

———— *Nazi Saboteurs on Trial.* Lawrence: University Press of Kansas, 2003.

———— "Who's Minding the Courts on Rights?" *Los Angeles Times,* Feb. 23, 2003, M2.

Fitton, Thomas. "From the Desk of Judicial Watch President Tom Fitton." Judicial Watch, Nov. 11, 2004. Available at www.judicialwatch.org/jwnews/111104.htm.

Ford, Gerald. Memo. "President's Talking Points at the Swearing In Ceremony of Edward Levi." Folder FG 17/A 8/9/74-2/10/75, Box 88, FG 17/A-Department of Justice. Gerald R. Ford Library. Ann Arbor, Michigan. Feb. 7, 1975.

Frankel, Glenn. "Europe, U.S. Diverge on How to Fight Terrorism." *Washington Post,* Mar. 28, 2004, A15. Available at www.washingtonpost.com/ac2/wp-dyn.

Freedman, Eric M. "Hamdi and the Case of the Five Knights." *Legal Times,* Feb. 3, 2003.

———— "Milestones in Habeas Corpus: Part I: Just Because John Marshall Said It, Doesn't Make It So: Ex Parte Bollman and the Illusory Prohibition on the Federal Writ of Habeas Corpus for State Prisoners in the Judiciary Act of 1789." *Alabama Law Review* 51 (Winter 2000): 531.

Freedom of Information Act. 5 U.S.C. § 552(e)(5). 2000.

Frieden, Terry. "Saudi Grad Student Cleared of Terror Charges; Mistrial Declared on Lesser Charges." CNN. June 15, 2004. Available at www.cnn.com/2004/LAW/06/11/computer.terrorism/index/html.

Frum, David. *The Right Man.* London: Weidenfeld and Nicolson, 2003.

Ganey, Terry, and Virginia Young. "Courts Reject Suits to Save Cruzan's Life." *St. Louis Post-Dispatch,* Dec. 21 1990, 1A.

Gearan, Anne. "New Info on Padilla Not Part of Court Case." Associated Press. June 2, 2004. Available at news.findlaw.com.

Gellman, Barton. "The FBI's Secret Scrutiny." *Washington Post,* Nov. 6, 2005, A1, A10, A11.

Gellman, Barton, and Susan Schmidt. "U.S., Pakistan Intensify the Search for Bin Laden." *Washington Post,* Mar. 7, 2003, A1. Available at www.washingtonpost.com/ac2/wp-dyn.

Government Accountability Office. "Freedom of Information Act: Agency Views on Changes Resulting from New Administration Policy." Report to the Ranking Minority Member, Committee on the Judiciary, U.S. Senate. Sept. 2003. GAO-03-981. Available at www.gao.gov/cgi-bin/getrpt?GAO-03-981. The GAO was formerly named the General Accounting Office.

———— "Justice Department: Better Management Oversight and Internal Controls Needed to Ensure Accuracy of Terrorism-Related Conviction Statistics." Report to Representative Dan Burton, House Committee on Government Reform. Jan. 2003. GAO-03-266. Available at www.gao.gov/cgi-bin/getrpt?GAO-03-266.

———— "Update on Freedom of Information Act Implementation Status." A Report to the Ranking Minority Member, Committee on the Judiciary, U.S. Senate. Feb. 2004. GAO-04-257. Available at www.gao.gov/cgi-bin/getrpt?GAO-04-257.

Gill, T. D. *The 11th of September and the International Law of Military Operations.* Amsterdam: Vossiuspers UvA, 2002.

Ginsberg, Thomas, and Bob Moran. "Ashcroft: Anti-terror Laws Are Working." *Philadelphia Inquirer,* Aug. 20, 2003. Available at philly.com/mld/inquirer/news/nation.

Gleckman, Howard. "John Ashcroft's Holy War." *Business Week Online,* Apr. 23, 2002. Available at www.businessweek.com/bwdaily/dnflash/apr2002.

Goldberg, Jonah. Ashcroft on My Mind." *National Review Online,* Jan. 17, 2001. Available at www.nationalreview.com/goldberg.

Golden, Tim. "Threats and Responses: Tough Justice; Administration Officials Split over Stalled Military Tribunals." *New York Times,* Oct. 25, 2004, A1.

Goldman, Sheldon. "Judicial Confirmation Wars: Ideology and the Battle for the Federal Courts." *University of Richmond Law Review* 39, no. 3 (Mar. 2005): 871–908.

Goldstein, Amy. "A Deliberate Strategy of Disruption: Massive, Secret Detention Effort Aimed Mainly at Preventing More Terror." *Washington Post,* Nov. 4, 2001, A1.

———— "Paige Calls NEA a 'Terrorist' Group." *Washington Post,* Feb. 24, 2004, A19. Available at www.washingtonpost.com/ac2/wp-dyn.

Goldstein, Amy, and Dan Eggen. "U.S. to Stop Issuing Detention Tallies." *Washington Post,* Nov. 9, 2001, A16.

Goldstein, David. "Ashcroft Mixes Religion, Action in Pitch to Christian Coalition." *Kansas City Star,* Sept. 14, 1997, A24.

Gordon, Diana R. "Ashcroft Justice." *Nation,* July 23–30, 2001, 20–24.

Government's Position on Competency and Defendant's Self Representation. *U.S. v. Moussaoui.* In the U.S. Court of Appeals for the Fourth Circuit, on Appeal from the U.S. District Court for the Eastern District of Virginia. No. 03-4792. June 7, 2002. Available at news.findlaw.com/hdocs/docs/Moussaoui/usmouss60702gcomp.pdf.

Green, John C., Mark Rozell, and Clyde Wilcox, eds. *The Christian Right in American Politics.* Washington, D.C.: Georgetown University Press, 2003.

Green, Joshua. "How Ashcroft Happened." *American Prospect,* Feb. 26, 2001, 16–17.

Green, Tanya. "U.S. Attorney General John Ashcroft Obtains Injunctions against Pro-Lifers." Concerned Women for America, Feb. 5, 2002, available at www.cwfa.org.

Greenberg, Karen, and Joshua Dratel, eds. *The Torture Papers: The Road to Abu Ghraib.* New York: Cambridge University Press, 2005.

Greenhouse, Linda. "Justices Hear Case on Using Death Photos of Official." *New York Times,* Dec. 4, 2003. Available at www.nytimes.com/2003/12/04/national.

———— "News Groups Seek to Open Secret Case." *New York Times,* Jan. 5, 2004. Available at www.nytimes.com/2004/01/05/national.

Gregg, Gary, and Mark Rozell, eds. *Considering the Bush Presidency.* New York: Oxford University Press, 2004.

Grimaldi, James V. "At Justice, Freedom Not to Release Information." *Washington Post,* Dec. 2, 2002, E1. Available at www.washingtonpost.com/ac2/wp-dyn/A58419-2002Nov30.

Grove, Lloyd. "Why Cher Is Steamed at John Ashcroft." *Washington Post,* Feb. 26, 2002, C3. Available at www.washingtonpost.com/ac2/wp-dyn.

Gullo, Karen. "Ashcroft Won't Name Detainees." *El Paso Times,* Nov. 27, 2001, 4A.

Gwyn, William B. "The Indeterminacy of the Separation of Powers and the Federal Courts." *George Washington Law Review* 57 (Jan. 1989): 474–505.

———— "The Indeterminacy of the Separation of Powers in the Age of the Framers." *William and Mary Law Review* 30 (Winter 1989): 263–268.

———— *The Meaning of the Separation of Powers.* New Orleans: Tulane Studies in Political Science, 1964.

H. 2526. "Restoration of Freedom of Information Act of 2003." Introduced June 19, 2003. Available at thomas.loc.gov.

Hakim, Danny. "Inquiries Begun into Handling of Detroit Terror Cases." *New York Times,* Jan. 29, 2004. Available at www.nytimes.com/2004/01/29/national/29TRIA.html.

———— "Man Acquitted in Terror Case Says Co-defendants Will Be Cleared." *New York Times,* June 6, 2003. Available at www.nytimes.com/2003/06/06/national/06DETR .html.

Halstuk, Martin. "In Review: The Threat to Freedom of Information." *Columbia Journalism Review* 40, no. 5 (Jan./Feb. 2002). Available at www.cjr.org/year/02/1/halstuk.asp.

Hamblett, Mark. "N.Y. Lawyer Lynne Stewart Convicted of Helping Terrorists." *New York Law Journal,* Feb. 11, 2005. Available at www.law.com.

Hamilton, Alexander. 1788. "The Judiciary Department." *The Federalist* No. 78. June 14, 1788. Available at www.constitution.org/fed/federa78.htm.

———— "The Real Character of the Executive." *The Federalist* No. 69. Mar. 14, 1788. Available at www.constitution.org/fed/federa69/htm.

Hanley, Charles. "Scientists Say Dirty Bomb Would Be a Dud." Associated Press. June 9, 2004. Available at customwire.ap.org/dynamic/stories/D/DIRTY_BOMB_DUD.

Hays, Tom. "Attorney Says Alleged Terror Suspect Held Unconstitutionally." *Washington Post,* June 11, 2002. Available at www.washingtonpost.com/ac2/wp-dyn/A32435-2002 Jun11.

Heiser, Peter, Jr. "The Opinion Writing Function of Attorneys General." *Idaho Law Review* 18 (1982): 9–41.

Henkin, Louis. *Foreign Affairs and the Constitution.* New York: Norton, 1975.

Hensen, Steven L. "The President's Papers Are the People's Business." *Washington Post,* Dec. 16, 2001, B1.

Hentoff, Nat. "Ashcroft's America." *Editor and Publisher,* Apr. 7, 2003, 46.

———— "John Ashcroft v. the Constitution: Giving the FBI a 'Blank Warrant.'" *Village Voice,* Nov. 26, 2001. Available at www.villagevoice.com/news/0148,hentoff,30259,6.html.

———— "Why Should We Care? It's Only the Constitution." *Progressive,* Dec. 2001, 24–30.

———— *The War on the Bill of Rights and the Gathering Resistance.* New York: Seven Stories Press, 2003.

Hersh, Seymour. *Chain of Command.* New York: HarperCollins, 2004.

Herz, Michael. "Washington, Patton, Schwarzkopf and . . . Ashcroft?" *Constitutional Commentary* 19 (Winter 2002): 663.

Holland, Gina. "White House Seeks Secrecy on Detainee." Associated Press. Jan. 5, 2004. Available at news.findlaw.com.

Holt, Pat. "Driving Dangerously with the Patriot Act." *Christian Science Monitor,* Oct. 2, 2003. Available at www.csmonitor.com/2003/1002.

Homeland Security Act. PL 107-296. Nov. 25, 2002.

Hulse, Carl. "Congress Shuts Pentagon Unit over Privacy." *New York Times,* Sept. 26, 2003. Available at www.nytimes.com/2003/09/26/national.

Human Life Act. S 2135. 1998.

Human Rights Watch. "U.S.: Guantanamo Tribunal Lacks Basic Knowledge of Law." Nov. 6, 2004. Available at hrw.org/English/docs/2004/11/05/usdom9615_txt.htm.

———— "Witness to Abuse: Human Rights Abuses under the Material Witness Law since September 11." Available at hrw.org/reports/2005/us0605/.

Hunt, Albert. "The Unaccountable Attorney General." *Wall Street Journal,* June 6, 2002, A15.

Immigration and Nationality Act. 8 U.S.C. 1231 (a). 2000.

Indictment. *U.S. v. Sattar.* U.S. District Court, Southern District of New York. Apr. 9, 2002, 11. Available at news.findlaw.com/hdocs/docs/terrorism/ussattar040902ind.pdf.

Indictment. *U.S. v. Ujaama.* U.S. District Court, Western District of Washington at Seattle. Aug. 28, 2002. Available at http://news.findlaw.com/hdocs/docs/terrorism/usujaama82802 ind.pdf.

Isikoff, Michael. "And Justice for All." *Newsweek,* Aug. 12, 2002. Available at www.msnbc.com/news/792462.asp.

———— "Double Standards?" *Newsweek.* Web exclusive. May 25, 2004. Available at www.msnbc.com/id/5032094/site/newsweek.

———— "Show Me the Money: Patriot Act Helps the Feds in Cases with No Tie to Terror." *Newsweek,* Dec. 1, 2003. Available at www.msnbc.com/news.

———— "Why Keating Didn't Cut It." *Newsweek,* Jan. 15, 2001, 28.

Isikoff, Michael, and Daniel Klaidman. "Ashcroft's Campaign to Shore Up the Patriot Act." *Newsweek,* Aug. 25, 2003, 6.

Issacharoff, Samuel, and Richard Pildes. "Between Civil Libertarianism and Executive Unilateralism: An Institutional Process Approach to Rights during Wartime." *Theoretical Inquiries in Law* 5, no. 1 (Jan. 2004): 2–44.

Ives, Nat. "Celebrities Line Up to Criticize Bush in A.C.L.U. Campaign." *New York Times,* Sept. 12, 2003. Available at www.nytimes.com/2003/09/12/business/media.

Jackman, Tom, and Dan Eggen. "'Combatants' Lack Rights, U.S. Argues." *Washington Post,* June 20, 2002, A1.

Jacoby Declaration on Padilla. "Declaration of Vice Admiral Lowell E. Jacoby (USN), Director of the Defense Intelligence Agency." Jan. 9, 2002. Available at findlaw.com.

Janofsky, Michael. "9/11 Panel Calls Policies on Immigration Ineffective." *New York Times,* Apr. 17, 2004. Available at www.nytimes.com/2004/04/17/national/17IMMI.html.

Jehl, Douglas. "Ex-C.I.A. Aides Ask for Leak Inquiry by Congress." *New York Times,* Jan. 22, 2004. Available at www.nytimes.com/2004/01/22/politics.

Johnson, Glen. "House Votes to Extend Patriot Act." *Washington Post,* July 22, 2005. Available at www.washingtonpost.com/wp-dyn/content/articles/2005/07/21/AR2005072100711 .html.

Johnson, Kevin, and Toni Locy. "Patriot Act at Heart of Ashcroft's Influence." *USA Today,* Sept. 15, 2003. Available at /www.usatoday.com/news/washington/2003-09-15.

Johnston, David, and Neil Lewis. "Religious Right Made Big Push to Put Ashcroft in Justice Dept." *New York Times,* Jan. 7, 2001, sec. 1, 1.

Johnston, David, Neil Lewis, and Douglas Jehl. "Security Nominee Gave Advice to the C.I.A. on Torture Laws." *New York Times,* Jan. 29, 2005. Available at www.nytimes.com/2005/01/ 29/politics/29homes.html.

Johnston, David, and Richard Stevenson. "Threats and Responses: Washington Memo; Ashcroft, Deft at Taking Political Heat, Hits a Rocky Patch." *New York Times,* June 30, 2004, A14.

Jones, Walter B. "Congressman Jones Continues to Fight for Senator Ashcroft's Nomination for U.S. Attorney General." Press release. Jan. 25, 2001. Available at jones.house.gov/html/ 12501.html.

Kairys, David. "Introduction." In David Kairys, ed., *The Politics of Law,* 1–20. 3rd ed. New York. Basic Books, 1998.

Kaiser, Robert. "That Giant Hissing Sound: What You Hear Is Congress Giving Up Its Clout." *Washington Post National Weekly Edition,* Mar. 22–28, 2004, 22.

Kaplan, Jonathan. "Ashcroft Joins K Street Legions." *The Hill,* May 1, 2005. Available at www .hillnews.com/thehill/export/TheHill/News/Frontpage/042805/ashcroft/html.

Kassop, Nancy. "The War Power and Its Limits." *Presidential Studies Quarterly* 33, no. 3 (Sept. 2003): 509–529.

Kayyem, Juliette. "The Sentencing of 'Shoe Bomber' Richard Reid." FindLaw's Writ Legal Commentary. Feb. 3, 2003. Available at writ.findlaw.com/commentary/20030203_kayyem.

Kennedy, Randall. "In Extremis." *American Prospect,* Feb. 26, 2001, 14.

Kent, Andrew. "Justice for Terrorists." *Commentary,* June 2004, 39–42.

Kiefer, Francine. "Backlash Grows against White House Secrecy." *Christian Science Monitor,* Mar. 25, 2002, 3.

——— "A Fight Brews over Ex-President's Papers." *Christian Science Monitor,* Nov. 6, 2001. Available at www.csmonitor.com/2001/1106.

Klein, Edward. "We're Not Destroying Rights, We're Protecting Rights." *Parade Magazine,* May 19, 2002, 4–6.

Knickerbocker, Brad. "Security Concerns Drive Rise in Secrecy." *Christian Science Monitor,* Dec. 3, 2001. Available at www.csmonitor.com/2001/1203.

Koh, Harold Hongju. "Against Military Tribunals." *Dissent* 49, no. 4 (Fall 2002): 58.

——— *The National Security Constitution.* New Haven, Conn.: Yale University Press, 1990.

——— "We Have the Right Courts for Bin Laden." *New York Times,* Nov. 23, 2001, A39.

Kondracke, Morton. "Ashcroft-Bashing Could End Up Hurting Democrats." *Roll Call,* Sept. 11, 2003. Available through Lexis-Nexis Congressional Universe.

Koontz, Linda. Letter from the Director, Information Management Issues, to Sen. Patrick Leahy. Sept. 3, 2003. General Accounting Office, GAO-03-981. Available at www.fas.org/sgp/foia/gao-03-981.pdf.

Koszczuk, Jackie. "Ashcroft Drawing Criticism from Both Sides of the Aisle." *Congressional Quarterly,* Sept. 7, 2002, 2286–2287.

——— "Lawmakers Struggle to Keep an Eye on Patriot Act." *Congressional Quarterly,* Sept. 7, 2002, 2284.

Kramer, Andrew. "Software Engineer Admits Aiding Taliban." Associated Press. Aug. 6, 2003. Available at www.news.findlaw.com.

Kristof, Nicholas D. "The 2000 Campaign: The Decision; For Bush, His Toughest Call Was the Choice to Run at All" *New York Times,* Oct. 29, 2000, 1.

Krugman, Paul. "Travesty of Justice." *New York Times,* June 15, 2004. Available at www.nytimes.com/2004/06/15/opinion.

Kulish, Nicholas. "Ashcroft Seeks More Antiterrorism Provisions." *Wall Street Journal,* June 6, 2003, B2.

LaFranchi, Howard. "U.S. vs. Europe: Two Views of Terror." *Christian Science Monitor,* Mar. 18, 2004. Available at www.csmonitor.com/2004/0318.

LaMarche, Gara. "Welcome to Watching Justice." Apr. 14, 2004. Available at www.watchingjustice.org/reports/article.php?docId=179.

Lamare, James, Jerry Polinard, and Robert Wrinkle. "Texas: Religion and Politics in God's Country." In John Green, Mark Rozell, and Clyde Wilcox, eds., *The Christian Right in American Politics.* Washington, D.C.: Georgetown University Press, 2003.

Lambrecht, Bill, and Patrick Wilson. "Abortion Activists Vow to Stress Moral Issues." *St. Louis Post-Dispatch,* Jan. 23, 1998, 4A.

Lane, Charles. "Fighting Terror vs. Defending Liberties: A New Debate Has Crystallized since Sept. 11." *Washington Post National Weekly Edition,* Sept. 9–15, 2002, 30.

——— "Justices Move to Define Detainees' Court Access." *Washington Post,* July 1, 2004, A7. Available at www.washingtonpost.com/ac2/wp-dyn.

——— "A Second Tier of Justice: A Parallel Legal System—without Constitutional Protections—Is in the Works for Terror Suspects." *Washington Post National Weekly Edition,* Dec. 9–15, 2002, 30.

——— "Unanswered Questions." *Washington Post National Weekly Edition,* July 22–28, 2002, 9.

Larry King Live. "Interview with John Ashcroft." CNN. Nov. 9, 2001. Available at http://www.cnn.com/TRANSCRIPTS/0111/09.

——— "Interview with John Ashcroft." CNN. Jan. 21, 2002. Available at www.cnn.com/TRANSCRIPTS/0201/21.

————— "Interview with John Ashcroft." CNN. May 31, 2002. Available at http://www.cnn .com/TRANSCRIPTS/0205/31.

————— "Interview with John Ashcroft." CNN. Sept. 11, 2003. Available at www.cnn.com/ TRANSCRIPTS/0309/11.

————— "Interview with John Ashcroft and Ted Olson." CNN. Dec. 17, 2002. Available at http://www.cnn.com/TRANSCRIPTS/0212/17.

————— "John Ashcroft Discusses His New Job as Attorney General." CNN. Feb. 7, 2001. Available at http://www.cnn.com/TRANSCRIPTS/0102/07.

————— "Secretary Powell on CNN's Larry King Live." CNN. Nov. 27, 2001. Available at http://www.cnn.com/TRANSCRIPTS/0111/27

————— "What Did John Ashcroft Say at Bob Jones University?" CNN. Jan. 12, 2001. Available at www.cnn.com/TRANSCRIPTS/0101/12.

Late Show with David Letterman. "Ashcroft to Appear on Letterman." Apr. 6, 2002. Available at www.allstarz.org/davidletterman.

Lawrence, J. M. "Justice Dept. Won't Turn Over Memo in Salvati Case." *Boston Herald,* Feb. 12, 2002. Available through Lexis-Nexis Academic Universe.

Lengel, Allan, and Susan Schmidt. "U.S. to Seek Dismissal of Terrorism Convictions." *Washington Post,* Sept. 1, 2004, A2. Available at www.washingtonpost.com/ac2/wp-dyn/ A50698-2004Aug31.

Leonnig, Carol. "Lawyers Seek Relief for 5 Detainees." *Washington Post,* July 3, 2004, A20. Available at http://www.washingtonpost.com/ac2/wp-dyn.

Lessenberry, Jack. "Ashcroft vs. Constitution." *Metro Times,* Nov. 28, 2001. Available at www .metrotimes.com/editorial/story.asp?id=2714.

Levi, Edward. *An Introduction to Legal Reasoning.* Chicago: University of Chicago Press, 1949.

Levin, Carl. Nomination of Alberto R. Gonzales to be Attorney General of the United States. Senate. 109th Cong., 1st sess., Feb. 3, 2005. 151 *Congressional Record* S293.

————— "Use of Force Authority by the President." U.S. Senate. Oct. 1, 2001. *Congressional Record,* S9951. Available at thomas.loc.gov/home/r107query.html.

Lewis, Charles, and Adam Mayle. "Justice Dept. Drafts Sweeping Expansion of Anti-terrorism Act." Center for Public Integrity. Feb. 20, 2003. Available at www.publicintegrity .org.

Lewis, Neil. "Bush Didn't Order Any Breach of Torture Laws, Ashcroft Says." *New York Times,* June 9, 2004. Available at www.nytimes.com/2004/06/09/politics.

————— "Court Overturns Limits on Wiretaps to Combat Terror." *New York Times,* Nov. 19, 2002. Available at www.nytimes.com/2002/11/19/national/19COUR.html.

Lewis, Neil, and Eric Schmitt. "Cuban Detentions May Last Years." *New York Times,* Feb. 13, 2004. Available at www.nytimes.com/2004/02/13/politics.

————— "Lawyers Decided Bans on Torture Didn't Bind Bush." *New York Times,* June 8, 2004. Available at www.nytimes.com/2004/06/08/politics/08ABUS.html.

Lichtblau, Eric. "Appeals Court Casts Doubt on Parts of Key Antiterrorism Law." *New York Times,* Dec. 4, 2003. Available at www.nytimes.com/2003/12/04/national/04USP.html.

————— "Ashcroft Criticized for Talks on Terror." *New York Times,* Aug. 22, 2003. Available at www.nytimes.com/2003/08/22/politics.

————— "Ashcroft Defends Detentions as Immigrants Recount Toll." *New York Times,* June 5, 2003. Available at www.nytimes.com/2003/06/05/national.

————— "Ashcroft Mocks Librarians and Others Who Oppose Parts of Counterterrorism Law." *New York Times,* Sept. 16, 2003. Available at www.nytimes.2003/09/16/politics.

———— "Ashcroft to Defend Ban on Some Abortion Protests." *New York Times,* Aug. 30, 2003. Available at www.nytimes.com/2003/08/30/politics.

———— "Ashcroft's Tour Rallies Supporters and Detractors." *New York Times,* Sept. 8, 2003. Available at www.nytimes.com/2003/09/08/politics.

———— "Enemy Combatant Decision Marks Change, Officials Say." *New York Times,* June 25, 2003. Available at www.nytimes.com/2003/06/25/politics/25TERR.html.

———— "Government Says It Has Yet to Use New Power to Check Library Records." *New York Times,* Sept. 19, 2003. Available at www.nytimes.com/2003/09/19/national.

———— "In a Reversal, Ashcroft Lifts Secrecy of Data." *New York Times,* Sept. 18, 2003. Available at www.nytimes.2003/09/18/politics.

———— "Justice Dept. Backs Off Its Demand for Abortion Records." *New York Times,* Mar. 23, 2004. Available at www.nytimes.com.2004/03/23/politics.

———— "Justice Dept. Lists Use of New Power to Fight Terror." *New York Times,* May 21, 2003. Available at www.nytimes.com/2003/05/21/international/worldspecial/21PATR.html.

———— "Justice Dept. Seeks Hospitals' Records of Some Abortions." *New York Times,* Feb. 12, 2004. Available at www.nytimes.com/2004/02/12/politics.

———— "Large Volume of F.B.I. Files Alarms U.S. Activist Groups." *New York Times,* July 18, 2005, A12.

———— "Libraries Say Yes, Officials Do Quiz Them about Users." *New York Times,* June 20, 2005. Available at www.nytimes.com/2005/06/20/politics/20patriot.html.

———— "Rising Fears That What We Do Know Can Hurt Us." *Los Angeles Times,* Nov. 18, 2001. Available at www.latimes.com.

———— "Sept. 11 Suspect May Be Set to Admit Guilt." *New York Times,* Apr. 20, 2005. Available at www.nytimes.com/2005/04/20/national/20moussaoui.html.

———— "Threats and Responses: The Attorney General; White House Criticizes Justice Dept. over Papers." *New York Times,* Apr. 30, 2004, A24. Available at www.nytimes.com/2004/04/30/national.

———— "Treatment of Detained Immigrants Is under Investigation." *New York Times,* June 26, 2003. Available at www.nytimes.com/2003/06/26/national/26DETA.html.

———— "Trucker Sentenced to 20 Years in Plot against Brooklyn Bridge." *New York Times,* Oct. 29, 2003. Available at www.nytimes.com/2003/10/29/national/29TERR.html.

———— "U.S. Spells Out Dangers Posed by Plot Suspect." *New York Times,* June 2, 2004. Available at www.nytimes.com/2004/06/02/politics.

———— "U.S. Uses Terror Law to Pursue Crimes from Drugs to Swindling." *New York Times,* Sept. 27, 2003. Available at www.nytimes.com/2003/09/27/politics.

———— "U.S. Will Tighten Rules on Holding Terror Suspects." *New York Times,* June 13, 2003. Available at www.nytimes.com/2003/06/13/national/13TERR.html.

———— "Whistle-Blowing Said to Be Factor in F.B.I. Firing." *New York Times,* July 29, 2004. Available at www.nytimes.com/2004/07/29/politics/29fbi.final.

Lichtblau, Eric, and Lawrence Altman. "Ashcroft in Hospital with Pancreatic Ailment." *New York Times,* Mar. 6, 2004. Available at ww.nytimes.com/2004/03/06/politics.

Lichtblau, Eric, and Janet Hook. "White House Angered by Leaks on Intelligence." *Los Angeles Times,* June 21, 2002, A15.

Lichtblau, Eric, and Adam Liptak. "On Terror and Spying, Ashcroft Expands Reach." *New York Times,* Mar. 15, 2003, A1.

Lichtblau, Eric, and Alissa Rubin. "Gay Issue Adds to Ashcroft Dispute." *Sun-Sentinel,* Jan. 26, 2001. Available at sns.sunsentinel.com/news/national.

Liptak, Adam. "Author of '02 Memo on Torture: 'Gentle' Soul for a Harsh Topic." *New York Times,* June 24, 2004. Available at www.nytimes.com/2004/06/24/politics.

———— "For Post 9/11 Material Witness, It Is a Terror of a Different Kind." *New York Times,* Aug. 19, 2004. Available at www.nytimes.com/2004/08/19/politics/19witness.html.

———— "The Pursuit of Immigrants in America after Sept. 11." *New York Times,* June 8, 2003. Available at www.nytimes.com/2003/06/08/weekinreview.

Locy, Toni, and Kevin Johnson. "How the US Watches Suspects of Terrorism." *USA Today,* Feb. 12, 2003.

Lowe, Brian. "Soviet and American Civil Religion: A Comparison." *Journal of Interdisciplinary Studies* 13 (2001): 73–96.

Luban, David. "The War on Terrorism and the End of Human Rights." *Philosophy and Public Policy Quarterly* 22, no. 3 (Summer 2002): 9–14.

Lumpkin, Beverley. "Justice Seeks to Interview 5,000." ABCNews, Nov. 13, 2001.

Lydersen, Kari. "The Civil Liberties Candidate?" AlterNet.org, Feb. 9, 2004. Available at www.alternet.org.

MacDonald, Sam. "Gun Control's New Language." *Reason.* 33, no. 10 (Mar. 2002): 16–18.

MAD magazine. Jan. 2003, 43.

Madison, James. "Notes on the Confederacy" (1787). In Philip R. Fendall, ed., *Letters and Other Writings of James Madison.* Published by order of Congress. Philadelphia: Lippincott, 1865.

———— "The Particular Structure of the New Government and the Distribution of Power among Its Different Parts." *The Federalist* No. 47. Jan. 30, 1788. Available at www.constitution.org/fed/federa47.htm.

———— "The Structure of the Government Must Furnish the Proper Checks and Balances between the Different Departments." *The Federalist* No. 51. Feb. 6, 1788. Available at www.constitution.org/fed/federa51.htm.

———— "These Department Should Not Be So Far Separated as to Have No Constitutional Control over Each Other." *The Federalist* No. 48. Feb. 1, 1788. Available at www.constitution.org/fed/federa48.htm.

Malhotra, Anjana. "Material Witness Law Is Being Abused." Human Rights Watch. May 27, 2004. Originally published in *The Oregonian,* May 27, 2004. Available at hrw.org/english/docs/20-04/05/27/usdom8631_txt.htm.

Margasak, Larry. "Feds: Moussaoui Aimed to Hit White House." Associated Press. Aug. 8, 2003. Available at news.findlaw.com/ap_stories/other/1110/8-8-2003/20.

———— "Judge: Moussaoui Case Fate Lies in Access." Associated Press. Aug. 8, 2003. Available at news.findlaw.com.

———— "Judge: Tribunal for Moussaoui Case?" Associated Press. June 3, 2003. Available at news.findlaw.com.

———— "Moussaoui Makes Plea for Live Testimony." Associated Press. July 24, 2003. Available at news.findlaw.com.

———— "Moussaoui Seeks Access to Gov't Documents." Associated Press. Apr. 23, 2003. Available at news.findlaw.com/ap_stories/other/1110/4-23-2003.

———— "Moussaoui Worried on Self-Representation." Associated Press. Aug. 22, 2003. Available at news.findlaw.com.

———— "U.S. Seeks to Block Moussaoui Request." *Washington Post,* June 3, 2003. Available at www.washingtonpost.com/wp-dyn/articles.

Markon, Jerry. "Judge Bars Death Penalty for Moussaoui." *Washington Post,* Oct. 2, 2003. Available at www.washingtonpost.com/ac2/wp-dyn?A34536-2003Oct2.

———— "Major Issues in Moussaoui Appeal." *Washington Post,* Nov. 30, 2003, A19. Available at www.washingtonpost.com.

———— "Moussaoui Barred from Hearing." *Washington Post,* May 3, 2003, A9. Available at www.washingtonpost.com/ac2/wp-dyn/A7582-2003May2.

———— "Moussaoui Is Spinning a Legal Web." *Washington Post,* May 26, 2003. Available at www.washingtonpost.com/wp-dyn/articles.

———— "Moussaoui Planning to Admit 9/11 Role." *Washington Post,* Apr. 19, 2005, A1. Available at www.washingtonpost.com/wp-dyn/articles/A64195-2005Apr18.html.

———— "Post 9/11 Probe Revived Stolen-Cereal Incident." *Washington Post,* June 12, 2005, A19. Available at www.washingtonpost.com/wp-dyn/content/article/2005/06/11/AR2005061100380_2.html.

———— "The Terrorism Case That Wasn't—and Still Is." *Washington Post,* June 12, 2005, A19. Available at www.washingtonpost.com/wp-dyn/content/article/2005/06/11/AR2005061100379.html.

———— "U.S. Tries to Block Access to Witness for Terror Trial." *Washington Post,* Apr. 2, 2003, A7. Available at www.washingtonpost.com/ac2/wp-dyn/A6605-2003Aprl.

Material Witness Statute. 18 U.S.C. § 3144. 1984.

Mathis, Deborah. "Religion—But Not Religious Groups—Drive Ashcroft." Gannett News Service, July 17, 1996.

Mayer, Jane. "Beyond Belief." *Washington Post National Weekly Edition,* Sept. 29–Oct. 5, 2003, 33.

McCaffrey, Shannon. "Ashcroft Opens PR Push for Patriot Act." *Philadelphia Inquirer,* Aug. 20, 2003. Available at philly.com/mld/inquirer/news/nation.

McCaughey, Betsy. "Ashcroft, Man of Principle: His Quest for a Restrained Judiciary." *National Review,* Jan. 8, 2001. Available www.nationalreview.com/comment.

McCoy, Donald. *Calvin Coolidge: The Quiet President.* New York: Macmillan, 1967.

McGee, Jim. "The Dragnet's Downside." *Washington Post National Weekly Edition,* Dec. 3, 2001, 8.

McIntire, Mike. "Terror Lesson Fading for Some, Ashcroft Says in Manhattan." *New York Times,* Sept. 10, 2003. Available at www.nytimes.com/2003/09/10/nyregion/10ASHC.html.

McIntyre, H. I. Memorandum from the Director, Directorate for Freedom of Information and Security Review. "Subject: DoD Guidance on Attorney General Freedom of Information Act (FOIA) Memorandum." Department of Defense. Nov. 19, 2001. Available at www.fas.org/sgp/foia/dod111901.pdf.

Meador, Daniel. *The President, the Attorney General and the Department of Justice.* Charlottesville, Va.: White Burkett Miller Center of Public Affairs, University of Virginia, 1980.

Means, Marianne. "John Ashcroft Will Not Be Missed." *Seattle Post-Intelligencer,* Nov. 11, 2004. Available at seattlepi.nwsource.com/opinion/199080_means11.html.

Meese, Edwin. "Introductory Remarks to True Faith and Allegiance by the Honorable John Ashcroft." Heritage Foundation Lecture no. 865. Feb. 11, 2005. Available at www.heritage.org/Research/LegalIssues/hl865.cfm.

Meller, Paul. "Europe Hacker Laws Could Make Protest a Crime." *New York Times,* Mar. 5, 2003. Available at www.nytimes.com/2003/03/05.

Memorandum opinion and order. *Khalid v. Bush; Boumediene v. Bush.* U.S. District Court for the District of Columbia. Civil Case No. 1:04-1142 and 1:04-1166. Jan. 19, 2005, 30.

Mensch, Elizabeth. "The History of Mainstream Legal Thought." In David Kairys, ed., *The Politics of Law,* 23–53. 3rd ed. New York. Basic Books, 1998.

Merry, Sally Engel. *Getting Justice and Getting Even: Legal Consciousness among Working-Class Americans.* Chicago: University of Chicago Press, 1990.

Meyer, Dick. "John Ashcroft: Minister of Fear." Against the Grain Commentary. CBSNews .com. June 12, 2002. Available at www.cbsnews.com/stories/2002.

Milbank, Dana. "DiIulio Saga Highlights Primacy Placed on Secrecy." *Washington Post,* Dec. 10, 2002, A27. Available at www.washingtonpost.com/ac2/wp-dyn/A32951-2002Dec9.

——— "GAO Backs Off Cheney Lawsuit." *Washington Post,* Feb. 7, 2003. Available at www .washingtonpost.com/ac2/wp-dyn/A40562-2003Feb7.

——— "In Cheney's Shadow, Counsel Pushes the Conservative Cause." *Washington Post,* Oct. 11, 2004, A21. Available at www.washingtonpost.com/ac2/wp-dyn/A2265-2004 Oct10.

——— "In War, It's Power to the President." *Washington Post,* Nov. 20, 2001. Available at www.washingtonpost.com/ac2/wp-dyn.

——— "Soaring Mightily into Retirement." *Washington Post,* Jan. 25, 2005, A13. Available at www.washingtonpost.com/wp-dyn/articles/A33675-2005Jan24.html.

Miller, John J. "Mr. Clean: John Ashcroft Has a Sterling Ethical Record and a Socially Conservative Base: But Does He Have What It Takes to Win?" *National Review,* Mar. 23, 1998, 36.

Mintz, John. "Al Qaeda Suspect Enters Legal Limbo: Few Precedents Available for Case, Experts Say." *Washington Post,* June 11, 2002, A10.

——— "Head of Muslim Charity Sentenced." *Washington Post,* Aug. 19, 2003, A2. Available at www.washingtonpost.com/wp-dyn/articles/2003Aug19.html.

——— "New Rules Shorten Holding Time for Detained Immigrants." *Washington Post,* Apr. 14, 2004. Available at www.washingtonpost.com/wp-dyn/articles/A9311-2004April13 .html.

Mintz, John, and Susan Schmidt. "Ashcroft Assailed on Terror Warning." *Washington Post,* May 28, 2004, A4. Available at www.washingtonpost.com/ac2/wp-dyn/A61742-2004 May27.

——— "Ridge, Ashcroft Issue Statement on Threat." *Washington Post,* May 29, 2004, A2. Available at www.washingtonpost.com/ac2/wp-dyn/A64374-2004 May28.

Moayedian, Ali. "Letter from Ayatollah Ashcroft to His CounterPart Ayatollah Shahroudi of Iran." *CounterPunch,* Nov. 21, 2002. Available at www.counterpunch.org/moayedian1121 .html.

Mobbs Declaration on José Padilla. "Declaration of Michael H. Mobbs, Special Advisor to the Undersecretary of Defense for Policy." Aug. 27, 2002. Available at findlaw.com.

Moe, Terry M., and William G. Howell. "Unilateral Action and Presidential Power: A Theory." *Presidential Studies Quarterly* 29, no. 4 (Dec. 1999): 850–872.

Montgomery, Alicia. "Conservatives Flex Muscles over Ashcroft." *Salon,* Jan. 11, 2001. Available at dir.salon.com/politics/feature/2001/01/11/conservatives.

Moore, David W. "Public Little Concerned about Patriot Act." Gallup News Service, Sept. 9, 2003. Available at www.gallup.com/poll/release.

Mosley, Jim, and Kathryn Rogers. "Ashcroft Takes Office, Urges Fight on Drugs, Porn." *St. Louis Post-Dispatch,* Jan. 10, 1989, 1A.

Mosley, Jim, and Virginia Young. "Missouri Upheld on Cruzan." *St. Louis Post-Dispatch,* June 26, 1990, 1A.

Motion to Dismiss. "Respondents' Reply in Support of Motion to Dismiss the Amended Petition for a Writ of Habeas Corpus." *Padilla ex rel. Newman v. Bush, Rumsfeld, Ashcroft, Marr.* U.S. District Court for Southern District of New York. 02 Civ. 4445. 2002.

Motion to Set Reasonable Conditions for Telephonic Communications and Visit. *U.S. v. Moussaoui.* Criminal No. 01-455-A. Filed in the U.S. District Court for the Eastern District of Virginia. Oct. 17, 2002. Available at news.findlaw.com/hdocs/docs/moussaoui/usmouss101702dmot.pdf.

Mowbray, Joel. "The Trouble with Ashcroft." Townhall.com. Dec. 20, 2001. Available at http://www.townhall.com/columnists/joelmowbray/jm20011220.shtml.

Murphy, Reg. *Uncommon Sense.* Atlanta: Longstreet Press, 1999.

Nagourney, Adam. "For Democrats Challenging Bush, Ashcroft Is Exhibit A." *New York Times,* July 13, 2003, A14.

Nathan, Debbie. "Oversexed." *Nation,* Aug. 29–Sept. 5, 2005, 28.

Nather, David, and Jill Barshay. "Hill Warning: Respect Level from White House Too Low." *Congressional Quarterly,* Mar. 9, 2002, 630.

National Academy of Public Administration. *Transforming the FBI: Progress and Challenges.* Washington, D.C.: National Academy of Public Administration, Jan. 2005.

National Association of Attorneys General. "Resolution: Congratulating Gale Norton and John Ashcroft." Adopted Mar. 14, 2001. Washington, D.C. Available at http://www.naag.org/naag/resolutions/res-spr01-norton_ashcroft.php.

National Public Radio. "Liberty vs. Security: An NPR Special Report." Dec. 6, 2001.

nbc17news.com. 2004. Accessed Mar. 17. Available at www.comand-post.org.

Neumeister, Larry. "2 Terrorism Charges against Lawyer Tossed." Associated Press. July 23, 2003. Available at news.findlaw.com.

———. "Verdict vs. Lawyer in Terror Case Upheld." SFGate.com, Oct. 25, 2005. Available at sfgate.com/cgi-bin/article.cgi?f=/n/a/2005/10/25/national/a203219D99.DTL.

Newsweek. "The Lindh E-Mails." June 24, 2002. Available at msnbc.com/news/767536.asp.

Newsweek/MSNBC. "Common Sense: Resistance to the Patriot Act Is Growing in the American Heartland." Nov. 20, 2003. Web exclusive. Available at www.msnbc.com/news.

Newton, Christopher. "FBI Probes Lawmakers for Leak." Associated Press. Aug. 2, 2002. Available at news.findlaw.com.

———. "U.S.: Terror Suspect Is 'Small Fish.'" Associated Press. Aug. 14, 2002. Available at news/findlaw.com.

New York Times. "Ashcroft Is Criticized for Remarks about Witness in Terror-Cell Case." Apr. 19, 2003. Available at www.nytimes.com/2003/04/19/international.

———. "The Trial of Zacarias Moussaoui." July 28, 2003. Available at www.nytimes.com/2003/07/28/opionion/28MON1.html.

———. "White House Push on Security Steps Bypasses Congress." Nov. 15, 2001, A1. Available at www.nytimes.com/2001/11/15.

9/11 Commission Hearing. "Chapter 6: The Illinois Charities Case Study." *Terrorist Financing Staff Monograph.* National Commission on Terrorist Attacks upon the United States, 2004. Available at www.9-11commission.gov/staff_statements/911_TerrFin_Ch6.pdf.

——— Transcript of Hearings with Attorney General John Ashcroft. National Commission on Terrorist Attacks upon the United States. FDCH E-Media. Apr. 13, 2004. Available at www.washingtonpost.com/wp-dyn/articles/A9088-2004Apr13.html#ashcroft.

——— Transcript of Hearings with Thomas Pickard. National Commission on Terrorist Attacks upon the United States. FDCH E-Media. Apr. 13, 2004. Available at www.washingtonpost.com/wp-dyn/articles/A9088-2004Apr13.html#pickard.

9/11 Commission Hearings. Transcript: National Security Adviser Condoleezza Rice. National Commission on Terrorist Attacks upon the United States. FDCH E-Media. Apr. 8, 2004. Available at www.washingtonpost.com/wp-dyn/articles/A61252-2004Apr8.html.

The 9/11 Commission Report. Final Report of the National Commission on Terrorist Attacks upon the United States. New York: Norton, 2004.

Nordlinger, Jay. "Ashcroft with Horns." *National Review,* May 24, 2002. Available at http://www.nationalreview.com/flashback/flashback-nordlinger.

Nosanchuk, Matthew. "The Embarrassing Interpretation of the Second Amendment." *Northern Kentucky Law Review* 29 (2002): 705–803.

Notice of Intent to Seek a Sentence of Death. *U.S. v. Moussaoui.* Criminal No. 01-455-A. Filed in the U.S. District Court for the Eastern District of Virginia. Mar. 28, 2002. Available at news.findlaw.com/hdocs/docs/moussaoui/usmoussaoui032802ntc.html.

Obama, Barack. Nomination of Alberto R. Gonzales to be Attorney General of the United States. Senate. 109th Cong., 1st sess., Feb. 3, 2005. 151 *Congressional Record* S923.

O'Hagan, Maureen. "A Terrorism Case That Went Awry." *Seattle Times,* Nov. 22, 2004, A1.

O'Harrow, Robert, Jr. "In Age of Security, Firm Mines Wealth of Personal Data." *Washington Post,* Jan. 20, 2005, A1. Available at www.washingtonpost.com/ac2/wp-dyn/A22269-2005 Jan19.

———. "The Pentagon Teams Up with Computer Sleuths." *Washington Post National Weekly Edition,* Nov. 18–24, 2002, 29–30.

Oliphant, Jim. "Justice during Wartime: Order on Military Trials Final Piece of Sept. 11 Response." *Legal Times,* Nov. 19, 2001, 1.

Online NewsHour. "Attorney General-Designate John Ashcroft." Dec. 22, 2000. Available at www.pbs.org/newshour/inauguration/transition.

———. "Confirmation Update." Jan. 24, 2001. Available at www.pbs.org/newshour/bb/politics/jan-june01/ashcroft_01-24.html.

Opinion and Order. *U.S. v. Benevolence International Foundation and Arnaout.* U.S. District Court for the Northern District of Illinois, Eastern Division. No. 02:cr414. Sept. 12, 2002. Available at news.findlaw.com/hdocs/docs/terrorism/usbif91302opn.pdf.

Order. *U.S. v. Moussaoui.* U.S. District Court for the Eastern District of Virginia, Alexandria Division. No. 01:01cr455. Apr. 20, 2005. Available at news.findlaw.com/hdocs/docs/moussaoui/usmouss42005ord.html.

Order. *U.S. v. Moussaoui.* U.S. District Court for the Eastern District of Virginia, Alexandria Division. Criminal No. 01-455-A. Oct. 2, 2003. Available at news.findlaw.com/hdocs/docs/Moussaoui/usmouss100203.ord.pdf.

Pallasch, Abdon. "Does Patriot Act Keep Us Safe or Go Too Far?" *Chicago Sun-Times,* Sept. 15, 2003. Available at www.suntimes.com.

Palmer, Elizabeth A. "Committees Taking a Critical Look at Ashcroft's Request for Broad New Powers." *CQ Weekly,* Sept. 29, 2001, 2263–2265. Available at CQ Electronic Library, CQ Public Affairs Collection: weeklyreport107-000000316148.

Paris, Michael. "Legal Mobilization and the Politics of Reform: Lessons from School Finance Litigation in Kentucky, 1984–1995. " *Law and Social Inquiry* 26 (2001): 631.

Partial Birth Abortion Ban Act of 2003. PL 108-105.

Pear, Robert, and Eric Lichtblau. "Administration Sets Forth a Limited View on Privacy." *New York Times,* Mar. 6, 2004. Available at www.nytimes.com/2004/03/06/politics.

People for the American Way. "Ashcroft's Missouri Record Found 'Deeply Disturbing' on Issues of Civil Rights, Reproductive Rights, and Other Fundamental Constitutional Freedoms." *Oppose Ashcroft.* Jan. 13. 2001. Available at www.opposeashcroft.com/press.

———. "A Record of Extremism." *Oppose Ashcroft.* Jan. 2001. Available at www.opposeashcroft.com.

Pfiffner, James. "Introduction." In Gary Gregg and Mark Rozell, eds., *Considering the Bush Presidency.* New York: Oxford University Press, 2004.

Philbin, Patrick. Memorandum Opinion for the Deputy Attorney General. "Limitations on the Detention Authority of the Immigration and Naturalization Service." Office of Legal Counsel. U.S. Department of Justice. Feb. 20, 2003. Available at www.usdoj.gov/olc/INSDetention.htm.

Pickler, Nedra. "Bush: Patriot Act Helped to Nab Terrorists." *San Francisco Chronicle,* June 9, 2005. Available at SFGate.comhttp://www.sfgate.com/cgi-bin/article.cgi?f=/n/a/2005/06/09/national/w092105D91.DTL.

Pierce, Emily. "Ashcroft Rapped over Oversight." *Roll Call,* June 9, 2003. Available through Lexis-Nexis Congressional Universe.

Pika, Joseph, John Anthony Maltese, and Norman C. Thomas. *The Politics of the Presidency.* 5th ed. Washington, D.C.: CQ Press, 2002.

Plea Agreement. *U.S. v. Arnaout.* U.S. District Court for the Northern District of Illinois, Eastern Division. Feb. 10, 2003. No. 02 CR 892. Available at news.findlaw.com/hdocs/docs/bif/usarnaout203plea.pdf.

Political MoneyLine. "Two New Lobbyists." Oct. 20, 2005. Available at www.fecinfo.com.

Poloma, Margaret M. "Charisma and Structure in the Assemblies of God: Revisiting O'Dea's Five Dilemmas." Prepared for the Organizing Religious Work Project. Feb. 6, 2002. Available at www3.uakron.edu/sociology/poloma.htm.

Ponemon Institute Report. "Privacy Trust Survey of the United States Government: Executive Summary Presented by Ponemon Institute and the CIO Institute of Carnegie Mellon University." Jan. 31, 2004. Available through www.ponemon.org/privacy-trust-survey.

Powell, Michael. "Padilla Case Puts Lawyers in Limbo, Too." *Washington Post,* June 5, 2004, A3. Available at www.washingtonpost.com/ac2/wp-dyn/A16691-2004Jun4.

Powell, Michael, and Michelle Garcia. "Amid Praise, Doubts about Nominee's Post 9/11 Role." *Washington Post,* Jan. 31, 2005, A1. Available at www.washingtonpost.com/ac2/wp-dyn/A49950-2005Jan30.

"President Bars 5 DOJ Agencies from Unionizing." *Federal Human Resources Week,* Jan. 21, 2002.

Presidential Records Act of 1978. 44 U.S.C. Chapter 22 § 2204 and § 2205.

Preston, Julia. "Judge Allows Peek into Challenge to Antiterrorism Law." *New York Times,* May 13, 2004. Available at www.nytimes.com/2004/05/13/politics/13suit.html.

Priest, Dana. "CIA Puts Harsh Tactics on Hold." *Washington Post,* June 27, 2004, A1. Available at www.washingtonpost.com/ac2/wp-dyn/A8534-2004Jun26.

——— "Reinterpreting International Law?" *Washington Post National Weekly Edition,* Nov. 1–7, 2004, 16.

Priest, Dana, and Dan Eggen. "Are We Ready to Thwart Attacks?" *Washington Post National Weekly Edition,* Nov. 18–24, 2002, 29.

Priest, Dana, and R. Jeffrey Smith. "Memo Offered Justification for Use of Torture." *Washington Post,* June 8, 2004, A1. Available at www.washingtonpost.com/ac2/wp-dyn/A23373-2004Jun7.

Project on Government Oversight Press Release. "Justice Department Caves In: Allows Publication of Retroactively Classified Information." Feb. 22, 2005. Available at www.pogo.org/p/government/ga-050202-Classification.html.

Purdum, Todd. "Bush Uses Speech to Nation to Get in Position for '04 Race." *New York Times,* Jan. 21, 2004. Available at www.nytimes.com/2004/01/21/politics.

Ragavan, Chitra. "Ashcroft's Way." *U.S. News & World Report,* Jan. 26, 2004. Available at www.usnews.com/usnews/news/articles/040126ashcroft.htm.

Ragavan, Chitra, and Sheila Kaplan. "Is Ashcroft Unsinkable?" *U.S. News & World Report,* Jan. 8, 2001, 13.

Ramasastry, Anita. "A Flawed Report Card: How DOJ Mishandled the Post–September 11 Detention Process." FindLaw's Writ Legal Commentary. Aug. 1, 2003. writ.news.findlaw .com.

Ranalli, Ralph. "Lawmakers Scold Justice Dept. over Shielded FBI Documents." *Boston Globe,* Feb. 7, 2002. Available through Lexis-Nexis Academic Universe.

Randolph, Edmund. Letter to the Speaker of the House of Delegates. Oct. 10, 1787. Reprinted in Paul Ford, ed., *Pamphlets on the Constitution of the United States.* Brooklyn, 1888.

Raspberry, William. "No!" *Washington Post,* Dec. 29, 2000, A33.

Regan, Tom. "Ashcroft Slams Critics as Patriot Act Backlash Grows." *Christian Science Monitor,* Sept. 16, 2003. Available at www.csmonitor.com.

Relyea, Harold. "Freedom of Information Act (FOIA) Amendments: 109th Congress." Congressional Research Service. CRS Report to Congress. RL32780. Updated May 16, 2005. Available at www.fas.org/sgp/crs/secrecy/RL32780.pdf.

Republican Policy Committee. "John Ashcroft: The Most Experienced Attorney General Nominee—in U.S. History." U.S. Senate. Jan. 18, 2001. Available at www.senate .gov/~rpc/releases/1999/jd011801.htm.

Reuters. "Ashcroft Defends Actions to Congress." Dec. 6, 2001. Available at news.findlaw .com.

——— "Ashcroft Says Walker Waived Right to Attorney." Jan. 16, 2002. Available at news .findlaw.com.

——— "Ashcroft Wins South Carolina Presidential Poll." May 17, 1998.

——— Transcript from Bush's television interview with *Meet the Press. New York Times,* Feb. 8, 2004. Available at www.nytimes.com/2004/02/08/politics.

——— "U.S. to Listen In on Some Inmate-Lawyer Talks." FindLaw Legal News and Commentary. Nov. 11, 2001. Available at news.findlaw.com.

——— "Web Sites Listed as 'Terror' Groups." Oct. 10, 2003. Available at news.findlaw.com.

Richey, Warren. "How Evidence Stacks Up on Military Tribunals." *Christian Science Monitor,* Mar. 22, 2002. Available at www.csmonitor.com/2002/0322.

——— "In Moussaoui Tangle, Glimpse of Terror's Legal Tug of War." *Christian Science Monitor,* July 18, 2003. Available at www.csmonitor.com/2003/0718/p04s02-usju .html.

——— "A Legal Tool Emerges in Terror War." *Christian Science Monitor,* June 19, 2002. Available at www.csmonitor.com/2002/0619.

——— "Secret 9/11 Case before High Court." *Christian Science Monitor,* Oct. 30, 2003. Available at www.csmonitor.com/2003/1030.

———"Supreme Court Asks for More Input on Secret Sept. 11 Case." *Christian Science Monitor,* Nov. 7, 2003. Available at www.csmonitor.com/2003/1107.

——— "Supreme Court Decision May Limit Access to Terror Cases." *Christian Science Monitor,* Feb. 24, 2004. Available at www.csmonitor.com/2004/0224.

Reichmann, Deb. "U.S. More Tightlipped since Sept. 11." Associated Press. Nov. 15, 2001. Available at news.findlaw.com.

Right to Financial Privacy. 12 USCS § 3414. 2005.

Ronald W. Reagan National Defense Authorization Act for Fiscal Year 2005. 118 Stat. 2070. PL 108-375. Oct. 28, 2004.

Roper, Jon. "George W. Bush and the Myth of Heroic Presidential Leadership." *Presidential Studies Quarterly* 34, no. 1 (Mar. 2004): 132–142.

Rosen, Jay. "John Ashcroft: National Explainer." *Press Think,* Sept. 16, 2003. Available at journalism.nyu.edu/pubzone/weblogs/pressthink/2003/09/16-ashcroft_rationale.html.

Rosen, Jeffrey. "Symposium on Security, Technology and Individual Rights." *Georgetown Journal of Law and Public Policy* 2 (Winter 2004): 17–38.

Rosenbaum, David. "A Nation Challenged: The Lawmakers; Congressional Leaders Offer Strong Endorsement of Attack." *New York Times,* Oct. 8, 2001, B11.

Rosenberg, Joel C. "Flashtraffic: Ashcroft Bulks Up Anti-terror Forces." *World Magazine,* Apr. 5, 2003. Available at Lexis-Nexis Academic Universe.

Rosenzweig, Paul. "Aiding Terrorists: An Examination of the Material Support Statute." Heritage Foundation. May 5, 2004. Available at www.heritage.org/Research/LegalIssues/tst050504a.cfm.

———. "The Ashcroft Legacy: Liberty and Security." Heritage Foundation, Web Memo No. 607. Nov. 10, 2004. Available at www.heritage.org/Research/HomelandDefense/wm607.cfm.

Rothschild, Matthew. "The Ashcroft Raids." *Progressive,* Apr. 25, 2003. Available at www.progressive.org.

Rozell, Mark. "Executive Privilege and the Bush Administration: Essay: Executive Privilege Revived? Secrecy and Conflict during the Bush Presidency." *Duke Law Journal* 52 (Nov. 2002): 403.

Runk, David. "Ashcroft Remarks 'Distress' Federal Judge." Associated Press. Apr. 18, 2003. Available at news.findlaw.com.

S. 609. "Restoration of Freedom of Information Act of 2003." Introduced Mar. 12, 2003. Available at thomas.loc.gov.

Safire, William. "Rights of Terror Suspects." *New York Times,* July 5, 2004. Available at www.nytimes.com/2004/07/05/opinion.

———. "Security with Liberty." *New York Times,* May 17, 2004. Available at www.nytimes.com/2004/05/17/opinion.

Salokar, Rebecca Mae. *The Solicitor General: The Politics of Law.* Philadelphia: Temple University Press, 1992.

Sanchez, Rene. "Librarians Make Some Noise over Patriot Act." *Washington Post,* Apr. 9, 2003. Available at www.washingtonpost.com/wp-dyn/articles/A1481-2003Apr9.html.

Sanders, Edmund. "The Court That Wields the Wiretaps." *Los Angeles Times,* Sept. 30, 2001. Available at www.latimes.com/news/nationworld/nation/la-09001fisa.story.

Sanger, David. "When Goals Meet Reality: Bush's Reversal on 9/11 Testimony." *New York Times,* Mar. 31, 2004. Available at www.nytimes.com/2004/03/31/politics.

Sarat, Austin. "The Law Is All Over: Power, Resistance and the Legal Consciousness of the Welfare Poor." *Yale Journal of Law and the Humanities* 2 (1990): 343–379.

Savage, David G., and Eric Lichtblau. "Ashcroft Deals with Daunting Responsibilities." *Los Angeles Times,* Oct. 28, 2001.

Sawyer, Jon, and Lia Dean. "Durbin, Ashcroft Let Others Pick Up the Tab for Travels." *St. Louis Post-Dispatch,* Aug. 3, 1998, 1A.

Schaeffer, Pamela, and Roger Signor. "Decision Hailed in Cruzan Case." *St. Louis Post-Dispatch,* Dec. 16, 1990, 1A.

Scheppele, Kim Lane. "Law in a Time of Emergency: States of Exception and the Temptations of 9/11." *University of Pennsylvania Journal of Constitutional Law* 6 (May 2004): 1001–1081.

Schlesinger, Arthur M., Jr. *The Imperial Presidency.* Boston: Houghton Mifflin, 1973.

Schmidt, Susan. "IG Probes Patriot Act Charges." *Washington Post,* July 22, 2003, A15. Available at www.washingtonpost.com/ac2/wp-dyn/A25296-2003Jul21.

Schmitt, Eric. "New Rules Are Proposed for Appeals of Immigrants." *New York Times,* Feb. 2, 2002, A9.

Schmitt, Eric, and Thom Shanker. "U.S. Officials Retool Slogan in Terror War." *New York Times,* July 26, 2005. Available at www.nytimes.com/2005/07/26/politics/26strategy .html?ex=1123214400&en=44a1e10bf887024d&ei=5070&emc=eta1.

Schmitt, Richard. "Patriot Act Author Has Concerns." *Los Angeles Times,* Nov. 30, 2003. Available at www.latimes.com/news/nationworld/nation/la-na-justice30nov30,1,5074199 .story.

Scott, Stephen. "In the U.S., Symbols of a Civil Religion Are Plentiful." *St. Paul Pioneer Press,* Oct. 25, 2001. Available through Lexis-Nexis Academic Universe.

Seelye, Katharine. "A Nation Challenged: Military Tribunals." *New York Times,* Mar. 21, 2001, A1.

———— "A Nation Challenged: The Trials." *New York Times,* Mar. 22, 2002.

———— "Study Confirms 'Stakeholders' Gave Advice to Energy Panel." *New York Times,* Aug. 26, 2003. Available at www.nytimes.com/2003/08/26/politics.

Senate Joint Resolution. 1998. SJ Res. 49.

Serrano, Richard. "The Nation: Rumsfeld Vows 'Fair and Impartial' Anti-terrorism Trials." *Los Angeles Times,* Mar. 22, 2002.

Shaffer, Jeffrey. "Commentary: Iraq Blurs the Line between Crime and War." *Christian Science Monitor,* Apr. 16, 2004. Available at www.csmonitor.com/2004/0416.

Shane, Scott. "Increase in the Number of Documents Classified by the Government." *New York Times,* July 3, 2005. Available at www.nytimes.com/2005/07/03/politics/03secrecy.html.

Shapiro, Ben. "Liars, Manipulators and the Great John Ashcroft." *Town Hall,* Nov. 27, 2003. Available at www.townhall.com/columnists/benshapiro/bs20030227.shtml.

Sheffer, Martin. "The Attorney General and Presidential Power." *Presidential Studies Quarterly* 12 (1982): 54–65.

———— "The Continued Need for the Prerogative Presidency." *White House Studies* 2, no. 3 (2002): 251–271.

Shenon, Philip. "Federal Appeals Court Restores Sept. 11 Prosecution." *New York Times,* Apr. 23, 2004. Available at www.nytimes.com/2004/04/23/politics/23 TERR.html.

———— "Hearing to Affect Government's Ability to Try Terror Suspects in Civilian Courts." *New York Times,* June 2, 2003. Available at www.nytimes.com/2003/06/02/politics/02USP .html.

———— "Judge Rules U.S. Must Provide Statements from Qaeda Leaders." *New York Times,* Apr. 23. 2003. Available at www.nytimes.com/2003/04/23/international/worldspecial/ 23USP.html.

———— "Justice Department Will Appeal Ruling in Trial Linked to 9/11." *New York Times,* Feb. 8, 2003. Available at www.nytimes.com/2003/02/08/politics.

———— "Justice Dept. Warns of Risk to Prosecution and Security." *New York Times,* June 4, 2003, A21.

———— "Moussaoui Case May Have to Shift from U.S. Court to Tribunal." *New York Times,* Feb. 7, 2003. Available at www.nytimes.com/2003/02/07/politics/07TERR.html.

———— "Prosecution Says Qaeda Member Was to Pilot 5th Sept. 11 Jet." *New York Times,* Apr. 16, 2003, B6.

———— "Report on USA Patriot Act Alleges Civil Rights Violations." *New York Times,* July 21, 2003. Available at www.nytimes.com/2003/07/21/politics21JUST.html.

Sheridan, Mary Beth. "Immigration Law as Anti-terrorism Tool." *Washington Post,* June 13, 2005, A1. Available at www.washingtonpost.com/wp-dyn/content/article/2005/06/12/AR2005061201441.html.

Shull, Steven A., ed. *The Two Presidencies: A Quarter-Century Assessment.* Chicago: Nelson Hall, 1991.

Siddiqui, Haroon. "Ayatollah Ashcroft's Law." *Toronto Star,* June 12, 2003. Available at http://www.commondreams.org/cgi-bin/print.cgi?file=/views03/0612-07.htm

Simmons, Wendy. "Ashcroft Receives Mixed Review from the Public." Gallup Organization. Jan. 18, 2001. Available at www.gallup.com.

Smith, R. Jeffrey. "Access to Memos Is Affirmed." *Washington Post,* Feb. 23, 2005, A17.

―――― "Justice Redacted Memo on Detainees." *Washington Post,* Mar. 22, 2005, A3. Available at www.washingtonpost.com/wp-dyn/articles/A55136-2005Mar21.html.

Smith, R. Jeffrey, and Dan Eggen. "Gonzales Helped Set the Course for Detainees." *Washington Post,* Jan. 5, 2005, A1. Available at www.washingtonpost.com/ac2/wp-dyn/A48446-2.

Society of Professional Journalists. "Ashcroft Speeches Should Be More Accessible to the Public and Media." Sept. 18, 2003. AScribe Law News Service. Available at web5.infotract.galegroup.com/itw/infomark/72/15/51032787w5/purl=rcl_EAIM_0_A107.

Spitzer, Robert J. "Gun Rights for Terrorists? Gun Control and the Bush Presidency." In Jon Kraus, Kevin McMahon, and David Rankin, eds., *Transformed by Crisis: The Presidency of George W. Bush and American Politics.* New York: Palgrave Macmillan, 2004.

Stephens, Bret. "Um, You're Right. (Not Really)." *Wall Street Journal,* Nov. 12, 2004. Available at www.opinionjournal.com/taste/?id=110005886.

Stevenson, Richard, and Eric Lichtblau. "As Ashcroft Warns of Attack, Some Question Threat and Its Timing." *New York Times,* May 27, 2004. Available at www.nytimes.com/2004/05/27/politics.

Szabo, Liz. "Senator Focuses on Themes of Faith, Family and Politics." *Virginia-Pilot & Ledger Star,* May 10, 1998, B1.

Tapscott, Mark. "More on the Right Get FOIA Right." *Dallas Morning News,* July 2, 2005, 35A.

Taylor, Stuart, Jr. "Let's Not Allow a Fiat to Undermine the Bill of Rights." *Atlantic* online, July 23, 2002. Available at www.theatlantic.com/politics/nj/taylor2002-07-23.htm.

Tocqueville, Alexis de. *Democracy in America.* Trans. and ed. Harvey Mansfield and Delba Winthrop. Chicago: University of Chicago Press, 2000.

Toobin, Jeffrey. "Profiles: Ashcroft's Ascent." *New Yorker,* Apr. 15, 2002, 50–63.

Trebilcock, Craig. "The Myth of Posse Comitatus." *Journal of Homeland Security,* Oct. 2000. Available at www.homelandsecurity.org/journal/articles/Trebilcock.htm.

Tribe, Laurence H. *American Constitutional Law.* 3rd ed. Vol. 1. New York: Foundation Press, 2000.

TrixiePix Graphics. Accessed Mar. 17, 2004. Available at www.trixiepixgraphics.com/books/ashcroft-constitution.

Turley, Jonathan. "You Have Rights—If Bush Says You Do." *Los Angeles Times,* June 3, 2004. Available at http://www.latimes.com/news/opinion/commentary.

United Press International. "Analysis: Ashcroft Trips but Carries On." Dec. 17, 2003. Available through infotrac.galegroup.com.

―――― "Analysis: Senate May Go Easy on Ashcroft." Dec. 22, 2000. P1008357u7573.

USA Patriot Act. PL 107-56. 2001.

U.S. Associate Deputy Attorney General David S. Kris Testimony. Statement before the Senate Judiciary Committee concerning the Foreign Intelligence Surveillance Act. Sept. 10, 2002. Available at www.usdoj.gov/dag/testimony.

U.S. Attorney General. News conference transcript. "Regarding Decision of Foreign Intelligence Surveillance Court of Review." Nov. 18, 2002. Available at www.usdoj.gov/ag/speeches/2002.

—— Guidelines. "FBI National Security Investigations and Foreign Intelligence Collection." Oct. 31, 2003. Available at www.usdoj.gov/olp/nsiguidelines.pdf.

—— Guidelines. "Federal Bureau of Investigation Undercover Operations." May 30, 2002. Available at www.usdoj.gov/olp/fbiundercover.pdf.

—— Guidelines. "General Crimes, Racketeering Enterprise and Terrorism Enterprise Investigations." May 30, 2002. Available at www.usdoj.gov/olp/generalcrimes2.pdf.

—— Letter to President George Bush from John Ashcroft. Feb. 1. 2002. Memo 9 in Karen Greenberg and Joshua Dratel, eds., *The Torture Papers: The Road to Abu Ghraib.* New York: Cambridge University Press, 2005.

U.S. Attorney General Remarks. "Attorney General Ashcroft Announces Indictment of Alleged Terrorist Financier." Chicago, Illinois. Oct. 9, 2002. Available at www.usdoj.gov/archive/ag/speeches/2002/100902agremarksbifindictment.htm.

—— "Attorney General Ashcroft Speaks about the Patriot Act, Boise, Idaho." Aug. 25, 2003. Available at www.lifeandliberty.gov/subs/speeches/patriotactroadspeech_boise.

—— "Attorney General Guidelines." May 30, 2002. Available at www.usdoj.gov/ag/speeches/2002/53002agpreparedremarks.htm.

—— "Attorney General Transcript: News Conference Regarding Zacarias Moussaoui." Dec. 11, 2001. Available at www.usdoj.gov/archive/ag/speeches/2001/agcrisisremarks12_11.htm.

—— "Commencement Address for the University of Missouri Columbia School of Law." May 18, 2002. Available at www.usdoj.gov/ag/speeches/2002.

—— "Eastern District of Virginia/Interview Projects Results Announcement." Mar. 20, 2002. Available at www.usdoj.gov/ag/speeches/2002.

—— "Eighth Circuit Judges Conference, Duluth, Minn." Aug. 7, 2002. Available at www.usdoj.gov/ag/speeches/2002.

—— "FBI Reorganization." May 29, 2002. Available at www.usdoj.gov/ag/speeches/2002.

—— "Federalist Society National Convention." Nov. 15, 2003. Available at www.usdoj.gov/ag/speeches/2003.

—— "Federalist Society 20th Anniversary Gala." Nov. 14, 2002. Available at www.usdoj.gov/ag/speeches/2002.

—— "Implementation of NSEERS." Nov. 7, 2002. Available at www.usdoj.gov/ag/speeches/2002.

—— "International Association of Chiefs of Police Conference." Oct. 7, 2002. Available at www.usdoj.gov/ag/speeches/2002/100702chiefsofpolicemn1.htm.

—— "Islamic Group Indictment/SAMS." Apr. 9. Available at www.usdoj.gov/ag/speeches/2002.

—— "National Security Entry-Exit Registration System." June 6, 2002. Available at www.usdoj.gov/ag/speeches/2002.

—— "Operation E-Con Press Conference." May 16, 2003. Available at www.usdoj.gov/ag/speeches/2003.

—— "Press Conference." Oct. 18, 2001. Available at www.usdoj.gov/ag/speeches/2001/agcrisisremarks.

—— "Press Conference." Oct. 4, 2002. Available at www.usdoj.gov/ag/speeches/2002/100402agnewsconferenceportlandcell.htm.

———— "Protecting Life and Liberty, Memphis, Tennessee." Sept. 18, 2003. Available at www .usdoj.gov/ag/speeches/2003/0918.

———— "The Proven Tactics in the Fight against Crime." Sept. 15, 2003. Available at www .usdoj.gov/ag/speeches/2003.

———— "Regarding Human Trafficking." Jan. 29, 2004. Available at www.usdoj.gov/ speeches/2004.

———— "Reorganization and Mobilization of the Nation's Justice and Law Enforcement Resources." Nov. 8, 2001. Available at www.usdoj.gov/ag/speeches/2001agcrisisremarks.

———— "Report from the Field: The USA Patriot Act at Work." July 13, 2004. Available at www.usdoj.gov/ag/speeches/2004/071304_patriot_report_remarks.htm

———— "Speak for Israel Meeting." Apr. 2, 2003. Available at www.usdoj.gov/ag/speeches/ 2003.

———— "The Transfer of Abdullah Al Muhajir (Born José Padilla) to the Department of Defense as an Enemy Combatant." June 10, 2002. Available at www.usdoj.gov/ag/speeches/ 2002.

———— "U.S. Attorneys Conference, New York City." Oct. 1, 2002. Available at www.usdoj .gov/ag/speeches/2002/1001012agremarkstousattorneysconference.htm.

———— "U.S. Conference of Mayors." eMediaMillWorks. Oct. 25, 2001. Available at www .washingtonpost.com/wp-svr/nation/specials/attacked/transcript/ashcroft.

———— "Violence against Women Act Symposium, 10th Anniversary." Sept. 13, 2004. Available at www.usdoj.gov/ag/speeches/2004/ag091304_ovw.htm.

———— "Violent Crime Initiative." PSN National Conference. Kansas City, Missouri. June 16, 2004. Available at www.usdoj.gov/ag/speeches/2004/agpns061504.htm.

U.S. Attorney General Transcript. News Conference—SEVIS, May 10, 2002. Available at www.usdoj.gov/ag/speeches/2002.

U.S. Bureau of Prisons. "National Security; Prevention of Acts of Violence and Terrorism; Final Rule." 28 CFR Parts 500 and 501, effective date. Oct. 31, 2001. Available at www .washingtonpost.com/ac2/wp-dyn/A64096-2001Nov8.

U.S. Congressman John Conyers Jr. Press release. "Conyers Condemns Today's FISA Court Decision." Nov. 18, 2002.

U.S. Department of Justice. "Attorney General Ashcroft Announces Citizen Corps' Volunteers in Police Service Initiative." May 30, 2002. Available at www.usdoj.gov/opa/pr/2002/May.

———— "Attorney General Ashcroft Announces Interagency Task Force to Review Ways to Combat Leaks of Classified Information." Dec. 14, 2001. Available at www.usdoj.gov/opa/ pr/2001.

———— Attorney General Memorandum to FBI Director, Assistant Attorney General for Criminal Division, Counsel for Intelligence Policy and U.S. Attorneys. "Intelligence Sharing Procedures for Foreign Intelligence and Foreign Counterintelligence Investigations Conducted by the FBI." Mar. 6, 2002.

———— "Department of Justice Releases New Numbers on Section 213 of the Patriot Act." Apr. 4, 2005. Available at www.usdoj/gov/opa/pr/2005/Apr./05_opa_160.htm.

———— "Department of Justice Success: The Past 4 Years." Nov. 9, 2004. Available at www .usdoj.gov/ag/speeches/2004/ag_successes_110904.htm.

———— Deputy Attorney General and Director, FBI. Memorandum for Michael Chertoff, Assistant Attorney General, James Baker, Counsel for Intelligence Policy, All U.S. Attorneys, All Anti-terrorism Task Force Coordinators, All FBI Special Agents. "Field Guidance on Intelligence Sharing Procedures for FI and FCI Investigations." Dec. 24, 2002.

―――― Deputy Attorney General Memorandum for all U.S. Attorneys and All Members of Anti-terrorism Task Forces. "Subject: Guidelines for the Interviews Regarding International Terrorism." Nov. 9, 2001. Available at www.usdoj.gov.

―――― "Earnest James Ujaama Sentenced for Conspiring to Supply Goods and Services to the Taliban." Feb. 13, 2004. Available at www.usdoj.gov/opa/pr/2004/February/04_crm_086.htm.

―――― Executive Office for U.S. Attorneys. Memorandum for All U.S. Attorneys, All First Assistant U.S. Attorneys, All Criminal Chiefs, All Civil Chiefs, All Appellate Chiefs and All Administrative Officers. "Departmental Guidance on Sentencing Recommendations and Appeals." July 28, 2003.

―――― "Fact Sheet: Attorney General's Guidelines for FBI National Security Investigations and Foreign Intelligence Collection." Nov. 5, 2003. Available at www.usdoj.gov/olp/nsi-fact sheet.pdf.

―――― "Fact Sheet: The Terrorist Screening Center." Sept. 3, 2003. Available at www.usdoj.gov/opa/pr/2003/September.

―――― "Instructions on Separation of Certain Foreign Counterintelligence and Criminal Investigations." Memorandum from Jamie S. Gorelick, Deputy Attorney General to Mary Jo White, Louis Freeh, Richard Scruggs, and Jo Ann Harris. 1995. Available at www.usdoj.gov.

―――― John Ashcroft Memorandum to Heads of All Federal Departments and Agencies. "Subject: the Freedom of Information Act." Oct. 12, 2001.

―――― "Justice Department Files Complaint against Oklahoma School District Seeking to Protect Student's Right to Wear Headscarf to Public School." Mar. 30, 2004. Available at www.usdoj.gov/opa/pr/2004/Mar.

―――― "Justice Department Files Motion to Intervene in Title IX Sexual Harassment Case against Rhinebeck Central School District." Mar. 18, 2001. Available at www.usdoj.gov/opa/pr/2004/Mar.

―――― Justice Department Statement. "Regarding Filing in Zacarias Moussaoui Case." Sept. 25, 2003. Available at www.usdoj.gov/opa/pr/2003/September.

―――― Letter from Vesper Mei to Michael Kirkpatrick, Public Citizen Litigation Group. Re: POGO v. Ashcroft, et al. 04-CV-1032 (JDB). Feb. 18, 2005. Available at www.pogo.org/m/gp/gp-02182005-JusticeDeptLetter.pdf.

―――― Letter of Barbara Comstock, Director of Public Affairs, to the Editor of *Time* magazine. May 13, 2003. Available at www.usdoj.gov/opa/pr/2003/May/03_opa_292.htm.

―――― Memorandum to Director of FBI, Assistant Attorney General Criminal Division, Counsel for Intelligence Policy, United States Attorneys, from the Attorney General. Subject: Intelligence Sharing Procedures for Foreign Intelligence and Foreign Counterintelligence Investigations Conducted by the FBI. Mar. 6, 2002. Available at www.fas.org/irp/agency/doj/fisa/ag030602.html.

―――― "New Attorney General FOIA Memorandum Issued." Oct. 16, 2002. Available at www.usdoj.gov/opa/pr/2001.

―――― Office of the Inspector General. "Report to Congress on Implementation of Section 1001 of the USA Patriot Act," Mar. 11, 2005, 6. Available at www.usdoj.gov/oig/special/0503/final.pdf.

―――― Office of the Inspector General. "A Review of the FBI's Actions in Connection with Allegations Raised by Contract Linguist Sibel Edmonds." Jan. 2005. Available at www.usdoj.gov/oig/special/0501/index.htm.

———— Office of the Inspector General. "The September 11 Detainees: A Review of the Treatment of Aliens Held on Immigration Charges in Connection with the Investigation of the September 11 Attacks." Apr. 2003. Available at http://www.usdoj.gov/oig/special/0304/index.htm.

———— Office of Inspector General. Special Reports. Accessed June 20, 2005. Available at www.usdoj.gov/oig/igspecr1.htm.

———— Office of Intelligence Policy and Review. Home page. Accessed June 4, 2004. Available at www.usdoj.gov/oipr.

———— Office of Legal Counsel. Guidelines of 18 U.S.C. § 1913. Anti-Lobbying Act. 1995. Available at www.amc.army.mil/amc/command_counsel/resrouces/documents/newsletter 97-6/enc118.pdf.

———— Office of Legal Counsel. "Memoranda and Opinions by Year." Accessed Apr. 5, 2005. Available at www.usdoj.gov.olc.opinions.htm.

———— Office of Legal Counsel. Memorandum for Alberto Gonzales, Counsel to the President, from Jay S. Bybee. "Application of Treaties and Laws to al Qaeda and Taliban Detainees." Jan. 22, 2002. Memo 6 in Karen Greenberg and Joshua Dratel, eds., *The Torture Papers: The Road to Abu Ghraib*. New York: Cambridge University Press, 2005.

———— Office of Legal Counsel. Memorandum for Alberto Gonzales, Counsel to the President, from Jay S. Bybee. "Re: Standards of Conduct for Interrogation under 18 U.S.C. §§ 2340-2340A." Aug. 1, 2002. Memo 14 in Karen Greenberg and Joshua Dratel, eds., *The Torture Papers: The Road to Abu Ghraib*. New York: Cambridge University Press, 2005.

———— Office of Legal Counsel. Memorandum for William J. Haynes III from John Yoo and Robert Delahunty. "Re: Application of Treaties and Laws to al Qaeda and Taliban Detainees." Jan. 9, 2002. Memo 4 in Karen Greenberg and Joshua Dratel, eds., *The Torture Papers: The Road to Abu Ghraib*. New York: Cambridge University Press, 2005.

———— Office of Legal Counsel. Memorandum for William J. Haynes III from Patrick Philbin and John C. Yoo. "Re: Possible Habeas Jurisdiction over Aliens Held at Guantanamo Bay, Cuba." Dec. 28, 2001. Memo 3 in Karen Greenberg and Joshua Dratel, eds., *The Torture Papers: The Road to Abu Ghraib*. New York: Cambridge University Press, 2005.

———— Office of Legal Counsel. Memorandum Opinion. To Glenn A. Fine, Inspector General. From Jack Goldsmith. Apr. 5, 2004. Available at www.aclu.org/SafeandFree/SafeandFree .cfm?ID=16253&c=282.

———— Office of Legal Counsel. Memorandum Opinion for the Associate Deputy Attorney General. 2001 OLC LEXIS 3. Nov. 5, 2001.

———— Office of Legal Counsel. Memorandum Opinion for the Attorney General. Aug. 24, 2004. Available at www.usdoj.gov/olc/secondamendment2.htm.

———— Office of Legal Policy. "Report to Congress on the Use of Administrative Subpoena Authorities by Executive Branch Agencies and Entities, Pursuant to Public Law 106-544." N.d. Available at www.usdoj.gov/olp/intro.pdf.

———— Office of Solicitor General. Amicus Curiae against Certiorari in *American Coalition of Life Activists v. Planned Parenthood of Columbia/Willamette*. No. 02-563. 2002. Available at www.usdoj.gov/osg/briefs/2002/2pet/6invit/2002-0563.pet.ami.inv.html.

———— Office of Solicitor General. Amicus Curiae on Merits in *Scheidler v. NOW* and *Operation Rescue v. NOW*. Nos. 01-1118; 01-1119. 2002. Available at www.usdoj.gov/osg/briefs/2002/3mer/1mi/2001-1118.mer.ami.html.

———— Organization chart. Accessed Apr. 1, 2004. Available at www.usdoj.gov/02organizations.

—— "Personnel Announcement." Mar. 1, 2001. Available at www.whitehouse.gov/news/releases/2001/03/20010301-3.html.

—— Speeches, Statements and Testimony. "Speeches by the Attorney General. 2003 Speeches." N.d. Available at www.usdoj.gov/ag/speeches.html.

—— Speeches, Statements and Testimony. "Speeches by the Attorney General. 2004 Speeches." N.d. Available at www.usdoj.gov/ag/speeches.html.

—— Statement of Associate Attorney General Jay Stephens. "Regarding the Sixth Circuit Decision in the Haddad Case." Apr. 19, 2002. Available at www.usdoj.gov/opa/pr/2002/Apr.

—— Statement of Associate Deputy Attorney General David S. Kris before the Senate Judiciary Committee Concerning the Foreign Intelligence Surveillance Act. Sept. 10, 2002. Available at www.usdoj.gov/dag/testimony/2002/kirssenjud091002.htm.

—— Statement of Attorney General John Ashcroft. "On Detroit Verdict." June 3, 2003. Available at www.usdoj.gov/opa/pr/2003/June/03_ag_331.htm.

—— Statement of Barbara Comstock, Director of Public Affairs. May 22, 2002. Available at www.usdoj.gov/opa/pr/2002/May.

—— Statement of Barbara Comstock, Director of Public Affairs. "Regarding Federal Prosecutions of Firearms Violations." May 14, 2003. Available at www.usdoj.gov/opa/pr/2003/May/03_opa_296.htm.

—— Statement of Barbara Comstock, Director of Public Affairs. "Regarding the IG's Report on 9/11 Detainees." June 2, 2003. Available at www.usdoj.gov/opa/pr/2003/June.

—— Statement of Barbara Comstock, Director of Public Affairs. "Regarding the Oral Argument in National Center for Security Studies v. Department of Justice." Nov. 18, 2002. Available at www.usdoj.gov/opa/pr/2002/November.

—— Statement of Barbara Comstock, Director of Public Affairs. "Regarding the Third Circuit Argument in North Jersey Media Group v. Ashcroft Today." Sept. 17, 2002. Available at www.usdoj.gov/opa/pr/2002/September.

—— Statement of Senator John Ashcroft. "Upon His Confirmation as Attorney General." Feb. 1, 2001. Available at www.usdoj.gov/ag/speeches/2001.

—— "Superseding Indictment Adds New Charges against Ahmed Abdel Sattar, Lynne Stewart, and Mohammed Yousry." Nov. 19, 2003. Available at www.usdoj.gov/opa/pr/2003/November.

—— Web site. "Dispelling the Myths." Sept. 11, 2003. Available at www.lifeandliberty.gov/subs/u_myths.

—— Web site. "Preserving Life and Liberty." Sept. 11, 2003. Available at www.lifeandliberty.gov.

U.S. House of Representatives. Committee on the Judiciary. "News Advisory: Sensenbrenner/Conyers Release Justice Department Oversight Answers Regarding USA Patriot Act and War on Terrorism." May 20, 2003. Available at www.house.gov/judiciary/news 052003.htm.

—— Committee on the Judiciary. "Oversight of the Justice Department: Testimony of Attorney General John Ashcroft." Federal Document Clearing House. June 5, 2003. Available at www.usdoj.gov/ag/testimony/2003/060503aghouseremarks.htm.

—— Committee on the Judiciary. "Testimony of Attorney General John Ashcroft on the USA Patriot Act." Sept. 24, 2001. Available at www.usdoj.gov/ag/testimony/2001/agcrisisremarks9_24.htm.

—— Subcommittee on Oversight and Investigations. House Committee on Financial Services. Testimony of Alice Fisher. 108th Cong., 1st sess. Mar. 11, 2003. Available at financialservices.house.gov/media/pdf/031103af.pdf.

U.S. Immigration and Naturalization Service. Office of the Chief Immigration Judge. Interim Operating Policies and Procedures Memorandum. "Protective Orders and the Sealing of Records in Immigration Proceedings." July 16, 2002.

—— Office of the Chief Immigration Judge. Michael Creppy Memorandum to All Immigration Judges and Court Administrators. "Subject: Cases Requiring Special Procedures." Sept. 21, 2001. Available at news.findlaw.com/hdocs/docs/aclu/creppy092101memo.pdf.

—— Release of Information Regarding Immigration and Naturalization Service Detainees in Non-federal Facilities. *Federal Register* 67, no. 77 (Apr. 22, 2002): 19508.

U.S. Senate. Committee on the Judiciary. "Ashcroft Comments on Anti-terror Policy." June 8, 2004. FDCH E-Media. Available at www.washingtonpost.com/wp-dyn/articles/A25211-2004Jun8.html.

—— Committee on the Judiciary. "Confirmation Hearing on the Nomination of John Ashcroft to Be Attorney General of the United States." 107th Cong., 1st sess. S. Hrg. 107-196. Jan. 16–19, 2001.

—— Committee on the Judiciary. "Department of Justice Oversight: Preserving Our Freedoms While Defending against Terrorism." Witness: Attorney General John Ashcroft. Dec. 6, 2001. 107th Cong., 1st sess. Federal News Service. Available at web.lexis-nexis.com/congcomp/document.

—— Committee on the Judiciary. "Department of Justice Oversight: Preserving Our Freedoms While Defending against Terrorism." Witness: Michael Chertoff. Nov. 28, 2001. 107th Cong., 1st sess. Available at www.frwebgate.access.gpo.gov/cgi-bin/getdoc.cgi?dbname=107_senate_hearings&docid=f:81998.wais

—— Committee on the Judiciary. "Hearings Concerning Oversight of the Department of Justice." Witness: Attorney General John Ashcroft. July 25, 2002. Available at www.usdoj.gov/ag/testimony/2002.

—— Committee on the Judiciary. "Hearings on the War against Terrorism." Witnesses: U.S. Attorney General John Ashcroft; Homeland Security Secretary Tom Ridge; Federal Bureau of Investigation Director Robert Mueller. Federal News Service. Mar. 4, 2003.

—— Committee on the Judiciary. "Text: Ashcroft Comments on Anti-terror Policy." June 8, 2004. FDCH E-Media. Available at www.washingtonpost.com/wp-dyn/articles/A25211-2004Jun8.html.

Vanderbilt Television News Index and Abstracts. Vanderbilt University Archives. Search of Mar. 15, 2004. Available at tvnews.vanderbilt.edu/TV-NewsSearch.

Vicini, James. "Supreme Court Declines Review on Right to Own Guns." Reuters, June 10, 2002. Available at news.findlaw.com/new/20020610/courtgunsdc.html.

—— "U.S. Says Error in Barring Moussaoui Death Penalty." Reuters. Oct. 31, 2003. Available at news.findlaw.com.

Vise, David, and Dan Eggen. "Ashcroft Names Key Aides to Senior Posts at Justice." *Washington Post,* Feb. 3, 2001, A4.

Walcott, Charles, and Karen Hult. "The Bush Staff and Cabinet System." In Gary Gregg and Mark Rozell, eds., *Considering the Bush Presidency.* New York: Oxford University Press, 2004.

Walsh, Edward. "High Court Stays Out of Secrecy Fray." *Washington Post,* May 28, 2003, A4. Available at www.washingtonpost.com/ac2/wp-dyn/A46103-2003May27.

—— "Treatment of Detainees Defended." *Washington Post,* June 25, 2003. Available at www.washingtonpost.com/ac2/wp-dyn/admin/A33233-2003Jun 25.

Walsh, Edward, and Dan Eggen. "Ashcroft Orders Tally of Lighter Sentences." *Washington Post,* Aug. 7, 2003, A1. Available at www.washingtonpost.com/ac2/wp-dyn.

Warren, Charles. "New Light on the History of the Federal Judiciary Act of 1789." *Harvard Law Review* 37 (1923): 49–132.

Warshaw, Shirley Anne. *Powersharing: White House–Cabinet Relations in the Modern Presidency.* Albany: State University of New York Press, 1996.

Washington Post. "Federal Prosecutors Defend Charges against Lindh." June 6, 2002, A12. Available at www.washingtonpost.com/ac2/wp-dyn.

———— "Transcript: Ashcroft on Terror Probe Suspects." On Politics. Nov. 27, 2001. Available at www.washingtonpost.com/ac2/wp-dyn.

———— "War on Terror Special Report." Internet archival search of John Ashcroft. Apr. 8, 2004. Available at www.washingtonpost.com.

Weekly Standard. "How Ashcroft Won." January 1–8, 2001, 2.

Weiser, Benjamin. "U.S. Asks Judge to Deny Terror Suspect Access to Lawyer, Saying It Could Harm Interrogation." *New York Times,* Jan. 10, 2003. Available at www.nytimes.com/2003/01/10.

White, Jack E. 2001. "The Wrong Choice for Justice." *Time,* Jan. 8, 30.

White House. "Fact Sheet: Counter-terrorism; The White House's Position on Terrorism." Office of the Press Secretary. 1995. Available at nsi.org/Library/Terrorism/policy/html.

———— Memorandum from Alberto R. Gonzales to President Bush. "Decision Re: Application of the Geneva Convention on Prisoners of War to the Conflict with al Qaeda and the Taliban." Jan. 15, 2002. Memo 7 in Karen Greenberg and Joshua Dratel, eds., *The Torture Papers: The Road to Abu Ghraib.* New York: Cambridge University Press, 2005.

———— Memorandum from Bill Clinton to the Vice President, Secretary of State, et al. Subject: U.S. Policy on Counterterrorism. June 21, 1995. Available at www.fas.org/irp/off-docs/pdd39.htm.

———— Memorandum from George W. Bush. "Humane Treatment of al Qaeda and Taliban Detainees." Feb. 7. 2002. Memo 11 in Karen Greenberg and Joshua Dratel, eds., *The Torture Papers: The Road to Abu Ghraib.* New York: Cambridge University Press, 2005.

———— Memorandum from George W. Bush to the Attorney General. "Congressional Subpoena for Executive Branch Documents." Dec. 12, 2001.

———— Memorandum from George W. Bush to the Secretary of Defense on the transfer of Jose Padilla as an enemy combatant. June 9, 2002.

———— Memorandum from George W. Bush to the Secretary of State, Secretary of Treasury, Secretary of Defense, Attorney General, Director of Central Intelligence, Director of FBI. "Disclosures to the Congress." Oct. 5, 2001.

———— "President Addresses the Nation in Prime Time Press Conference." Office of the Press Secretary. Apr. 13, 2004. Available at www.whitehouse.gov/news/releases/2004/04.

———— "President Thanks Attorney General Ashcroft." Office of the Press Secretary. Nov. 9, 2004. Available at www.whitehouse.gov/news/releases/2004/11/20041109-18.html.

———— Press briefing by Attorney General, Secretary of HHS, Secretary of Transportation, and FEMA Director. Sept. 11, 2001. Available at www.whitehouse.gov/news/releases/2001/09.

———— "Press Conference by the President." Mar. 31, 2002. Available at www.whitehouse.gov/news/releases/2002/03/20020313-8.html.

———— Press release. "Joint Resolution to Authorize the Use of United States Armed Forces Against Iraq." Office of the Press Secretary. Oct. 2, 2002. Available at www.whitehouse.gov/news/releases/2002/10/20021002-2.html.

———— Press release. "On the Executive Order to Establish a Presidential Task Force on Citizen Preparedness in the War on Terrorism." Office of the Press Secretary. Nov. 9, 2001. Available at www.whitehouse.gov/news/releases/2001/11.

———— Press release. "President Addresses Military Families, Discusses War on Terror." Office of the Press Secretary. Aug. 24, 2005. Available at www.whitehouse.gov/news/releases/2005/08/20050824.html.

———— "Remarks Via Satellite by the President to the National Association of Evangelicals Convention." Office of the Press Secretary. Mar. 11, 2004. Available at www.whitehouse.gov/news/releases/2004/03.

White House, Office of the Press Secretary. Press briefing by Ari Fleischer. Dec. 13, 2001. Available at www.whitehouse.gov/news/releases/2001/12/20011213-7.html.

———— Press briefing by Ari Fleischer. Jan. 17, 2002. Available at www.whitehouse.gov/news/releases/2002/01/20020117-8.html.

———— Press briefing by Ari Fleischer. May 21, 2002. Available at www.whitehouse.gov/news/releases/2002/05/20020521-9.html.

———— "Remarks by President Bush and Chancellor Schroeder of Germany in Press Availability." May 23, 2002. Available at wwwwhitehouse.gov/news/releases/2002/05/20020523-1.html.

White House Counsel's Office. Letters from Alberto R. Gonzales to John W. Carlin, Archivist of the United States, National Archives and Records Administration. Mar. 23, June 6, and Aug. 31, 2001.

Wildavsky, Aaron. "The Two Presidencies." *Trans-Action* 4, no. 2 (1966). Reprinted in Aaron Wildavsky, ed., *Perspectives on the Presidency*, 448. Boston: Little, Brown, 1975.

Willing, Richard. "John Ashcroft to Teach Class at Va. College." *USA Today,* Mar. 16, 2005. Available at www.usatoday.com/news/nation/2005-03-16-ashcroft-teach_x.htm.

Wilkinson, Todd. "Boise Terror Case Tests Patriot Act's Reach." *Christian Science Monitor,* Apr. 22, 2004. Available at www.csmonitor.com/2004/0422/p03s01-usju.htm.

Wilson, Michael. "Judge Dismisses Terror Charges against Lawyer." *New York Times,* July 23, 2003. Available at www.nytimes.com/2003/07/23/nyregion.

Wood, Daniel B. "Registration for Arabs Draws Fire." *Christian Science Monitor,* Feb. 6, 2003. Available at news.findlaw.com.

Woodward, Bob. *Bush at War.* New York: Simon and Schuster, 2002.

———— "Cheney Upholds Power of the Presidency." *Washington Post,* Jan. 20, 2005, A7. Available at www.washingtonpost.com/wp-dyn/articles/A22190-2205Jan19.html.

———— *Plan of Attack.* New York: Simon and Schuster, 2004.

York, Byron. "Democrats Need John Ashcroft to Kick Around." *The Hill,* Oct. 8, 2003. Available through Lexis-Nexis Congressional Universe.

Yost, Pete. "Federal Prosecutor Sues Ashcroft." *Washington Post,* Feb. 17, 2004. Available at www.washingtonpost.com/ac2/wp-dyn/A47812-2004Feb17.

Young, Virginia. "Ashcroft Backs Fight against Moving Patient." *St. Louis Post-Dispatch,* Feb. 12, 1991, 7A.

———— "Ashcroft Gets Right-to-Die Bill." *St. Louis Post-Dispatch,* May 16, 1991, 1A.

———— "Cruzan Testifies for Bill." *St. Louis Post-Dispatch,* Jan. 22, 1991, 4A.

Zengerle, Jason. "The Gospel According to John: Senator Ashcroft's Longshot Presidential Bid." *New Republic,* Dec. 22, 1997. Available at www.tnr.com/archive/12/122297/zengerle122297.html.

Interviews

Bell, Griffin. U.S. attorney general, 1977–1980. Interview with author. Atlanta, Georgia. May 16, 2005.

Bingaman, Jeff. U.S. senator, New Mexico. Interview with author. Las Cruces, New Mexico. Mar. 31, 2005.

Brewer, C. Madison (Brick). Retired career attorney with Justice Department, including service with the Executive Office of the U.S. Attorneys and the Information and Privacy Unit. Telephone interview with author. May 24, 2005.

Hatch, Orrin. U.S. senator, Utah. Interview with author. Washington, D.C. May 10, 2005.

Thornburgh, Richard. U.S. attorney general 1988–1991. Interview with author. Washington, D.C. May 12, 2005.

List of Cases

Ashcroft v. North Jersey Media Group. 122 S.Ct. 2655; 536 U.S. 954. 2002 U.S. LEXIS 4898 (2002)

Barry v. United States ex relatione Cunningham. 279 U.S. 597 (1927)

Brandenburg v. Ohio. 395 U.S. 444 (1969)

Center for National Security Studies, et al., v. Department of Justice. 215 F. Supp 2d 94; 2002 U.S. Dist. LEXIS 14168 (2002)

Center for National Security Studies, et al., v. Department of Justice. 2003 U.S. App. LEXIS 11910 (2003)

Curtiss Wright Export Corp. v. U.S. 299 U.S. 304, 57 S.Ct. 216 (1936)

Dames & Moore v. Regan. 453 U.S. 654 (1981)

Detroit Free Press, et al., v. John Ashcroft, et al. 195 F. Supp. 2d 937 (2002)

Detroit Free Press, et al., v. John Ashcroft, et al. 303 F. 3d 681; 2002 U.S. App. LEXIS 17646 (2002)

Detroit Free Press, et al., v. John Ashcroft, et al. 2003 U.S. App. LEXIS 1278 (2003)

Edmonds v. Department of Justice. 2005 U.S. App LEXIS 8116 (2005)

Elmaghraby and Iqbal v. Ashcroft, et al. 2005 U.S. Dist. LEXIS 21434 (2005)

Ex Parte Quirin. 317 U.S. 1 (1942)

FMC v. South Carolina State Ports Authority. 535 U.S. 743, 122 S.Ct. 1864 (2002)

Grosjean v. American Press Co. 297 U.S. 233 (1936)

Haddad v. Ashcroft. 221 F. Supp. 2d 799; 2002 U.S. Dist. LEXIS 17990 (2002)

Hamdan v. Rumsfeld. Memorandum opinion. U.S. District Court for the District of Columbia. Civil Action. No. 04-1519 (2004)

Hamdan v. Rumsfeld. U.S. Court of Appeals for the District of Columbia Circuit. No. 04-5393 (2005)

Hamdi v. Rumsfeld. U.S. Court of Appeals for the Fourth Circuit. 2002 U.S. App. LEXIS 12547 (2002)

Hamdi v. Rumsfeld. 294 F. 3d 598 (2002)

Hamdi v. Rumsfeld. 316 F. 3d 450; 2003 U.S. App. LEXIS 198 (2003)

Hamdi v. Rumsfeld. 542 U.S. 507; 124 S.Ct. 2633 (2004)

Higazy v. Millennium Hotel. 346 F. Supp. 2d 430; 2004 U.S. Dist. LEXIS 19605 (2004)

Humanitarian Law Project v. Ashcroft. 309 F. Supp. 2d 1185; 2004 U.S. Dist. LEXIS 4411 (2004)

Humanitarian Law Project v. Reno. 205 F. 3d 1130 (2000)

Humanitarian Law Project v. U.S. Department of Justice. 352 F. 3d 382; 2003 U.S. App. LEXIS 24305 (2003)

In re: All Matters Submitted to the Foreign Intelligence Surveillance Court. U.S. Foreign Intelligence Surveillance Court. 218 F. Supp. 2d 661 (2002)

In re: Application of the United States for Material Warrant. 214 F. Supp. 2d 356. 2002 U.S. Dist. LEXIS 14355 (2002)

In re: Guantanamo Detainees Case. 355 F. Supp. 2d 443; 2005 U.S. Dist. LEXIS 1236 (2005)

In re: Sealed Case no. 02-001, Consolidated with 02-002. U.S. Foreign Intelligence Surveillance Court of Review. Attachments 310 F. 3d 717 (2002)

Johnson v. Eisentrager. 339 U. S. 763; 70 S.Ct. 936 (1950)

M.K.B. v. Warden. 124 S.Ct. 1405 (2004)

Morrison v. Olson. 487 U.S. 654 (1988)

North Jersey Media Group v. Ashcroft. 205 F. Supp. 2d 288; 2002 U.S. Dist. LEXIS 10136. May 28 (2002)

North Jersey Media Group v. Ashcroft. 308 F. 3d 198. 2002 U.S. App. LEXIS 21032 (2002)

North Jersey Media Group v. Ashcroft. 538 U.S. 1056; 123 S.Ct. 2215 (2003)

Northwestern Memorial Hospital v. Ashcroft. Seventh Circuit Court of Appeals. No.04-1379. March 26 (2004)

Oregon v. Ashcroft. U.S. District Court for the District of Oregon. 192 F. Supp. 2d 1077; 2002 U.S. Dist. LEXIS 6695 (2002)

Padilla ex rel. Newman v. Bush. U.S. District Court for the Southern District of New York. 233 F. Supp. 2d 564. Dec. 4 (2002)

Padilla ex rel. Newman v. Rumsfeld. U.S. District Court for the Southern District of New York. 02 Civ. 4445, Mar. 11 (2003)

Padilla v. Rumsfeld. U.S. App. LEXIS 25616 (2003)

Padilla v. Rumsfeld. U.S. Court of Appeals for the Second Circuit. No. 032235 (2003)

Planned Parenthood v. Casey. 510 U.S. 1309; 114 S.Ct. 909 (1994)

Planned Parenthood Association of Kansas City, Missouri v. Ashcroft. 462 U.S. 476; 103 S.Ct. 2517; 1983 U.S. LEXIS 64 (1983)

Rasul, Bibi as Next Friend, et al., v. Bush and *al Odah, et al.* Memorandum opinion. U.S. District Court for the District of Columbia. July 2002. Available at www.findlaw.com (2002)

Rasul, et al., v. Bush. 525 U.S. 466; 124 S.Ct. 2686 (2004)

Roe v. Wade. 410 U.S. 113; 93 S.Ct. 705 (1973)

Rumsfeld v. Padilla. 542 U.S. 426; 124 S.Ct. 2711 (2004)

Scheidler v. National Organization for Women. 537 U.S. 393 (2004)

State of Missouri v. National Organization for Women. 620 F. 2d 1301; 1980 U.S. App. LEXIS 19133 (1980)

Turkmen, et al., v. Ashcroft, et al. 2004 U.S. Dist. LEXIS 14537 (2004)

U.S. v. Arnaout. Plea agreement. U.S. District Court for the Northern District of Illinois, Eastern Division. Feb. 10, 2003. No. 02 CR 892. Available at news.findlaw.com/hdocs/docs/bif/usarnaout203plea.pdf.

U.S. v. Awadallah. U.S. District Court for the Southern District of New York. 2002 U.S. Dist. LEXIS 7536 (2002)

U.S. v. Awadallah. 349 F. 3d 42, U.S. App. LEXIS 22879 (2003)

U.S. v. Moussaoui. 333 F. 3d 509 (2003)

U.S. v. Moussaoui. U.S. Court of Appeals for the Fourth Circuit. No. 03-4792. Decided Sept. 13, 2004. Available at news/findlaw.com/hdocs/docs/Moussaoui/usmouss91304opn.pdf.

U.S. v. Moussaoui and ABC, Associated Press, Cable News Network, et al. Order on motion to intervene. No. 03-4162 (2003)

U.S. v. Sattar, Al-Sirri, Stewart and Yousry. Opinion and order. 02 Cr. 395. U.S. District Court for the Southern District of New York. July 22 (2003)

Vermilya-Brown Co. v. Connell. 335 U.S. 377 (1948)
Walker v. Cheney. 230 F. Supp. 2d 51; 2002 U.S. Dist. LEXIS 23385 (2002)
Youngstown Sheet and Tube Co. v. Sawyer. 343 U.S. 579 (1952)
Zadvydas v. Davis. 533 U.S. 678; 2001 U.S. LEXIS 4912 (2001)

Index